Quantitative Methods in the Humanities and Social Sciences

Quantitative Methods in the Humanities and Social Sciences is a book series designed to foster research-based conversation with all parts of the university campus – from buildings of ivy-covered stone to technologically savvy walls of glass. Scholarship from international researchers and the esteemed editorial board represents the far-reaching applications of computational analysis, statistical models, computer-based programs, and other quantitative methods. Methods are integrated in a dialogue that is sensitive to the broader context of humanistic study and social science research. Scholars, including among others historians, archaeologists, new media specialists, classicists and linguists, promote this interdisciplinary approach. These texts teach new methodological approaches for contemporary research. Each volume exposes readers to a particular research method. Researchers and students then benefit from exposure to subtleties of the larger project or corpus of work in which the quantitative methods come to fruition.

Giacomo Landeschi · Eleanor Betts
Editors

Capturing the Senses

Digital Methods for Sensory Archaeologies

Springer

Editors
Giacomo Landeschi
Department of Archaeology and Ancient History
Lund University
Lund, Sweden

Eleanor Betts
School of Arts and Humanitie
The Open University
Milton Keynes, UK

ISSN 2199-0956 ISSN 2199-0964 (electronic)
Quantitative Methods in the Humanities and Social Sciences
ISBN 978-3-031-23132-2 ISBN 978-3-031-23133-9 (eBook)
https://doi.org/10.1007/978-3-031-23133-9

This Springer imprint is published by the registered company Springer Nature Switzerland AG
The registered company address is: Gewerbestrasse 11, 6330 Cham, Switzerland

In memory of Hanna Stöger

Preface

This volume was inspired by a symposium held at Lund University in 2017 which focused on the theme of digitally informed sensory archaeologies. As organisers of the event, we felt it would be extremely fruitful to write a book focused on the contribution provided by digital/quantitative methods to the study of a sensorial past. As a result, this work comes as a product of a collective effort made by scholars who have been working intensively on the theme of sensory archaeologies and digital methods.

At the time of writing, there is no comprehensive work that systematically investigates the role played by computational methods in supporting and promoting sensory-based archaeologies. This is an opportune time to raise a methodological discussion as an increasing number of university departments and research centres all over the world have been designing courses and curricula centred around the theme of Computational Archaeology/Digital Heritage. It is therefore urgent to reflect on the possibilities that this can open up for investigating senses and sensory-based approaches to the study of the past. In this respect, the contributors of this volume, based on their research experience, propose innovative approaches where digital methods are presented as a fundamental tool to (a) promote the dissemination of cultural heritage-related contents, (b) simulate the sensory experience of peoples of the past and (c) re-interpret information mediated by ancient authors by examining their descriptions of the landscape.

What can be argued about past people's minds? How can we cope with the problem of our situated perspective as modern people? What sort of engagement should we design to enable visitors to a museum, exhibit or archaeological site to approach and confront past people's mindsets? These are only some of the questions that this book addresses, by relying on real-world case studies where interdisciplinary approaches are employed and presented. To provide readers with the broadest picture of research scenarios, we were keen to select chronologically and geographically diverse case studies, spanning Prehistory to the Modern Age, and Northern Africa to Central America.

Giacomo Landeschi is Associate Professor of Archaeology and Researcher at Lund University. His research interests include archaeological computing, landscape and field archaeology, archaeological method and theory. His current research is focused on the development of advanced computational methods for analysing the perceptual experience of a past landscape. Eleanor Betts is Lecturer in Classical Studies at The Open University. Her research explores Roman urbanism and religion in Roman and Iron Age Italy (Picenum), underpinned by sensory studies. She develops and applies multisensory approaches to understand people's construction, experience and use of urban and ritual space and landscapes.

Lund, Sweden Giacomo Landeschi
Milton Keynes, UK Eleanor Betts

Acknowledgements

For the possibility of organising the symposium and the opportunity to release this multi-authored volume as a full open-access source, we wish to give a special thanks to the Lund University Library, the Marcus Wallenberg Foundation, the King Gustaf VI Adolf's Fund for Swedish Culture in Sweden, the Riksbankens Jubileumsfond, fil. Dr. Uno Otterstedts Fund, who generously supported our initiatives. We are particularly grateful to the Digital Archaeology Lab and the Humanities Laboratory at Lund University for providing access to the facilities and the technical equipment employed during the symposium.

A special thank you goes also to the colleagues in the Department of Archaeology and Ancient History, Lund University and all the students and attendees who took part in the symposium.

Contents

Contributors

Eleanor Betts School of Arts and Humanities, Faculty of Arts and Social Sciences, The Open University, Milton Keynes, UK

Eleni Bozia Department of Classics, University of Florida, Gainesville, USA

Stuart Dunn Department of Digital Humanities, King's College London, London, UK

Stuart Eve Department of Archaeology and Anthropology, Bournemouth University, Poole, UK

Anna Foka Digital Humanities Uppsala, Department of ALM (Archive, Library and Information Science, Museum and Cultural Heritage Studies), Uppsala University, Uppsala, Sweden

Mark Gillings Department of Archaeology and Anthropology, Bournemouth University, Poole, UK

Graham Goodwin University of California, Merced, CA, USA

Giacomo Landeschi Department of Archaeology and Ancient History, Lund University, Lund, Sweden

Mattis Lindmark Humlab, Umeå University, Umeå, Sweden

Maria Cristina Manzetti Department of History and Archaeology, University of Cyprus, Nicosia, Cyprus

Anna Misharina Studio CRIT, CA, Orinda, USA

Marinella Pasquinucci Department of Civilizations and Forms of Knowledge, University of Pisa, Pisa, Italy

Chiara Piccoli Faculty of Humanities, University of Amsterdam, Amsterdam, The Netherlands

Kristy E. Primeau New York State Office of Renewable Energy Siting, Albany, NY, USA

Heather Richards-Rissetto School of Global Integrative Studies, Nebraska College of Arts and Sciences, Lincoln, NE, USA

Jim Robertsson Humlab, Umeå University, Umeå, Sweden

Claudia Sciuto Department of Civilizations and Forms of Knowledge, University of Pisa, Pisa, Italy

Elaine A. Sullivan Department of History, University of California at Santa Cruz, Santa Cruz, USA

David E. Witt Department of Anthropology, University at Buffalo, Buffalo, NY, USA

Introduction: Digital Methods and Experiential Approaches to the Past

Giacomo Landeschi and Eleanor Betts

Abstract In this chapter, the authors introduce the theme of computational/digital methods in the realm of sensory archaeologies. To this purpose, the concept of sensoriality and its relevance for the archaeological discourse is rediscussed. Key concepts such as perception of material culture help us in better defining possible modalities through which archaeologists can benefit from the use of formal methods to answer questions related to the relationship between ancient space and its original inhabitants. In this context, recent advances in the field of computational methods can now provide a significant contribution to the development of 'digitally mediated' sensory archaeologies.

Keywords Sensory archaeologies · Digital archaeology · Perception · Material culture · Phenomenology

Is it possible to combine computational methods with the study of sensory archaeologies? To answer this question, it is important to reflect on what lies behind the concept of 'sensoriality' and its relevance for archaeological discourse. A sensory-informed approach to the analysis of landscape was sought long before any statistical inferential method was in use within the discipline. When thinking about the definition of archaeology as the discipline dealing with 'thought transmuted into things' (Frothingham 1911), it is quite apparent that the material manifestation of past human existence can inform us about the mindset of peoples of the past.

What an archaeology of the senses can allow us to do is perhaps to define new modalities through which we can engage with 'the Past'. It is therefore crucial to reinforce the concept of perception as a pivotal element in linking the world to our

G. Landeschi (✉)
Department of Archaeology and Ancient History, Lund University, Lund, Sweden
e-mail: giacomo.landeschi@ark.lu.se

E. Betts
School of Arts and Humanities, Faculty of Arts and Social Sciences, The Open University, Milton Keynes, UK
e-mail: eleanor.betts@open.ac.uk

G. Landeschi and E. Betts (eds.), *Capturing the Senses*,
Quantitative Methods in the Humanities and Social Sciences,
https://doi.org/10.1007/978-3-031-23133-9_1

knowledge about the world: to put it simply, perception can be understood as the relationship between sensation and cognition (Frieman and Gillings 2007). In this respect, as stated by Pollock (1967), 'the data of all our senses are combined in perception to make us aware of the entire object at once'. If we take perception as an essential part of our process of understanding the world, then the experience, intended as the synesthetic sum of multiple perceptual stimuli through which we gain knowledge about the external reality, becomes the key point for us to interpret and infer also about a past reality.

When it comes to the definition of experiential or phenomenological approaches, there is still the problem of replicating and verifying what has been found, which is typically the result of a single researcher's personal observation (Day 2013).

For us as modern people, the main challenge is to define possible workflows to reach as close as possible to a plausible insight into the world of the past or to quote Lock (1995:13) 'to make coherent and meaningful statements of it'. To fulfil this scope, archaeology typically combines the study of material culture with the examination of multiple sources. When it comes to the definition of methods applicable to the study of material culture, it is possible to identify at least two macro-categories: the autoptic, individual examination of the objects under scrutiny and the formal examination conducted through inferential, quantitative methods.

Autoptic examination is conducted by the archaeologist who typically approaches any form of material culture (artefacts, buildings, landscapes) and raises hypotheses and interpretations about their significance or cultural value based solely on his/her own observation. Phenomenological, experiential approaches have been widely applied throughout the last 30 years (Tilley 1994; Fleming 1999; Brück 2005; Hamilton et al. 2006; Skeates 2010; Johnson 2012; Hamilton and Whitehouse 2020) with embodiment representing an important aspect reflecting the role of body as a metaphor (Meskell 1996; Hamilakis et al. 2002; Joyce 2005; Crossland 2010) through which our modern selves get in touch with our past predecessors. One of the main limitations with this approach is the bias of the individual experience that can hardly be generalised to allow us to get plausible conclusions on past humans' behaviours and their relationship with the landscape (Fleming 2006; Tringham 2013).

1 The Role of GIS-based Visual Studies/Space Syntax Analysis

A way to cope with the 'subjectivity' inducted by most of the traditional phenomenological studies is to introduce formal methods of enquiry. Early attempts to investigate the archaeological landscape through quantitative/statistical methods are described by Lake et al. (1998) who refer to works conducted by a few scholars during the 1980s and termed 'non-GIS visibility studies'. Although these methods were not based on computational approaches, the idea to adopt formal procedures to test assumptions and formulate hypotheses around the perception of sites or monuments based on their relational (visual) structure with the surrounding landscape laid the foundation for a more digitally informed post-processual archaeology that developed during the 1990s (Gaffney and Stančić 1991; Wheatley 1995; Llobera 1996, 2003; van Leusen 1999; Lock et al. 2014). That approach was characterised by the attempt to include an understanding of the symbolic dimension of past space based on the theoretical strands raised by processual cognitive archaeology (Renfrew 1994). Prehistoric monuments, mounds, cairns and other prominent features in the landscape became the target of such studies, where the visual impact, but also the movement (Van Leusen 1999; Verhagen and Jeneson 2012; Herzog 2013), was assessed in order to find possible patterns connected to the way prehistoric peoples lived and interacted with their surrounding landscape.

On a similar note, Space Syntax methods, first introduced by Hillier and Hanson (1984), developed with the goal of generating insights into the architectural configuration of ancient buildings, relying on concepts intimately related to a perceptual dimension of the space, such as accessibility, movement and exposure/concealment (Banning and Byrd 1989; Van Dyke 1999; Chatford Clark 2007; Stöger 2015).

In this context, and partially as a consequence of the 'phenomenological turn', Gillings and Goodrick (1996) questioned the role of GIS and its very static nature as a tool not really capable of grasping the complexity of the social aspects of ancient space. The main points of criticism focussed on the significant limitations imposed by computational capabilities and traditional map visualisation standards, which reflected on the impossibility of providing a detailed representation of the palaeolandscape. For this reason they introduced the notion of a sensuous GIS, where the simulation of the past reality becomes a pivotal element. Indeed, it was essential to explore alternative ways to data representation and to find a suitable option to integrate multi-dimensional contents in order to cope with the complexity of an experiential approach to the past landscapes. The authors proposed VR as a possible means to provide a more 'humanised' perspective of the (pre)historic space and subsequently VRML as a standard computing language for representing VR contents.

2 VR-based Applications

It is thus partly due to the dramatic advances in computer graphics and partly to the discussion of the role of more dynamic landscape representations raised in the frame of post-processual archaeology (Ingold 1993; Tilley 1994; Llobera 1996) that more scholars started to focus their interest on digitally oriented (multi)sensory approaches to the investigation of archaeological or ancient space. This included some of the first experiments with sound analysis of prehistoric monuments (Watson and Keating 1999; Watson 2001). In the Iron Age site of Danebury, Earl (1999) presents an analytic use of VRML in combination with CAD software for creating controlled viewpoints in a digital landscape where a rendered view is derived and first-person view associated to each viewpoint. This visually based simulation provided some insights into the original functions associated with the hillfort and allowed archaeologists to question the defensive scope of that space (Earl 1999). The role of senses in relation to the development of a digital ecosystem capable of providing the user with an experience similar (but not equal) to the one lived by the original inhabitant of a prehistoric space is then discussed by Forte (2003), drawing upon Barcelo's idea of developing models to reproduce complex behaviours of agents (human and non-human) interacting with the landscape (Barceló 2001). The main challenge at this point was to move on to an interpretative use of 3D modelling in archaeology (Earl and Wheatley 2002), in which multi-dimensionality and sensory-enriched virtual reconstructions could have provided the users with a formal set of tools for evaluating the experiential qualities of a landscape.

In the attempt to overcome limitations due to the 2–2.5-D visualisation of digital landscapes, texture viewshed was presented as a possible analytical tool to be applied in combination with 3D modelling software to perform visibility analysis in a virtually reconstructed built space of a Roman villa (Earl 2005), where visual prominence, impact and control were measured as a way to understand the sensory-mediated meaning of the social space in an ancient building. In this respect, a more comprehensive and systematic work for interpreting the architectural and iconographic apparatus within the Minoan palace of Akrotiri along with their agency in the frame of liturgical processions is conducted by Paliou (2011), who integrates 3D modelling and GIS functions to perform the analysis. On a related note, Paliou also tried to combine visual and acoustic analysis to explore the sensory dimension of Byzantine churches (Paliou and Kinight 2013).

Additional efforts were made in the attempt to cope with the issue of natural and artificial illumination, an aspect often neglected in most VR-based reconstructions but that has an important agency in affecting the actual perception of an object in the space (Papadopoulos and Earl 2009; Earl et al. 2013).

To further improve the reliability of the visual assessment for ancient or prehistoric monuments, simulated through VR application, Opitz (2017) proposed an assessment based on the evaluation of visual acuity and the capability of the human eye to discern details in an object's view. Richards-Rissetto (2017) explored instead multisensory modalities of analysis for the Mayan site of Copan by combining well-established GIS-based spatial analysis techniques with VR-oriented solutions for increasing the experiential value of the experiment.

3 Where Are We Now?

Throughout its chapters, organised according to a chronological order of the different case studies presented, this volume provides an insight into state-of-the-art research on digital methods and sensory-based studies of the past and the contribution they can bring to the discipline.

In Chap. 2, Eve and Gillings invite the reader to overcome the traditional reliance on representation and analysis of sensory modalities, to explore affects and invitations-to-act engendered by such sensory encounters. To demonstrate this, the authors present a case study in which a combination of GIS-based mapping and analysis plus virtual, mixed, augmented reality approaches are employed to evoke affects.

A special role in sensory-based investigation of the ancient space is played by the study of sacred or ritual space. In this respect, Sullivan in Chap. 3 explores the sacred space of an Egyptian necropolis by combining multiple sources including textual, art historical and archaeological evidence, with 3D GIS-based technology for answering questions related to the way ancient people create a physical and emotional sense of specialness or distinction in their ritual places.

Concerning the role of Virtual Reality and sensory immersion for archaeological enquiry, in Chap. 4, Sciuto et al. introduce and examine a few case studies where VR was used, respectively, (a) to support the interpretation process in a Mesolithic site in northern Sweden, (b) to capture the intangible art of Roman pantomime in the virtually reconstructed theatre of Pompeii and (c) to study through an immersive approach the photogrammetric models of mediaeval rock-cut settlement and to assess VR Google Earth as an educational students learning ancient topography.

In Chap. 5, Dunn introduces some reflections on the role of digitisation as a freeze-frame process to represent natural movement. Drawing upon a selection of case studies, the author explores and compares the possibilities provided by digital tools to cope with the problem of representing a dynamic phenomenon such as movement in order to improve our understanding of past landscapes and their inhabitants.

Visibility and acoustic analyses represent an important tool also for increasing our understanding of ancient architecture and the original structure of Roman theatres. In Chap. 6, Manzetti introduces an analytical approach to hypothesise the original architecture of Roman theatres in Crete. Her analysis is based on the combination of multiple data source, including 'legacy' data that form the basis for 3D reconstructions that were further analysed in 3D GIS.

A synesthetic investigation of a Mayan urban landscape is presented by Rissetto et al. in Chap. 7. The authors take advantage of GIS, 3D and acoustic tools to create multisensory experiences in VR with spatial sound using an immersive headset and touch controllers for movement. Interestingly, the authors explore the role of landscape in facilitating movement, sending messages and influencing social interaction.

Concerning the possibilities for artefact study and dissemination offered by sensory-oriented digital tools, in Chap. 8, Bozia presents a research project focussed on possibilities for natural interaction, physicality and contextualisation of digitally acquired artefacts and the opportunities provided by 3D printing for hands-on study and experience of the artefacts.

In Chap. 9, Pasquinucci and Landeschi illustrate the contribution that integrated sources can provide to reconstruct a narrative of the past based on a sensory account of a few coastal landscapes in Northwestern Etruria as they were perceived and described by ancient authors. The study of these passages is compared with the output of recent integrated research in the same districts described by the ancient authors.

In Chap. 10, Piccoli discusses about the use of 3D digital reconstructions for providing users with visual cues to increase their perception and so their understanding of historical places by relying on a transparent and philological process of digital anastylosis based on heterogeneous data set which includes the surviving architecture of a room in a seventeenth-century Dutch home.

Misharina and Betts, in Chap. 11, present a methodology for recording sensory data in an urban landscape and consider how the results of such sensory surveys might enable multisensory mapping of ancient urban spaces. This work draws upon Lefebvre's philosophy of social space, according to which it is impossible to make a single map of a city without overlapping temporal, monumental, social and sensory spaces.

References

Banning, E.B. and Byrd, B.F., 1989. Alternative approaches for exploring Levantine Neolithic architecture. Paléorient, pp. 154–160.

Barceló, J.A., 2001. Virtual reality for archaeological explanation. Beyond "picturesque" reconstruction. Archeologia e calcolatori, (XII), pp. 221–244.

Brück, J., 2005. Experiencing the past? The development of a phenomenological archaeology in British prehistory. Archaeological dialogues, 12(1), pp. 45–72.

Chatford Clark, D.L., 2007. Viewing the liturgy: a space syntax study of changing visibility and accessibility in the development of the Byzantine church in Jordan. World Archaeology, 39(1), pp. 84–104.

Crossland, Z., 2010. Materiality and embodiment. The Oxford handbook of material culture studies.

Day, J. ed., 2013. Making senses of the past: toward a sensory archaeology. SIU Press.

Earl, G., Porcelli, V., Papadopoulos, C., Beale, G., Harrison, M., Pagi, H. and Keay, S. (2013) Formal and informal analysis of rendered space: the Basilica Portuense. In, Bevan, Andrew and Lake, Mark (eds.) Computational Approaches to Archaeological Spaces. Walnut Creek, US. Left Coast Press/Routledge, pp. 265–305.

Earl, G.P. 1999. Visualising Danebury: Modelled Approaches to Spatial Theory, in: Dingwall, L., S. Exon, V. Gaffney, S. Laflin and M. van Leusen (eds.) Archaeology in the Age of the Internet. CAA97. Computer Applications and Quantitative Methods in Archaeology. Proceedings of the 25th Anniversary Conference, University of Birmingham, April 1997 (BAR International Series 750). Archaeopress, Oxford, pp. 259–264.

Earl, Graeme and Wheatley, David (2002) Virtual reconstruction and the interpretative process: a case-study from Avebury. In, Wheatley, David, Earl, Graeme and Poppy, Sarah (eds.) Contemporary Themes in Archaeological Computing. Oxford, UK. Oxbow Books, pp. 5–15.

Earl, G. 2005. *Wandering the house of the birds: reconstruction and perception at roman italica.* In (Fellner, D.W. and Spencer, S.N. eds.) VAST 2005: The 6th International Symposium on Virtual Reality, Archaeology and Intelligent Cultural Heritage, Incorporating 3rd EUROGRAPHICS Workshop on Graphics and Cultural Heritage, ISTI-CNR, Pisa, Italy, November 8–11, 2005 : Short and Project Papers Proceedings

Fleming, A. 1999. Phenomenology and the megaliths of Wales: a dreaming too far?. Oxford journal of archaeology, 18(2), pp.119–125.

Fleming, A., 2006. Post-processual landscape archaeology: a critique. Cambridge Archaeological Journal, 16(3), pp. 267–280.

Forte, M. 2003. "Mindscape: Ecological Thinking, Cyber-Anthropology and Virtual Archaeological Landscapes." BAR International Series 1151: 95–108.

Frieman, C. and Gillings, M., 2007. Seeing is perceiving?. World Archaeology, 39(1), pp. 4–16.
Frothingham, A.L., 1911. Where Archaeology Comes in an Open Sesame. The North American Review, 194(671), pp. 576–588.
Gaffney, V. and Stančić, Z. 1991 GIS Approaches to Regional Analysis: A Case Study of the Island of Hvar. Ljubljana.
Gillings, M., and G. T. Goodrick. 1996. "Sensuous and Reflexive GIS: Exploring Visualisation and VRML." Internet Archaeology 1 (1).
Hamilakis, Y., Pluciennik, M. and Tarlow, S., 2002. Introduction: Thinking Through the Body. In, Hamilakis, Yannis, Pluciennik, Mark and Tarlow, Sarah (eds.) Thinking Through the Body: Archaeologies of Corporeality. London; New York. Kluwer Academic/Plenum, pp. 1–21.
Hamilton, S., Whitehouse, R., Brown, K., Combes, P., Herring, E. and Thomas, M.S., 2006. Phenomenology in practice: Towards a methodology for a 'subjective' approach. European Journal of Archaeology, 9(1), pp. 31–71.
Hamilton, S. and R. Whitehouse, eds. 2020. Neolithic Spaces: Social and sensory landscapes of the first farmers of Italy, Vols 1 and 2. London: Accordia.
Herzog I. 2013, Theory and practice of cost functions, in F. Contreras, M. Farjas, F.J. Melero (eds.), Fusion of Cultures. Proceedings of the 38th Annual Conference on Computer Applications and Quantitative Methods in Archaeology (Granada, Spain 2010), BAR International Series 2494, Oxford, Archaeopress, 375–382.
Hillier, B. and Hanson, J., 1984. The social logic of space. Cambridge university press.
Ingold, T. 1993 'The temporality of the landscape', World Archaeology 25(2), 152–75.
Johnson, M.H., 2012. Phenomenological approaches in landscape archaeology. Annual Review of Anthropology, 41, pp. 269–284.
Joyce, R.A., 2005. Archaeology of the body. Annu. Rev. Anthropol., 34, pp. 139–158.
Lake, M. W., P. E. Woodman, and S. J. Mithen. 1998. "Tailoring GIS Software for Archaeological Applications: An Example Concerning Viewshed Analysis." Journal of Archaeological Science 25 (1): 27–38.
Llobera, M. 1996. "Exploring the Topography of Mind: GIS, Social Space and Archaeology." Antiquity 70 (269): 612–622.
Llobera, M. 2003 'Extending GIS-based visual analysis: the concept of visualscapes', International Journal of Geographical Information Science 17(1), 25–48.
Lock, G. 1995. Archaeological Computing, Archaeological Theory, and Moves towards Contextualism, in: Huggett, J. and N. Ryan (eds.), CAA94. Computer Applications and Quantitative Methods in Archaeology 1994 (BAR International Series 600). Tempus Reparatum, Oxford, pp. 12–18.
Lock, G., M. Kormann, and J. Pouncett. 2014. "Visibility and Movement: Towards a GIS-based Integrated Approach." In Computational Approaches to the Study of Movement in Archaeology: Theory, Practice and Interpretation of Factors and Effects of Long Term Landscape Formation and Transformation, edited by S. Polla and P. Verhagen, 23–42. Boston, MA: De Gruyter.
Meskell, L., 1996. The somatization of archaeology: institutions, discourses, corporeality. Norwegian archaeological review, 29(1), pp. 1–16.
Opitz, R., 2017. An experiment in using visual attention metrics to think about experience and design choices in past places. Journal of Archaeological Method and Theory, 24(4), pp. 1203–1226.
Paliou, E. 2011. "The Communicative Potential of Theran Murals in Late Bronze Age Akrotiri: Applying Viewshed Analysis in 3D Townscapes." Oxford Journal of Archaeology 30 (3): 247–272.
Paliou, E., and D. J. Knight. 2013. "Mapping the Senses: Perceptual and Social Aspects of Late Antique Liturgy in San Vitale, Ravenna." In the Proceedings of CAA 2010, Computer Applications and Quantitative methods in Archaeology, International Conference, Granada 6–9 April, 2010, pp. 229–236.
Papadopoulos, C. and Earl, G.P., 2009, September. Structural and lighting models for the Minoan cemetery at Phourni, Crete. In Proceedings of the 10th International conference on Virtual Reality, Archaeology and Cultural Heritage (pp. 57–64).

Pollock, J.L., 1967. Criteria and our knowledge of the material world. The Philosophical Review, 76(1), pp. 28–60.
Renfrew, C. 1994 'Towards a cognitive archaeology', in C. Renfrew and E.B.W. Zubrow (eds) The Ancient Mind, Cambridge, 3–12.
Richards-Rissetto, H., 2017. What can GIS+ 3D mean for landscape archaeology?. Journal of Archaeological Science, 84, pp. 10–21.
Skeates, R. 2010. An archaeology of the senses: prehistoric Malta. Oxford University Press.
Stöger, J.J., 2015. Roman neighbourhoods by the numbers: A space syntax view on ancient city quarters and their social life. The Journal of Space Syntax, 6(1), pp. 61–80.
Tilley, C. 1994. A Phenomenology of Landscape: Places, Paths, and Monuments. Vol. 10. Oxford: Berg.
Tringham, R. 2013. A sense of touch–the full-body experience–in the past and present of Çatalhöyük, Turkey. Making senses of the past: Toward a sensory archaeology, pp.177–195
Van Dyke, R.M., 1999. Space syntax analysis at the Chacoan outlier of Guadalupe. American Antiquity, 64(3), pp. 461–473.
Van Leusen, M. 1999. "Viewshed and Cost Surface Analysis Using GIS (Cartographic Modelling in a Cell-Based GIS II)." BAR International Series 757: 215–224.
Verhagen, P. and Jeneson, K., 2012. A Roman puzzle. Trying to find the Via Belgica with GIS. Thinking beyond the tool. Archaeological computing and the interpretive process, pp. 123–130.
Watson, A. and Keating, D., 1999. Architecture and sound: an acoustic analysis of megalithic monuments in prehistoric Britain. Antiquity, 73(280), pp. 325–336.
Watson, A., 2001. Composing avebury. World archaeology, 33(2), pp. 296–314.
Wheatley, D. 1995. "Cumulative Viewshed Analysis: A GIS-based Method for Investigating Intervisibility, and Its Archaeological Application." In Archaeology and Geographical Information Systems: A European Perspective, edited by G. Lock and Z. Stancic, 171–185. London: Taylor & Francis.

More than Modal? Exploring Affect, Affordance, Invitation and Solicitation

Stuart Eve and Mark Gillings

Abstract The aim of this chapter is to make a strong case for the adoption of a radically different approach to the archaeology of the senses. This is an approach that focuses not on what is sensed per se (or any ingenious mapping or digital representation of such) but instead the emergent *affects* that may have arisen in any given sensory encounter, and the impact(s) of such on the assemblage of individuals, things, animals, environments, landscape elements, memories, expectations and anticipations (to name but a few) that were bound up within it. This is not to say that we should abandon attempts to, for example, delineate, visualise, map and analyse what could be seen, heard or smelled. Instead, it is to stress that such efforts should always be treated as a means-to-an-end and never taken as definitive end-products. In the discussion that follows, we build the theoretical framework needed to effect such a re-orientation, drawing upon affect theory and notions of relational capacity and affordance. We then go on to demonstrate the value of this through a case study involving the mapping and exploration of visibility and foreground the unique (yet largely untapped) interpretative potential of virtual, mixed and augmented reality approaches to move beyond mere representation, to instead evoke affects directly.

Keywords Affect · Affordance · Aura · GIS · Gaming · Augmented-reality

1 Introduction

In this chapter we argue that to get the most out of computational approaches to the senses we need to treat the results of our analyses as heuristic building blocks rather than end-products, solutions or answers. This requires not only methodological innovation, but also careful theory-building, as whilst a range of computationally

S. Eve · M. Gillings (✉)
Department of Archaeology and Anthropology, Bournemouth University, Poole, UK
e-mail: mgillings@bournemouth.ac.uk

S. Eve
e-mail: seve@mola.org.uk

G. Landeschi and E. Betts (eds.), *Capturing the Senses*,
Quantitative Methods in the Humanities and Social Sciences,
https://doi.org/10.1007/978-3-031-23133-9_2

elegant approaches to the investigation/mapping/modelling/exploration of sensory modalities have been (and as this volume demonstrates, continue to be) developed, we still lack the theoretical frameworks needed to unlock their full interpretative potential. It is often the case that we construct elaborate theoretical justifications for carrying out our analyses or simulations of seeing, hearing, smelling, touching etc. most commonly through various strands of phenomenology and the archaeologies/anthropologies that have themselves drawn upon them (e.g. Tilley 1994) qualified and quantified through thresholds and metrics derived from the formal modelling of sensory capacities (e.g. Mlekuz 2004; Ogburn 2006). When it comes to interpreting the results of such studies—i.e. what does knowing what was potentially seen, heard, smelled etc. tell us about the past that we did not know (or suspect) before the study was carried out?—we are largely left to our own devices. This then is a chapter about how we can best use the results of modal simulations in order to shed light on the past.

Our basic argument is that our current focus is wrong. We should not concern ourselves with the senses at all, but instead *affect*, and as a result we should abandon efforts to delineate a sensory archaeology and focus instead upon the development of a coherent and persuasive archaeology of affect. This is an archaeology where methodological and theoretical developments are closely entwined. To demonstrate the value of such a shift we explore one pathway for moving beyond simple modalities to consider instead the impact a particular bundle of sensory engagements may have had on a perceiving animal. Rather than limit ourselves to mapping or quantifying what could be seen, heard, felt etc. the aim is to explore what emergent impacts a given tangle of sensory impacts may have had in the particular context of engagement in which they occur. The aim is not to restrict or formalise, but instead to offer a helping-hand for thinking beyond the senses. The key point is that rather than set out to explore perception, studies should always set out to explore affect, treating individual sensory engagements as at best partial proxies and always means to an end. As we demonstrate, the benefits of doing so can be enormous.

We explore this through the study of elements of the prehistoric monument complex at Avebury (Gillings and Pollard 2004). Reaching across 3.5 km of chalkland, this takes the form of an intensive collection of earthen, timber and megalithic structures spanning the 4th–3rd millennia BC, centred upon the standing stone circles of the Avebury henge (Fig. 1). Recent research focusing on the heart of this landscape (Gillings et al. 2019) has argued that the very beginnings of what would become the largest standing stone circle in the world lay with a small, unremarkable domestic house dating to the very introduction of Neolithic ways of life in this part of Britain. After gradually falling into disrepair and decay, the footprint of this short-lived house would come to be marked and dramatically amplified by a series of monumental constructions that radiated out from it, like ripples on the surface of a pond; each new addition enclosing and enfolding the last. To date the explanation for this has been couched in terms of memory-work and memorialisation; the location of the very first settlement and thus the site of a founder's house, being successively re-inscribed, albeit on an increasingly dramatic scale and in very different media. Kept in active memory, as the physical remains of the house proper were lost to the forces of entropy and decay. Whilst this explanatory framework certainly accounts

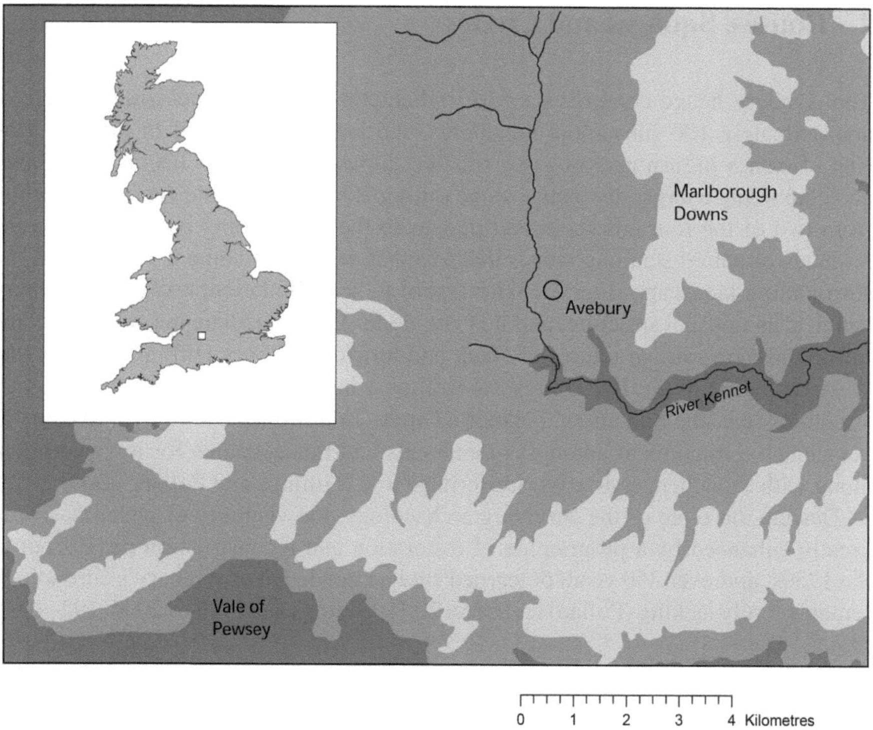

Fig. 1 General location plan of the Avebury region

for the progressive (aggressive?) monumentalisation that took place at the site, it has little to say about how exactly, this memory-work manifested itself in everyday practice or the complex relationships that may have existed between the memory (as a malleable fluid thing) and the thing it was purported to be memorialising (the fragmentary remains of a rather unprepossessing rectangular house). Or to put this another way, how did this memory-work *work*?

We explore this through the development of a new interpretative framework based upon the closely linked concepts of affect and relational capacity (or affordance), using computational approaches to capture and explore not sensory modalities but instead the affective atmospheres or fields that emerged from the coming together of certain configurations of people, structures, materials, imperatives and motivations. Here we treat the construction of elements of the monumental fabric as the creation of deliberate engines for shaping and focusing sensory affordances and thus affects; mechanisms that could have undesired as well as desired consequences and that are bound up in the emergence of new constructions and new affects. Our argument is that rather than passive entities to memory—memorials in the traditional sense of the word—the various standing stone settings that were progressively constructed around the house were active engines of affect—deliberate mechanisms of fascination that through their particular configuration and relations with other material objects served to intensify and shape a particular set of affective atmospheres (sensu Ash 2013).

2 Houses, Squares and Circles

The Avebury henge comprises a 420 m diameter earthwork enclosing a circle of approximately 100 substantial megaliths—the largest of its kind in Europe. This ring of stones in turn encloses two smaller circles each around 100 m in diameter and containing a large, distinctive stone setting at its approximate centre. Extending from two of the four entrances that punctuate the surrounding bank and ditch are Avenues of paired standing stones that together extend for some 3.5 km across the surrounding landscape (Fig. 2). With regard to scale and complexity, the Avebury henge is an unusual structure, and it is not alone. The immediate landscape is home to further enormous structures of chalk and turf (e.g. Silbury Hill) and timber (the West Kennet Palisade Enclosures) as well as a host of more modest monumental structures (e.g. the Sanctuary, Falkner's Circle, Longstones enclosure). Avebury is very much a monument amongst monuments and this accounts for its inscription, along with Stonehenge, as a World Heritage Site (Gillings and Pollard 2004).

Despite the scale of the surviving archaeology, the visibility of which has been greatly enhanced by a programme of restoration and reconstruction carried out in the 1930s, and over 350 years of learned study, knowledge of Avebury's chronology remains sorely lacking (Pollard and Cleal 2004; Gillings and Pollard 2004: 192–193).

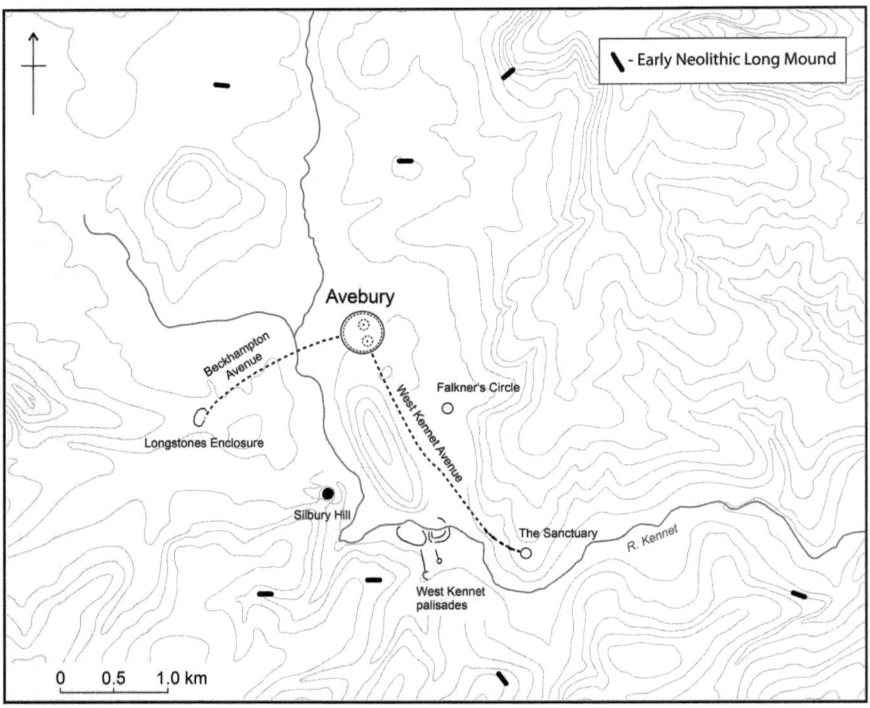

Fig. 2 The Avebury henge and surrounding monumental structures

This situation results in large part from the lack of excavation within the henge since 1939 compounded by a tendency for excavated features (such as stone holes) to be largely free of material that can be used for radiocarbon determinations. Whilst we are confident that the main phases of construction took place in the 3rd millennium BC, the precise sequence of earth-working and stone erection remains elusive. We do not know when the first activity at the site took place or the form it took.

The scale of the challenge is brought into stark focus by the small suite of C14 dates we do have, which suggest that alterations and additions were being made to the stone circles well into the 2nd millennium BC, possibly extending into the Iron Age/early Romano-British periods (Pollard and Cleal 2004: 127).

Recent archival and survey work has raised the distinct possibility that the largest prehistoric stone circle in the world began its life a millennium or so earlier as a small domestic house (Gillings et al. 2019). The proposed sequence can be summarised as follows. At some point, most likely during the first half of the 4th millennium BC, a small domestic house was constructed, square in shape and some 7 m across (Fig. 3a). After this had fallen into disuse and collapsed (Fig. 3b), a large standing stone (called the Obelisk by 18th century observers) was erected in the corner of the house; a thick pillar of unworked stone standing some 6 m high (Fig. 3c). By this stage, all that would have been left of the house were a few low earthworks. At some point the

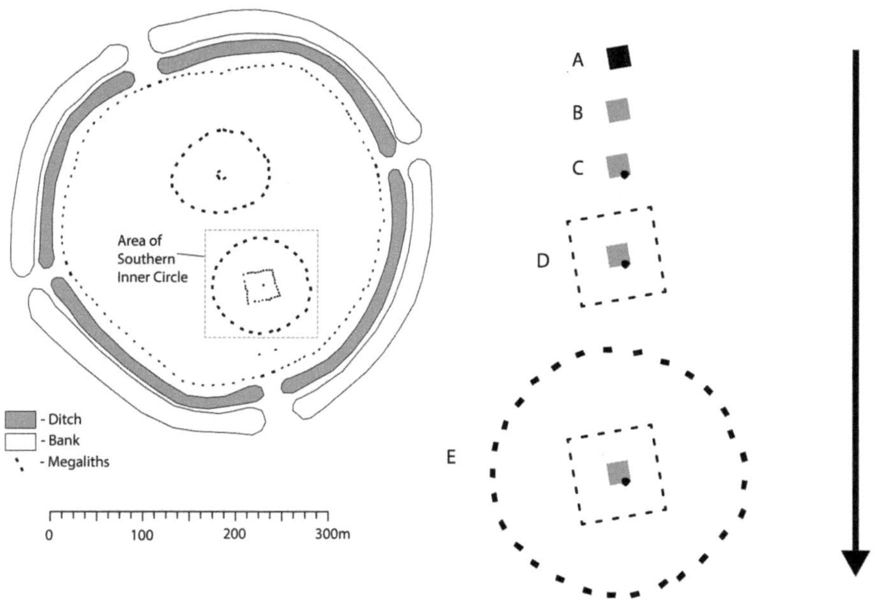

Fig. 3 The location of the house structure and surrounding settings. The published phasing begins with a rectangular house (**A**). After a century or so all that is left of the house are subtle surface traces (**B**). At some point a substantial megalith—the 6 m high Obelisk—is erected in the southeast corner of the former structure (**C**). A 30 m wide square of megaliths is then erected around the house respecting, yet exploding and exaggerating, its orientation and proportions (**D**). The final phase of activity sees the square itself enclosed by the 100 m diameter Southern Inner Circle (**E**)

footprint of the house was quite literally exploded and monumentalised. A square setting of standing stones 30 m across was raised centred upon the earlier structure and echoing its shape and orientation (Fig. 3d). As far as can be reconstructed, this megalithic square comprised alternating large and small standing stones though the precise frequency and pattern are not clear (nothing of this setting survives apart from geophysical anomalies, some excavated stoneholes and a line of small megaliths re-erected in the 1930s). This square was in turn enclosed by a 100 m diameter circle of very large megaliths, with an average height of 3.4 m), forming what is today referred to as the Southern Inner Circle (Fig. 3e). The picture is essentially one of the sequential ripples or progressive 'wrappings' (sensu Richards 2013: 16–23). The lack of conclusive evidence for any re-working (i.e. the reconfiguration of existing stone settings) suggests progressive elaboration and enhancement, the remains of the house structure receding behind enclosing settings of substantial standing stones.

3 Affect and Affordance

So what exactly do we mean by affect? Having highlighted the way in which affect emerges in contexts as varied as language, narrative, poetics and performance, as well as the complex relationships that exist between affect and terms such as emotion, feelings, personality and attitude, Besnier has argued that 'adopting a broad (but malleable) definition of "affect" can be seen as a wise empirical stance' (1990: 421). We agree and in the current discussion follow Bonta and Protevi (2006: 49) and Seigworth and Gregg (2010: 1) in using the term 'affect' to refer broadly to the profoundly relational capacity of bodies to both act (affect) and be acted upon (be affected). Looking to the latter, this is to acknowledge that certain processes, activities, practices, dispositions, happenings, events, encounters and assemblages can provoke/invite responses—emotional, anticipatory, practical, reflective, evaluatory etc.—and through these lead to tangible change and transformation in the bodies bound up in them. One of the most interesting developments to emerge from the 'affective turn' that has taken place across the humanities and social sciences (see Gregg and Seigworth 2010) has been the notion of the affective field or atmosphere (Harris and Sørenson 2012; Anderson 2009, 2014) and the idea that certain relations (or motleys and entanglements) of and between things can, and do, have an affective reach that can be both spatial and temporal. The notion of the affective atmosphere was introduced by Anderson and is a concept that, in Anderson's work at least, seems to work tirelessly to elude concise definition. The key element we would like to draw from his discussions is the attention that is placed upon atmospheres as collective affects—the 'shared ground from which subjective states and their attendant feelings and emotions emerge' (2009: 78). Atmospheres have an inherent spatiality and can be strongly agentic. They are singular yet (in Anderson's terms) indeterminate—qualities that 'exceed that from which they emanate' (2009: 80). Bille and Simonsen have stressed that these atmospheres emerge ("unfold") as relations located in spatially embedded practices—'created by both materiality and the presence and practices of people' (2019: 12). In an important discussion, Harris and Sørenson have introduced the notion of the affective field as an adjunct to that of atmosphere. The former comprises an active, dynamic field of relations that emerges from tangles between things and locations. Perhaps most importantly, these relational fields are 'productive' of practice (2012: 150). In distinction, they use the term atmosphere to refer to the instantiation of a particular affective field through (for example) certain combinations of materials such as architecture (2012: 152). Put another way, certain affective fields are revealed, intensified or actualised by certain configurations of materials and people. This echoes Thrift's suggestion that specific combinations of locales, things and systems can create what he terms *fields of captivation* and *mechanisms of fascination* (2012: 290). We will return to these notions later in our discussion of Avebury. Clearly, the distinction Harris and Sørenson draw between fields and atmospheres is subtle and whilst we would support the emphasis they place upon temporality and spatiality in their consideration of atmosphere, we are less comfortable with the distinction that is drawn in relation to practice. To Harris and Sørenson, whilst atmospheres can shape and texture practices, it is argued that they need not necessarily emerge from them, which seems a little arbitrary. As a result, in the current discussion we have folded the affective field into our consideration of atmosphere. Atmospheres are spatial, temporal and (following Bille and Simonsen (2019) and practice theorists such as Reckwitz (2017)) for atmospheres to affect—whether through emergent fields of relations or as generators/enhancers/focusing-devices—they need to be fully embedded in practice.

Some stark illustrations of precisely the kind of affective atmosphere we are evoking can be gleaned from archaeological and ethnographic studies of place and place-making. In her seminal study of the 'hills and hollers' of the decaying coal mining communities of southern West Virginia, Kathleen Stewart stressed how place inscription could be small and deeply personal; the resultant places emerging as a series of vignettes—complex affective fields that bound together the location, the visitor and events that had unfolded there (1996). Clearly, places such as this could serve a didactic role (e.g. Basso 1996), but they could also be rawly affective—serving to weave emotion and feeling into the very fabric of the landscape. In Stewart's case nostalgia, yearning, tragedy and suffering were articulated through a scatter of places into a starkly visceral geography of loss and despair. This was a deeply relational and emergent approach insofar as the place was made less by any given event/doing/happening (and simple memory of that event) but instead the way the echoes and ripples of the event reached out across space and time to shape practices in the present. This has echoes in Lorimer's claim that certain places exert a 'holding power' and have the ability to 'charm' (Darling cited in Lorimer 2006: 501). We might just as well simplify this to say that as a consequence of the web of performances and relations of which they are part, certain places *affect*.

Having introduced our use of the term affect, through the notion of the affective atmosphere, we would now like to argue that critical to understanding the relations that lie at the heart of any given affective atmosphere, is the notion of affordance. If affect is a relatively recent addition to our heuristic toolbox, affordance has a longer history within the discipline, particularly in the context of computational approaches that deal, in one way or another, with archaeology and the senses (e.g. Llobera 1996; Gillings 2009, 2012; Eve 2014). Since its introduction by Gibson (1979), the attractiveness and utility of the term has resulted in it being co-opted across a range of disciplines and in a range of contexts, including archaeology (e.g. Gillings 1998; Knappett 2005; Hodder 2011; Eve 2012). However it has proven rather slippery in each case, with more (or less) orthodox definitions emerging and arguably as much intellectual energy spent on policing its boundaries as developing it as a useful heuristic (e.g. Chemero 2003; Burlamaqui and Dong 2014). This is a consequence of Gibson's failure to define exactly what he meant by the term in the first instance. The definition of affordance followed here takes its inspiration from DeLanda's concept of *relational capacity*, and Ingold's *affordance*, both drawing upon specific readings of the foundational work of Gibson (DeLanda 2013: 66–67; Ingold 1992: 46). In short, we are using it to refer to relational rather than intrinsic (or essential) properties that emerge in the context of practical activities carried out by animals (like us) in an environment. In this formulation, relations or assemblages (containing things, animals, materials, expectations, motivations, memories etc.) afford certain experiences or engagements, that are integral to the emergence and/or realisation of specific affects. This is not to argue that affects are somehow built from affordances in a simple and direct way, or that the former represents a higher-order phenomenon. The particular value of affordance here is in its direct link to sensory perception and the framework it offers for interpreting our carefully modelled sensory data. To give the explicitly sensory example of vision, to an animal seeking to hide, a location that affords seclusion and concealment (i.e. that is not over-looked or perceived to be so) may allow an atmosphere of security, relief and even confidence to emerge and saturate it. Likewise, a particular assemblage of materials (whether deliberately assembled or emergent) can afford a particular odour that if only sporadically encountered, can immediately and vividly evoke other times and places, feelings and responses (alongside a host of other affects ranging from disgust and pleasure to indifference).

For a more concrete example we can turn to Kassung and Schwesinger's (2016) first-person simulation of the Forum Romanum (http://www.soundstudieslab.org/events/how-to-sound-out-the-past/). Through careful acoustic modelling, the simulation allows a virtual participant to explore the relationship between an orator, their speech and the surrounding architecture in order to map the degree to which specific locations impacted one's ability to hear and understand. Degree of audibility mapped as an affordance. Once mapped, that affordance can then be employed as a frame through which to explore the atmosphere of relative satisfaction, comprehension and clarity on the part of a listener seeking to actively hear the words being spoken. Likewise, in Paliou's (2014) study of past built environments (https://eleftheria121.wordpress.com/research/visibility-analysis-in-fully-3d-spaces/) we can use isovists to map the visibility of wall paintings through apertures such as doors and windows as an affordance, and then go on to study the changing textures of frustration and revelation that this partial obscurement encourages in a curious viewer desperate to see what is going on. The range of affordances possible in any relationship therefore helps us to frame, characterise and interpret the likely atmospheres it engenders. They offer us a methodological 'way-in' to investigate affect. For example, we can map degrees of in-view/out-of-view (affordance) in order to explore relative concealment and feelings of security, comfort versus insecurity, fear and frustration (affect).

So far so good, but this reliance upon affordance raises the thorny issue of how we decide which affordances or relations (out of what is often a large field of possibilities) are germane in a certain situation or context. A useful way of filtering the almost infinite set of potential affordances that could theoretically playout in a given relational context, is through the notion of 'invitations' (Withagen et al. 2012; Käufer and Chemero 2015). The argument here is that whilst any potential set of relations may indeed afford a near infinite set of possibilities, the nature of the practices being carried out will mean some affordances are more inviting than others. For example, to return to the example of Cicero, a raised piece of architecture may well afford the opportunity to rest, but to an individual trying to catch a glimpse of the illustrious orator, it is its ability to raise their viewpoint that will be more inviting. In a similar way, in his application of assemblage theory to the analysis of Cache Cave, California, Robinson has used the notion of value and the technique of capacity analysis to identify, characterise, compare and contrast, the range of relational capacities that emerge from creating and engaging with material culture at different locations in the site (Robinson 2017).

4 Exploring Affective Atmospheres

To return to our case study, as the importance of the house as a foundational structure grew over time, its physical presence diminished as it decayed; its traces subtle (a change in vegetation, some slight lumps and bumps, a spread of artefactual material in and on the surface of the soil). This was a site that had to be carefully looked for if it was to be found, the intimate visual clues it afforded perhaps conjuring an atmosphere of reverence and deep memory. If the proposed sequence is correct (Fig. 3) with the construction of the Obelisk this atmosphere would have changed. Once raised, the 6 m high bulk of the Obelisk made visible the fact that there was something there that demanded to be seen and left the viewer in no doubt as to where it was. As a result it generated its own affects, drawing viewers in; orienting them towards the location of the house traces and stoking the expectations they carried with them. The Obelisk affords visibility that in turn evokes an atmosphere of anticipation and reverence, an anticipation that intensifies the closer the viewer gets. It is almost as though the Obelisk had to be constructed on the exaggerated scale that it was, towering above the other megalithic settings at the site, as a direct consequence of the virtual invisibility of the structure it was signalling. In this sense it is interesting (but not surprising) that over time it was the Obelisk itself that took on this role—moving from a 'signpost towards', to the object of veneration itself as the house structure finally slipped from memory (or perhaps more properly, relevance). This was certainly the case by the early 18th century and persists to the present day. With the construction of the surrounding square of stones, the atmosphere was transformed once again, as whilst the Obelisk itself was clearly visible, and the presence of the foundational house structure was re-inscribed and amplified, the lumps and bumps at the foot of it and the aura they radiated were now partially hidden from view, shuttered by the interrupted lines of standing stones. The use of aura is deliberate here, referring to Benjamin's use of the term (2008) to denote authenticity, and the particular quality that encounters with originals (rather than reproductions) can have. Aura offers another productive way of thinking about affect, particularly in the context of digital reproductions such as VR models (Gillings 2005). In many ways we might think of aura as an atmosphere in its own right. The key point is that the creation of the square subtly altered the atmosphere which now began to take on a more teasing texture of frustration, anxiety and potential confusion. From a free field-of-view viewers now had to actively jostle and manoeuvre to catch a glimpse. This in turn was amplified and extended further from the site of the former house by the construction of the enclosing circle.

Over time the memory-work taking place in Avebury became characterised by a growing tension between a visitor's desire to gaze upon and perhaps touch the object of veneration, and the degree to which this was actually possible. As physical traces slipped away, the increasingly elaborate proxies and signposts that radiated out from them, like ripples in a pond, served as much to inhibit access as permit it, allowing a series of complex and textured atmospheres to emerge in the web of relations between the traces of the house, the megalithic settings, desires, memories and movement. Needless to say, if we can begin to unravel and explore the sequence of perceptual affordances that emerged, we can begin to understand these changing atmospheres and in turn begin to shed light upon the practices and engagements that would, over the course of a millennium and a half, result in the construction of one of Europe's pre-eminent prehistoric monument complexes.

In seeking to explore affective atmospheres two approaches are offered—abstraction and evocation. The first relies upon familiar modes of cartographic representation. In this a 2D abstraction of affect is mapped through the delineation of a single sensory modality (vision) as an affordance. The aim here is to render affect as something tangible, the atmosphere or field (however fuzzily defined) translated to a definable spatial footprint. The result is a thematic map whose novelty lies in the theme that is being represented. The second seeks to eschew representation all together by seeking to evoke the very affect the analysis is seeking to explore. In this case frustration-revelation. This is through the sketching out of an approach that employs AR and sound to prompt emplaced performances of seeking and glimpsing.

5 Methodology

To explore the affective power of the fragmentary remains of the founder house, four analyses have been carried out. In the first of these a GIS has been used to map the affective field generated by the aura of the house using a specific visual affordance—glimpsing—as a proxy for affective atmosphere. This is produced in relation to an individual (or group of such) who wants to directly see (and perhaps physically engage with) these original traces, and is comprised of a variable cocktail of curiosity, revelation, awe, impatience and frustration; different elements rising to the surface as glimpses become progressively more snatched and elusive.

The data used for this analysis comprises a Digital Elevation Model (DEM) of the henge which incorporates a reconstruction of the original final phase earthwork; a substantial bank and ditch reaching maximum heights/depths of six and ten metres respectively. Although undoubtedly later than the megalithic phases discussed, this serves as a useful frame for the analysis. Standing stone positions likewise represent a blend of known megalithic settings, former stone holes recorded through survey and excavation (Gillings et al. 2019), and educated guesswork, using known patterns to infill areas currently under the modern village (Fig. 4). Although there would undoubtedly have been significant variation in the shapes and heights of the standing stones (these were unmodified blocks of locally available sandstone) for the purposes of the analyses carried out the stones have been modelled as regular lozenges with the heights of the megalithic settings estimated at a conservative 1 m for the stones of the square setting and 3 m for the southern inner circle (for structural detail of the Avebury henge please see Gillings and Pollard 2004).

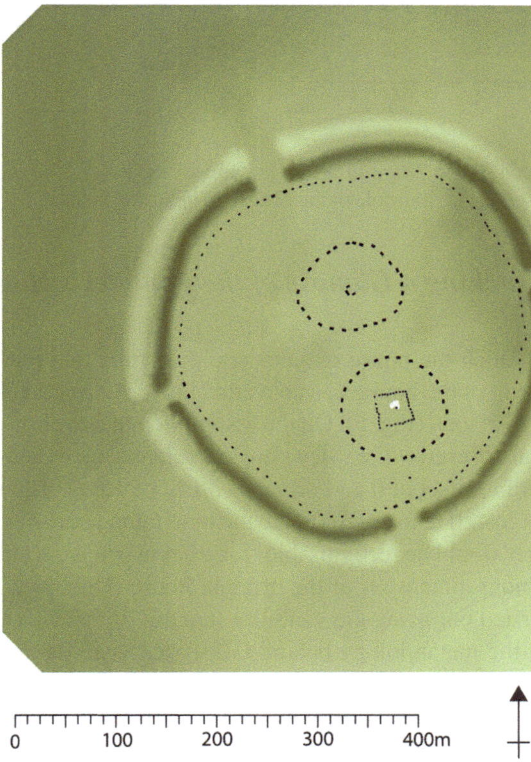

Fig. 4 The reconstructed DEM and stone setting positions used in the analyses. The footprint of the house structure is indicated in white

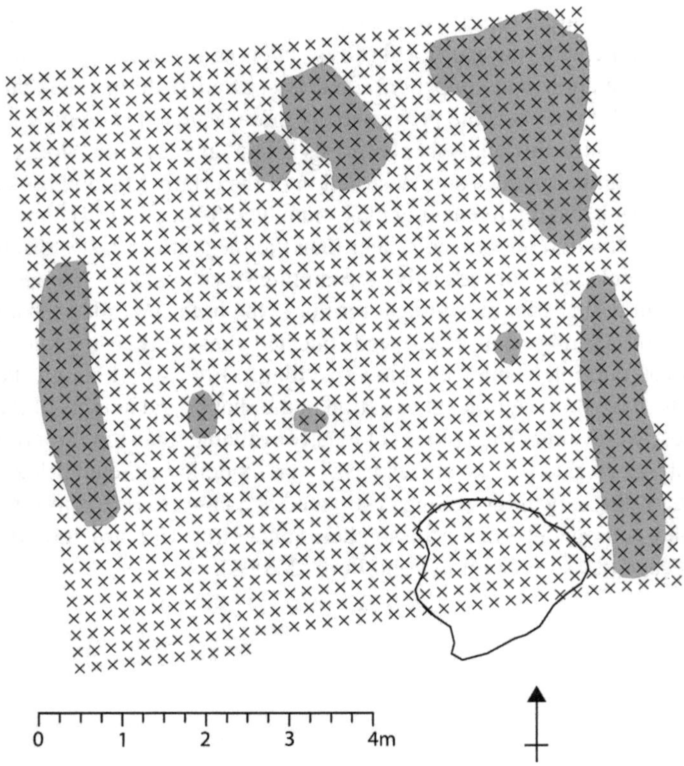

Fig. 5 The viewpoints spaced on a 0.2 m grid across the area of the house. The gulleys of the former structure are shaded grey; the stonehole of the obelisk in indicated in black

5.1 Analysis 1—Catching a Glimpse of the Founder's House

To map the areas from which the house remains could be fully and partially seen (i.e. glimpsed) the footprint of the house was converted into a 0.2 m grid of potential viewpoints—1,271 points in total (Fig. 5). On the assumption that the house remains would be essentially flat a reverse (i.e. views-to) cumulative viewshed was then generated, with a viewpoint offset of 0 and observer offset of 1.6 m. The maximum viewing distance was set to 420 m to approximate the maximum short-distance view (i.e. view where the target would be recognisable) for a 7.4 m spread of subtle earthwork traces—the maximum dimension of the original house (Ogburn 2006, Table 1). The analysis was carried out using the visibility function in ArcGIS 10.6.1 (for a detailed discussion of the methodology behind GIS-based visibility analyses see Gillings and Wheatley 2019). The resulting summed viewshed identified the areas from which a viewer would see the house remains (Fig. 6). With the exception of some partial views beyond the east and southern entrances, these were full views, with the entire area of the house either visible or not; the affective field an otherwise

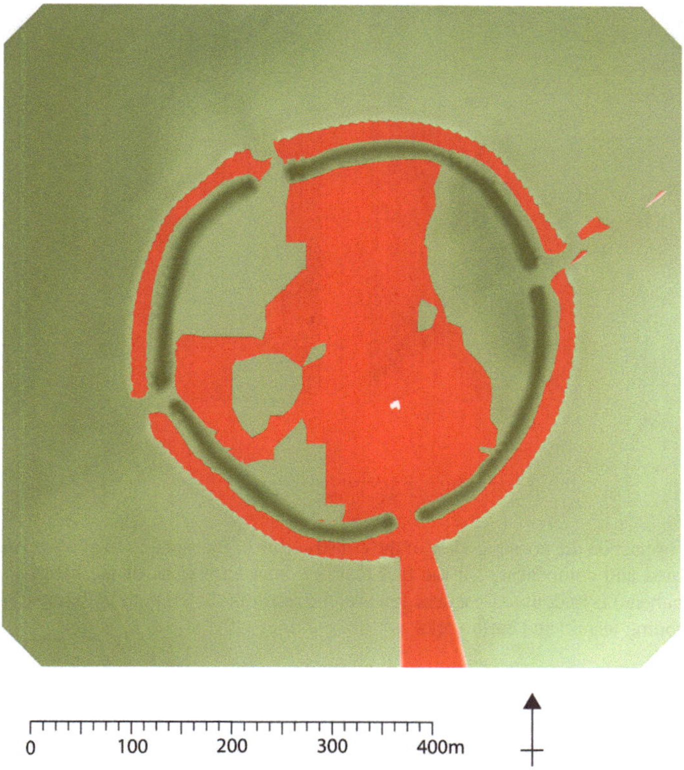

Fig. 6 The area (red) from which a viewer would have had an unobstructed view of the former house structure assuming no megalithic settings

undifferentiated block of clear views. The impact upon this field of the construction of the square setting of megaliths was dramatic; put simply the atmosphere of revelation had changed (Fig. 7). The effect of exploding and exaggerating the footprint (and thus visual signature) of the house was to create an intense zone within and around the square of direct and total visual engagements, whereas beyond the square acts of looking and seeing were now broken down into a complex, spoke-like pattern of partial views—glimpses. The original atmosphere was now restricted to the interior and immediate border of the square; outside of it, a viewer would need to position themselves carefully, and potentially jockey and jostle, just to catch a glimpse. Frustration, exploration and negotiation (not to mention strategy and tactics) would come to the fore as they sought, and evaluated, a sequence of partial, fragmentary views. What is interesting is that there is a directionality to the strength of the fragmentary views available, with more rewarding channels to the south and west. These coincide broadly with what would later become the southern and western entrances, monumentalised breaks in the earthwork bank that connected to lines of paired megaliths (the West Kennet and Beckhampton Avenues) that together extended out into the surrounding landscape (Fig. 2).

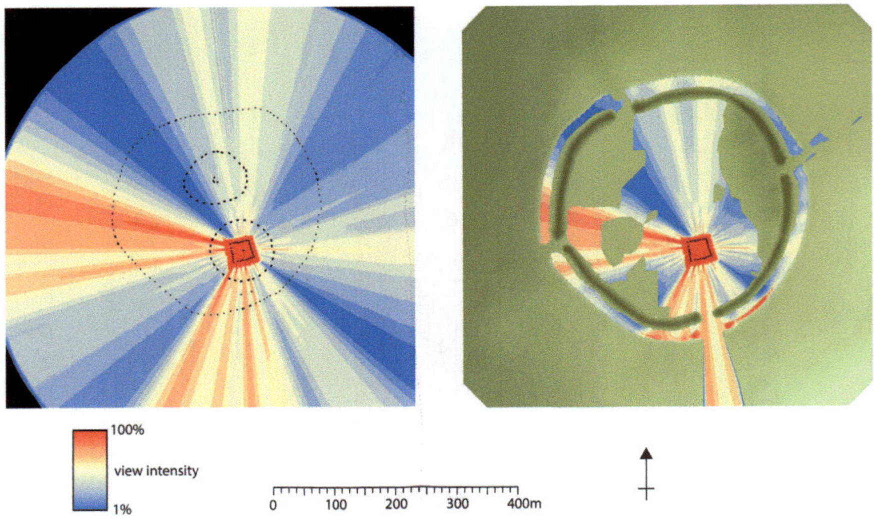

Fig. 7 The impact on the possible view of the construction of the square. To allow broader patterns to be discerned and compensate for the fact that the outer earthwork of the henge (used here to frame the analysis) is undoubtedly a later feature, the result is shown both with (right) and without (left) surrounding terrain and earthworks

With the construction of the Southern Inner Circle surrounding the square, the atmosphere changes once again (Fig. 8) becoming more fractured and frustrating beyond the exploded footprint of the square and more intensified within, the channels that afforded glimpses of the founder structure becoming narrower and the chance of losing sight entirely increasing. The alignment of the broadest of the southern enhanced visibility bands with the southern entrance is again worthy of note. Here a sensory modality has been simulated as the first step in mapping out the extent and form of an affective atmosphere and dramatic changes in the form and composition of that atmosphere have been suggested. Throughout, the remains of the founder's house served as a powerful engine of fascination, however its aura was progressively focused, intensified and contained; that which managed to seep out past the nested layers of megaliths generating a very different kind of atmosphere.

The analysis presented here is undoubtedly crude—not least in its depiction of the standing stones as undifferentiated, uniform rectangular slabs. A sensitivity study would be required to compensate for this, carrying out multiple iterations of the analysis whilst varying both the precise positions of the stones and their heights and widths (using the surviving fabric of Avebury to set ranges). Following Fisher (1994) one solution to this would be to employ a Monte-Carlo approach in order to generate a probable viewshed, only with the modelled 'error' relating to the stones themselves rather than underlying DEM.

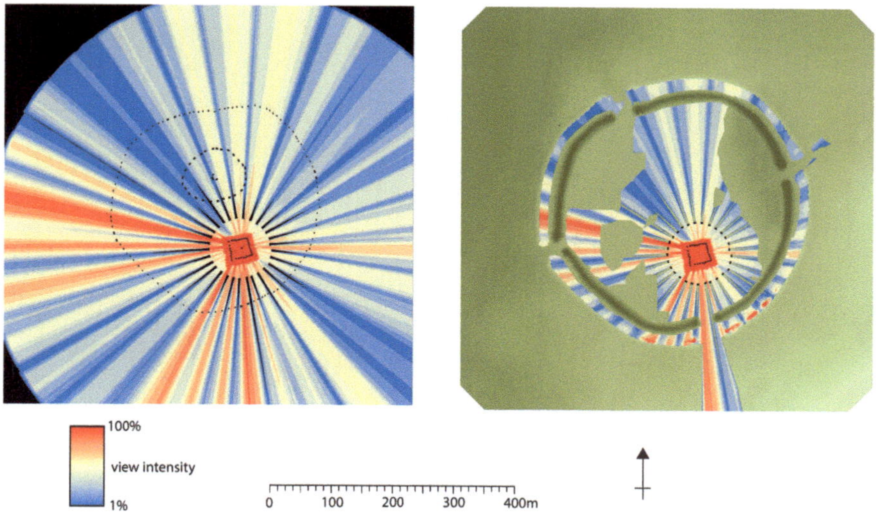

Fig. 8 The impact of adding the Southern Inner Circle. As with Fig. 7, the result is shown both with (right) and without (left) surrounding terrain and earthworks

5.2 Analysis 2—But What is Being Glimpsed?

In his seminal study of the visual impact of the megalithic settings at Stonehenge, Wilson made the important observation that whilst knowing whether the monument as a whole could, or could not, be seen from points in the surrounding landscape was useful, the real interpretative gold lay in establishing which specific parts of the monument were visible or not (Wilson 2012: 65–141). To explore this he developed a unique 'hybrid' viewshed approach that combined traditional 2D GIS approaches with modelled environments visualised using 3D Studio Max and analysed using multiple in-world camera positions (Wilson 2012: 23–64).

The approach adopted here has been to generate a view-to viewshed for each of the 1,271 viewpoints spaced in a grid across the house footprint (as per analysis 1), extracting the viewshed area which was then written as an attribute to each vector viewpoint using a bespoke Python script. In this way each viewpoint is given a value that corresponds to the area that it could be seen from. The resultant gradient of values was then mapped across the area of the house to identify the view intensity for each location. The results for the open terrain (i.e. before any megaliths were placed) confirmed that the full area of the house was in view (mean viewing area for each point = 902,845 m^2 with a Standard deviation of just 4.2 m^2 and Relative Standard Deviation (RSD) of 0.0004%). In the case of the Square (RSD = 1.75%) and combined Square & Southern Inner Circle (RSD = 12.5%) the results were much more patterned, with the most highly visible elements consistently towards the southeast (Fig. 9). Full and open views of the whole house progressively became partial views of parts of the house. The most visible element of the house is precisely

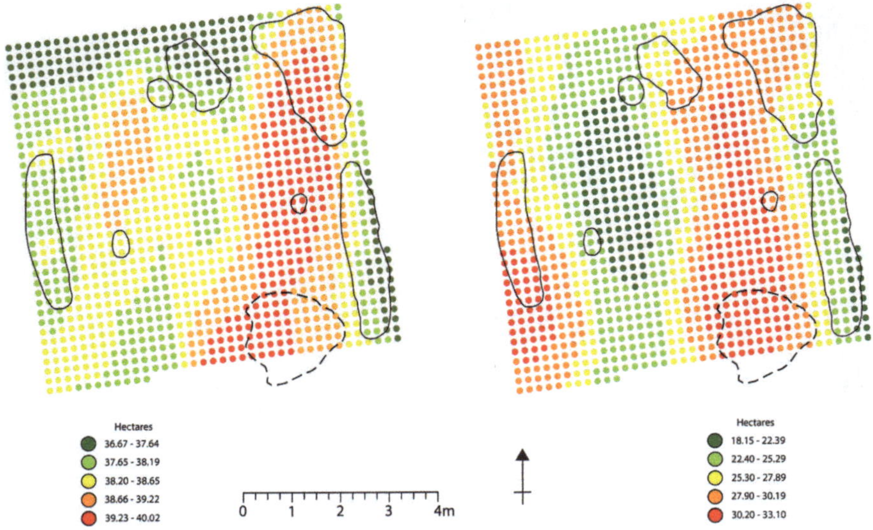

Fig. 9 View intensity of the footprint of the house structure with the square (left) and square and Southern Inner Circle (right). In each case the legend indicates the area that the particular element is viewable from

where the 6 m high Obelisk was erected, and this result raises some interesting questions regarding the sequence of construction in this part of the henge. The published sequence assumes a progressive 'spreading out' with the raising of the Obelisk the first intervention and then the successive wrapping offered by the square and then the Southern Inner Circle progressively enclosing it. However, as the visibility of this area of the house footprint was only concentrated and intensified as a result of the construction of the Square and Southern Inner Circle, it could be argued that the Obelisk came at the end of the sequence. This may very well have been an attempt to address the growing disconnection that was taking place as a result of the megalithic settings by enhancing the most visible portion of the former structure. At this point the atmosphere changes again, as the Obelisk is fully visible from across the area of the henge (Fig. 10); the 6 m high megalith becoming a very literal omphalos.

5.3 Analysis 3—On the Outside, Looking in

So far, so flat. Although the results of the initial GIS-based analyses were stimulating, we were conscious that any approach that relied upon the projection of complex 3D worlds into a two dimensional plane may result in a loss of information; this was a particular concern given the known variability in shape and proportion of Avebury's standing stones. Using a 3D engine to explore the viewshed, and thus potential affective atmosphere may counteract this. Greenwood et al use the example of a

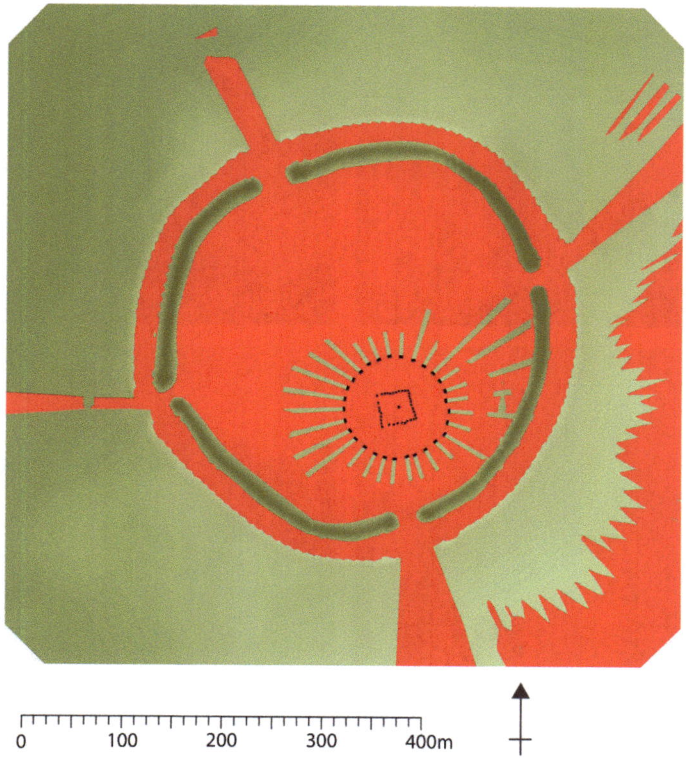

Fig. 10 The visual envelope of the Obelisk

viewshed performed next to an overpass. From the plan it would appear that all views are obstructed by the overpass, in reality, however, only a small part of the view would be obscured and views would still be possible under and above the structure (Greenwood et al. 2009: 2234). In our Avebury example, this effect would translate to the shapes of the stones, many of which taper to a point, or have very irregular profiles (Fig. 11). The basic GIS analysis reduces these irregularities to a single square pixel value that can either be seen over or else obscures the view. As we are interested in the power of 'glimpsing' and the associated satisfaction/frustration of seeing/not seeing the founder's house—it seemed sensible to also attempt to model the subtleties of seeing 'around' the stones.

Once we had completed the GIS-based viewshed analysis, we decided to expand on the basic viewshed concept and undertake a similar analysis, but this time using a 3D gaming engine. The use of 3D modelling software and gaming engines to undertake 3D viewsheds has been applied successfully in the past for diverse applications such as the assessment of road infrastructure (Greenwood et al. 2009), lightscapes (Kaufman 2014), humanistic views of the landscape (Richards-Rissetto 2017), and, as already mentioned analysing the relative visibility of the individual elements that together make up Stonehenge (Wilson 2012).

Fig. 11 Examples of surviving Avebury megaliths. This gives a sense of the variability and irregularity of the component standing stones

The methodology developed uses a 3D engine (Unity) to create different views to the founder's house across the landscape that are then analysed to assess how much of the house is visible from each location. One of the challenges when using gaming engines to represent real world locations is the translation from real world coordinates to 'game-space' coordinates. Whilst Unity can support vast gaming areas, experimentation has shown that due to performance issues it is necessary to keep the maximum terrain size quite small (e.g. a 10 km × 10 km grid). Therefore a mechanism is needed to translate the real world coordinate of each stone's centroid to the game space. This was achieved using the Real World Terrain asset (Infinity Code 2019) which has a built-in converter for moving between real world and game space coordinates. The basic digital elevation model (as used in the GIS-based viewshed analysis above) was imported into Unity using the methodology laid out by Eve (2013). The Real World Terrain plugin was then extended through custom written C# code, to batch place objects according to a Comma Separated Values file of the megalith centroids, exported from the GIS. Each megalith centroid included a path to a 3D model that would represent the specific standing stone within the 3D space (Fig. 12).

Once the basic reconstruction of Avebury was imported, the area of the founder's house was textured bright red, and the rest of the model black. A virtual camera was then created representing the field of view of a human standing 1.6 m above

Fig. 12 Examples of the 3D models used to depict the stones

the ground surface. This camera was programmatically moved along a 1 m grid of viewpoints (in total 21316 unique viewpoints) that encompassed the area of the Southern Inner Circle (Fig. 13). At each point the camera was rotated to face the area of the founder's house and a screenshot was taken of the camera's view. This procedure was completed for three different scenarios: no stones present; only the stones of the square present; and the stones of the square and southern inner circle present; and resulted in three sets of 21316 screenshots (Fig. 14).

Using a python script and the cv2 computer vision library each of the screenshots was analysed and the number of red pixels that were present in each were counted (after Wilson 2012)—a relative measure of how much of the founder's house could be seen from each of the viewpoints. The results of this analysis were fed back into the GIS and surfaces were created showing the areas of highest and lowest 'glimpsability' of the founder's house (Fig. 15). Once again, it is clear that the raising of the megalithic settings had a direct impact on the affective atmosphere. As with the GIS analysis, visual access becomes progressively more channelled, albeit this is in a much more subtle and graded fashion than was suggested by the first set of analyses. As for why this is the case, this is undoubtedly a consequence of the shape of the megaliths (see Fig. 12). Put simply, the irregularity of the stones creates more opportunities to glimpse than the undifferentiated blocks implemented by the raised raster cells in the original analyses. In this sense, in the absence of extensive sensitivity testing (as discussed earlier) it might be best to view the results of the GIS analyses as representing the most extreme scenario.

Taken together the results would argue that whilst we can begin to map affective fields using either approach, in the case of more organic, or complex structures a 3D

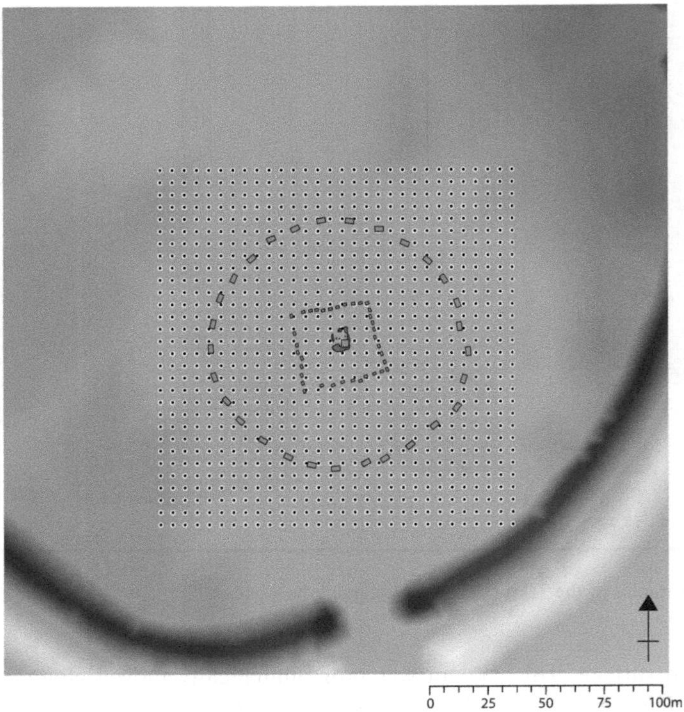

Fig. 13 The location of the viewing points. For clarity only a subset of the 21,316 actual viewpoints have been depicted

approach is preferable. However the 3D approach tendered is very much an experiment, and does not yet represent a full set of stress-tested results. For example, at this stage we are using representative digital stone models—what might be thought of as regularly irregular stone proxies—rather than 3D models created by photogrammetry or laser-scanning. This is because the bulk of Avebury's standing stones have been either buried or destroyed, with their precise locations (and in many cases size and shape) either known only from excavation and geophysical survey, else estimated. A further confounding issue is that the majority of the stones which are currently standing have been re-erected or reconstructed in the past, therefore their locations and orientations may not be original. As with the GIS analyses, the next stage in the research project will be to carry out sensitivity analyses to explore the impact of varying stone shape, size and position on the trends identified.

There is, however, a further—and we would argue critical—limitation with the methodology developed that derives from our stated aim to 'model the subtleties of seeing 'around' the stones'. If curious viewers feel a sense of frustration or disappointment when a view is partially blocked, they rarely slide their position sideways whilst maintaining a rigid sightline. Particularly when trying to see around irregular obstacles. Instead, they bob, stoop, dip and lift themselves in order to catch the elusive

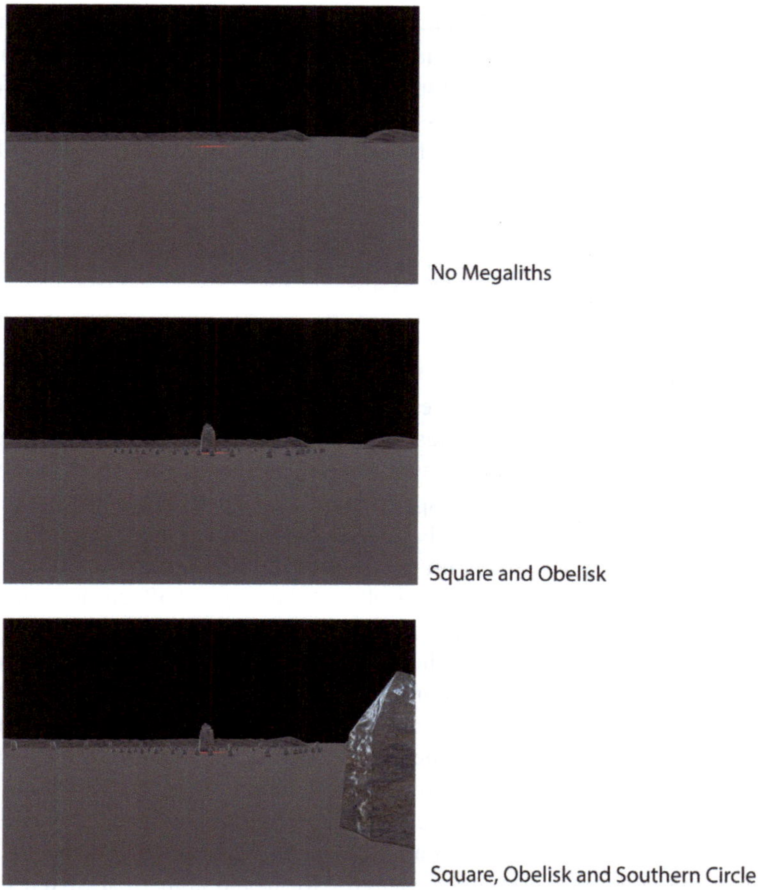

Fig. 14 A representative view to the founder's house, in the three different scenarios

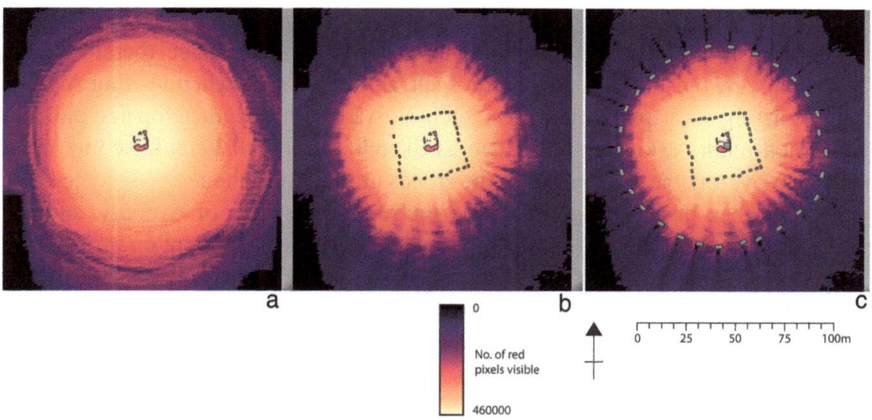

Fig. 15 The amount of the founder's house visible from each of the 21,316 viewpoints

glimpse. This would require our cameras to be mounted (effectively) on springs at each viewpoint location and in potentially constant motion. Whilst this is technically achievable, using a comparable multiple iteration approach to that sketched for the GIS analyses, another solution is possible. That is to replace indifferent, simulated cameras with curious people. This leads us to our final mode of analysis for exploring affective atmospheres.

5.4 *Analysis 4—Being Affected*

For our final analysis, we would like to sketch out a very different approach to the exploration of affect and one that we feel exploits the power of Mixed Reality to move beyond representation to instead offer powerful new heuristics for making sense of the past. The point of departure is straightforward; why simplify, abstract and represent (map) fields and atmospheres when we can generate and evoke them directly? In this way researchers will be encouraged to engage more viscerally; being directly affected as opposed to distilling out particular impacts and emotions for the purposes of calculated study. This may well reveal a range of affects not considered as well as inform on the likelihood and character of those presumed.

Mixed Reality (MR) offers a methodology to combine digital data with the real world, usually through the medium of a smartphone or virtual reality headset. MR is an all-encompassing term that covers both Virtual Reality (the entire experience created within a computer environment) and Augmented Reality (the experience involving virtual objects appearing to be placed within the real environment). MR techniques are being increasingly used within archaeology to enhance the experience of heritage sites, museums and artefacts (see Eve 2017; Ellenberger 2017 for examples). Building on our previous analyses we would argue that Mixed Reality offers perhaps the most useful pathway for engaging with the affective power of the founder's house.

One approach would be to re-use the virtual 3D environment already created within analysis 3. The model is already mapped to geographic space, therefore could theoretically be presented at the correct scale and orientation when visiting Avebury itself. Existing smartphone libraries, such as ARKit (https://developer.apple.com/augmented-reality/arkit/) or apps such as Sketchfab (https://sketchfab.com), could be used to overlay the 3D models of the stones onto a smartphone video screen. The user would then be able to walk around the real monuments of Avebury, and also encounter the virtual models as well. We could create the 'viewpoint on springs' that was lacking in analysis 3—effectively making the smartphone of the user a dynamic viewpoint, allowing the user to duck, sidestep or peer over the stones at will.

A more mischievous implementation would be to model not the obstructions but instead the target, the house itself. This would only be stable and visible from the correct locations (as determined by analyses 1–3), flickering and becoming increasingly fractured and ghostlike (i.e. frustrating) as the views become more partial. If a group of potential viewers were engaged in 'seeing' the house then they would end up carrying out precisely the kinds of movement, exploration, evaluation, negotiation, flocking, jostling and clumping we have speculated about.

This process, however, is much easier to write down than it is to actually make happen. Most AR applications have been designed for indoor use and their use in outdoor situations is problematic due to GPS and compass inaccuracy. This leads to virtual objects being placed in the incorrect spatial location in relation to the viewer and a certain amount of spatial drift (Eve 2014). Our preliminary attempts to put the virtual stones in the real location by using 'off-the-shelf' apps were not successful. The spatial drift resulted in the stones appearing to float above the ground surface and also moving slightly when the user moved—so rather than providing a fixed set of virtual monuments to glimpse around, the monuments were in constant motion, swimming across the video feed. This was certainly strongly and directly affective, evoking a feeling of intense frustration, and as a result, achieving in a way exactly what we intended. However, the frustration was directed and prompted by the break in the presence (Turner 2007; Eve 2012) caused by the software, rather than by the placement of the stones themselves. To counteract this inaccurate and inappropriate rendering of the stones, a dedicated AR application could be written—perhaps using fixed markers to anchor the virtual objects in their correct spatial locations, however this would require significant extra resources.

Rather than concentrating on recreating the visual appearance of the missing stones, we could also use more abstract methods to conjure the affective atmosphere we want to investigate. Sound has been increasingly used in AR applications to both guide and surprise the user (Eve and Graham 2020). By re-framing the results of our GIS analyses to be measures of volume or pitch it would be possible to walk across the real landscape and 'hear' the visibility of the founder's house. Following the methodology used for the 'Historical Friction' application by Graham et al. (2019), the GPS location of the smartphone can be continually queried against the results of the visibility mapping—which then returns the value (in the case of analysis 2 how much of the founder's house can be seen from that location). This value can then be used to set the volume of the sound that is playing in the user's headphones. The volume changes as the user moves around Avebury—getting louder or quieter depending on how much of the founder's house they should be able to 'see'. As we are exploring the frustration of *not* seeing the founder's house, the volume increases as the founder's house goes out of view—becoming louder and louder as the calculated view becomes more obstructed. Immediately, the user is actively engaged in attempting to find the location within the monuments where the cacophony is muted by the unrestricted view of the founder's house. With no monuments at all silence reigns across the entire site, but as the square, obelisk and finally the circle are (virtually) erected, it becomes increasingly more difficult, and frustrating, to find somewhere that is not noisy and that does not disrupt quiet contemplation. As with the example of the flickering house, if a group is involved then the listener may well find themselves far from alone, allowing etiquettes and behaviours to emerge.

6 Conclusions

In this chapter we have argued that whilst considerable energy has been spent in developing increasingly ingenious methodologies for the analysis and simulation of sensory engagements, we still lack the theoretical frameworks to reap their full interpretative potential. Here we have argued that an archaeology of affect offers precisely the framework needed, particularly through the concept of the affective atmosphere, and the ideas of affordance, relational capacity and aura that it encapsulates. Through a case study exploring the affective power of a founder's house, we have showcased how the analysis of a single sensory modality can serve as the building block for a more nuanced study of the changing character of place. Through the complex memory-work bound up in their emergence as the genius loci of a founder lineage, the surviving traces of a flimsy house structure gained an aura that in turn acted as a powerful mechanism of fascination. Subsequent structural elaborations, bound up in the practices of lifting and raising standing stones, served as lenses, focusing, distorting, moulding and shaping the affective atmosphere thus generated. If the house was an affect generator, the megalithic settings were affect manipulators.

It is perhaps an irony that the sheer scale of this process ultimately resulted not in heightened memory of the house but eventual forgetting. In this case (and with apologies to McLuhan) the megalithic medium became the message. By mapping and analysing sensory affordances we have been able to conjure the affective atmospheres that emerged in the complex interplay between materials, people and practices that were bound up in the recognition and elevation of a 'founder' lineage. This revealed a fundamental tension as successive attempts to emphasise and reify the physical traces of a single, small structure led instead to its distancing and obscuration, to the point where it was able to slip from memory entirely. In the last centuries of the 3rd millennium BC the result was a monumental complex of stone and earth spanning some 3.5 km of the surrounding landscape, yet one whose own origins had been lost.

Although we have focused in the present study on archaeological reconstructions and the modelling of sensory affordances as a way to access affective atmospheres, it is important to stress that we can instead model affect directly. To put this another way, the possibilities offered by AR/VR allow us to move beyond the mere representation and abstraction of affect as a heuristic device, to instead evoke the very affects we are seeking to understand. This is to eschew verisimilitude completely and instead use AR/VR models as direct provocations (see Goodrick and Gillings 2000). This can be achieved through deliberate anachronism, play, disruption and a host of other techniques. For example, if we made the Obelisk 50 m high and covered in polka dots, we may directly engender on the part of the viewer the same feelings of disbelief and incredulity as the erection of a 6 m high column of stone back in the early 3rd millennium BC. This would open the methodological doors to a completely new kind of archaeology. Take for example Augmented Reality; could we use emerging AR techniques to create a form of what Grossberg has termed *mattering maps* (Grossberg 1992; Seigworth and Gregg 2010: 21). To Grossberg, such maps constitute the way in which the affective world is structured—they "are deployed in relation to the formations in which they are articulated. They tell people where, how and with what intensities they can become absorbed—into the world and their lives" (Grossberg 1992: 82). To this we might add 'the past' as well.

To conclude, in this chapter we have presented a new theoretical framework for GIS/AR/VR applications in archaeology and have developed a range of methodologies through which it can be put into practice. In each case these methodologies can be further developed. For example, in the case of analyses 1–3, given the uncertainties that exist with regard to many of the stone positions and the shape of the stones themselves, an obvious next step is to carry out a series of sensitivity analyses. Here the aim would be to vary: the positions and dimensions of the various megaliths; the heights of the viewing points that represent the footprint of the collapsed house; and the heights of the prospective viewers. This will allow more confidence in establishing the veracity of any patterns or trends revealed in the affective fields. In the case of the augmented methodologies we have sketched in analysis 4, the challenge lies more with field-testing and delivery. Only then will be able to assess the effectiveness of the mechanisms of fascination and affect generators we have put in place. This is not only in conjuring the anticipated affects we are striving for, but the unexpected affects that emerge amongst viewer-participants through the practices of moving, glimpsing, listening and jostling that takes place.

Acknowledgements The research was funded by the Arts and Humanities Research Council (AHRC) as part of the *Living with Monuments* project.

References

Anderson, Ben. 2009. Affective atmospheres. *Emotion, Space and Society* 2: 77–81.

Anderson, Ben. 2014. *Encountering Affect: capacities, apparatuses, conditions*. London: Routledge.

Ash, James. 2013. Rethinking affective atmospheres: Technology, perturbation and space times of the non-human. *Geoforum* 49: 20–28.

Basso, Keith. 1996. Wisdom sits in places: notes on a western Apache landscape. In *Senses of Place*, eds. Steven Feld and Keith Basso, 53–90. Santa Fe: School of American Research Press.

Benjamin, Walter. 2008. *The Work of Art in the Age of Mechanical Reproduction*. London: Penguin.

Besnier, Niko. 1990. Language and Affect. *Annual Review of Anthropology* 19: 419–451.

Bille, Mikkel and Kirsten Simonsen. 2019. Atmospheric Practices: On Affecting and Being Affected. *Space and Culture* [Online First - https://doi.org/10.1177/1206331218819711].

Bonta, Mark and Protevi, John. 2006. *Deleuze and Geophilosophy*. Edinburgh: Edinburgh University Press.

Burlamaqui, Leonardo and Andy Dong. 2014. The use and misuse of the concept of affordance. *Presented at the Sixth International Conference on Design Computing and Cognition, London, UK*: 1–20. https://doi.org/10.13140/2.1.2722.6242.

Chemero, Anthony. 2003. An Outline of a Theory of Affordances. *Ecological Psychology* 15(2): 181–195.

DeLanda, Manuel. 2013. *Intensive Science and Virtual Philosophy*. London: Bloomsbury.

Ellenberger, Kate. 2017. Virtual and Augmented Reality in Public Archaeology Teaching. *Advances in Archaeological Practice*, 5(3): 305–309.

Eve, Stuart. 2012. Augmenting Phenomenology: Using Augmented Reality to Aid Archaeological Phenomenology in the Landscape. *Journal of Archaeological Method and Theory*, 19(4): 582–600. https://doi.org/10.1007/s10816-012-9142-7.

Eve, Stuart. 2013. "Embodied GIS How To: Part 1 – Loading Archaeological Landscapes into Unity3D (via Blender) | Dead Men's Eyes." http://www.dead-mens-eyes.org/embodied-gis-howto-part-1-loading-archaeological-landscapes-into-unity3d-via-blender/.

Eve, Stuart. 2014. *Dead Men's Eyes: Embodied GIS, Mixed Reality and Landscape Archaeology.* BAR British Series 600, Archaeopress.

Eve, Stuart. 2017. The Embodied GIS. Using Mixed Reality to explore multi-sensory archaeological landscapes. *Internet Archaeology* 44. https://doi.org/10.11141/ia.44.3.

Eve, Stuart and Shawn Graham. 2020. Spatial Data Visualisation and Beyond. In *Archaeological Spatial Analysis: A Methodological Guide, eds.* Mark Gillings, Piraye Hacıgüzeller and Gary Lock, 459–473. London: Taylor & Francis.

Fisher, Peter. 1994. Probable and fuzzy models of the viewshed operation. In *Innovations in GIS: selected papers from the First National Conference on GIS Research UK. London,* ed. Mike Worboys, 161–75. London: Taylor & Francis.

Gibson, James. J. 1979. *The ecological approach to visual perception.* New York: Psychology Press.

Gillings, Mark. 1998. Embracing uncertainty and challenging dualism in the GIS-based study of a palaeo-flood plain. *European Journal of Archaeology* 1(1): 117–144.

Gillings, Mark. 2005. The real, the virtually real and the hyperreal. In *Envisioning the Past: Archaeology and the image,* eds. Sam Smiles and Stephanie Moser, 223–239. New York: Blackwells.

Gillings, Mark. 2009. Visual affordance, landscape and the megaliths of Alderney. *Oxford Journal of Archaeology* 28 (4): 335–356.

Gillings, Mark. 2012. Landscape Phenomenology, GIS and the Role of Affordance. *Journal of Archaeological Method and Theory.* 19(4): 601–611.

Gillings, Mark. and Pollard, Joshua. 2004. *Avebury.* London: Duckworths.

Gillings, Mark, Pollard, Joshua and Kris Strutt. 2019. The Origins of Avebury. *Antiquity* 93(368): 359–377.

Gillings, Mark and David Wheatley, 2019. GIS-based visibility analysis. In *Archaeological Spatial Analysis: A Methodological Guide, eds.* Mark Gillings, Piraye Hacıgüzeller and Gary Lock, 4313–332. London: Taylor & Francis.

Goodrick, Glyn and Mark Gillings. 2000. Constructs, simulations and hyperreal worlds: the role of Virtual Reality (VR) in archaeological research. In *On the theory and practice of archaeological computing*, eds. Gary Lock and Kate Smith, 41–58. Oxford: Oxbow.

Graham, Shawn, Eve, Stuart, Morgan, Colleen and Alexis Pantos. 2019. Hearing the Past. In *Seeing the Past with Computers: Experiments with Augmented Reality and Computer Vision for History*, eds. Kevin Kee and Timothy Compeau, 347–366. Michigan: University of Michigan Press.

Greenwood, Philip, Sago, Jesse, Richmond, Sam and Vivi Chau. 2009. Using Game Engine Technology to Create Real-Time Interactive Environments to Assist in Planning and Visual Assessment for Infrastructure. *18th World IMACS/MODSIM Congress*: 2229–2235.

Gregg, Melissa and Gregory Seigworth, eds. 2010. *The Affect Theory reader*. Durham: Duke university Press.

Grossberg, Lawrence. 1992. *We gotta get out of this place: popular conservatism and postmodern culture*. London: Routledge.

Harris, Oliver and Tim Flohr Sørensen. 2012. Rethinking emotion and material culture. *Archaeological Dialogues* 17(2): 145–163.

Hodder, Ian. 2011. Human-thing entanglement: towards an integrated archaeological perspective. *Journal of the Royal Anthropological Institute* 17: 154–177.

Infinity Code. 2019. Real World Terrain - Asset Store. 2019. https://assetstore.unity.com/packages/tools/terrain/real-world-terrain-8752.

Ingold, Tim. 1992. Culture and the perception of the environment. In *Bush Base: Forest Farm,* eds, Elizabeth Croll and David Parkin, 39–56. London: Routledge.

Kassung, Christian and Sebastian Schwesinger. 2016. How to Hear the Forum Romanum. On Historical Realities and Aural Augmentation. In *Kultur und Informatik. Mixed Reality,* eds. Carsten Busch, Christian Kassung and Jürgen Sieck, 41–54. Glückstadt: Hülsbusch.

Käufer, Stephan and Anthony Chemero, A. 2015. *Phenomenology: an introduction.* Cambridge: Polity.

Kaufman, Andrew. 2014. Shedding Light on GIS: A 3D Immersive Approach to Urban Lightscape Integration into GIS. West Virginia University. https://search.proquest.com/openview/8df376a009c86dfe028c973380864ef4/1?pq-origsite=gscholar&cbl=18750&diss=y.

Knappett, Carl. 2005. *Thinking through Material Culture.* Philadelphia: University of Philadelphia Press.

Llobera, Marcos. 1996. Exploring the topography of mind: GIS, social space and archaeology. *Antiquity* 70: 612–622.

Lorimer, Hayden. 2006. Herding memories of humans and animals. *Environment and Planning D: Society and Space* 24: 497–518.

Mlekuz, Dmitrij. 2004. Listening to Landscapes: Modelling Past Soundscapes in GIS. *Internet Archaeology* 16. https://doi.org/10.11141/ia.16.6.

Ogburn, Dennis. E. 2006. Assessing the level of visibility of cultural objects in past landscapes. *Journal of Archaeological Science, 33*: 405–413.

Paliou, Eleftheria. 2014. Visibility analysis in 3D spaces: a new dimension to the understanding of social space. In *Spatial analysis and social spaces: interdisciplinary approaches to the interpretation of prehistoric and historical built environments*, eds. Eleftheria Paliou, Undine Lieberwirth and Silvia Polla, 91–113. Topoi, Berlin Studies of the Ancient World: De Gruyter: 91–113.

Pollard, Joshua. and Rosamund Cleal. 2004. Dating Avebury. In *Monuments and Material Culture*, eds. Joshua Pollard and Rosamund Cleal, 120–9. East Knoyle: Hobnob Press.

Reckwitz, Andreas. 2017. Practices and their Affects. In *The Nexus of Practices: connections, constellations, practitioners*, eds. Allison Hui, Theodore Schatzki and Elizabeth Shove, 114–125. London: Routledge.

Richards, Colin. 2013. Interpreting Stone Circles. In *Building the Great Stone Circles of the North*, ed. Colin Richards, 2–30. Oxford: Windgather Press.

Richards-Rissetto, Heather. 2017. What Can GIS + 3D Mean for Landscape Archaeology? *Journal of Archaeological Science, Archaeological GIS Today: Persistent Challenges, Pushing Old Boundaries, and Exploring New Horizons,* 84 (August): 10–21.

Robinson, David. W. 2017. Assemblage Theory and the Capacity to Value: An Archaeological Approach from Cache Cave, California, USA. *Cambridge Archaeological Journal*, 27 (1): 155–168.

Siegworth, Gregory. J. and Melissa Gregg 2010. An Inventory of Shimmers. In *The Affect Theory Reader*, eds. Melissa Gregg and Gregory Seigworth, 1–26. Durham: Duke University Press.

Stewart, Kathleen. 1996. An Occupied Place. In *Senses of Place,* eds. Steven Feld and Keith Basso, 137–166. Santa Fe: School of American Research Press.

Tilley, C. 1994. *A Phenomenology of Landscape.* Oxford: Berg.

Turner, Phil. 2007.The intentional basis of presence. In *Proceedings of the 10th international workshop on presence* (pp. 127–134).

Wilson, Andrew. T. 2012. *Hybrid Approaches to Visual Analysis in Archaeological landscapes.* University of Liverpool: Doctoral Thesis.

Withagen, Rob, de Poel, Harjo. J., Duarte Araújo and Gert-Jan Pepping. 2012. Affordances can invite behaviour: Reconsidering the relationship between affordances and agency. *New Ideas in Psychology* 30: 250–258.

Stuart Eve is the Director of Creativity at Museum of London Archaeology. His research concentrates on the intersection between the virtual and the real in archaeological method and practice. He is also the Co-Director of the Waterloo Uncovered project in Belgium.

Mark Gillings is a Professor in the Department of Archaeology and Anthropology at Bournemouth University. His research interests concentrate on the productive spaces that emerge through the integrated study of landscape, archaeological theory and digital archaeology, with a particular focus on the potentials of all things geospatial and virtual. Much of his recent research has centred upon the prehistoric landscapes of southern Britain, and the relationships that animated the complex, multi-scalar motleys of monument and everyday dwelling that characterise this region.

The Senses & the Sacred: A Multisensory and Digital Approach to Examining an Ancient Egyptian Funerary Landscape

Elaine A. Sullivan

Abstract What makes a space feel sacred? How did ancient people create a physical and emotional 'sense' of specialness or distinction in their ritual places? The ancient Egyptians created at least two major zones of ritualised space (demarcated from the secular parts of their cities and towns), the temple and the cemetery. While scholars have addressed the multisensory techniques utilised by kings and priests to craft the temple precinct into a sacred landscape, the sensory experience of the necropolis remains undertheorized. This gap results from the challenge of comprehending the vast funerary landscapes that have experienced dramatic change since ancient times, changes which have obscured ancient ground level and pathways as well as dramatically altered the appearance of monumental tomb architecture. In this chapter, I combine textual, art historical, and archaeological evidence for the sounds, smells, and visual experiences of ancient people at an Egyptian necropolis with 3D GIS technologies that attempt to virtually represent ancient ritual spaces in their form during the Pharaonic Period. The necropolis of Saqqara, bordering the administrative centre Memphis and one of Egypt's oldest elite burial grounds, is used as a case study to explore the ancient Egyptian funerary landscape from a multisensory perspective.

Keywords Archaeological landscapes · Funerary landscapes · 3D reconstruction modelling · Sensory archaeology · Cyber-archaeology · Ancient Egypt · Historical geographic information systems (HGIS) · Funerary ritual

1 Introduction

Ancient Egyptian towns and cities included two important spheres of sacred space distinguished geographically or architecturally from the rest of the urban settlement: the temple and the cemetery. The temple served as the 'house' for the local manifestation of the god, and the sensory aspects of the elaborate structures and ceremonies used by the kings and priests to create a sanctified home for the divine have been

E. A. Sullivan (✉)
Department of History, University of California at Santa Cruz, Santa Cruz, USA
e-mail: easulliv@ucsc.edu

G. Landeschi and E. Betts (eds.), *Capturing the Senses*,
Quantitative Methods in the Humanities and Social Sciences,
https://doi.org/10.1007/978-3-031-23133-9_3

studied extensively by scholars (Shafer 1997; Dorman and Bryan 2007). The sensory experience of the necropolis, final resting place and site of elaborate funerary rituals for royals and elites, in contrast, remains undertheorized. Cemetery landscapes have been greatly altered by environmental and human forces in the intervening millennia since their use. These changes have obscured ancient ground horizon, erased original processional routes, and modified the visual and physical relationships between buildings and those inhabiting the landscape. Multisensory consideration of these spaces, examining how the ancient Egyptians produced a physical and emotional 'sense' of specialness or distinction in the funerary landscape, have thus been limited.

In this chapter, I use primary source texts and artistic depictions related to funerary and mortuary cult events at the site of Saqqara, as well as the archaeological traces of these ceremonial activities, to explore the visual, audio and olfactory world of the necropolis in Egypt's New Kingdom. These records are augmented with data gleaned from a 3D GIS model of the site that visualises physical and material elements of the cemetery frequently indiscernible today. Following the ideas of Day (2013: 6), this work thus attempts to embed visual analysis in its larger sensory network, exploring how visual impressions could have been integrated with other sensory experiences, while grounding the examination in archaeological and historical evidence. It also claims to show how 3D modelling can contribute to the study of sacred landscapes, especially those that have altered tremendously over time.

2 Sensory Archaeology and Egyptology

The wider discipline of Archaeology's interest in a robust examination of sensory and embodied aspects of the lives of ancient peoples (Fahlander and Kjellström 2010; Day 2013; Hamilakis 2013; and Skeates and Day 2019) has not yet found major traction in the field of Egyptology.[1] Currently, no single work addresses the senses in Egypt in a comprehensive manner. This is despite extensive consideration of the senses in Egyptology's sister field of Classical Studies, such as a recent a six-volume multi-authored set covering sight, smell, taste, sound, touch and synaesthesia (Butler and Purves 2013, 2017; Bradley 2015; Squire 2016; Rudolph 2017; Butler and Nooter 2019). However, relevant topics occasionally appeared in late twentieth-century publications, including the sensuous aspects of Egyptian religion (Finnestad 1999), music (Manniche 1991), and the composition, sourcing, use and representation of fragrance in daily life and ritual activities (Cherpion 1994; Manniche 1999). A number of more recent analyses centering individual or multiple senses in their investigations suggest interest is growing, and these include studies on the relationship between smells and religious concepts of the divine (Wise 2009; Lieven 2016a; Price 2018; Goldsmith 2019), sound inside the temple (Elwart and Emerit 2019) and

[1] Perhaps telling is that the otherwise informative UCLA Encyclopedia of Egyptology (UEE) entry on 'the Body' (Riggs 2010) does not include a discussion of the senses in the Egyptian context.

in literary contexts (Manassa 2011), the soundscapes of war (Matić 2018), and experiential elements of taking part in Egyptian festivals (Pellini 2015). Because there is still a lack of general discussion of the senses in the Egyptian conception, I will provide a brief review here, focusing on ritual contexts.

3 The Human Sensorium in Pharaonic Egypt

The ancient Egyptians identified the importance of the five Aristotelian physical sensations, including touch, taste, smell, hearing and seeing, yet they did not classify them together as a distinct group connoting 'the senses'. Perhaps the closest categorization was their designation of the seven important orifices on the human head (two ears, mouth, two nostrils, two eyes), conceived of as the 'seat of the principal faculties' of a person (Van de Walle 1985: 365, my translation from the French). To 'taste', the verb ***dp***in the Egyptian language, also connoted 'to experience', indicating the broad metaphorical understanding of that sense (Manassa 2011: note 3). Touching was a critical part of diagnosis in Egyptian medicine, deemed necessary for comprehension of illnesses, and the connection to its practice in medicine suggests a conceptual link between that sense and knowledge acquisition (Manassa 2011: note 4; Allen 2005: 70–115). Sound (both hearing and speaking), breathing and smell, and sight were the focus of the sensorium in the Egyptian worldview, as these were the aspects of the person deemed most critical for individual understanding. The heart (*ỉb*) was deemed the seat of justice, free-will, cognition, memory and action (Assmann 2002, 2005), and Egyptian theology construed it as guided by those sensations (Van de Walle 1985: 368): 'Sight, hearing, breathing—they report to the heart, and it makes every understanding come forth. As to the tongue, it repeats what the heart has devised' (Lichtheim 1973: 54).[2] Speaking, seeing and breathing were actions of the living body imagined as revivified magically at the tomb in the 'opening of the mouth' ceremony, the climax of the funerary service in which religious spells engendered eternal life to the deceased. Funerary text recitations explicitly aspired to both the 'opening of the mouth and eyes' of the corpse (Assmann 2005: Chap. 13). A New Kingdom purification spell at Theban tomb 23 affirmed the final purpose of the ceremony of bodily reactivation was the transformation of the deceased into a divine being:

> May the divine words purify you,
>
> may your mouth be opened by the chisel of Ptah.
>
> May your two eyes be opened for you...
>
> May linen belong to your mummy
>
> and breath be at your nose, that you not suffocate
>
> May you emerge as a living ba (Assmann 2005: 323)

[2] Text from the so-called 'Memphite Theology,' inscribed on a granite stela in the Third Intermediate Period by Dynasty 25 king Shabaqo, possibly based on an earlier text.

These funerary concepts ran parallel to the creation myths recorded at Esna temple in which the god Khnum shaped the first man, and to make him live, 'he opens his eyes and his ears' (Emerit 2011: 68).

The actions of hearing, smelling and seeing all held strong ritualised meanings in Egyptian culture. *sḏm* 'to hear', or 'to listen', could connote 'to obey', and the living went to great lengths to hear, address, and follow the will of the gods, as well as their deceased ancestors, all of whom they communicated with via ritualised practices (Emerit 2011: 65–66, 83). The material expression of these practices resulted in a number of charmingly literal votive offerings of model ears (Pinch and Waraksa 2009) and stelae with inscribed depictions of ears, interpreted by scholars as 'encouraging…the deity to hear a prayer' (Pinch 1993: 253). Hearing was closely tied in the Egyptian language to the concept of speaking, and the term *ḫrw*, 'voice', also connoted music, noise, or sound (von Lieven 2016b: 25). Chanting, clapping and the playing of musical instruments, especially the sistrum, were an integral aspect of temple ritual and religious festivals (Finnestad 1999: 113; Manniche 1991: 60–73). The act of speaking was itself a form of creation, and a number of Egyptian myths recount how a creator god, existing in a primordial ocean, spoke aloud and the world came into being (von Lieven 2016b: 32). Invocation offering formulae, repeated on hundreds of elite tombs, requested a voice offering (*prt ḫrw*), literally 'the going forth of the voice', from the visitor. The repetition aloud of the names of offerings magically gave them existence in the tomb and sustained the deceased in the necropolis (Strudwick 2005: 31–32):

> O you who live on earth… who shall pass by this tomb: pour water, make invocation offerings from that which you have! If you have nothing, (then) speak with your mouth and offer with your hands: 'a thousand of bread and beer…' (Strudwick 2005: 223).[3]

Sounds and the spoken word thus held 'inherent power', with divine and ritualized words effective[4] on the cosmic and earthly level (von Lieven 2016b: 34).

Smell offered a potent means to interact with the divine. The most common Egyptian term for 'to breathe' or 'smell', *šn*, was utilised in mythological texts and relief scenes where the gods interacted with the king; the intimacy of exchanging breath and scents with the gods demarcated the king as super-human (Beaux 2015: 68–69). In the temple, priests burned fragrant incense and anointed the small statues of the gods (protected in the temple interiors) with fragrant oils, many of which were imported at substantial cost from sub-Saharan Africa or Arabia (Manniche 1999: 25–26). The heady scents were imagined as originating in and emanating from the bodies of the gods themselves, and thus 'by means of odour the officiants could reach parts of the divine power which they could not even see' (Manniche 1999: 25–26, 34). These divine smells operated in the funerary sphere as well, as such

---

[3] Text from the architrave of the tomb of Mehi (reign of Teti I-Pepy I) at Saqqara.

[4] Egyptian magical practice, which consisted of the repeating of spells, was closely tied to speech. Ritner suggested that the Egyptian terms for 'word,' 'speech,' and 'statement' often held "magical connotations" (2008: 40).

unguents were imagined to remove the stink of death and heal the dissociated dead,[5] reuniting their parts and turning them into divine beings (Manniche 1999: 35), a concept already developed in the first recorded funerary spells (dated to the Old Kingdom), the Pyramid Texts:

> Ho, Pepi Neferkare! I have come to you too, that I might fill you with the oil that comes from Horus's eye. I fill you with it so that it will tie together your bones, join together your limbs for you, collect your flesh for you, and release your bad sweat. When you have received its scent on you, your scent will be sweet like the Sun when he comes from the Akhet…(Allen 2005: spell 637, from pyramid of Pepi II)

One of the most effective forms of ritual communication and connection in Egyptian culture was sight. *Seeing* (*m33*, 'to see', or ***ptr***, 'to perceive/behold') was a reciprocal act, with the eye an active agent that reached out—a concept likely stemming from the myth of the powerful 'divine eye' (Van de Walle 1985: 370). In looking upon the god (or the king in his divine form), a person interacted with him or her, benefited from their divine presence, and could even be healed by this sight, and thus prayers to 'see the god' were repeated in a variety of types of texts: 'May my body be renewed at seeing Amon-Re…' (Tosi and Roccati 1972: 209, object 50259; Van der Plas 1989: 27, from a chapel at Deir el Medina, Thebes). Viewing or being seen was participatory and included the viewer in ritual practice and allowed him or her to acquire sustenance, sacral knowledge, and advantage through the visual relationship (Sullivan 2020: Sect. 3. 2).

Vision was key for both the living and the dead. Images of the dead (in statue form or carved in relief in the tomb) perpetuated their existence eternally (Robins 1997: 12). The dead were imagined as retaining their ocular functions, and the sides of coffins sometimes included representations of eyes, to assure that the deceased could peer outward (Van der Plas 1989: 6). Indeed, the effective dead could act upon what they saw, as is clear from tomb inscriptions describing the transformation of the dead into their mobile *ba* form in death:

> Transforming into a living ba
>
> So as to alight on his grove
>
> And enjoy the shade of its sycamores
>
> and sit in the rear part of the pyramid,
>
> while his statues endure in his house
>
> and receive the offerings…
>
> …transforming into a living ba.
>
> May he again see his house of the living,

[5] Assmann interpreted death in the Egyptian conception as a breaking down of the person into "its various aspects of constituent elements," a process he labeled *dissociation* (2005: 87). The goal of the mortuary rituals focused on reuniting these elements (including the *ba*, *ka*, corpse, shadow, name, heart, etc.) into one eternal being (Assmann 2005: 87–112).

so as to be a protection to his children daily,

forever and ever (Assmann 2005: 216).

Hearing/speaking, smelling/breathing, and seeing/being visible all thus had specialised sacral connotations in the Egyptian worldview. The senses were not only a means for a person to acquire knowledge about their surroundings, but additionally instruments to access the divine and to bridge the gap between the living and the dead. This is crucial to understanding the experience of Egyptian sacred spaces—royal and elite spaces were orchestrated to activate the senses in particular ways, to create unique places that smelled, sounded, looked, and felt distinct from the mundane world. This was true within the thick enclosure walls of the protected temple precinct, but also in the open necropolis. This work will explore how a 'sense of the sacred' was reinforced within the elite funerary landscape, using the cemetery of Saqqara as a case study.

4 The Egyptian 'Funerary Landscape' and Digital Archaeology

Funerary landscapes are particular types of archaeological landscapes where social and community identity, as well as structures of social and political power, are created and maintained through the repeated activities revolving around the death, burial and commemoration of the deceased (Härke 1997; Daróczi 2012). They are loci for 'intense' human experiences, where emotional and phenomenological encounters may be significantly tied to place and memory (Daróczi 2012: 200), and thus especially useful locations for the study of sensory experience. From the Early Dynastic through the Late Period in Egypt, the elite necropolis was often a high desert site bordering the town areas where corpses were meant to be protected in closed underground burials, usually marked by some type of chapel above. The burial was celebrated by a community procession to the tomb, at which a priest performed rituals meant to facilitate the regeneration of the deceased. Because the dead were conceived of as joining the ancestors and continuing to exist after death, a key element of Egyptian culture was the perpetuated mortuary cult. This centred on an accessible part of the tomb superstructure, where priests and family members presented offerings to the blessed dead, who needed the same types of sustenance as the living (Ikram 2015: 27). The hope was that this familial offering practice would endure for generations, but even passing visitors were encouraged to participate in cult veneration (Dodson and Ikram 2008: 21–22; Martin 1997: 22; Martin et al. 2012: 19–20). Cemeteries therefore were not closed off from the population (like temples), but instead offered continued access to the chapels of the ancestors, eternally reifying social hierarchies and relationships that developed out of the state system.

Elite cemeteries in ancient Egypt were specialised, highly structured spaces, with monumental tomb constructions and their related texts and artistic imagery following strict precedents (albeit with some room for innovation) within the major periods of state power throughout the Pharaonic Period. In some cases, elite tombs were grouped around royal monuments, or located in direct relationship with royal tombs nearby. The repetition of architectural forms[6] and descriptions and depictions of funerary and mortuary activities within the tombs[7] demonstrated great consistency and continuity in the events that took place at these cemeteries, with major differences focusing less on the form of proceedings, but rather the elaborateness of the ceremonies, depending on the wealth of the individual. Thus, here I trace a sensory path through the necropolis of the New Kingdom, utilising primary sources woven together from a variety of tomb and funerary materials representative of broader cultural patterns. These sources include inscriptions carved into the architectural elements of tombs, painted representations of funeral activities, and archaeological remains that document human behaviour on the ground. I focus when possible on materials from the site of Saqqara, but augment these with information from comparable sites.

While the richness of the Egyptian textual and artistic record makes such an exploration possible, with direct reference from an emic perspective on elements of sounds, smells and actions in the funerary landscape, understanding of the original spatial context of cult rituals remains incomplete.[8] Here is where digital methods can expand our capacities. Specifically, the affordances of cyber-archaeology, where scholars can consider 'potential pasts' in a virtual environment (Forte and Siliotti 1997), are brought to bear on the funerary landscape of Saqqara. Although archaeologists today can walk through the ruins of Saqqara's monumental pyramids and tombs, the necropolis and associated city of Memphis are tremendously altered from Pharaonic times. In some locations, ground level has risen many metres, burying or obscuring superstructures that were once highly prominent. Grand stone and mud-brick monuments that formerly towered over the cemetery stand in various states of collapse, their stones removed in both ancient and Mediaeval times by resourceful 'recyclers', or their bricks deflated due to thousands of years of rain and abrasive blowing sand. The monumental temples of Memphis are today barely visible, swallowed up by the rising Nile floodplain. Digital methods are here used to therefore investigate aspects of the visual landscape inaccessible for study in the field today.

The material expression of monumental tombs is particularly important for a sensory evaluation of the funerary landscape, as sensory experiences are not individual, isolated perceptions, but instead emerge from the interaction between person and the material object (Riggs 2016: 249–250). The tomb monument at Saqqara structured the performance of, and interaction between, participants in funeral services

[6] Elite tomb types changed over time, for example, the stone *mastaba* tomb style characteristic of the elite in the Old Kingdom (especially Dynasties 4–6 in the Memphis area, ~2600-2200 BCE) was abandoned in favor of stone and mud-brick 'temple tombs' and tombs cut into the edge of the rock escarpment at Saqqara in the New Kingdom (~1548-1086 BCE). However, the style of tomb popular within each period (spanning more than 400 years each) was highly consistent.

[7] Hays contended that there was a "fundamental commonality in belief and in practice" in Egyptian funerary religion running throughout the Pharaonic period (2010: 1–2).

[8] Barrowclough and Malone (2007: 1–3) discussed the dominance of artistic and textual sources in the study of ritual practice, leaving spatial context under-theorized.

and mortuary cults, staging ritual practice in highly formalised ways. The monument's specific type of temporality, quasi-permanent (built or lined with stone blocks) manifesting centuries of cultural continuity, yet chronologically distinct (with superstructure forms easily demarcated by time period) and vulnerable to the processes of deflation and collapse (displaying the passage of time and 'ancientness'), signalled social and political messages about the position of the present in terms of the past.[9] Yet building prominence, as well as the original visual impact of architectural materials, colours and textures, has significantly diminished due to the ravages of time. Later constructions are layered on top of or around those of the earlier periods. Key elements that contributed to the visual power of the sacred funerary landscape at any given point in the Pharaonic Period—the physical and visual links that would have constituted a powerful sense of place, but that are rarely referred to in Egyptian funerary literature in specific ways[10]—have faded in modern times. It is precisely these material aspects of the landscape that can be visualised in 3D GIS models, allowing the archaeologist to reimagine and hypothesise how such elements contributed to the sensory experience of the necropolis.

In the digital model utilised for this study, informed 'reconstruction' of original building heights, shapes, materials, placement and lighting was based on GIS data, published excavation reports, comparative examples, modern digital imagery, and even artistic depictions of Saqqara monuments. Using this information, simple 3D massing models of basic architectural elements of building superstructures were built for more than eighty-five key monuments at Saqqara. The 3D model takes a 'maximalist' approach, including not only those well-documented monuments, but also adding in hundreds of *mastaba* tombs (many excavated in the early twentieth century) as procedural models, whose form in the visualisation is a schematic one, generated by the software program based on the recorded 2D footprint (length and width) of the tomb. Each monument was linked to a time-slider, appearing chronologically in the 3D model during the Egyptian dynasty in which it was built. Four terrain models, each representing ground horizon across a different timespan, were produced from topographic line maps of the site. These were each modified to reflect the changing ancient ground levels documented by the continuous rise of building threshold and floor levels over the centuries. The terrains were also linked to the time-slider, so that monuments and topography in the 3D visualisation change in parallel across space and time. This combination of temporally reimagined terrains and monuments has allowed for the hypothetical placement of elements of the sacred landscape back into the virtual scene for consideration, expanding our opportunities to evaluate how the material impacted the creation of meaning at Saqqara. Because this type of virtual

[9] I follow the ideas of Bauer and Kosiba (2016), who consider "the physicality and constant dynamism of things" in interpreting the relationship between material culture and historical processes, and suggest that "things become particular kinds of actors that can affect historical processes precisely because of how their material properties articulate with cultural values.".

[10] The size and cost of tomb superstructures show that these buildings were one of the most important aspects of the funerary landscape, but elite funerary literature focused primarily on the tomb owner's biography and highly standardised offering rituals and did not comment on the tomb's individual setting in the necropolis, or provide general descriptions of the cemetery layout or overall structure.

'reconstruction' of an entire ancient landscape necessitates a great deal of hypothesis—and each individual building reconstruction includes various levels of uncertainty in form—the building and publication of the model was robustly annotated with descriptive metadata and paradata.[11] Such layered and complex 3D visualisations admittedly ask a great deal of the viewer, and necessitate engagement with the base data through various channels—in the case of this project, through metadata available via the online 3D GIS web-browser and through the documentary metadata and paradata included in the model's full publication, both available elsewhere (Sullivan 2020).

This article argues that it is the combination of robust primary sources with the capabilities of cyber-archaeology toolkits that opens up exciting possibilities for exploring aspects of the sensory landscape. Historical sources have been supplemented with digital engagement in the material world to assess the impact of the original structures on the funerary landscape. While the culturally conditioned nature of the senses may not allow modern researchers to grasp any individual's experience or emotional response to sensory stimuli (Houston and Taube 2000: 262; Squire 2016; Nyberg 2010), we can seriously assess the potential for sensory engagement of specific material objects within a known cultural framework, as well as consider aspects of material culture that do not easily survive in the archaeological record (Hurcombe 2007).

5 A Multisensory and Digital Exploration of the Saqqara Funerary Landscape in the New Kingdom

The necropolis of Saqqara extends north and south along a high plateau west of the Nile floodplain. Although a dry, desert-like environment in the New Kingdom, it was an active landscape. At any given moment, labourers would have moved materials up the escarpment to the multiple elite tombs under construction.[12] The sounds and vibrations of hammers and chisels on stone, and the murmurs of workmen would have been common. Annually, festival events would have transformed the cemetery into a space where the living comingled directly with the god (and the dead), at events like the festival of Sokar, where that deity emerged from the temple and paraded through the necropolis on a special barque, preceded by a night of rituals

---

[11] Following documentation recommendations laid forth in the London Charter (https://web.archive.org/web/20190708161510; http://www.londoncharter.org/principles/documentation.html), a full discussion of the base data, including research sources, process, and methods for the 3D model construction was included in the online publication of the model (Sullivan 2020: Sects. 6 and 8).

[12] At New Kingdom Saqqara, multiple elites serving under the same king built individual tombs, and construction on those tombs would have lasted many years. For example, work on the tomb of Maya, which was never completed, began during the reign of Tutankhamun, and likely extended until Maya's death in year 9 of king Horemheb (Staring 2014: 493).

where participants wore garlands of onions (Brovarski 1984).[13] At the death of the Apis bull, housed at the Ptah temple in Memphis, the body of the mummified bull (imagined as an incarnation of the god) was dragged up the escarpment in procession to the Serapeum for burial, and the cemetery again manifested the direct presence of the divine.[14] The related sounds, smells and sights of such intermittent activities would have blended with those tied to the everyday ritual activities at Saqqara, the funeral and the elite mortuary cults, described in detail below.

5.1 *Funerals*

When an elite member of the New Kingdom royal court or administration died, he likely would have already spent many years preparing a tomb in his chosen necropolis.[15] Those selecting to be buried at Saqqara often held careers in state administration, the temple of Ptah at Memphis, or one of the solar deities at Heliopolis, all located in the floodplain settlement areas east across the Nile river. After death, numerous funerary texts describe the ceremonial transport of the body over water to the west, approaching the necropolis from the town (Hays 2010: 3). The open court of the tomb of Mose depicts the beginning of a funeral procession, which may have started soon after dawn, with mourners and the coffin rowed in boats across the Nile. The corpse, protected by a series of coffins and outer shrine, was then laid on a sledge and pulled up over the sands of the Saqqara plateau by oxen. Priests 'opened the way', pouring milk to smooth the path, while burning incense to purify the route, the pungent scents probably of frankincense or myrrh (Gaballa 1977: 16–17 and pl. XXXV). Family members and professional colleagues joined the procession, making it a major community event. The tomb of Meryneith represents large groups of people taking part in the procession, including priests, officials, mourners and even horse-drawn chariots (Raven et al. 2014: 94–96). Relief scenes suggest a cacophonous affair, with professional mourners in accompaniment, including women and men (some with titles of 'singer') who wailed in grief and covered themselves in dust.[16] Porters are shown carrying grave goods, such as chests, baskets, and furniture, and

[13] Sokar was a Memphite god associated closely with the temple of Ptah at Memphis by the Old Kingdom. His festival continued to be celebrated in the New Kingdom.

[14] These ceremonies would have only taken place irregularly (~16–17 years), based on the average lifespan of the bulls as recorded in later data. The funerary events took place at Saqqara from the mid-New Kingdom and after; nothing is known about how the body was treated during the Old or Middle Kingdoms at Memphis (Dodson 2001).

[15] In most cases, elite tomb owners were male. Frequently, the tomb owner's wife, or immediate male and female family members, were included in tomb decoration and buried within. The major exception to this rule is royal women, who were often accorded individual burials due to their unique status in relationship to the king.

[16] The middle and bottom registers of the south wall of the cult chapel at the tomb of Raia registers depict male and female mourners throwing dust on their heads and "weeping and wailing." (Martin et al. 1985: 13–14). The tomb of Meryneith depicts six women mourners, and at least thirteen male mourners, all in dramatic poses of grief, including prostrated; parallel scenes represent additional

vessels filled with drink, oils and fragrances. Mourners may have carried or worn fragrant bouquets of lotus flowers (Hays 2010: 6; Teeter 2011: 138–139; Assmann 2005: 302, 318; Manniche 1999: 108–109). Groups of male dancers, called the *muu*, joined the procession, performing a series of steps and elaborate arm gestures (Teeter 2011: 143–4). The dance, deriving from the Old Kingdom or earlier, was meant to demarcate the liminal space between the living and dead opened at the funeral, the dancers personifying the powerful ancestral spirits linked with early kingship (Meyer-Deitrich 2009: 5; Kinney 2004).[17]

Somewhere behind the coffin, other mourners pulled shrines with the canopic jars, statues of the deceased to serve the ongoing mortuary cult,[18] as well as elaborately wrapped remnants of the embalming process (Assmann 2005: 299–303). Later New Kingdom tomb reliefs, like those in the tombs of Horemheb, Meryneith and Maya, show the procession serviced by shaded arbours supplied with offerings for the deceased, including fruits, garlands of lotus flowers, vessels of liquid and meats (Raven et al. 2014: 94–95; Martin 1989: 101–102, pls. 123–4; Martin et al. 2012: pl. 32 scene 42) which may have sustained the mourners on their journey and filled the air with their scents (Assmann 2005: 309).

Tomb texts do not specify the route travelled on any New Kingdom funeral procession at Saqqara, and it is possible each funeral traced a unique path. But for the living climbing the escarpment, the visual and physical presence of hundreds of funerary structures passed on any route, including already ancient stone pyramids and *mastaba* tombs, must have offered great potential to invoke an emotional response. The renewed mortuary cults of select Old Kingdom kings —deified into local gods— included two whose pyramids were located northeast of the step pyramid enclosure, Menkauhor and Teti. These Old Kingdom royal spaces were reclaimed and reinterpreted by the elite New Kingdom Egyptians (1000 years later); for example, king Teti was newly envisioned as 'beloved of Ptah', linking him to the New Kingdom Memphite temple that housed the living Apis bull and the associated processional that passed nearby extending to the Serapeum (Málek 1992: 67–72). Wealthy officials clustered their tombs around the Old Kingdom pyramids, presumably seeking a connection to divinity for their burial.[19] New Kingdom Memphites erected dedicatory stelae and statues to the former kings, like the one depicting a man named Amenwahsu adoring Teti-Merenptah (Naville 1878: Tafel IV; Porter and Moss 1981: 729). The god was represented as standing in his pyramid, suggesting the monument still served as a key visual marker in the New Kingdom (Fig. 1).

---

mourners (Raven et al. 2014: 94–95). Maya and Meryt's tomb also portrays mourners (Martin et al. 2012: pl. 32).

[17] The earliest depictions of the *muu* come from Old Kingdom tombs at Saqqara; New Kingdom tombs in Thebes also represent them (Kinney 2004: 63–65).

[18] The dragging of statues of the tomb owner in the procession is shown in the tomb of Maya and Meryt (Martin et al. 2012: 36 and pl. 32 scene 43).

[19] An image of Menkauhor was carved on the exterior door jamb of the tomb of Amenemone, presumably a sort of 'public statement' of the official's devotion to that god, in hopes of attracting supplicants visiting the king's temple to enter his tomb as well (Ockinga et al. 2004: 73–76).

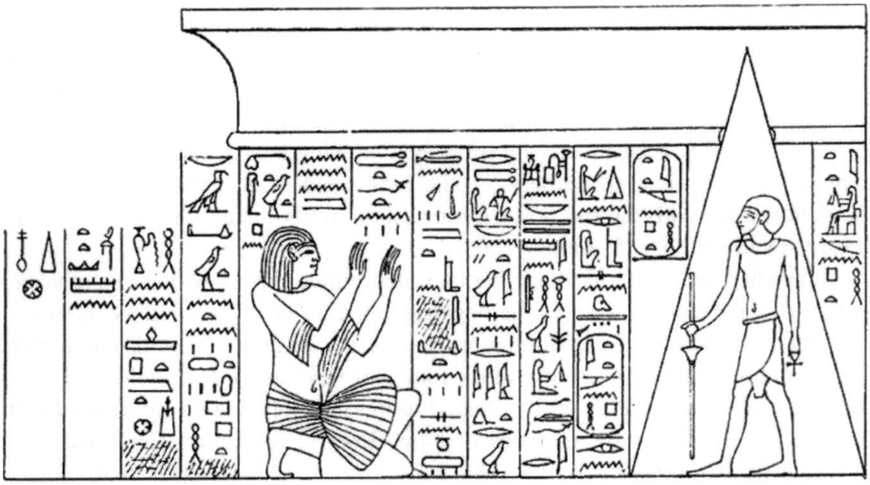

Fig. 1 Line drawing of a relief scene on the side of an unprovenanced statue probably from Saqqara, now in the Musée d'archéologie in Marseille, showing the scribe Amunwahsu (left) kneeling and praising the king (right) 'Teti-Merenptah' (his name labelled in the cartouche), published in Naville (1878: tafel IV)

The 3D GIS model suggests that the ruins of the Menkauhor (potentially 35 m tall)[20] and Teti (originally 52.5 m tall) pyramids would indeed have constituted the defining visual feature for those approaching the small New Kingdom temple-tombs erected in this part of the necropolis (Fig. 2).

New Kingdom elites potentially sited their tombs near these ruins to evoke an impression of continuity that asserted the New Kingdom tomb owner as the direct inheritor of the glorious (Old Kingdom) past (Bauer and Kosiba 2016), turning the early kings into eternal and beneficent neighbours, and confirming the newcomers' place in the immortal order. The funeral participants approaching this area may have been meant to feel awe at such antiquity and reverence for the more contemporary dead now buried nearby.

Once the procession reached the tomb at midday, the priests, family members and body of the deceased would have entered into the outermost court or forecourt.[21] The coffins were opened and the mummy placed upright, facing the south of the court. The deceased was meant to be purified and recharged by the powerful rays of the

[20] Menkaure's pyramid superstructure has almost completely disappeared today, and its original height and state of completion is unknown; potentially contributing to its reduced state was the reuse of its stone blocks for the construction of the Late Period and Ptolemaic terraces for the neighboring Anubieion (Berlandini 1979: 7–8).

[21] Imagery of female family members, including the tomb owner's wife, mourning before the mummy or coffin at the tomb clearly demonstrates that many members of the household witnessed the final rituals at the tomb, regardless of gender. Example scenes from Saqqara come from the south wall of the cult chapel at the tomb of Raia (Martin et al. 1985: 13) and the north wall of the North Chapel of Khay (Martin et al. 2001: 13 and plates 8, 52).

Fig. 2 3D model render of the area around the New Kingdom private tombs (small buildings with mud-brick pyramids, right, near the three small queen's pyramids) located north of the Old Kingdom Teti and Menkaure pyramids (shown as deflating ruins, left), with late morning lighting and shadow, view is looking southwest, render by the author in e-on Vue software

solar disc Re, now at its peak in the noon sky (Assmann 2005: 318–320).[22] Light here acquired a religious role, converting 'daytime' into something with religious power in the funerary space.[23] The court, a space designed to be open to the sky, but enclosed with walls and often lined with pillars,[24] would have been almost blinding in the intense Egyptian sun. Examples like that of Amenemone (Figs. 3 and 4) would have provided only small amounts of shade under its portico at noon, and none in the court itself.

If tomb reliefs do not tremendously exaggerate the quantity of funeral participants, the court may have stood packed with observers, most fully exposed to the sunlight. In Egypt's invariably cloudless sky, the participants positioned in the open court would have felt the heat of the solar rays radiating through their bodies, and

[22] A stela from the tomb of Pay at Saqqara repeats the desire for the face of tomb owner to be exposed daily to the light of the sun, to allow him to see the solar disk, and explains the benefits of this interaction for the deceased: "*...my body [shall be rejuvenated] at beholding your perfection...*" (Raven 2005: 44).

[23] See Bille and Sørensen (2007) for the social uses of light.

[24] Assmann interpreted these spaces (called *wsḫ.t*) in the Theban tombs as the enclosed courts with pillars, frequently decorated by stelae, in front of the entrance to the rock-cut section of the tomb, and suggested the development of these spaces was directly related to the performance of funerary cult activities (2005: 318–320). The parallel space at a free-standing Memphite tomb would be the columned first court. A relief in the tomb of Meryneith shows funeral activities taking place in a court with four columns and two pilasters, which corresponds architecturally to that tomb's inner courtyard (west portico), not the outer forecourt, which was not columned (Raven et al. 2014: 59, fig. III.3, and 99–100 scene 16).

Fig. 3 3D model render of the interior of the court of the New Kingdom tomb of 'the overseer of craftsmen and chief goldsmith' Amenemone near the Teti pyramid at Saqqara, visualising light in the courtyard at midday, with only the area of the western portico in shade; note that the tomb reconstruction is highly schematic and does not include exact column details, reconstruct relief or painting in the court, or include the cult statue in the central chapel; render by the author in e-on Vue software

Fig. 4 Archival photo showing view of the cult statue, courtyard, and western portico of the tomb of Amenemone near the Teti pyramid at Saqqara during its discovery by Victor Loret in 1898, copyright Biblioteca e Archivi di Egittologia, Università degli Studi di Milano

perhaps this added to the communal belief in the 'recharge' of the mummy. With the mummy released from the enclosed coffins and bathed with direct sun, the warming embalming chemicals may have diffused the potent scent of natron to those standing in front.

The priests performed the 'opening of the mouth' ritual, and in a practice derived from one enacted on tomb statuary in the Old Kingdom, encircled the mummy four times, burned incense, and repeatedly intoned the wish to 'Be pure! Be pure!'[25] (Assmann 2005: 313; Teeter 2011: 139–140). The ritual included touching the mouth of the mummy with special instruments, an act intended to magically re-animate the image of the dead with the ability to breathe and speak, essential to defend himself during his final judgement by the gods (Hays 2010: 7–8). The priest offered to the face of the mummy the foreleg of a calf, in theory butchered at this moment in the tomb, 'the still warm vital energy streaming out of it', imagined as transferring its own power of life to the mummy and reanimating it (Assmann 2005: 324–5).[26] If the butchering indeed took place at or immediately outside the tomb, the cries of the dying animal, the smell of the fresh blood, and the dripping red limb could have created a moment of intense sensory drama for witnesses.[27]

The chief lector priest recited spells to guarantee the transfiguration of the dead. An offering ritual was performed, meant to supply the deceased with sustenance for the afterlife. Sets of new vessels carried up during the procession, elaborately painted with blue floral motifs, held food and drink to be presented.[28] Family members burned incense, as depicted in the north chapel of the tomb of Khay, which shows the tomb owner's son Neferbau censing before the mummy (Martin et al. 2001: 13 and plates 8, 52). At some point in the service, the mummy was likely anointed with fragrant oils, such as moringa oil, examples of which were found at the tomb of Maya.[29] Perhaps at sunset, torches of fine linen were lit and offered to the deceased, their flames doused in bowls of scented milk only after a priest had chanted related spells from the Book of the Dead. The darkening of the sky and the simultaneous extinguishing

---

[25] This scene is shown and described in great detail in the Theban tomb of the royal domain administrator Nebsumenu (Assmann 2005: 312).

[26] A fragmentary relief from an unknown tomb near the Teti complex depicts these two actions from the opening of the mouth ritual (Martin 1987: object 92, pl. 54).

[27] After an ethnographic exploration of animal sacrifice practices in modern Muslim communities in Istanbul, Weddle suggested the sight, sound, and smell of dripping blood from the slaughter of bulls as part of the Roman Imperial cult could have made a significant sensory impression on the viewer of the ritual sacrifice (2013: 151–152).

[28] Large deposits of new, blue painted offering vessels were found buried between the Dynasty 18 tomb of Horemheb and the neighboring tomb of Iniuia at Saqqara, in parallel with pottery deposits found outside the exterior pylon of the tomb of Maya. Maya's pottery was designed in sets and was theorized as commissioned for the funeral of either Maya or his wife Meryt (Raven et al. 2011: 238).

[29] Maya and Meryt's burial included vessels with residue inside, including one labeled "sweet moringa oil for the funeral procession of 'Osiris', royal scribe, overseer of the treasury, Maya." Moringa oil was commonly applied to the body, and often used as a base oil then scented with frankincense or cyperus grass (Manniche 1999: 30, 110).

of the fire symbolised the beginning of the deceased's nocturnal journey through the netherworld.[30]

Finally, the mummy was returned to his protective coffins and processed from the court to the entrance of the burial shaft. Once manoeuvred into the proper burial chamber, the priests dragged it into the final location (Assmann 2005: 328). The chamber was then closed and sealed; the shaft filled to protect the burial (Teeter 2011: 147). Vessels involved in serving the funerary meal, as well as those providing food and drink in the arbours, were at various points during the ceremonies shattered intentionally and left in or around the tomb (Ritner 2008: 145–7; Martin 1989: 101). Some of the ceramic vessels could have been smashed on the stone-paved floors of the open court,[31] the piercing sounds part of an execration act thought to offer protection at moments of transition like death (Winlock and Arnold 2010).[32] The funerary event completed, the mourners descended from the high desert escarpment and ferried back across the Nile.

5.2 *Elite Mortuary Cults at Saqqara*

While the procession and funeral must have served as the most dramatic event related to the death of an elite community member, the ritualised relationship between the living and the deceased was far from complete at the cemetery. Most impactful was the continued mortuary cult, led by specialised priests, who (ideally) daily and in tandem with seasonal festival occasions, visited the open tomb chapel to chant or sing aloud a series of recitations.[33] The liturgies were intended to entice the *ba* of the tomb owner to return briefly from the netherworld and receive sustenance, engender the effective power of the deceased, and aid him on his transition to the netherworld. Theoretically the son of the deceased tomb owner acted as main officiant, but professional priests, family, and friends may have also participated in various ways.[34] Purification rituals

[30] Evidence for this practice comes from New Kingdom funerary papyri (Strong 2018).

[31] Many of the New Kingdom temple-tombs had courts lined with stone pavers.

[32] Blue painted offering vessels made for funerary use were frequently found buried between the New Kingdom temple-tombs at Saqqara. The ceramicist studying the tomb of Horemeheb suggested that pottery used in the funeral was either immediately taken outside and buried or moved at least to the outer court for disposal (Raven et al. 2011: 238). At the tomb of Paser at Saqqara, a cache of over 150 vessels likely used during the funerary rituals was found in a shallow pit in the forecourt, and they appear to have been intentionally broken before deposit (Martin et al. 1985: 47). At the tomb of Ramose at Saqqara, ceramics likely from the funeral were deposited in chapel D, inside the tomb (Martin et al. 2001: 54).

[33] But see Baines and Lacovara (2002) for the frequent neglect of mortuary duties.

[34] Clear traces of repeated, long-term mortuary cult celebrations for the elite at Saqqara comes from the New Kingdom temple-tombs south of the Unas causeway. In the forecourt and inner court of tomb of Maya, archaeologists uncovered objects likely used in cult ceremonies, including offering stands, an offering table and basin, and inscribed tablets (Raven et al. 2001: 8). A stela discovered near the tomb was inscribed by the lector priest Yamen and shows him making offerings to Maya and his wife Meryt (Raven et al. 2001: 9). A second stela, identified in a museum in Warsaw, depicts a

were performed, including censing and the presenting of fragrant oils, which would have filled the small chapels in the rear of the temple-tombs with strong scent. The priests made invocations to the dead, pouring water on a stone table with offerings represented, the libation action activating their power (Hays 2010; Assmann 2005: 244, 330–32, 348; Willems 2001; O'Neill 2015: 58–59). A wall relief in the central chapel of the tomb of Amenemone shows the owner's son making an invocation offering to his father, the text inscribed before his image stating:

> Words spoken by his son, the Scribe of the Treasury Ptahmose, true of voice: Take to yourself an offering of provisions, libations, incense, offerings consisting of offering loaves of your god of your city… May they give you invocation offerings of bread, beer, oxen, fowl, libations, wine, milk, all good and pure things upon which a god lives; may you breathe air with myrrh and incense when one summons (to a meal) in the great place; may you eat bread and food offerings, namely that which the great gods give you; may you hear the voice when the offerings are announced, when giving the food offering to its lord; may you see the lord when he goes forth at the appearance of the god for his city. Your real heart belongs to you, your heart of being on earth…" (Ockinga et al. 2004: 55 and pl. 12, line numbers removed).

It was the sound of the priest's voice, the distinguishing of his words by the dead, and the flow of the water that made this practice, which went back as far at least as the Old Kingdom, effective (Assmann 2005: 330–32, 348). Finally, protective rituals, likely the breaking of vessels, concluded some rituals (Willems 2001). In the Old Kingdom at least, the words would have been accompanied by the alternating beating of the priest's breast with his fists, creating a type of 'corporal music' that Assman interpreted as expressing 'emotion at the presence of a superhuman power', here, the empowered dead (2005: 243). Middle Kingdom coffin texts interpreted as mortuary liturgy suggest that some oral spells were highly repetitive, to demarcate them aurally as distinct from regular speech (Willems 2001: 368).

Imagined thus as dwelling within the tomb, and maintaining their capacities to hear, breathe, taste and see, the sensory experience of the *dead* must be considered in structuring experience in the necropolis. Most of the New Kingdom Memphite temples, including the main temple of Ptah and the royal memorial temples nearby (whose locations remain yet undiscovered), have succumbed to the rising floodplain and modern development, and thus their ancient visual connection with Saqqara is not preserved in modern times. 3D GIS viewshed studies, which calculate all aspects of a 3D space that would have been visible and not visible from a single observer point (computationally taking into account building heights and shape, terrain topography, and any natural or built forms that would have obstructed the view of the observer),

---

man named Peraaerneheh, who described himself as a "lector priest of the Overseer of the Treasury Maiay," (which almost certainly refers to Maya) and represents this priest offering to "Tyia" below, likely the Ramesside princess Tia buried in the neighboring tomb. If Maya's mortuary cult was still being celebrated, it would have lasted then at least two, possibly three decades (year 9 of Horemheb to the first half of the reign of Ramesses II, who reigned over 65 years). Other individuals left small stelae or carved their names onto Maya's relief scenes in the pylons (Raven et al. 2001: 9). At other nearby tombs, including those of Iniuia, Meryneith, and Tia and Tia, deposits of late New Kingdom pottery were interpreted by excavators (based on pottery date or find spot) as related to the continued offering of mortuary service to the deceased (Raven et al. 2014: 261–2; Schneider et al. 2012: 139; Martin 1997: 64).

suggest the Memphite temples would originally have maintained high prominence from the area of the New Kingdom tombs. That the dead desired to 'see the god' is clear from contemporary texts (discussed above), and I have elsewhere argued that the southern groups of New Kingdom tombs were positioned to allow the deceased to maintain a visual connection with the temple of the god or the contemporary divinized king (Sullivan 2020). Visual links to the royal memorial temple could have been especially desirable, as the king was officially the official patron of mortuary offerings, distributing them to the houses of the gods and eventually reverting to the deceased in the necropolis (Strudwick 2005: 31–32).

The mechanisms of the dead's sight were not defined; potentially through their mobile *ba* spirit, which could leave the tomb and ascend to the sky (Assmann 2005: 90–94). The stones capping the small mud-brick or stone-faced pyramids, positioned directly above or behind the cult chapel seem to have acted as one conduit for sacred vision for the deceased, as a number of examples at Saqqara included sculpted figures of the tomb owner (and sometimes his wife) kneeling and praising the sun.[35] The imagery was carved on the west and east sides of the pyramidion, placing the dead to directly face the rising and setting sun each day. The inscribed text on the east face of the pink granite capstone of Iniuia makes an explicit request for sacred vision:

> An offering which the King gives (to) Re-Horakhte, the Great God, Lord of the sky, may he give that one sees his beauty when he rises, to the Osiris, the King's Scribe, the Steward, Iniuia, justified, of Memphis" (Schneider et al. 2012: 78).

The position of these objects, five or more metres above ground level, at the highest point of the tomb, would have also offered excellent 'sight-lines' to the temples of Memphis on the flood plain to the east (Figs. 5 and 6).

The topography of the necropolis may therefore have been arranged in order to facilitate sacred vision, an aspect no doubt observable to the living approaching or leaving the tombs for funerary or mortuary cult performance, but designed to serve the sensory desires of the dead emerging out from the tomb.

6 Conclusion

Scholars have defined ritual as the physical expression of social concepts about the sacred and the divine (Barrowclough and Malone 2007: 1–2). Ritual actions were repeatedly performed and concretized through highly specialised architectural forms at Saqqara in ways creating the potential for significant sensory stimulation. The recurring events and their sensory signatures were an important means of demarcating the funerary landscape as a special form of 'sacred space'. That these experiences were repeated over and over at various locations across the cemetery by a variety of people is clear, and these would have constituted the sounds, smells and sights

[35] Examples from New Kingdom Saqqara include those from the tomb of Amenemone (Cairo JE 41665), Iniuia (Louvre D 14), Pay (Louvre D 21) (Rammant Peters 1983: Docs 20, 50, 55).

Fig. 5 (Left) 3D model render of the interior court of the New Kingdom tomb of Iniuia at Saqqara with the suggested position of the red and black granite capstone on the mud-brick pyramid superstructure indicated, render by the author in e-on Vue software; (Right) cropped digital photo of the west face of the pyramidion of Iniuia now in the Louvre museum (D 14), image courtesy of WikiMedia Commons, under a CC BY-SA 2.0 FR license: https://commons.wikimedia.org/wiki/File:Louvres-antiquites-egyptiennes-img_2865.jpg

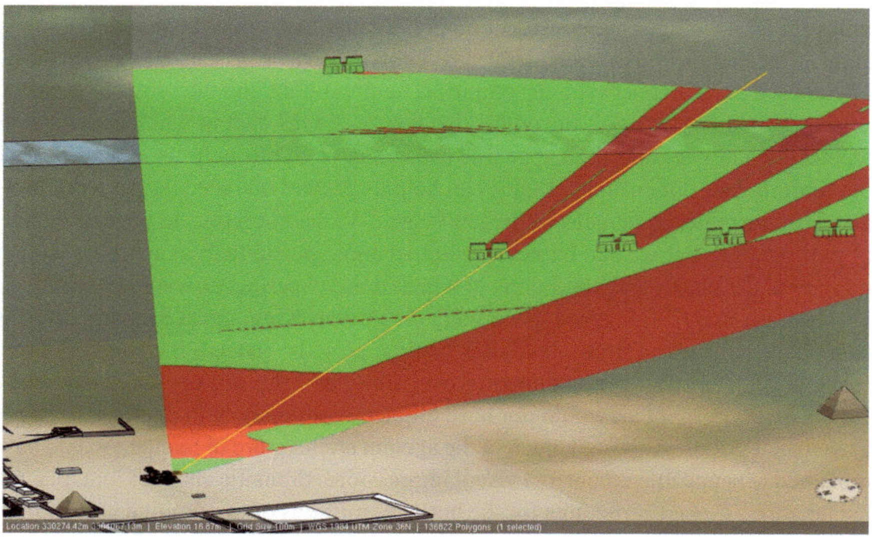

Fig. 6 3D analysis of visibility showing elements that would be blocked (red) and visible (green) from an observer point at the centre of the pyramidion of Iniuia looking towards known (Ptah temple, background) and hypothetical (royal memorial temples, foreground) New Kingdom temples at Memphis represented by New Kingdom-style pylons (~25 m in height), analysis performed by the author in CityEngine 2018.0

that most characterised the necropolis landscape for the living. The dead too were imagined to tangibly benefit from these powerful sensations, but desired additional sensory capacities, to be able to look outward and see the god (or king in divinized form) from the tomb.

In this work, I have argued that although the artistic and textual record provides tremendous information on human experience at the necropolis, some vital elements of that experience—specifically the physical and visual impact of related monumental architecture—must be sought elsewhere. Using 3D GIS technologies, this study visualised aspects of the site of Saqqara in the New Kingdom that are inaccessible today to the modern scholar. These include the original form, materials, and lighting effects of individual New Kingdom tombs, the many existing monuments spread across the landscape of the cemetery that time (those both newly constructed and then-ancient structures in a state of collapse or deflation), and the contemporary temples (whose positions are variously known and still hypothetical) at the neighbouring site of Memphis. This digital material was directly integrated within the larger sensory discussion, to avoid isolating conclusions based on the digital from more traditional historical sources. Using the 3D visualisations and 3D viewshed calculations, I suggested ways that the physical space of the elite New Kingdom monuments, as well as views of royal monuments at Saqqara and Memphis, shaped embodied experience of the living, offered sacred sight-lines to the dead, and imbued places with a sense of 'perpetuity'. 3D GIS visualisations thus create new opportunities for archaeologists to consider complex spatial and temporal elements of sites, and I argue that the digital can operate profitably *in service of* sensory examinations. I do not see a conflict between the empirical nature of GIS and the subjective aspects of sensory studies. Instead, the embedded nature of GIS data in real locations at an archaeological site, and the expansive capacities of 3D to help us extend beyond the limiting two dimensions of GIS, can help us ground our speculative work more firmly in the material remains of the landscape. We cannot replicate the experiences of past peoples, but we can harness digital technologies to help us more rigorously reimagine the places and conditions in which those experiences were generated.

This case study has focused specifically on the New Kingdom at Saqqara, drawing cautiously on sources from other sites or time periods. Indeed, the funerary landscape at Saqqara changed continually over time, and the sensory experience of a New Kingdom Egyptian would not have aligned seamlessly with one in the Late or Ptolemaic Periods. Although much of the ancient architecture of Saqqara would have remained to shape movement and visual impressions, dramatic changes took place at the necropolis. Huge structures for the burial of millions of mummified cult animals were erected, including temples and facilities for priests and pilgrims. The area of the monumental New Kingdom tombs was repurposed for lower- and non-elite burials, and mummification workshops popped-up around the tombs themselves. Pilgrims visited and slept in the temple of the Greek *Asklepieion*, hoping to receive divine messages through dreams (Bagnall and Rathbone 2004). New smells, sounds, and sights would have characterised the landscape as the nature of the site shifted. One of the main strengths of using digital landscape visualisations is their facility in showing multiple past moments in time, highlighting the complex histories of ancient places, which remind us that human experiences would have transformed in tandem with the spaces they inhabited.

References

Allen, James. 2005. *The Art of medicine in ancient Egypt*. New York: Metropolitan Museum of Art.

Assmann, Jan. 2002. *The mind of Egypt: History and meaning in the time of the Pharaohs*. New York: Metropolitan Books.

Assmann, Jan. 2005. *Death and salvation in ancient Egypt*. Ithaca: Cornell University Press.

Bagnall, Roger, and Dominic Rathbone. 2004. *Egypt: From Alexander to the Early Christians, an archaeological and historical guide*. Los Angeles: The J. Paul Getty Museum.

Baines, John, and Peter Lacovara. 2002. Burial and the dead in ancient Egyptian society: Respect, formalism, neglect. *Journal of Social Archaeology* 2: 5–36. https://doi.org/10.1177/146960530 2002001595.

Barrowclough, David, and Caroline Malone. 2007. *Cult in context: Reconsidering ritual in archaeology*. Oxford: Oxbow.

Bauer, Andrew, and Steve Kosiba. 2016. How things act: An archaeology of materials in political life. *Journal of Social Archaeology* 16: 115–141. https://doi.org/10.1177/1469605316641244.

Beaux, Nathalie. 2015. Odeur, souffle et vie. *Bibliotheque d'Etude* 164: 61–74.

Berlandini, Jocelyne. 1979. La pyramide <<ruinée>> de Sakkara-nord et le roi Ikaouhor-Menkaouhor. *Revue d'Égyptologie* 31: 3–28.

Bille, Mikkel, and Tim Flohr Sørensen. 2007. An Anthropology of luminosity: The agency of light. *Journal of Material Culture* 12: 263–284. https://doi.org/10.1177/1359183507081894.

Bradley, Mark. 2015. *Smell and the ancient senses*. Senses in antiquity. London: Taylor & Francis Group.

Brovarski, Edward. 1984. Sokar. Edited by Eberhard Otto, Wolfgang Helck, and Wolfhart Westendorf. *Lexikon der Ägyptologie*. Wiesbaden: O. Harrassowitz.

Butler, Shane, and Sarah Nooter. 2019. *Sound and the ancient senses*. Routledge.

Butler, Shane, and Alex Purves. 2013. *Synaesthesia and the ancient senses*. University of California at Los Angeles.

Cherpion, Nadine. 1994. Le "cone d'onguent." *Bulletin de l'Institut français d'archéologie orientale* 94: 79–106.

Daróczi, Tibor-Tamás. 2012. Death, disposal and social memory – Towards a definition of funerary landscapes. *eTopoi Journal for ancient studies* Special volume 3: 199–207. https://doi.org/10.17171/5-3-28.

Day, Jo. 2013. *Making senses of the past: Toward a sensory archaeology*. Center for Archaeological Investigations Occasional Paper; No. 40. Carbondale: Center for Archaeological Investigations, Southern Illinois University Carbondale and Southern Illinois University Press.

Dodson, Aidan. 2001. Of bulls, Pharaohs, Persians and Ptolemies: The latter years of the Serapeum of Saqqara. *Bulletin of the Egyptological Seminar* 15: 27–38.

Dodson, Aidan, and Salima Ikram. 2008. *The tomb in Ancient Egypt: Royal and private sepulchres from the early dynastic period to the Romans*. London: Thames & Hudson.

Dorman, Peter, and Betsy Bryan, ed. 2007. *Sacred space and sacred function in ancient Thebes*. Studies in Ancient Oriental Civilizations 61. Chicago: Oriental Institute of the University of Chicago.

Elwart, Dorothée, and Sibylle Emerit. 2019. Sound studies and visual studies applied to ancient Egyptian sources. In *Sounding sensory profiles in the ancient Near East*, ed. Annette Schellenberg and Thomas Krüger, 315–334. Atlanta: SBL Press.

Emerit, Sibylle. 2011. Listening to the gods: Echoes of the divine. In *Laut und Leise: Der Gebrauch von Stimme und Klang in historischen Kulturen*, ed. Erika Meyer-Dietrich, 61–88. Bielefeld: Transcript Verlag.

Fahlander, Fredrik, and Anna Kjellström, ed. 2010. *Making sense of things: Archaeologies of sensory perception*. Stockholm: Dept. of Archaeology and Classical History, Stockholm University.

Finnestad, Ragnhild. 1999. Enjoying the pleasures of sensation: Reflections on a significant feature of Egyptian religion. In *Gold of Praise: Studies on Ancient Egypt in Honor of Edward F. Wente*, 111–119. SAOC 58. Chicago: The Oriental Institute of the University of Chicago.

Forte, Maurizio, and Alberto Siliotti. 1997. *Virtual archaeology: Re-creating ancient worlds*. New York: H.N. Abrams.

Gaballa, G. 1977. *The Memphite tomb-chapel of Mose*. Warminster: Aris & Phillips.

Goldsmith, Dora. 2019. Fish, fowl, and stench in Ancient Egypt. In *Sounding sensory profiles in the Ancient Near East*, ed. Annette Schellenberg and Thomas Krüger, 335–360. Atlanta, GA: SBL Press.

Hamilakis, Yannis. 2013. *Archaeology and the senses: Human experience, memory, and affect*. New York, NY: Cambridge University Press.

Härke, Heinrich. 1997. The nature of burial data. In *Burial & society: The chronological and social analysis of archaeological burial data*, ed. Claus Kjeld Jensen and Karen Høilund Nielsen, 19–27. Aarhus: Aarhus University Press.

Hays, Harold. 2010. Funerary Rituals (Pharaonic Period). Edited by Willeke Wendrich and Jacco Dieleman. *UCLA Encyclopedia of Egyptology*. https://escholarship.org/uc/item/1r32g9zn.

Houston, Stephen, and Karl Taube. 2000. An archaeology of the senses: Perception and cultural expression in ancient Mesoamerica. *Cambridge Archaeological Journal* 10: 261–294. https://doi.org/10.1017/S095977430000010X.

Hurcombe, Linda. 2007. A sense of materials and sensory perception in concepts of materiality. *World Archaeology* 39: 532–545. https://doi.org/10.1080/00438240701679346.

Ikram, Salima. 2015. *Death and burial in ancient Egypt*. Cairo: The American University in Cairo Press.

Lichtheim, Miriam. 1973. *Ancient Egyptian literature. The Old and Middle Kingdoms*. Vol. I. Ancient Egyptian Literature. Berkeley: University of California Press.

Lieven, Alexandra van. 2016a. 'Thy fragrance is in all my Limbs': On the olfactory sense in ancient Egyptian religion. In *Religion für die Sinne – Religion for the Senses*, ed. Philipp Reichling and Meret Strothmann, 309–325. Oberhausen: Athena-Verlag.

Lieven, Alexandra van. 2016b. Sounds of power: The concept of sound in ancient Egyptian religion. In *Religion für die Sinne – Religion for the Senses*, ed. Philipp Reichling and Meret Strothmann, 25–35. Oberhausen: Athena-Verlag.

Kinney, Lesley. 2004. The dance of the MWW. *The Bulletin of the Australian Centre for Egyptology* 15: 63–77.

Málek, Jaromír. 1992. A meeting of the old and new: Saqqara during the New Kingdom. In *Studies in Pharaonic religion and society: In honour of J. Gwyn Griffiths*, ed. Alan Lloyd, 57–76. London: Egypt Exploration Society.

Manassa, Colleen. 2011. Soundscapes in ancient Egyptian literature and religion. In *Der Gebrauch von Stimme und Klang in historischen Kulturen*, ed. Erika Meyer-Dietrich, 147–172. Bielefeld: transcript Verlag.

Manniche, Lise. 1991. *Music and musicians in ancient Egypt*. London: British Museum Press.

Manniche, Lise. 1999. *Sacred luxuries: Fragrance, aromatherapy, and cosmetics in Ancient Egypt*. New York: Cornell University Press.

Martin, Geoffrey. 1987. *Corpus of reliefs of the New Kingdom from the Memphite Necropolis and Lower Egypt*. London: KPI.

Martin, Geoffrey. 1989. *The Memphite tomb of Horemheb, commander-in-chief of Tutankhamun: I: reliefs, inscriptions, and commentary*. Vol. I. Excavation Memoir 55. London: Egypt Exploration Society.

Martin, Geoffrey. 1997. *The tomb of Tia and Tia: A royal monument of the Ramesside Period in the Memphite necropolis*. Excavation Memoir 58. London: Egypt Exploration Society.

Martin, Geoffrey, Hans Schneider, Maarten Raven, Janine Bourriau, Jacobus Van Dijk, and David Aston. 1985. *The tomb-chapels of Paser and Ra'ia at Saqqâra*. Excavation Memoir 52. London: Egypt Exploration Society.

Martin, Geoffrey, Jacobus Van Dijk, and Kenneth Frazer. 2012. *The tomb of Maya and Meryt I: The reliefs, inscriptions, and commentary*. Vol. I. Excavation Memoir 99. London: Egypt Exploration Society.

Martin, Geoffrey, Jacobus Van Dijk, Maarten Raven, Barbara Aston, David Aston, Eugen Strouhal, and Ladislava Horackova. 2001. *The tombs of three Memphite officials: Ramose, Khay and Pabes*. Excavation Memoir 66. London: Egypt Exploration Society.

Matić, Uroš. 2018. 'They were like lions roaring upon the mountain-crests': Soundscapes of war in New Kingdom Egypt. In *Current research in Egyptology 2017. Proceedings of the eighteenth annual symposium.*, ed. Ilaria Incordino, Stefania Mainieri, Elena D'Itria, and Maria Pubblico, 103–115. Oxford: Archaeopress.

Meyer-Dietrich, Erika. 2009. Dance. Edited by Willeke Wendrich and Jacco Dieleman. *UCLA Encyclopedia of Egyptology*. https://escholarship.org/uc/item/5142h0db.

Naville, Edouard. 1878. Le roi Teta Merenphtah. *Zeitschrift für ägyptische Sprache und Altertumskunde* 16: 69–71. https://archive.org/details/zeitschriftfr16brug.

Nyberg, Jenny. 2010. A peaceful sleep and heavenly celebration for the pure and innocent. The sensory experience of death during the long eighteenth century. In *Making sense of things: Archaeologies of sensory perception*, ed. Fredrik Fahlander and Anna Kjellström, 15–34. Department of Archaeology and Classical History, Stockholm University.

Ockinga, Boyo, K. Sowada, Jacobus van Dijk, and Mark Spiegelman. 2004. *Amenemone, the chief goldsmith: A New Kingdom tomb in the Teti Cemetery at Saqqara*. Reports of the Australian Centre for Egyptology 22. Oxford: Aris and Phillips.

O'Neill, Barbara. 2015. Setting the scene: The deceased and regenerative cult within offering table imagery of the Egyptian Old to Middle Kingdoms BC. Oxford: ArchaeoPress.

Pellini, José Roberto. 2015. Remembering through the senses: The funerary practices in ancient Egypt. In *Coming to senses: Topics in sensory archaeology*, ed. José Roberto Pellini, Melisa Salerno, and Andrés Zarankin, 39–63. Newcastle upon Tyne: Cambridge Scholars Publishing.

Pinch, Geraldine. 1993. *Votive offerings to Hathor*. Oxford: Griffith Institute, Ashmolean Museum.

Pinch, Geraldine, and Elizabeth Waraksa. 2009. Votive practices. Edited by Willeke Wendrich and Jacco Dieleman. *UCLA Encyclopedia of Egyptology*. https://escholarship.org/uc/item/7kp4n7rk.

Porter, Bertha, and Rosalind Moss. 1981. *Topographical bibliography of ancient Egyptian hieroglyphic texts, reliefs, and paintings: Memphis*. Vol. III: Part 2: Saqqara to Dahshur. VII vols. Oxford: Clarendon Press.

Price, Robyn. 2018. Sniffing out the gods: Archaeology with the senses. *Journal of Ancient Egyptian Interconnections* 17: 137–155.

Purves, Alex. 2017. *Touch and the ancient senses*. Routledge.

Raven, Maarten. 2005. *The tomb of Pay and Raia at Saqqara*. Excavation Memoir 74. Leiden: National Museum of Antiquities Leiden.

Rammant-Peeters, Agnes. 1983. *Les pyramidions Egyptiens du Nouvel-empire*. Orientalia Lovaniensia Analecta 11. Leuven: Peeters.

Raven, Maarten, Hans Schneider, Eugen Strouhal, Georges Bonani, and Willy Woelfli. 2001. *The tomb of Maya and Meryt 2: Objects and skeletal remains*. Excavation Memoir 65. Leiden & London: National Museum of Antiquities & Egypt Exploration Society.

Raven, Maarten, Vincent Verschoor, Marije Vugts, and Rene Van Walsem. 2011. *The Memphite tomb of Horemheb, commander-in-chief of Tutankhamun: The forecourt and area south of the tomb with some notes on the tomb of Tia*. Vol. V. Papers on Archaeology of the Leiden Museum of Antiquities 6. Belgium: Brepols.

Raven, Maarten, René van Walsem, Willem Beex, Amanda Dunsmore, Ladislava Horáčkova, Dorothea Schulz, P. J. Bomhof, and Anneke de Kemp. 2014. *The Tomb of Meryneith at Saqqara.* Brepols, Belgium: Turnhout.

Riggs, Christina. 2010. The Body. Edited by Willeke Wendrich and Jacco Dieleman. *UCLA Encyclopedia of Egyptology*. https://escholarship.org/uc/item/8f21r7sj.

Riggs, Christina. 2016. Beautiful burials, beautiful skulls: The aesthetics of the Egyptian mummy. *The British Journal of Aesthetics* 56: 247–263. https://doi.org/10.1093/aesthj/ayw045.

Ritner, Robert K. 2008. *The mechanics of ancient Egyptian magical practice*. Chicago: Oriental Institute of the University of Chicago.

Robins, Gay. 1997. *The art of ancient Egypt*. Cambridge: Harvard University Press.

Rudolph, Kelli. 2017. *Taste and the ancient senses*. Routledge.

Schneider, Hans, Barbara Aston, Jacobus Van Dijk, Christine Dijkstra, Rutger Perizonius, and Eugen Strouhal. 2012. *The tomb of Iniuia in the New Kingdom necropolis of Memphis at Saqqara*. Papers on Archaeology of the Leiden Museum of Antiquities 8. Turnhout: Brepols.

Shafer, Byron, ed. 1997. *Temples of ancient Egypt*. Ithaca: Cornell University Press.

Skeates, Robin, and Jo Day, ed. 2019. *The Routledge handbook of sensory archaeology*. Routledge.

Squire, Michael, ed. 2016. *Sight and the ancient senses*. Senses in Antiquity. London: Routledge.

Staring, Nico. 2014. The tomb of Ptahmose, mayor of Memphis: Analysis of an early 19th Dynasty funerary monument at Saqqara. *Bulletin de Institut Français d'Archéologie Orientale* 114: 455–518.

Strong, Meghan. 2018. A great secret of the West: Transformative aspects of artificial light in New Kingdom Egypt. In *Archaeology of the night: Life after dark in ancient world*, ed. Nancy Gonlin and April Nowell, 249–264. Boulder: University Press of Colorado.

Strudwick, Nigel. 2005. *Texts from the pyramid age*. Writings from the Ancient World no. 16. Atlanta: Society of Biblical Literature.

Sullivan, Elaine. 2020. *Constructing the sacred: Visibility and ritual landscape at the Egyptian necropolis of Saqqara*. Palo Alto: Stanford University Press. http://constructingthesacred.org.

Teeter, Emily. 2011. *Religion and ritual in ancient Egypt*. New York: Cambridge University Press.

Tosi, Mario, and Alessandro Roccati. 1972. *Stele e altre epigrafi di Deir el Medina*. Torino: Edizioni d'arte Fratelli Pozzo.

Van der Plas, Dirk. 1989. "Voir Dieu" - Quelques observations au sujet de la fonction des sens dans la culte et la devotion de l'Egypte ancienne. *Bulletin de la Société Française d'Egyptologie: Réunions trimestrielles et communications archéologiques* 115: 4–35.

Van de Walle, Baudouin. 1985. Le sens de la vue et la vertu du regard dans la mentalité égyptienne. In *Mélanges offerts à Jean Vercoutter*, 365–374. Paris: Editions Recherche sur les civilisations.

Weddle, Candace. 2013. "The sensory experience of blood sacrifice in the Roman imperial cult." In *Making senses of the past: Toward a sensory archaeology*, ed. by Jo Day, 137–59. Center for Archaeological Investigations Occasional Paper 40. Carbondale: Southern Illinois University Press.

Willems, Harco. 2001. The social and ritual context of a mortuary liturgy of the Middle Kingdom (CT Spells 30–41). In *Social aspects of funerary culture in the Egyptian Old and Middle Kingdoms. Proceedings of the international symposium held at Leiden University, 6–7 June, 1996*, 253–372. Orientalia Lovaniensia Analecta 103. Leuven.

Winlock, Herbert, and Dorothea Arnold. 2010. *Tutankhamun's funeral*. Metropolitan Museum of Art.

Wise, Elliott. 2009. An "odor of sanctity": The iconography, magic, and ritual of Egyptian incense. *Studia Antiqua* 7: 67–80.

Elaine A. Sullivan (M.A. and Ph.D. at Johns Hopkins University) is an Associate Professor of History at the University of California, Santa Cruz. She is an Egyptologist and a Digital Humanist whose work focuses on applying new technologies to ancient cultural materials.

Kinesthetic Archaeologies: Digital Methods and the Reconstruction of Movement

Stuart Dunn

Abstract Digitization, defined as the capture of data into computable 1 and 0 s, is a freeze-frame process: a digital image, a piece of text, a video or audio file are a fixed set of data that is only rendered dynamic when it is read or played, or otherwise executed. What, therefore, are the implications of digitising movement? Digital technologies and methods employed for such digitization take a variety of forms, but broadly, they can be divided into two categories: those which capture and record motion directly (such as motion capture), and those which reconstruct it (such as GIS cost pathways). This chapter will consider and compare these two classes of approach. By considering them in the context of their "digital epistemology," it will seek to situate these two highly complementary methods between performance studies and the digital humanities. By combining historical perspectives from both areas, the chapter will offer an evaluation of how the digital capture and recording of movement can contribute to our understandings of past environments and processes.

1 Introduction: The Idea of "Retro-Documentation"

The two processes of capturing and documenting human movement in a form that can be reproduced, analysed and communicated have an interdisciplinary significance. Examples of where one needs to understand movement might include analysing past events in history and archaeology, choreography and performance studies, architecture, cartography and urban design. Doing so, however, presents numerous methodological and interpretive challenges. Techniques commonly used for the purpose include video, gyroscopic motion capture and visualisation, whether based on evidence or conjecture, of movement from secondary sources through graphical means such as mapping. More recently, we might add Global Positioning Systems (GPS) as a means for tracking human movement in real time (Barber and Sammon n.d.). At some point, all such techniques must address an inherent contradiction:

S. Dunn (✉)
Department of Digital Humanities, King's College London, London, UK
e-mail: stuart.dunn@kcl.ac.uk

G. Landeschi and E. Betts (eds.), *Capturing the Senses*,
Quantitative Methods in the Humanities and Social Sciences,
https://doi.org/10.1007/978-3-031-23133-9_4

their subject is ephemeral, transitory and above all *dynamic*, yet the form into which it is being documented is *static*. A photograph or a painting of a dancer in mid-performance, for example, records movement at one particular point in time and in a particular place, but the act of documenting those attributes at that one point repalces movement with stasis. The remediation of movement into a form in which it can be analysed, critiqued, assessed, transmitted and archived is therefore problematic both practically and philosophically.

Classical rhetoricians were preoccupied with the transmission of value-bearing objects, such as artworks, or indeed humans, into other forms. In the case of our dancer, this means transfering them from the dynamic/physical/embodied world to a static/visual/disembodied one. The branch of rhetoric associated with such transformation is *ekphrasis*, the expression of (artistic) physical objects in other forms, usually literary or spoken ones (Foka and Arvidsson 2016). Mitchell states that:

> [t]he crucial rule of ekphrasis [...] is that the 'other' medium, the visual, graphic or plastic object, is never made visible or tangible except by way of the medium of language. One might call ekphrasis a form of nesting without touching or suturing, a kind of action-at-distance between two rigorously separated sensory and semiotic tracks, one which requires completion in the mind of the reader. (Mitchell 2005: 263).

Ekphrasis, therefore, is a form of remediation through understanding and semantic description. In order to adapt this principle to the dancer's movement motion, whether in the past or the present, needs to be added to Mitchell's list of visual, graphic or plastic objects. In all these cases, there is a chain of creativity and interpretation, consisting of five "links": (1) the point (in both time and space) in which the movement is executed, (2) the point at which it is observed or captured, (3) the point at which a further "object" is made recording that movement, (4) the point at which that object is augmented or enriched and (5) the point at which it is observed and received. The idea of this "ekphrastic chain" is crucial to the arguments developed below.

This framing highlights the distinction between *capturing* the dancer's movement and *documenting* it. The first three links in this chain (execution, observation, recording) deal with *capture*, an act that must inevitably take place in some physical and/or temporal proximity to the movement. If one tried to draw the dancer's movements a fortnight after they executed them from memory, for example, the new object (the drawing) is unlikely to be as faithful a rendition as a drawing made co-temporally and co-locationally from direct observation. Having been captured, the movement itself is obviated or even supressed. The last two links in the chain (augmentation and reception of the new object) refer to documentation, where the captured movement is rendered into a form in which it can be shared—and manipulated, consumed, appreciated, and critiqued—in different ways. One is a product of direct observation, physically co-spatial and/or co-temporal—and by implication containing a degree of objectivity—and the other is augmentative and interpretive. All five links are part of an ekphrastic processes, but for the purposes of this discussion, "capture" refers to movement remediated through direct observation, whereas "documentation" is a process of augmentation of the "object" thus created, in which the movement is described with further information and/or new perspectives. This could be contextual information, other remediated movement "objects," artistic interpretation, etc. This allows for the complexity and variety of humanistic interpretation: what the movement means to the observer. For example, if the image is a drawing rather than a photograph, then a facet of human interpretation (the artist's eye) is introduced. The image is a subjective rendering of the physical situation *at a particular point* between (to extend the example above) Positions A and B. One could add at this point other material or metadata, such as a choreographer's instruction, or a critic's comments, interpretations or explanations of that particular section of the movement's meaning.

Framing the capture and documentation of movement in this way allows us to deal more easily with problems of timescale. For both capture and documentation, a significant complication occurs where there is a large temporal separation between the movement being captured, and the (documented) "object" being observed. Many would argue that it is impossible to empirically reconstruct the movement of human beings in the past, and that the cognitive, social and cultural processes which drive that movement, through a variety of means and in a variety of media, are similarly shrouded in the mists of history and archaeology. This assumption accounts for many of the sceptical reactions to phenomenology in archaeology (of which more below) (Barrett and Ko 2009), and also to experimental archaeology. It also fits into a context of more recent discussion about the "archaeology of mobility," an approach to archaeological research which seeks explicitly to transcend the static nature of the archaeological record and recognise that it is a product of the movement and motion of multiple agents over a long period of time (Leary 2014). However, if we consider movement itself as an "object," with the possibility of both an original (captured) and secondary (documented) manifestation in the terms framed above, and if we draw on the idea of the ekphrastic chain to trace that object's transmission through time, then it becomes possible to think in more structured terms about the documentation we create in the process. This in turn allows us to consider how a formal understanding of motion, can contribute to broader historical, cultural and archaeological questions.

I argue below that to gain this formal understanding, we need to think of the interpretation of "captured" (with the word used in a very broad sense) motion in terms of "retro-documentation". Retro-documentation refers to information associated with, and explicating, movement captured, whether directly or through contemporary observation, either in the past, or in the present day. In both cases, retro-documentation allows us to address the separation in time of the movement and its reception; be that scaled in minutes or seconds, or of years, decades or centuries. Thus framing retro-documentation, this chapter offers a brief overview of the histories of both the media and the standards which have been used to describe and document movement in the human record. The augmentation of past movement, whether captured or observed (be it the near or distant past) in the present with information increases its interpretive or scholarly value. This provides background and context for a discussion of the retro-documentation of motion capture, and how it can it can be applied to remediate and understand human movement in both the past and the present. I then reflect how "the digital," both in terms of hardware and the physical technologies which are used to capture it overlap conceptually with digital data standards which—as noted above—do not lend themselves to such tasks. It will be argued that retro-documentation exposes a creative tension therein which offers new possibilities for both academic researchers and creative practitioners (recognising that one individual can occupy both categories simultaneously) to document, explore and understand the role of physical movement in the human record.

2 Digital Capture, Digital Documentation

In theory, the digital age has ushered in a new paradigm of possibilities for both the capture and the documentation of movement, not least by allowing contemporary direct capture in three dimensions. Most obviously, the development of motion capture equipment to record human movement directly emerged in the 1970s, as hardware in general became cheaper and more widespread (Moeslund and Granum 2001). Such technologies are now extensively employed in the creative industries, most notably film and animation. The method allows direct, observational capture of movement in real time using calibrated gyroscopic sensors to record the trajectories of the body's joints end extremities. This would enable the user to record that the hypothetical dancer's arm, for example, moved from position A to position B in Cartesian space, with both defined in an X, Y, and Z coordinate system along with all stages in between, with other attributes such as the speed of the movement. In this way, direct motion capture can recreate movement in real time, i.e. it can restore the actual movement of human body parts. It could also be observational, however, in that the data generated could be translated into commands executable by a machine, i.e. the dancer's arm movement could cause the machine to act in a certain way. In all cases, however, the equipment used for the capture and recording must be co-located with the object that is actually moving.

The use of digital methods to capture and document movement generates further questions for the ekphrastic chain. As noted above, motion is dynamic and analogue and continuously variable. Conversely, any digital file composed of 1 and 0 s, which represents a movement (for example, the X, Y, and Z coordinates of the dancer's arm) applies only to one particular series of points in time: is inherently static, whereas movement by definition encompasses and crosses multiple points in time. Like any inert physical medium, digital media is fixed, motionless and atemporal, although not necessarily aspatial. However, the whole basis of computing relies on sequences—"programmes" of such sets of 1 and 0 s running *in sequence*, itself an epistemologically new form of "motion". To put it another way, the structure of motion, like any other formal structure, can always be replaced by computer code (Dyson 2012: 275). In this case, computer code forms a series of representations of movement at sequentially differing points, but as will be explored later, the digital world, including technologies such as GPS and the GeoWeb, has created a new context in which both the capture and the documentation of movement in real time can be understood.

3 Movement and the Human Record

This context relates to the capture and documentation of movement outside of real time, movement in the past, what I call retro-documentation. Despite—and in some cases because of—the methodological concerns and questions that capturing and documenting movement produces, the analysis and understanding of movement are central to many broad questions of human history, culture and society. Accordingly, different humanities domains have developed different approaches—or rather, in many cases different workarounds—to retro-documentation. In the field of history, for example, retro-documenting the movement of individuals, or groups of individuals (such as armies) is essential to the interpretation of particular events and processes; even if movement is only one part of a complex array of factors. Such examples throw into contrast the role of individuals and large bodies of interacting individuals, who may make very different contributions to larger movement macro-patterns. For example, in one application of Agent-Based Modelling (ABM), the logistical question of how the Seljuk Turkish army was able to move as quickly as it did to engage the Byzantine Army at the Battle of Manzikert in AD 1071 was addressed. In this study (Murgatroyd et al. 2012), the contribution made by individual members of the army to its overall trajectory, and that trajectory's timescale; historical factors which are known from historical sources, were modelled and visualised. Individual agents' movements, from the Emperor down the social hierarchy to the common soldiery were hypothesised according to different variables of terrain and environment (ibid). The likeliest set of historical scenarios that enabled the movement that actually occurred was thus constructed. This may be seen as "retro-documentation" of the army's movement, achieved by starting with a known trajectory and extrapolating the causes and impetuses behind it from other known data.

This highlights that for many historical scenarios, especially scenarios involving the more distant past, informed simplification is a key component of movement retro-documentation. Retro-documenting collective movement, like that of an army, inevitably involves abstracting it at scale. This is the approach adopted by the Orbis project (Scheidel 2015). Orbis, developed by Stanford University, allows one to estimate the cost, in terms of time and expense of traversing distance between any two given points in the Roman Imperial period, depending on whether the traveller is crossing sea or land. A variety of historical sources are factored in, and the cost is generated according to factors of distance, terrain, mode of transport, etc. Whilst, as with the ABM application described above, this technique involves retro-documenting hypothesised movement based on known variables, this approach allows the user to define a series of "what if?" questions, and then view mapped movement models which fit certain bespoke historical hypotheses. Both are examples of retro-documentation involving the creative blending of empirical and interpretive evidence.

As the final part of the interpretive chain, retro-documentation is inevitably conditioned by the medium in which it is executed. As noted above, remediating motion in a static medium highlights the tension of embodiment versus separation, a core concern of ekphrasis, as Mitchell notes. Before the advent of relatively widespread photography in the nineteenth century, and then motion pictures, computing and associated technological developments in computer graphics in the twentieth, documentation of movement was inevitably undertaken on paper. It is therefore worth examining in greater depth some "milestone" examples of how historians came to use the print medium to problematize movement in this medium.

4 Recording Movement in Print

The print medium lends itself to abstraction (Ingold 2016), which in turn channels the kind of "informed simplification" highlighted in the two examples above. We can reinforce this view by turning to some early examples of visualisation used to document multi-causal dynamism which, like the Manzikert example above, can be found in the field of military history, specifically the French military engineer Jean Charles Minard's work on the mapping of the Napoleonic wars. Minard was one of the first engineers to recognise the importance of mapping geographical location and, working in the first half of the nineteenth century, was doing so in the context of the war in Europe on an industrial scale. His *Carte figurative des pertes successives en hommes de l'Armée Française dans la campagne de Russie 1812–1813* is a masterpiece in data visualisation. It describes, in multidimensional visual form, the French advance on Moscow in 1812; an early-modern example of a large-scale military campaign, involving the movement of thousands of troops in the abstract, which may be considered an example of "flow mapping" rather than "movement mapping" (Bahoken et al. 2015). Like the movement of the Turkish army to Manzikert, this campaign is well understood in terms of times, dates and locations; but less so in terms of causes, and which processes "flowed" between static events. Minard's map sought to deepen causal understanding by retro-documenting the army's path with six different dimensions of analogue-dynamic data: the spatial route of the army in the form of latitude and longitudes, its size in terms of numbers of men (denoted by the thickness of the line), the temperature, distance between key events, and the army's location in relation to specific dates and key events, such as the battle of the Berezina river. Whilst of course this map does not in any way transcend the limitations of the static print medium, it nonetheless brings these six aspects of data together in such a way that they can be meaningfully read visually and collectively on the static page. Whilst the Minard map is thus often seen in terms of its importance to the history of data visualisation (Friendly 2002), it can also be seen as a key moment in the history of conceptual flow capture and subsequent documentation.

Minard's dynamic flow map reflects a more general nineteenth-century Eurocentric concern with the theme of Imperial and military expansion, of the fate of empires, and of how the visualisation of movement across space and time could be realised in the print medium. The possibilities of this medium, and the hyper-nationalistic worldviews which accompanied the rise of powerful (often imperial) political entities in this period, arguable encouraged a new genre of retro-documentation. Minard's map is a one visual response to this. Another, more abstract form, can be found in a map produced some years later to accompany Emma Willard's *Universal History in Perspective*, an "*Atlas, To Accompany A System Of Universal History; Containing, I. A Chronological Picture of Nations, Or Perspective Sketch of the Course of Empire*" (see Davis et al. 2016). Forming part of an educational text aimed at children, this map charts the progress through time, in the form of movement from distance in both time and space to proximity in both time and space of the "great empires" of history, starting with the Creation, traditionally placed in pre-Darwinian terms in 4004 BC. Visually mimicking the flow of a series of rivers, the streams of the different civilizations appear to move towards the viewer, the visualisation seeking to provide context to the emergence of the United States after the Revolutionary War. This hyper-abstracted view of the movement through time is entirely non-spatial—or rather space (i.e. the width and length of the trails representing the empires) is rendered entirely in non-geographical and conceptual terms.

The obvious common factor for both of the examples listed above is that they represent retro-documentation of the movement of large groups at a macro level: armies, empires, traders and merchants travelling across country; and in the latter example the entirely non-spatial documentation of abstract movement through time. In many cases, it is difficult or impossible to trace the movements of individual persons in any kind of evidence-based way, or to know anything significant about the individual identities or histories which motivated that movement. An exception in the examples above might be certain points in the personal histories of the officers and senior leaders of the French army in the Moscow campaign; but in most cases the ekphrastic chain of movement > observation > contemporary documentation > retro-documentation obscures any chance of understanding the *particular* movements embodied/executed by *particular* people. So can our "ekphrastic chain" relate to individuals, or only to large groups?

5 Movement and GIS

Digital mapping tools allow such abstract and reconstructive methods for movement retro-documentation at a micro level but require different forms of hypothesised inference. Such methods include Geographic Information Systems (GIS). GIS enables researchers to interrogate data with a spatial component in different ways and has been extensively used in archaeology (Lock 2001), history (Bodenhamer 2007) and literary studies (Cooper et al. 2016). However, notably, one well-known criticism of GIS is that it generally is not effective at dealing with time, or with change through time. In most cases, GIS deploys the "freeze frame" methodologies implicit above, without accounting, or offering any basis for interpreting, movement. However, some forms of GIS analysis do seek to address this limitation of the methodology. One example is the "least-cost pathway" model, which allows researchers to estimate how much cost in terms of energy consumption and time it would take, under certain conditions, for an individual to move between certain points, and to define a route which requires the least expenditure of one or both. One good example of the least-cost pathway methodology in action concerns an analysis of the effort required to traverse between different points of the Ridgeway path in southern England, now a national walking trail, but historically a trading route dating back until at least the Iron Age (Bell and Lock 2000). This application enabled researchers to establish that the least-cost route, and the route of the modern footpath, matched remarkably well but differed in the location of hillforts positioned along the way. In other words, the actual path for individuals more or less followed the modelled least-cost, but the sections where there were forts represented variations to this. Therefore, assuming that the pathway once connected with the forts at some point in its history (a reasonable historical assumption), this suggested that they post-dated the original route, which reverted to the original "least-cost" when the forts fell out of use (ibid.). This is a good example of how GIS, a methodology and class of software designed for spatial analysis, can move the discourse relating to movement forward beyond the entirely freeze-frame affordances of the print medium. This also hints at a broader significance for the digital in-motion capture and (retro)documentation, which I come to later in the chapter.

That said, however, the GIS example just described enables a deeper understanding (or at least better inference) about the significance of historical movement, and helps to explain changes it wrought in the archaeological and historical records, but it still does not address the problem of abstraction where individuals are concerned. This work may help us guess as to how an ancient traveller might have interacted with the landscape, how they came to leave their impression on it, and how it impacted on their behaviours; however, we cannot use it to retro-document individual travellers' stories. By definition, the pathways, movements or motions of actual historical persons must be confined to scenarios where there is direct historical or literary, as opposed to archaeological, evidence. Where such evidence exists, the movement patterns of a particular individual at a particular time and through a particular place can also be reconstructed with GIS. One example is the literary description of journeys from first-hand experience. In contrast to the examples above, where the movement of unidentifiable people is documented in the abstract, GIS can be used to interrogate the experiences of actual individuals as they describe them. Such approaches hint at engagement with the phenomenological experiences of the landscapes described (of which more below); in that they seek to unpack personal experiences at particular moments.

6 Textual Approaches

In literary studies, the "eventfulness" of the processes of reading and writing is often framed in terms of bridging the distances (whether physical or conceptual) between the writer and the reader, and/or between different real or fictional characters (Hones

2008): these either concern or describe, processes of movement, yet—in the intellectual context of ekphrasis—the movement is secondary to the static description. As explored further below, in history, as in archaeology, the movements and motions of individual actions needed to construct a particular type of artefact can be reconstructed through processes of experimentation. However, in most cases these are documented as *text descriptions* of the process and the output, with a little systematic attempt to capture the movement itself.

In the case of authorial narratives describing journeys, GIS can be used as a retro-documentation mechanism for motion, framing the phenomenological experience as described by the author. This works particularly well (as one might expect) for travel literature, where the narrative is structured around a route or routes taken by the author. For example, George Jeffrey was an administrator in British-controlled Cyprus, who published a monolithic study in 1918, *Studies in the Archaeology and Architecture of the Island, with Illustrations from Measured drawings and Photographs*, which aims at an encyclopaedic overview of Cyprus's antiquities—then of growing interest to the educated sections of the British colonial hierarchy, which assumed direct control of the island after the First World War. In his work, Jeffrey takes an itinerant, travelogue-like approach to the island, giving detailed textual and visual descriptions of significant antiquities. This in itself plays to a kind of "stop-motion" mode of writing, where the purpose and emphasis is on recording (and thus retro-documenting) particular monuments at particular places at particular times. However, if we detach the objects (= the monuments) described and focus instead on the named places, it is possible to gain a different perspective on the text. We can map one section of Jeffrey's itinerary, for example, Chap. 9, which describes his journey between Perakhorio and Nicosia, as a composite viewshed, showing what Jeffrey (or anyone else) could have seen from the points he names. Figure 1 shows this journey, with the linear route purposefully left off, but with each place mapped at the centre of a viewshed, using a 30 m Digital Elevation Model (DEM) of the terrain. That is to say each 30 m square which Jeffrey could have seen from the points he describes is coloured in blue. This shows that, travelling up the eastern flank of the Troodos mountains, the view of this journey was predominately characterised by east-facing panoramas. This allows us to construct a more overarching, composite perspective of the experience of the journey, and not necessarily one that is tied to anything that Jeffrey wrote in particular—and thus less constrained by the print medium. GIS thus becomes, in itself, a method for the retro-documentation of a particular individual's journey.

7 Movement: The Medium Suppresses the Message

To fully appreciate the possibilities of retro-documentation, we need to acknowledge that it does not necessarily have to employ the print or screen medium; and that, for the purposes of the "ekphrastic chain" this necessarily requires divergence from Mitchell's view (2005: 263) that objects (in this case motion) are "never made visible

Fig. 1 George Jeffrey's Perakhorio-Nicosia journey mapped as a viewshed. The South East/North West axis of his journey becomes clearly visible as the viewshed fans out towards the east. The two aberrations to the west are caused by visits, and references, to monasteries

or tangible except by way of the medium of language" (see above). This is a truth that has been explored not only by academic researchers (of which more below), but also by myriad performance artists, choreographers, creative practitioners and dancers who have used non-textual media to convey and interpret movement. Richard Long, in his 1967 photographic work, *A Line Made By Walking*,[1] now in the Tate Collection in London, experimented with the tension between transience and permanence, and its capture through photography. The work records the line made as Long walked repeatedly backwards and forwards in a field in Wiltshire as the sun hit a certain angle and made the line visible. This not only expresses the tension between the transience of Long's walking motion and the transience of the line in the grass, but also between both of these and the permanence of the photographic medium which recorded it (see Dunn 2019, Chap. 5).

[1] See https://www.tate.org.uk/art/artworks/long-a-line-made-by-walking-p07149.

The illusion of pathways' permanence, as explored in Long's work, was further exposed in the Covid-19 lockdown period in the summer 2020. At this time, public social distancing requirements bought in to limit the spread of the virus required people not part of the same household to maintain a physical distance of 2 m at all times. This altered fundamental habits of pedestrianism and transience, and these found themselves temporarily etched into the landscape, in much the same way as Long's *Line* was. Figure 2 illustrates this, by showing the creation of a new path alongside an established path along the River Thames in Berkshire, UK. These examples show that not only should retro-documentation not be assumed to be always textual, but sometimes it also represents a one or more stages in a process of *embodied* documentation that can be textual, visual, embodied or all three.

These issues become more complex when tracing the ekphrastic chain back further in time, to the creation of artefacts for which there is no kind of documentation or contextual knowledge. Here, we turn to the practices of experimental archaeology, which involves the re-creation of artefacts, features or any other object visible in the archaeological record in the present day using the same materials and methods of construction identified by experiment, thus drawing inferences as to how the archaeological objects were made.

As a discipline, experimental archaeology emerged in the 1970s in the context of "uniformitarianism," the belief that processes, including movement processes, as well as cognitive and physical ones (and perhaps therefore flows, in Minard's sense), can be viewed as uniformly objective, and thus replicable. Today it is employed with a greater degree of theoretical nuance, which acknowledges the limitations, most significantly by being a critically selective as to the type of activity being reconstructed, and whether it is likely to sustain an assumption that a particular process is unlikely to have changed over time. The butchery of animal carcasses using hand tools is one example of this, as Seetah states: "butchery has remained largely unchanged as a technological exercise since its inception; what differs amongst regions, periods and groups are the socioeconomic and socio-technological drivers behind the observed practice" (Seetah 2008: 143). Experimental archaeologists thus deal with embodied action as a primary resource, within a robust critical and theoretical framework.

This is necessary for the results to have interpretive value. The re-creation of, say, a Palaeolithic hand axe in a way which causes the artefact created to reflect those which are millions of years old can only be done by physically enacting a particular series of movements which demonstrably lead to that finished physical artefact. It follows that a key limitation of experimental archaeology is the medium in which the results are, or can be, communicated. There is no empirical basis for documenting the movements that "successfully" reconstruct the hand axe by physically replicating it, nor are there even any clear criteria for what defines "success" (i.e. showing that the process reconstructed and enacted by the modern archaeologist definitely the same process as that originally enacted in the distant past). To frame the question in the terms of the discussion at the opening of this chapter, if an ekphrastic chain begins with the creation of a hand axe in Tanzania in 900,000 BCE, how does experimental reconstruction end it in the twenty-first century? It can take the form of entertainment (one thinks of the opening scenes of Kubrick's *2001: A Space Odyssey*, which

Fig. 2 Diverging pathways as a result of the 2020 Covid-19 lockdown illustrate the collective/accidental capture, and retro-documentation, of human movement in the landscape. Here the "insurgent" pathway re-joins the established one as they both have to negotiate a narrow gap between a field boundary and the river

re-enacts the initial invention of bone tools by pre-human apes), or of public education. However, in order to constitute methodologically solid archaeological inference about the creation of tools, documentation and replicability are required. There is no critical documentation framework where, for example, information about the sensory experience of the creator (who is likely to be a highly skilled and trained technician) might be recorded, or cross-referenced to other attempts to recreate the same process (except with video); nor is there any way of ensuring that the sequence enacted is the "right" series of movements.

This is a limitation which is fully recognised within the discipline of experimental archaeology. John Coles states the matter succinctly in his book *Archaeology by Experiment* (1979), which laid the theoretical groundwork for the field:

> A multiplier effect applies here: if the action of B and only B upon material A produces an answer Z, then the inference is that B might have been the only method in the past to get Z. However, if Z is also produced by C, and perhaps D as well, then the possibility exists that any one of B, C or D might have been used in the past to get Z. (Coles 1973: 15).

Despite the clear differences in scale and content, a formally documented academic argument (as expressed in a research paper for example) would require the kind of narrative structure we saw unpacked in George Jeffrey's Cypriot itinerary, encoding provable statements based on cited evidence; however, when it comes to the deployment and impact of movement and the results thereof, such statements cannot be made. They also cannot be expressed in written form. Rather, we might characterise formal descriptions of the production of artefacts produced by experimentation to the descriptive narrative, of the sort found in other genres. One might put it another way by asking what, in the experimental movement-based reconstruction of Palaeolithic hand axes, is the equivalent of academic citation?

Both the literary GIS case of Jeffrey's journey, and the case of experimental archaeology require retro-documentation to transcend the constraints of the textual narrative form. This means transcending an implicit Cartesian and Westernised form of movement's spatial representation; and becomes even more apparent when we turn to the retro-documentation of movement in non-Western societies, which do not make the same sort of use of Cartesian or formalist structures to create understanding. Indeed the art history of non-Western cultures, including the art histories of pre-literate societies, often rejects such linear literary assumptions. It is possible to detect in those societies' artistic practices approaches to movement which reflects their own cultural outlooks—which may differ markedly from Western world views, and the Cartesian approaches to mapping movement which often goes with these.

The study of aboriginal rock art is an excellent example of this. In particular, in Australian rock art iconography, much emphasis is made on the emplacement of the art, of the fact that it is immovably anchored to a particular location, which contrasts with the non-settled nature of the communities which produced it. Westernised interpretations of the art which fail to take into account the nomadic lifestyle and culture of the societies which produced them leads to what Ursula K. Frederick calls a "site-focussed and sedentarist line of thinking" in the historical and cultural understanding of the art. This in turn leads to "sedentarist" assumptions about the art's interpretation, (which might be perfectly valid and applicable to art in Western contexts) whereas in reality "a fusion of motion and stasis as potentially coinciding attributes, may serve as a useful metaphor for comprehending both the constant and the dynamic aspects of rock art" (Frederick 2014: 64).

The "sedentarist" approach highlighted by Fredrick is key for rock art research, which is characterised by its physical fixity, and standing in contrast to the kinds of knowledge generated by experimental archaeology. The latter cannot be executed without physical engagement with the physical world in the present day, yet any method for capturing and further disseminating the "movement objects" produced which does not take account of this is inherently sedentrist. Sedentarism pervades the medium of print and text (consider that reading is rarely an activity carried out while walking). When retro-documentation takes printed form, it reflects the physical constraints and characteristics of that medium. However, it also becomes dependent on the shared epistemological frameworks—the standards and metadata which describe each movement "object". Standards are crucial to regulate the creation of any dataset and to make it reusable. Yet, as noted above, the very concept of a "standard" implies fixity: the alignment of data to a set of standards *at one particular point in time*. Mapping a landscape according to fixed geographical standards and conventions, such as latitude and longitude, or the colouring of rivers as blue, is one example.

8 Retro-Documentation and Standards

The example of mapping a landscape, like the example of the Ridgeway above, highlights the reliance for retro-documentation of this kind on fixed maps and plans of space. More generally maps, or any other form of fixed diagram, as static frameworks of representation, themselves deal with movement in an imperfect and temporally detached manner. A particular square mile of landscape can be entirely accurately mapped according to such standards, but such a map will only represent the terrain at one fixed point in time. It will not document (for example) the lateral movement of a river as it changes course over centuries, on the emergence of forests over the same period; nor can it reflect the changing perspectives of a user as they traverse a landscape on foot. The instinctive metaphor of "map reading" in fact implicitly links paper maps to the narrative extratemporal fixity of the written word.

Landscape dynamism may be more inferable from static photography, when combined with a map—strengthening the implication introduced above that retro-documentation of movement must, in many case span different forms of media. For examine Fig. 3 was taken from the bridge over the River Irving near Birdoswald Roman Fort on Hadrian's Wall in Northumberland. In the middle distance (marked), is the bridgehead constructed at the time of the Wall, when the river was in a different location. It is clearly visible, and its removal in physical space, as well as time, from the modern day bridge strikes the (physically present) viewer as incongruous. It is a change that can only be appreciated phenomenologically by immediate human presence: by a somatic understanding of the landscape that contains both the ancient and the modern bridge. One can apply the principles set out by Frederick for aboriginal rock art (above) to archaeological landscapes: mobility is key to *their* access, making and maintenance, and "sedentarist" principles of standards, on which data creation, maintenance and curation are based, must be if not rejected, then augmented with critical cross-media frameworks that allow for the subjective vagaries of human enactment and experience of movement. This is what phenomenological archaeologists such as Christopher Tilley have called "societal space" (Tilley 1994: 34). Such

Fig. 3 River Irving in Cumbria (photo: the author). The Roman bridgehead is visible in the middle distance, marked by the red arrow, illustrating the extent of the lateral movement of the river through the landscape since the Roman period

space cannot be understood only through sedentarist documentation and metadata structures; rather there has to be a mechanism for feeding in the embodied and sensory experience of movement as well.

This is an idea which is fundamental to Tilley's influential book, written in 1994, "A phenomenology of landscape". As with the examples above, "the digital" has significantly impacted on the phenomenological experience of *information*, as well as the experience of the physical world. The most obvious example of this is the emergence of devices which are able to geolocate in real time: for the first time, it can be argued, the key distinction for this chapter, the distinction between captured movement and documented movement has finally been collapsed by the medium/technology of GPS, which captures movement in three dimensions at the same time as being part of it.

The challenges faced by different disciplines in dealing with movement are therefore very distinct; however, they share one very significant factor. That is that the way in which movement is documented is conditioned by the medium in which that documentation takes place—whether physical, digital or embodied. An example is provided by the case of experimental archaeology highlighted above.

9 Movement and the Digital

The most obvious way in which the digital realm has collapsed the fixity of the map with the somatic engagement of physical presence in, and dynamic movement through, a landscape, is with GPS. Once the preserve of the military and scientific establishments, GPS draws on a constellation of satellites to allow receivers to triangulate their exact position on the earth's surface; and it has emerged as a major feature in the digital age. It is most familiar to public users as a means for allowing mobile devices to draw on georeferenced information in real time, and connect it immediately with other useful forms of information such as routes that the user needs to find, amenities that they wish to use, services that they wish to employ, and so on.

GPS traces can be uploaded to various web services and shared. This essentially allows users to capture their own movement through the environment and save it to a local device or server—which, in the context of this discussion, is a form of retro-documentation. However, as noted above, *digital* retro-documentation allows the capture of movement as a series of static data points, in the form of a latitude and longitude value, rectified according to a trusted geodetic world data standard, and a time stamp. Therefore, while the sedentrist/dynamic tension of the ekphrastic chain connecting the GPS user's movement with the GPS trace's view is not removed, it nonetheless represents a closer, more embodied and more direct relationship between capture, documentation and retro-documentation than any of the methods discussed above, since the data points directly represent the user's actual movement in real time and in real place.

Just as Richard Long challenged notions of sedentrism in photography with *A Line Made By Walking* (see above), so contemporary artists in the twentieth century have used GPS as a medium to deconstruct the static nature of the digital as a means for encoding embodied human movement using GPS. One notable example is the genre of "GPS art," in which an artist will either use the composite overlay of multiple GPS layers to illustrate things like increased footfall in urban areas, or they use their own movement through a landscape in order to render a 2D, and greatly scaled down image of that journey. One notable example of this genre is the "walking artist" Jeremy Wood, who uses GPS to construct first-person perspectives of particular areas, using GPS traces that only make sense in their entirety, once the walk is complete. In doing so, he uses motion and place to challenge human perceptions and notions of scale, recognising that the "map" produced in fact exists at a scale of 1:1, and is itself a product of phenomenological engagement with the landscape. As Wood himself puts it:

> Our personal navigation is evolving from looking up at the stars to looking down from satellites mediated by digital devices held in our palm. The two meridian lines are the edges of maps that don't meet up: between them are places that don't exist. (Wood 2006, quoted in Lauriault 2009: 361).

GPS motion traces are a key feature of the so-called "GeoWeb," the subsection of the Internet which caters explicitly to the standards, practices and infrastructures of geographic data, and which is increasingly used as a guide, mediator and facilitator of human movement. However, unlike Wood's motion-as-art, most GPS traces on the GeoWeb are uncurated, or at least only partly curated. Numerous platforms for the sharing and use of GPS traces; and a notable feature of most of these is that the only form of structure or organisation is rectification to the same systems of latitude/longitude/timestamp (**ref**). One of the best-known GeoWeb repositories for GPS data is the open mapping platform OpenStreetMap, a user-generated and open source map of the world.[2] Users can add geographical features to the map, but the site also contains a repository for GPS traces which supports the **.gpx** format. People do so for a variety of reasons, for example, to share details of a walk or a run they have done, a favourite route or path, etc. Sharing captured and retro-documented traces, whether intestinally or unintentionally, can have unintended consequences. One such issue arose in January 2018, when the GPS data company Strava, which provides services to a number of companies dealing in fitness tracking products such as Fitbit, produce a global "Heatmap," providing a composite global picture of anonymized GPS traces generated by athletes using the third-party mobile devices for monitoring speed, heart rate, etc. This led to the internal geography of the US air force base at Kandahar, Afghanistan, being exposed in the form of a very clear set of outlines, composed of the traces left by the base's personnel using fitness trackers as they navigated the base. This led to the US military reviewing its rules on personnel's use of such equipment.[3]

The collectivization of GPS traces, of the retro-documented movement of multiple actors through a landscape, can thus build up a detailed somatic picture of that landscape, and of human interaction with it. As well as unintended consequences such as those just described, this can also allow us to trace the impact of conscious design decisions. For example, the area of west-Central London between Piccadilly Circus and Oxford Circus was laid out by the architect John Nash in the first two decades of the nineteenth century, one of the first designed parts of London. Nash based his approach on the idea that Regent Street should act as a connector between these two hubs; but also that it should act as a divider, separating the two areas of Mayfair to the west, and Soho to the east. This was a straightforward piece of social engineering: Mayfair was (and is) a highly affluent part of London, the base of high-end residences and businesses, whereas Soho was characterised by tenement-type dwellings and commercial premises. Nash made his methodology of separation plain, stating that his intention was

> ...a complete separation between the streets occupied by the Nobility and Gentry, and the narrower Streets and meaner houses occupied by mechanics and the trading part of the community ... My purpose was that [Regent street] should cross the eastern entrance to all the streets occupied by the higher classes and to leave out to the east all the bad streets (John Nash, quoted in Johnson 2006: 20).

Thus, the west-facing exits of Regent Street are broad and accessible and facilitate the free flow of pedestrian and vehicular traffic, whereas the east-facing exits are narrow, often one-way and/or pedestrianised, and do not facilitate the free

[2] See www.openstreetmap.org.

[3] See https://www.wired.com/story/strava-heat-map-military-bases-fitness-trackers-privacy.

flow of any traffic. This is clearly visible on the relevant area of OpenStreetMap (Fig. 4), where the exits east to Vigin, New Burlington, Maddox and Conduit streets, towards Mayfair, are relatively heavily populated with GPS traces, whereas the east-facing exits are not. Thus, whilst the area's urban configuration is at least substantially informed by eighteenth-century class preoccupation, unstructured GPS retro-documentation allows us to visualise the impact of those preoccupations in the present day urban landscape.

This brings us back to direct motion capture itself. In 2010–12, the author participated in a series of experiments using motion capture to test contemporary human responses to historical environments, notably Iron Age round houses, of the kind known from archaeological excavation to have been widespread in Britain before the Roman invasion (Woolford and Dunn 2014); the project was called *Motion in Place Platform*. In this sense, therefore, we were not undertaking direct experimental reconstruction in the sense illustrated above with the examples of butchery and hand axes. The movements necessary to (re)construct an Iron Age domestic roundhouse were not explored, rather the affordances of motion capture were used to examine the use of the domestic environment *once it had been created*. The aim of the experiment was to see how humans reacted to the physical characteristics of the environment such as the cramped space occasioned by the sloping of the roof at the edges, and the obstruction caused by the inner ring of posts; and also sensory aspects of the environment such as the dark (experimental archaeology has established that round houses could not have had windows), the presence of smoke from a central fire, and the acoustic compression. To one not familiar with such a space, these factors are disorientating and unsettling. The experiment sought to establish how people who were familiar with the space contrasted with those who were not while carrying out

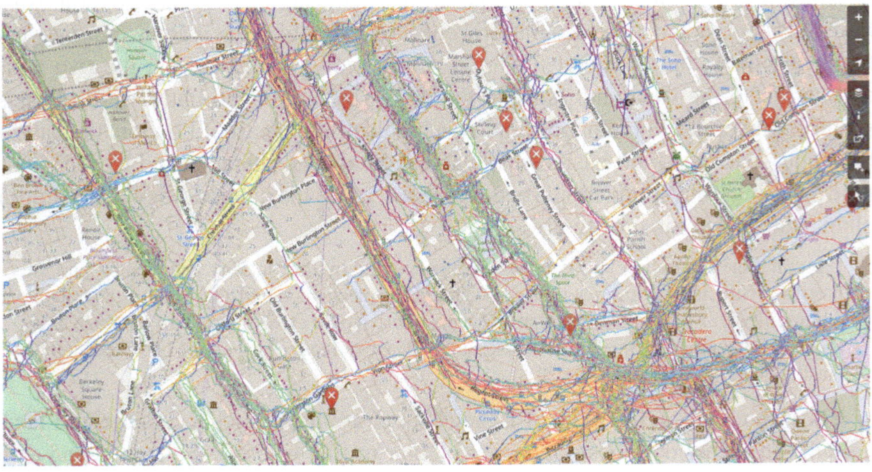

Fig. 4 GPS traces from OpenStreetMap (OSM contributors). The dominant flows of user traffic noth and south along Regent Street and towards Piccadilly Circus clearly show up, accentuating pedestrian activity towards Mayfair in the west, and limiting it in the direction of Soho to the east

basic domestic tasks such as using a quern stone and sweeping. The motion traces produced through gyroscopic motion capture analysed how those unfamiliar oriented themselves in contrast to those who were familiar, as well as the fluid, ergonomic efficiency of the way in which an expert used a quern stone, versus, one who was not (see Woolford and Dunn 2014, Figure 5).

The outcomes of the experiment itself have been published elsewhere (Woolford and Dunn, 2013; Woolford and Dunn 2014). However, the discussion above allows us to illustrate the digital objects produced by MiPP into the context of the ekphrastic chain, and as examples of elements of retro-documentation. At some point in the first or second century BCE an unidentified Iron Age inhabitant of Britain undertook the use of a quern stone and a broom in a round house dwelling. The fact that they did so is inferred from archaeological evidence; but the embodied movements themselves are transitory and lost. 2000+ years later, a round house reflecting the one in which they undertook these tasks is reconstructed, experimentally reproducing the environment. Those tasks are undertaken again—it is inappropriate to use the term "re-enactment," as the specific original enacted task is unknown—and remediated using direct capture. The motion, ultimately sourced to routine activities in distant antiquity is essentially reconstructed and re-understood in a different time, and by a different audience.

10 Conclusion

This chapter has traced a trajectory from the very broad scale of historical events (Emma Willard's map of Empires, Minard's map the Napoleonic campaign), to the scale of individual people, through media from paper, to the digital to the landscape itself. It has been shown that the concept of retro-documentation of movement is a key element for historical understanding of events such as those described in these examples. It has also been shown that as digital methods for recording and analysing movement, such as GPS and GIS are introduced, it becomes easier to retro-document the movement of individuals, but that the "ekphrastic chain" linking the original movement to its documentation remains key to problematizing movement embodied in the past and re-created, and retro-documented, in the present.

The MiPP experiment provides an example of how direct, immersive interaction with the environment can be retro-documented through a combined process of direct engagement, digital capture and archaeological interpretation. It fits into a far broader landscape of how "the digital" has both introduced new challenges of understanding movement in the humanities, but also into the possibilities it offers. Direct observation such as gyroscopic motion capture, or even GPS, does not remove the documentary links in the ekphrastic chain, but rather it illustrates that those links should be regarded as effective, possibly non-textual and experimental. It should that motion in the past can be investigated, just as any other archaeological "object" can be; but just as archaeology has had to re-think its approaches to object analysis in the light of ideas such as processualism, uniformitarianism and experimentalism; so it has an opportunity to re-think its approaches to motion in the light what digital capture has to offer. This chapter has sought to offer the beginnings of a framework, in the form of retro-documentation, for doing so.

References

Babrber, G., & Sammon, A. (n.d.). A Brief History of GPS—from James Bond to Pokémon Go – Mother Jones. Retrieved September 13, 2017, from http://www.motherjones.com/media/2016/11/brief-history-gps-military-timeline/.

Bahoken, F., Grasland, C., & Zanin, C. 2015. Flow mapping vs movement mapping: a theoretical and cartographic demonstration of their significance at a world scale. Plurimondi, 3p. Retrieved from https://hal.archives-ouvertes.fr/hal-01217237.

Barrett, J. C., & Ko, I. 2009. A phenomenology of landscape: A crisis in British landscape archaeology? Journal of Social Archaeology, 9(3), 275–294. https://doi.org/10.1177/1469605309338422.

Bell, T., & Lock, G. 2000. Topographic and cultural influences on walking the Ridgeway in later prehistoric times. In Nato ASI Series A Life Sciences 321 (pp. 85–100).

Bodenhamer, D. J. D. J. 2007. Creating a landscape of memory: The potential of humanities GIS. International Journal of Humanities and Arts Computing, 1(2), 97–110. https://doi.org/10.3366/E1753854808000207.

Coles, J. 1979. Archaeology by Experiment. Routledge.

Cooper, D., Donaldson, C., & Murrieta-Flores, P. (Eds.). 2016. Literary mapping in the digital age. Literary mapping in the digital age. Abingdon: Routledge. Retrieved from https://searchworks.stanford.edu/view/11748577.

Davis, S. B., Vane, O., & Kräutli, F. 2016. Using Data Visualisation to tell Stories about Collections. BCS Learning & Development. https://doi.org/10.14236/ewic/eva2016.44.

Dunn, S. 2019. A history of place in the digital age. Routledge.

Dyson, G. 2012. Turing's cathedral: the origins of the digital universe. Pantheon.

Foka, A., & Arvidsson, V. 2016. Experiential Analogies: A Sonic Digital Ekphrasis as a Digital Humanities Project. Retrieved December 9, 2019, from http://www.digitalhumanities.org/dhq/vol/10/2/000246/000246.html.

Frederick, U. K. 2014. Suspended Animations: Mobilities in Rock Art Research. In Past Mobilities: Archaeological Approaches to Movement and Mobility (pp. 63–78). Farnham: Ashgate.

Friendly, M. 2002. Visions and Re-Visions of Charles Joseph Minard. Journal of Educational and Behavioral Statistics, 27(1), 31–51. https://doi.org/10.3102/10769986027001031.

Hones, S. 2008. Text as it happens: Literary geography. Geography Compass, 2(5), 1301–1317. https://doi.org/10.1111/j.1749-8198.2008.00143.x.

Ingold, T. 2016. Lines: a brief history. Routledge.

Johnson, S. 2006. The Ghost Map, a Street, a City, an Epidemic and the Hidden Power of Urban Networks.

Lauriault, T. P. 2009. GPS Tracings-Personal Cartographies. Art & Cartography Special Issue, 46(4), 360–365. https://doi.org/10.1179/000870409X12549997389628.

Leary, J. 2014. Past mobilities: Archaeological approaches to movement and mobility. Ashgate Publishing, Ltd.

Lock, G. 2001. Theorising the practice or practicing the theory: archaeology and GIS. Archaeologia Polona.

Mitchell, W. J. T. 2005. There Are No Visual Media. Journal of Visual Culture, 4(2), 257–266.

Moeslund, T. B., & Granum, E. 2001. A survey of computer vision-based human motion capture. Computer Vision and Image Understanding, 81(3), 231–268. https://doi.org/10.1006/cviu.2000.0897.

Murgatroyd, P., Craenen, B., Theodoropoulos, G., Gaffney, V., & Haldon, J. 2012. Modelling medieval military logistics: An agent-based simulation of a Byzantine army on the march. Computational and Mathematical Organization Theory, 18(4), 488–506. https://doi.org/10.1007/s10588-011-9103-9.

Scheidel, W. 2015. Orbis: The Stanford Geospatial Network Model of the Roman World. SSRN Electronic Journal. https://doi.org/10.2139/ssrn.2609654.

Seetah, K. 2008. Modern analogy, cultural theory and experimental replication: A merging point at the cutting edge of archaeology. World Archaeology, 40(1), 135–150. https://doi.org/10.1080/00438240701843652.

Tilley, C. 1994. A phenomenology of landscape: places, paths, and monuments. Berg Oxford.

Wood, J. 2006. Can't be elsewhere when GPS drawing. In Else/Where Mapping: New Cartographies of Networks and Territories, eds. J. Abrams, P. Hall (pp. 274–275). Minneapolis, MN: University of Minnesota Design Institute.

Woolford, K., & Dunn, S. 2013. Experimental archaeology and games: Challenges of inhabiting virtual heritage. Journal on Computing and Cultural Heritage, 6(4). https://doi.org/10.1145/2532630.2532632.

Woolford, K., & Dunn, S. 2014. Micro mobilities and affordances of past places. Past Mobilities: Archaeological Approaches to Movement and Mobility.

Stuart Dunn is Professor of Spatial Humanities at King's College London. He has interests in the history of cartographic technologies and methods, GIS approaches in archaeology and history and digital placemaking. His most recent monograph is *A History of Place in the Digital Age* (Routledge 2019) and, in 2020, he co-edited the *Routledge International Handbook of Research Methods in Digital Humanities.*

Exploring Fragmented Data: Environments, People and the Senses in Virtual Reality

Claudia Sciuto, Anna Foka, Mattis Lindmark, and Jim Robertsson

Abstract Taking into consideration that archaeologists and historians are today more frequently encouraged to think in terms of digital transduction of historical materials, this chapter focuses on the potentials and pitfalls of 'visualizing' 'recreating' and 're-enacting/experiencing the senses' in Virtual Reality (thereon VR) environments. More precisely, we focus on the very idea of sensory immersion for archaeological enquiry, research, study and dissemination. This chapter draws upon four VR projects at Humlab, Umeå University. The first is an example of using archaeological data for supporting the interpretation process in a Mesolithic site, environment from GIS to an immersive platform. The second is a result of collaborative work with the project ancient dance modern dancers (Slaney et al. 2018) in capturing the intangible art of Roman Pantomime in the theatre of Pompeii on Virtual Reality. The third is the implementation of interactive tools for an immersive study of photogrammetric models of medieval rock-cut settlements while the fourth is an assessment of the implementation of VR Google Earth in teaching ancient topography for undergraduate archaeology students. We show how important and interesting research is made in the process of tool experimentation and tool development.

Keywords Virtual reality · Sensory engagement · Digital craft · Fragmented data

C. Sciuto
Department of Civilizations and Forms of Knowledge, University of Pisa, Pisa, Italy
e-mail: claudia.sciuto@cfs.unipi.it

A. Foka (✉)
Digital Humanities Uppsala, Department of ALM (Archive, Library and Information Science, Museum and Cultural Heritage Studies), Uppsala University, Uppsala, Sweden
e-mail: anna.foka@abm.uu.se

M. Lindmark · J. Robertsson
Humlab, Umeå University, Umeå, Sweden
e-mail: mattis.lindmark@umu.se

J. Robertsson
e-mail: jim.robertsson@umu.se

G. Landeschi and E. Betts (eds.), *Capturing the Senses*,
Quantitative Methods in the Humanities and Social Sciences,
https://doi.org/10.1007/978-3-031-23133-9_5

1 Introduction

Virtual Reality (VR) environments that build around historical and archaeological data have been created and studied for a few decades already. There is a well-established scholarly tradition of reconstructing historical sites in 3D, focusing on estimated architectural and environmental properties of a certain place in time (landscapes, buildings and artefacts), broadly considered as Virtual Archaeology (Forte and Siliotti 1997). The methods and rendering of Virtual Archaeology (approximately from 1990 to early 2000) have been criticised as maintaining static and sanitised depictions of historical space and place without displaying the complexity of archaeological data.

In the mid-2000s, Cyber Archaeology (Forte 2010), has challenged these ocularcentric modes of knowledge production through participatory and interactive design practices. Reflection and cooperative efforts in investigations of sensory engagement with space, architecture and artefacts of the past have the potential to generate new knowledge (Forte 2010). Cyber Archaeology promises, through interactive virtual immersion, to operate as a testbed for linking archaeological information to intangible data about the past. Inspired by the theoretical premises of cyber archaeological inquiries, this chapter advocates Virtual Reality as a participatory, interactive method with great potential, and ought to be addressed with a sensibility to pedagogy and digital infrastructure for optimal results.

This chapter offers an in-depth analysis of the practice of virtual model building, as well as potential scholarly and pedagogical benefits based on four case studies. We argue that VR, as infrastructure, has the potential to engage researchers and students in direct interaction with multiple datasets and may help them reflect on sites that are otherwise inaccessible and remote. Such an enterprise requires transparency throughout the process of annotation and interpretation of data. Beyond the visual component of alternative (e.g. augmented, VR, Mixed) realities, an analysis of already fragmented datasets can be mediated through a sensorial engagement and this process is generative of both knowledge about the past and the discipline of archaeology itself.

For the purpose of this chapter, we have chosen to discuss four examples thematically from the perspectives of fragmented data about past people/spaces and the sensory properties of the VR prototypes. These prototypes were deliverables from research projects that have been carried out at Humlab, Umeå University, in 2017–2018, and were supported by a community of students, researchers and developers. All the described prototypes have been developed using an HTC Vive set, with a field of view of 110°, resolution of 1080×1200 pixels, refresh rate 90 Hz, audio output with headphones, positional tracking and head tracking. The prototypes were implemented through a game engine technology, Unity, a cross-platform development software mainly used for games, digital art and entertainment.[1] Unity tends

[1] https://unity.com/.

to support a wide range of file formats, making it particularly suitable for experimentations and data import from other applications (for example from GIS software, photogrammetry models or mocap data).

Our inquiry encompasses the analysis of an immersive interactive visualisation of the data from a multiproxy investigation of a Mesolithic dwelling in Northern Sweden, where a palaeoenvironmental reconstruction of the VR environment was completed by applying a reflexive approach (Berggren et al. 2015; Hodder 2000). The second case study is a motion-capture experimental reproduction of roman pantomime that involves the exploration of the sense of self-movement (Slaney et al. 2018). The third example presents a workflow for importing a photogrammetric model of a rock-cut settlement in Unity and implementing customised drawing tools, crucial for the analysis of the rock surface in VR. Finally, we will evaluate the use of VR in undergraduate archaeology classes as a medium for exploring space of a multi-layered urban centre.

With this chapter, we aim to show how the process of building and displaying VR models has pedagogical value and how the potential of VR prototypes to mediate sensory information helps reflect on data at a deeper level. By doing so, we further feedback on how customised tools are created to interact with the models function and recommend possible solutions for technical issues or desirable future improvements.

2 Broken Data and Multivocality

Potentials of experiential learning in VR environments have been investigated in various disciplines, including both humanities and natural sciences. The development of VR prototypes focusing on educational aspects has triggered a broad theoretical reflection over pedagogical prospects of immersive environments (Fowler 2015). In archaeology and ancient history, VR has been used mostly for 'time travels', i.e. the re-enactment of ancient scenarios in which the user can interact with avatars or objects. These models are certainly interesting for communication as they generate a fully reconstructed past setting in which the visitor is projected, with little or no access to metadata and paradata.

Nevertheless, the creation of any VR prototype that relies on archaeological/historical data should be correlated to the theoretical reflection over the way raw information is transduced in virtual environments. Since its early applications, it has been clear that 'virtual reality is geographically, culturally and temporally situated as much as the context that it aims at visualizing' (Brody 1991), and therefore depends on the archaeological set of data available at the moment of the creation of the models, the theoretical standpoint of the developers and the technology used. Examining the creation of a VR prototype, we can gain an insight into the process of constructing archaeological interpretation and use the digital platform as a support for the exegesis of raw datasets.

A lot has been written on archaeological documentation and data collection including digital and analogue methods currently used by archaeologists to register and store observations on traces that are, most of the time, ephemeral. The majority of archaeological recording is done in the field, where the observation of features and objects demands a specific set of competences. Data collection is based on the assumption that the researcher deconstructs the material trace in distinct sets of information as complete and as accurate as possible. Archaeological data necessarily comprise gaps and uncertainty, due to the difficulty of capturing all aspects of material remains. In fact, the documentation of archaeological evidence is made more difficult by the fact that all objects and traces are subject to a multitude of interactions, as part of a lively ecological system. In order to represent the complexity of the interplay human environment, archaeologists usually divide up the record into proxies that can be measured individually, such as the case of various types of artefacts (ceramics, lithics), soil geochemistry, pollen analysis, etc. According to Caraher, this forced simplification and segmentation of the archaeological record relies, at its core, on a meticulous observation that requires time and dedication, the so-called 'slow archaeology' (Caraher 2015).

Sets of data concerning geographical/environmental and chronological attributes of sites can be acquired by means of standardised practices. Digitised or digital data can then be combined and intertwined in a VR environment, where criteria for visualisation are mediated by the judgement of researchers and programmers.

Due to the high variability of hardware and software used for visualising and recreating the past, there are no clear guidelines for the rendering of models but rather some collections of broad principles that provide a benchmark for each community of practice (that is, for example, the case of the London charter). In this context, a lot of choice about prototyping procedures and display of information is left to the specialists.

For instance, the geographical dimension of a site/landscape can be reproduced partially or highlight prominent features, according to the specific research goals and available information. In our case study, creating an interactive prototype of rock-cut sites, the accurate representation of the internal surface of the excavated room was considered a relevant landmark, while the location of the site in its original landscape was not essential. The choice of representing only part of the original environment resulted in a carved chamber floating in a space without geographical connotations in which the user is demanded to focus on the carved features inside the cave rather than the eternal context.

Another example of a rendering of ecological interactions in a complex space is the creation of a VR prototype for the study of a dwelling discovered in Lillsjön, Angermånland, excavated in 2010/2012 by a team of researchers and students from Umeå University, consisting of a pit house dated to mid-late Mesolithic (7200-5800 BP) BC. The site was excavated following a grid of small test pits covering a total area of 0.4 ha and documenting archaeological features and findings mostly on notes and paper drawings. In order to reconstruct the Mesolithic palaeoenvironment context of the area, the excavators collected samples for macrofossils, pollen sequences and soil geochemistry. The dataset resulting after excavation and laboratory analysis was multifaceted, including different types of information in various formats and scales:

- More than 850 soil samples (analysed for phosphate, elemental composition and organic content);
- Position and amount of findings (bones and lithics, characterised according to raw materials and typology);
- Features and C14-dated samples;
- Core samples for pollen analysis.

In May 2016, the digitalisation and systematisation of data from the excavation in Lillsjon were carried out using Esri ArcScene (the use of tridimensional mapping platforms—particularly GIS—for the study of archaeological sites is becoming a common practice amongst archaeologists; Dell'Unto 2014; Dell'Unto et al. 2016). The information gathered during the excavation was stored in a geodatabase connected to 3D features corresponding to the excavated trenches. Height values (z) of features and 14C-dated samples were interpolated in order to reconstruct the various phases and, in particular, the earliest Mesolithic tramping levels. The dataset modelled in ArcScene included a high-definition set of palaeoenvironmental proxy, but while the spatial analysis performed through GIS could highlight important information and link different datasets, ArcScene could not be used to render the delicate balance of ancient soils and vegetation. Paleoecological information was implemented in Unity, developing a VR prototype that could be used to visualise artefacts, features and environmental data.

The 3D GIS, primarily designed for quantitative analysis, was used to interpolate the trampling level dated to the earliest Mesolithic phase and associate that to various features (postholes, hearths and waste pits). The geographic attributes of the scene were created importing both the original terrain model and the interpolated surfaces that represented the prehistoric trampling levels. The vegetation was reconstructed thanks to macrofossils and pollen sequence, combined together with palaeogeomorphology and soil properties. The features documented during the excavation were represented on the interpolated surface, and flagged using floating tags (Fig. 1).

In this case, the reconstruction of the ecological context from various proxies is based on the establishment of links and correspondence between distinct datasets rendered through the immersive environment (Buckland et al. 2018). The VR scene was used as a tool for knowledge production, offering a peculiar space for exploring connections and overlapping between various branches of information. The data-driven VR prototype facilitated the visualisation of interactions between different data sources, supporting an experience-based interpretative process. In these terms, the design of a VR prototype is the product of a reflexive and collaborative practice, based on a scrupulous monitoring and the development of specific skills. Modelling becomes a digital craft, a slow process in which segments of information are interlaced to constitute a wider knowledge network (Goodrick and Earl 2004).

The reconstruction of the Mesolithic dwelling structure was approached as a participative workshop. The structure of the dwelling was suggested according to literature and ethnoarchaeological comparisons (Bergman et al. 2004; Olofsson 2003). Post-holes documented during the excavation were marked and used as a

Fig. 1 The VR prototype of a Mesolithic dwelling site in northern Sweden. The two images represent two moments of the making: importing and flagging features from 3D GIS to Unity and reconstructing the ancient vegetation according to paleoecological data

reference to propose possible structural solutions for the shelter. The position of the posts was tested and discussed as a digital experimental workshop involving several researchers that could experience the virtual scene both with the headset and projected on a screen (Dunn and Woolford 2012). The VR prototype fulfilled its potential of rendering the analytical process, from the visualisation of archaeological data, studded with gaps and uncertainties, to the complicated task of formulating interpretative hypotheses on a shifting ground.

Transparency is a crucial attribute of VR prototypes, fundamental in order to verify and validate the models. In fact, defined codes can be applied to feature metadata and paradata, acknowledge the source of information and recall the interpretative process. This is the case, for example, of the extended matrix, a formal language that uses the stratigraphic approach to create a taxonomic system for virtual reconstruction (Demetrescu 2015; Demetrescu and Fanini 2017). An open rendering of immersive environments with the integration of interactive tools for browsing the making of virtual models can trigger discussion and collaborative practice, as shown by reconstruction of the house of Caecilius Iucundus within the Swedish Pompeii project (Nicolò Dell'Unto et al. 2013; Demetrescu et al. 2016), the 3D repository and model-building protocol of the MayaArch3D project (Von Schwerin et al. 2013) or the Second Life model of Çatalhöyük (Morgan 2009).

Both raw data and virtual models represent the consecutive steps of an archaeological investigation: from raw data to narrative reconstructions (Pietroni et al. 2005). Stages in the interpretation process of our Mesolithic dwelling were rendered creating a distinct user interface, with the possibility to switch from one visualisation to another. In each scene, geographical landmarks (e.g. the lake) were left unaltered while the models of the dwelling area were modified. In the first scene, data from the excavation are represented fragmented, correlated by tags and symbols that specify the field description of the evidence. In this interface, features are represented as blank shapes on the interpolated surface. The graphic choice highlights gaps and discontinuity within the dataset offering at the same time a projection of the original paper drawings and the 3D GIS visualisation. In the second scenario, a simple rendering of the dwelling structure displays the result of the experimental digital workshop. The reconstruction is intentionally synthetic; the poles are rendered as simple geometries and can be moved and rearranged as the hypothesis is modified. The third scene aims at a rather phenomenological experience of the reconstructed environment, with the soft light of the dusk lightened up by a fire rustling in the shelter. The three settings display different stages of the embodied interaction as parallel and complementary narratives.

The re-enactment of past intangible characters can be mediated by using immersive platforms for experimenting avatar implementation. For the project Digitizing Ancient Pantomime, the goal was to create a virtual environment of a pantomime performance, using the language that describes movement and the relevant libretti to create 3D avatars of dancers. The process of building an ancient environment (roman) to accommodate the avatar of a dancer required a much simpler solution. 3D Models of Roman and Greek amphitheatres can be found online, and are easy and cheap to purchase.[2] The research team decided to use a 3D photo-realistic representation of the theatre of Pompeii that could be openly accessible and reused in Sketchfab. We further embedded different weather and light conditions as options in our prototype. Darkness, light, torches and even rain were options by which the user could experience a pantomime performance. As pointed out by Papadopoulos and Earl (2014), illumination can have an impact on the perception of a reconstructed environment, enabling a better understanding of the space and inducing different experiences (Boyce2014; Parisinou 2007). Instead of recreating a specific environment, the attention was placed on building a number of conditions that could correspond to environmental properties.

For the purpose of recording the dancers, we collaborated with members of the Lausanne academy of dance *Les Marchepieds*, and used the 'Black Box', an isolated motion capture laboratory in the ground floor of the Sliperiet facility at Umeå University. In a space of approximately 20 m^2 (4 × 5 m), we positioned a wooden flooring (3 × 3 m), and 12–15 cameras close to the ceiling of the Black Box. The dancers slipped into motion sensor costumes and dancing movements were recorded with the help of the motion capture software (OptiTrack 13 W) and using Motive as interface software. Motive offered several different options for visualisation including:

- an ungendered avatar, that could be characterised using male or female default models; and
- motion tracking avatars with strings that display direction and velocity of the motion capture.

The technological complexities of recording the dancers and their bodies in full are covered extensively in Slaney et al. (2018). For example, custom sensors on the costume proved too few to capture dancing movements accurately and in turn, the dancers felt constrained by technology. Constructing an appropriate avatar was a gradual process. The final avatar used was a synthesis of disparate gender and age features: a conventional female face on a young/early teenager male body with an olive skin complexion and African hair. The reason for the combination of these aesthetic elements was to reflect that professional dance training started from a young age in antiquity (Libanius, *Oration* 64, cf. Slaney et al. 2018). When envisaging the final deliverable, we wanted to break the shackles of dominant thinking about people in the Roman Empire: recent discussions of representation and reception dictate that we see entertainers as slaves or freedmen that may have arrived there from all points of the empire (Fig. 2).

[2] At the time when the article was written the available online repositories were: https://3dmdb.com/en/3d-models/amphitheater/; https://sketchfab.com/tags/amphitheater; https://www.cgtrader.com/3d-models/amphitheatre.

Fig. 2 The virtual reality environment and avatar in the digitizing ancient pantomime project

3 Critical Senses

As argued in the previous paragraph, the deduction of intangible attributes from fragmentary tangible evidence is the most challenging responsibility of historical disciplines. The use of VR platforms supports the visualisation of the interpretative process, bolstering the digital representation of links and interactions amongst physical findings. Involving various degrees of multisensorial engagement, VR relies on sensory feedback for generating a user-centred analysis of the models.

A scholarly exploration of sensory experience may provide gateways to both the mind and the body; it mediates cultural values between the individual and the social world (Betts 2011; Favro 1996; Witmore 2006). By situating an enactment into the sensory sphere, the user has the possibility to learn by experiencing, and reflect on a distant and intangible past.

Gaps and ambivalence encountered through a sensorial examination of virtual models could also represent a key for comprehension of a complex set of data. As Tarr and Warren pointed out 'the critical element provided by virtual reality is the ability to break the laws of optics and physics, or to disconnect physical reality as specified by a subject's body senses from the world he/she is seeing' (Tarr and Warren 2002, 1090). In fact, new knowledge is generated through the virtual experience of breaking the laws of physics: something that happens and our brain perceives as odd or 'unnatural'. Brain responses to VR computer interface have been studied especially with regard to medical rehabilitation and specific treatments. Understanding sensorial responses to VR models helps maximise the potential of information transfer within immersive environments. According to Dalgarno and Lee's model of learning, users develop a sense of presence in an immersive environment through a realistic representation of space, a consistency of the objects' behaviour and audio mapping. These features enable the sense of presence, defined as an 'act of selection between two hypotheses' (e.g. I am here or there, (Slater 2002, 435). Interaction as co-presence is then achieved through control of objects' behaviours in the virtual environment, embodied action and communication (Dalgarno and Lee 2010).

According to these models, the cognitive ability of the observer is influenced by the hardware performance. Visuals and tracking accuracy deeply influence users' responses and ecological validity, meaning that an observation made in the virtual environment remains valid in the real world (Sjölie 2011). For example, the view is significantly enhanced when coupled with head tracking.

As argued, an important feature to consider when re-constructing a sense of presence in VR is audio mapping. Within Digitizing Roman Pantomime, we adopted a methodological approach, termed *synaesthetic prototyping* (Foka and Arvidsson 2016). Inspired by post-processual thinking in archaeology, the proposed approach aimed at turning attention from sensory accuracy to experiential analogy. While there was a lack of tangible evidence about the sonic experience of a roman pantomime dance, we enabled multiple interpretations possible of any sensory experience (Hodder and Hutson 2003) and to treat sensory data, in this case, sound, as materially situated in both space and time (Hodder 2012).

While there have been studies on the acoustics of the theatre of Pompeii and others (Berardi et al. 2016), as well as music in antiquity (e.g. Armand D'Angour's study of Ancient Greek music), we unfortunately had none of these audio materials at our disposal. With all our sound settings (reverberation, impact, etc.) set to analogue, we aimed for the sonic impression of a pre-industrial setting. We then divided natural sounds (birds, rain, etc.) from artificial (human-generated) sounds, and as our environment took different configurations we created soundscapes by analogy. This method recognises that information data will always be incomplete and gaps therefore need to be filled imaginatively. Nevertheless, even the sound reconstruction can be made explicit by introducing different tracks and the relative metadata (Bruno et al. 2010). For example, we experimented with drum sound samples and rhythms from around the Mediterranean (e.g. 9/8) in order to examine phenomenal patterns of communal approval (if any), thus renegotiating social and ethnic diversity in the Roman Empire.

Contemplating sounds was a lesson for all of us as researchers, which we wished to pass onto our students. During our course on Heritage Implementations we presented the prototype to discuss how sounds and their meanings are considered as shaped by the cultural, economic, and political contexts in which they are produced and heard (Ihde 1970; Smith 2001). Indeed, sound studies have been referred to as 'the interdisciplinary ferment in the human sciences that takes sound as its analytical point of departure or arrival. By analysing both sonic practices and the discourses and institutions that describe them, it re-describes what sound does in the human world, and what humans do in the sonic world' (Sterne 2012, 2).

The actual aspect of the VR environment also plays an important role for generating a captivating scene. In order to trigger brain responses to the virtual environment and enhance the immersive feeling, archaeological VR models have been designed to be more and more appealing, through improving the acquiring techniques, the generation of models and textures (Slater 2009). Despite the exceptional quality of some renderings, a few unavoidable flaws occur in the transliteration of archaeological objects into virtual models. For example, some inconsistencies can arise when juxtaposing the represented place of the immersive environment with the real space (the room) in which the user is situated. Most of the time, the scene represented in the VR model does not match the physical environment in which the user is located. While the digital landscape is defined by spatial attributes that can be explored, users' motion is usually limited by material constraints, such as walls, furniture or the position of the tracking devices.

A main idiosyncrasy when dealing with material evidence in a virtual space is the lack of materiality, a physical texture to handle. In archaeology, the understanding of sedimentary record and artefacts is largely achieved through touch, while in a VR environment the loss of solidity could affect the immersive feeling (Allison 2008). The implementation of interactive touching features could represent an important goal for developing historical and pedagogical VR. At the current state, specific hardware for handling virtual objects are being developed, such as haptic gloves, but standard solutions for regular users are not yet available.

Particularly interesting to enhance synergic and immersive feelings is the design of an interactive apparatus to engage with the model. A VR prototype can be implemented with a number of tools and widgets that allow the user to perform predefined actions in the defined space. The architecture of these tools correspond to the needs and aims of the designers and respond to precise research questions. While VR software does not incorporate specific tools, quite a lot of freedom is left to programmers to implement the interactions according to the use.

An illustrative example of the advantages of VR in rendering immersive spaces can be found in the study and documentation of rock-cut chambers, caves or rock shelters: spaces opening from a vertical cliff and characterised by engraved features. The documentation and interpretation of these sites begin with a meticulous mapping of the inner rock surface in order to identify tool marks and carved features, crucial for understanding the use and transformation of the space. Rock-cut sites do not usually incorporate thick sediment deposits and therefore excavations in these specific sites are almost impossible. Consequently, data collection and interpretation are mostly done by mapping carving techniques and discontinuities on the rocky surface. The entire characterisation of the stone walls, including volumes and position of the niches, is hardly described through a two-dimensional mapping system and requires a tridimensional representation. The inside perspective, necessary for observing the carved surfaces, could be recreated thanks to the immersive potential of VR environments, establishing a workflow for importing photogrammetric models and implementing interactive tools (Fig. 3).

The experiment was carried out on a medieval rock-cut settlement situated in the Puy de Dôme, Auvergne, France. The site is located in the district of Murol and consists of eight rooms arranged on two floors and carved in a volcanic cliff. The dwelling is nowadays located in a dense woodland with the entrance of the lowest caves lying a few metres above the ground, making the access to the site extremely

Fig. 3 Tests for importing a photogrammetric 3D model of a rock-cut room in unity for creating an immersive and interactive prototype

difficult. The documentation and study of these caves are also restricted by the poor lighting conditions that limits the visibility of carved features on the rock surface.

A rectangular room of about 12 m^2 was documented using photogrammetry, the photos were taken creating and oblique lighting in order to capture the micro-relief. The resulting model and the corresponding mesh were then scaled to the real dimensions and imported into Unity for further processing. The user was set to be inside the cave and could freely move within the space delimited by the model. The VR environment was built as a single user interface without possibility to switch to other visualisations. The focus of the prototype was the development of interactive tools, in particular a painting tool, suitable for marking specific features, map the surface of the room and visualise interpretative hypotheses. Using various brushes the user can directly annotate the rock-cut room, marking features, chronological elements and tool marks. The immersive model can be used as a notepad, observing, exploring and interpreting the tridimensional space as an open and transparent process.

For the cave prototype, we envisage a collaborative multi-user development, inviting researchers to draw their annotation in the virtual cave at the same time. All the tridimensional sketches should then be considered as single geometries and linked to controlled vocabularies, implementing a searchable database. Finally, the use of haptic gloves in such a context would enhance the potential of the interplay between the user and the material evidence. In fact, touch could be used to uncover discontinuities and asperities on the rock surface that would not be detectable through visual observation.

Developing both the Mesolithic dwelling prototype and the rock-cut cave, the use of Unity allowed for quick prototyping and a short iteration span between the conception and the test implementation in a virtual space. Unity relies on a large user community online, providing a handful of premade assets and comprehensive solutions that can speed up the frame development in order to focus more on project-specific features. Unity disposes of a large palette of tools and ways for creating a customised apparatus that encourages a participatory development. Researchers with different skills and background were invited to take part in the actual development, focusing on the process of building the VR prototype and fostering a reflexive approach to the digital craft. Inviting researchers to use the technology and participate in the development process helps perceive the potential of the application and recognise its limitations. Finally, the close collaboration of various experts helped define priorities and adjust to technical optimisations. In capturing dancing data, the multidisciplinary collaboration and direct involvement in the post-production processes helped toward the realisation of the prototype. Collaborative and iterative development, including several prototyping and testing phases, has shown to be the key for the progression of VR environments. In fact, this meticulous phase of apprenticeship is crucial for exploring potential and pitfalls hidden in the data. While ease of use makes it possible for non-developers to take part in the actual development, the collaborative prototyping helps reach a common understanding. Iteration and testing, as part of a reflexive approach, support an informed development of prototypes that rely on data availability and present new interactive tools.

4 Dynamic Cyberspace as Formative Resource

VR modelling has been designated as a potential 'workshop of scientific research, an active and measurable space where to compare datasets, models, hypotheses, archives, and cyberspaces of interactive knowledge' (Forte 2008, 97). In our experience, VR helped comparison and interaction amongst data supporting a transparent rendering of the interpretation process. This was the case of the Mesolithic site in Lillsjön, where the multiproxy dataset could be re-assembled without missing the archaeological spatial information and qualitative data from the dig. Discontinuity and gaps in the documentation (due to the limited excavated surface) were made visible through the import of GIS layers representing features and trampling levels. The spatial reference and position of findings established an important landmark for recreating the structure of the shelter through a participatory study.

Information generated through the programming and use of interactive tools reinforced the collaboration amongst researchers for the development of interpretative hypotheses. Sketching the lost apparatus of the rock-cut settlement was crucial for understanding an empty space and conceiving its biographic narrative. Itineraries of objects could be outlined in an immersive model acting as a digital canvas, while gaps in the information flow could be filled through a virtual depicted commentary.

Pedagogical aspects of the making emerged while combining different pieces of information in an attempt at rendering the complexity of the archaeological or historical record. The immersive simulation arena allows an interaction with the archaeological evidence that is not constrained by spatial or temporal hindrances. Users can browse an immersive fluid representation of space and time; visualise together data collected in different excavation campaigns and swiftly change position and point of view. VR can bolster the generation of new knowledge and the representation of archaeological data through ubiquity of time and space. Students participating in a Roman Pantomime performance were able to ask questions about place and people, as well as to reflect on the ephemerality of the senses and sound perception before electricity.

The pedagogical contribution of VR for understanding of ancient topography and the evolution of an urban space was tested using Google Earth for teaching ancient topography and the evolution of the centre of Rome to the students of the bachelor programme in archaeology at Umeå University. Google Earth supplies an interactive model for VR that reaches an acceptable level of 3D accuracy in the representation of buildings in urban centres. The urban fabric of a layered city such as Rome must be observed from different perspectives in order to acknowledge the complexity of scattered elements of the past persisting in modern buildings. Most of the time, undergraduate students do not have direct access to visiting historical city centres where the palimpsest of urban development is conspicuous. Thematic maps, in which the archaeological evidence is organised according to the chronology, represent the graphic support used for teaching and learning urban topography. While being very clear and useful for the comprehension of the ancient urban space, two-dimensional maps struggle to represent transformations and resilience.

Browsing a virtual photorealistic model of the city centre, students could cross a steady virtual space, move fast through different scales of observation and annotate significant benchmarks.

Two-dimensional maps representing some specific areas in a precise chronology were presented to the students (from Coarelli 2007) who were challenged to find and explore the corresponding space in the contemporary city, highlighting persistence and transformations. One student at time could act as a guide, wearing VR googles, being in control of the field of view and the proximity to the buildings. The goggles view was then projected on two big screens allowing the other students to respond as spectators/annotators, giving directions and pointing out relevant details. Users moved across two representations of the same space, overlapping the information coming from two separate sources (the map and the model) and creating links between the immersive environment and the 2D selected representation. During the exercise, students developed cooperative strategies to gain the best perspective on the monuments, unfolding details of the metamorphoses of the urban fabric.

An augmented immersive environment strengthens users' sense of presence, bypassing in some cases the lack of a complete sensorial engagement. The implementation of VR prototypes in archaeology classes could promote a broad understanding of the geographical context in which the sites are situated and stimulate student's enthusiasm and engagement. A first-person interaction with the digital model reinstates the slowness of the interpretation reconnecting the user to the craft of digitally rendered evidence and hypothesis. VR appears compelling in order to paraphrase archaeological practice and deliver it as a transparent pedagogical process.

5 Conclusions

VR prototype development supplies a powerful tool for interacting with the production of historical knowledge from an immersive viewpoint. The development of a new approach to historical information, allowing the rendering of mechanisms of knowledge production, seems the most compelling feature of VR applications. The interactive environments can be designed for the analysis of 3D features in a way that GIS cannot provide, through collaborative and iterative prototyping.

The collaboration with different research content in producing VR prototypes offered new insights. There is no comprehensive research about how such multidisciplinary collaborations may illuminate the value of technology as a tool for knowledge processes. Nevertheless, through the process of capturing and placing in a virtual environment the movements of Roman pantomime, we examined how the entanglements between technology, scholarship and performance art enable new knowledge production. Virtual reality in that sense acted as a lens that affects the way we conduct empirical and experimental research: it brings new conditions and demands for research.

The flexibility of game engines like Unity offers virtually no limits to the implementation of new tools to process and visualise information. Digital objects can render ideas, as in the case of the rock-cut settlement, where 3D annotations can frame lost objects and gestures. The sensorial engagement can confuse the users in their perception of space outside the VR environment, due to technological limits. VR allows the enhancement of some senses feedback, like vision and hearing, while, most of the time, disabling other ones such as touch and smell. The disproportionate sensorial experience of the cyber prototype supports a unique approach to the archaeological evidence. Tangible traces are partially deprived of their materiality in the digital representation while acquiring new properties that are embedded in features driving sensorial experiences.

The educational value of prototype-making is specifically expressed throughout collaborative practice. Cooperation amongst students was enhanced through experiential learning and sharing of information regarding the topography of Rome. Similarly, an instructive dialogue was generated through the virtual experimental workshop on reconstructing the wooden structure of the Mesolithic dwelling.

The development of VR prototypes represents an opportunity to explore technological agency within the disciplines of archaeology and ancient history. In all case studies, we have shown how VR applications can assist researchers in generating information both about the past and about the process of historical reconstruction itself. Immersive environments encourage a different approach to data processing and visualisation that must be mediated through an epistemological reflection over paradigms of knowledge production.

References

Allison, J 2008. 'History Educators and the Challenge of Immersive Pasts: A Critical Review of Virtual Reality "Tools" and History Pedagogy'. *Learning, Media and Technology* 33 (4): 343–52. https://doi.org/10.1080/17439880802497099.

Berardi, U., G. Iannace, and L. Maffei. 2016. 'Virtual Reconstruction of the Historical Acoustics of the Odeon of Pompeii'. *Journal of Cultural Heritage* 19 (May): 555–66. https://doi.org/10.1016/j.culher.2015.12.004.

Berggren, Å., N. Dell'Unto, M. Forte, S. Haddow, I. Hodder, J. Issavi, N. Lercari, C. Mazzucato, A. Mickel, and J. S. Taylor. 2015. 'Revisiting Reflexive Archaeology at Çatalhöyük: Integrating Digital and 3D Technologies at the Trowel's Edge'. *Antiquity* 89 (344): 433–48.

Bergman, I., A. Olofsson, G. Hörnberg, O. Zackrisson, and E. Hellberg. 2004. 'Deglaciation and Colonization: Pioneer Settlements in Northern Fennoscandia'. *Journal of World Prehistory* 18 (2): 155–77.

Betts, E. 2011. 'Towards a Multisensory Experience of Movement in the City of Rome'. *Rome, Ostia, Pompeii: Movement and Space*, 118–32. Oxford University Press.

Boyce, P. R. 2014. 'Human Factors in Lighting'. Routledge.

Brody, F. 1991. 'How Virtual Is Reality?' In *Feldman T. (Ed.) Proceedings of the First Annual Conference on Virtual Reality 91*, 18–20. London.

Bruno, F., S. Bruno, G. De Sensi, M.-L. Luchi, S. Mancuso, e M. Muzzupappa. 2010. 'From 3D Reconstruction to Virtual Reality: A Complete Methodology for Digital Archaeological Exhibition'. *Journal of Cultural Heritage* 11 (1): 42–49. https://doi.org/10.1016/j.culher.2009.02.006.

Buckland, P. I., N. Dell'Unto, and G. Palsson. 2018. 'To Tree, or Not to Tree? On the Empirical Basis for Having Past Landscapes to Experience.' *DHQ: Digital Humanities Quarterly* 12 (2). http://www.digitalhumanities.org/dhq/vol/12/3/000383/000383.html.

Caraher, W. 2015. 'Slow Archaeology'. *North Dakota Quarterly* 80 (2): 43–52.

Coarelli, F. 2007. *Rome and Environs: An Archaeological Guide.* University of California Press.

Dalgarno, B., and M. J.W. Lee. 2010. 'What Are the Learning Affordances of 3-D Virtual Environments?' *British Journal of Educational Technology* 41 (1): 10–32.

Dell'Unto, N. 2014. 'The Use of 3D Models for Intra-Site Investigation in Archaeology'. In *S. Campana and F. Remondino (Eds.) 3D Recording and Modeling in Archaeology and Cultural Heritage. Theory and Best Practices.* BAR International Series.

Dell'Unto, N., G. Landeschi, A.-M. Leander Touati, M. Dellepiane, M. Callieri, and D. Ferdani. 2016. 'Experiencing Ancient Buildings from a 3D GIS Perspective: A Case Drawn from the Swedish Pompeii Project'. *Journal of Archaeological Method and Theory* 23 (1): 73–94.

Dell'Unto, N., A.-M. Leander Touati, M. Dellepiane, M. Callieri, D. Ferdani, and S. Lindgren. 2013. 'Digital Reconstruction and Visualization in Archaeology: Case-Study Drawn from the Work of the Swedish Pompeii Project'. In *Digital Heritage International Congress (DigitalHeritage), 2013*, 1: 621–28. IEEE.

Demetrescu, E. 2015. 'Archaeological Stratigraphy as a Formal Language for Virtual Reconstruction. Theory and Practice'. *Journal of Archaeological Science* 57 (May): 42–55. https://doi.org/10.1016/j.jas.2015.02.004.

Demetrescu, E., and B. Fanini. 2017. 'A White-Box Framework to Oversee Archaeological Virtual Reconstructions in Space and Time: Methods and Tools'. *Journal of Archaeological Science: Reports* 14 (August): 500–514. https://doi.org/10.1016/j.jasrep.2017.06.034.

Demetrescu, E., D. Ferdani, N. Dell'Unto, A.-M. Leander Touati, and S. Lindgren. 2016. 'Reconstructing the Original Splendour of the House of Caecilius Iucundus. A Complete Methodology for Virtual Archaeology Aimed at Digital Exhibition.' *SCIRES-IT - SCIentific RESearch and Information Technology* 6 (1): 51–66. https://doi.org/10.2423/i22394303v6n1p51.

Dunn, S., and K. Woolford. 2012. 'Reconfiguring Experimental Archaeology Using 3D Reconstruction'. In *Dunn S., J. F. Bowen and K. Ng (Eds.), EVA London 2012 Electronic Visualisation and the Arts*, 172–78. BCS London.

Favro, D. G. 1996. *The Urban Image of Augustan Rome.* Cambridge University Press.

Foka, A., and V. Arvidsson. 2016. 'Experiential Analogies: A Sonic Digital Ekphrasis as a Digital Humanities Project'. *Digital Humanities Quarterly* 10 (2).

Forte, M. 2008. 'Cyber-Archaeology: An Eco-Approach to the Virtual Reconstruction of the Past'. In *Proceedings of International Symposium on Information and Communication Technologies in Cultural Heritage, Ioannina, Greece*, 91–106.

Forte, M. 2010. *Cyber-Archaeology.* Archaeopress Oxford.

Forte, M., and A. Siliotti. 1997. 'Virtual Archaeology'. *Thames and Hudson.*

Fowler, C. 2015. 'Virtual Reality and Learning: Where Is the Pedagogy?' *British Journal of Educational Technology* 46 (2): 412–22. https://doi.org/10.1111/bjet.12135.

Goodrick, G., and G. Earl. 2004. 'A Manufactured Past: Virtual Reality in Archaeology'. *Internet Archaeology*, no. 15. https://doi.org/10.11141/ia.15.2.

Hodder, I. 2000. 'Developing a Reflexive Method in Archaeology'. *Towards Reflexive Method in Archaeology: The Example at Çatalhöyük*, 1–3. McDonald Institute Monographs.

Hodder, I. 2012. *Entangled: An Archaeology of the Relationships between Humans and Things.* John Wiley & Sons.

Hodder, I., and S. Hutson. 2003. *Reading the Past: Current Approaches to Interpretation in Archaeology.* Cambridge University Press.

Ihde, D. 1970. 'Auditory Imagination'. In *Smith P.J. (Ed.), Phenomenology in Perspective*, 202–15. Springer.

Morgan, C. L. 2009. '(Re) Building Çatalhöyük: Changing Virtual Reality in Archaeology'. *Archaeologies* 5 (3): 468.

Olofsson, A. 2003. 'Pioneer Settlement in the Mesolithic of Northern Sweden'. Doctoral dissertation, Umeå University Press.

Papadopoulos, C., and G. Earl. 2014. 'Formal Three-Dimensional Computational Analyses of Archaeological Spaces'. In *Paliou E., U. Lieberwirth and S. Polla (Eds.), Spatial Analysis and Social Spaces*. De Gruyter. https://www.degruyter.com/view/book/9783110266436/10.1515/9783110266436.135.xml.

Parisinou, E. 2007. 'Lighting dark rooms: some thoughts about the use of space in early Greek domestic architecture'. *British School at Athens Studies* 15: 213–23.

Pietroni, E., S. Pescarin, M. Forte, and N. Dell'Unto. 2005. 'The Narrative Approach of Virtual Heritage Real-Time Applications'. In *ISPRS Congress, 2005*. Archaeopress.

Sjölie, D. 2011. 'Reality-Based Brain-Computer Interaction', Doctoral dissertation, Umeå University Press.

Slaney, H., A. Foka, and S. Bocksberger. 2018. 'Ghosts in the Machine: A Motion-Capture Experiment in Distributed Reception.' *DHQ: Digital Humanities Quarterly* 12 (3).

Slater, M. 2002. 'Presence and The Sixth Sense'. *Presence: Teleoperators and Virtual Environments* 11 (4): 435–39. https://doi.org/10.1162/105474602760204327.

Slater, M. 2009. 'Place illusion and plausibility can lead to realistic behaviour in immersive virtual environments'. *Philosophical Transactions of the Royal Society B: Biological Sciences* 364 (1535): 3549–57. https://doi.org/10.1098/rstb.2009.0138.

Smith, M. M. 2001. *Listening to Nineteenth-Century America*. UNC Press Books.

Sterne, J. 2012. 'Sonic Imaginations'. *The Sound Studies Reader*, 1–17.

Tarr, M. J., and W. H. Warren. 2002. 'Virtual Reality in Behavioral Neuroscience and Beyond'. *Nature Neuroscience* 5 (11): 1089–92. https://doi.org/10.1038/nn948.

Von Schwerin, J., H. Richards-Rissetto, F. Remondino, G. Agugiaro, and G. Girardi. 2013. 'The MayaArch3D Project: A 3D WebGIS for Analyzing Ancient Architecture and Landscapes'. *Literary and Linguistic Computing* 28 (4): 736–53.

Witmore, C. L. 2006. 'Vision, Media, Noise and the Percolation of Time: Symmetrical Approaches to the Mediation of the Material World'. *Journal of Material Culture* 11 (3): 267–92.

Claudia Sciuto is a research fellow at the University of Pisa, Italy. Her work focuses on environmental archaeology as well as digital methods for the study of the past and archaeological theory. Contact: claudia.sciuto@cfs.unipi.it

Anna Foka is the Director of the Centre for Digital Humanities Uppsala and Professor in Digital Humanities at the department of ALM, at Uppsala University. Her research outputs to date focus on digital cultural heritage, heritage data and information science more generally, its classification, representation and related methods, tools and infrastructures.

Mattis Lindmark is a developer at Humlab, Umeå University, mainly focused on 3D visualisation, virtual/augmented reality, digital art and gaming culture.

Jim Robertsson is developer at Humlab, and specialises in IT issues, operation and maintenance at Humlab with technical purchases and inventory. He also works with technical support and development. He participates in cultural and humanistic research projects, and supervise students at the Programme for Museums and Heritage Studies. His fields of interest include IT-technology, Prototype Development, Sensor Technology, Motion Capture and Physical Computing.

Combining 3D Visibility Analysis and Virtual Acoustics Analysis for the Architectural Study of Ancient Theatres

Maria Cristina Manzetti

Abstract The research presented in this chapter demonstrates the fruitful combination of interdisciplinary and multisensory approaches in the field of archaeology. Several disciplines, such as architecture, archaeology, computer science, acoustics and geophysics, cooperated to obtain new data and to elaborate new hypotheses about the original structure of the Roman theatres in Crete. All the information available about these monuments (such as ancient drawings, descriptions of travellers, plans, archaeological reports, aerial pictures and geophysical anomalies) were the basis to hypothesise their original architecture, together with the support of comparisons with well-preserved Roman theatres and with Vitruvius' proportions. These reconstructive hypotheses were visualised by 3D models and their accuracy was verified through a new methodology that sees the application of 3D visibility analysis and virtual acoustics analysis. The 3D visibility analysis was useful to verify the level of visibility of the stage by the spectators in the seating area. The virtual acoustics analysis was used to obtain quantitative values of acoustic parameters helpful to judge the acoustic quality of the 3D reconstructions. The auralisation was also carried out to attain a subjective parameter about acoustic perception. In particular, by 3D visibility analysis and virtual acoustics analysis, it is possible to verify the reliability and the accuracy of hypothetical reconstructions, assuming that every spectator was able to watch the stage and able to listen and to comprehend any performance. The case study presented here is the theatre at the acropolis of Gortyna. Two different 3D reconstructions were tested and it has resulted that the 3D model of the theatre which maintains some Greek characteristics is the most reliable one. This approach made it possible to obtain data that could not be obtained otherwise, as well as raising new questions and opening up new perspectives.

Keywords Roman theatres · 3D visibility analysis · Virtual acoustics analysis · Gortyna

---

M. C. Manzetti (✉)
Department of History and Archaeology, University of Cyprus, Nicosia, Cyprus
e-mail: cristinamanzetti@gmail.com; manzetti.maria-cristina@ucy.ac.cy

G. Landeschi and E. Betts (eds.), *Capturing the Senses*,
Quantitative Methods in the Humanities and Social Sciences,
https://doi.org/10.1007/978-3-031-23133-9_6

1 Introduction

The sector of Cultural Heritage has always been characterised by collaboration among several disciplines. We cannot achieve a thorough study of a monument if we do not consider its historical context, its architecture and its graphical representation. Besides, we cannot completely understand an archaeological site if we do not take into account its geographical context, history, geology, artefacts and social and religious functions. History, architecture, history of art, geography, sociology, anthropology and theology are only some of the disciplines that together contribute to a better and deeper knowledge of what we now consider symbols of the past, representing our culture.

In the last three decades, a new bailiwick has been involved in the field of Cultural Heritage: information technology (IT) and virtual reality. Virtual analyses, 3D modelling, virtual reality and digital media are some of the very useful instruments borrowed from the technological sector and applied to the field of Cultural Heritage, above all to archaeology. This research project exploits these recently developed tools and proposes an interdisciplinary approach that sees the cooperation and the integration of archaeology, architecture, 3D modelling, virtual analyses and acoustics. New and peculiar disciplines can take shape through interdisciplinarity. An example of a new field born from the combination of archaeology and information technology is Virtual Archaeology. The expression 'Virtual Archaeology' was coined by Reilly (1991) and since then its success has increased until it has been recently chosen to give the name to a biennial international forum organised by the State Hermitage Museum of Saint Petersburg (http://www.virtualarchaeology.ru/). With the expression virtual reality, Reilly explains that archaeologists can virtually reproduce an archaeological excavation through 3D modelling, and thus visualise and analyse the excavated area over and over again, without losing the possibility to verify the excavated layers once they have been removed. Many steps have been made since then but there is still a long way to go; for example, developing a more systematic application of interdisciplinary approaches in archaeology.

The fundamental contribution of interdisciplinarity, rather than multidisciplinarity, in the archaeological sector, is also expressed by the Principles of Seville, which are the eight international principles of Virtual Archaeology. The first principle is 'interdisciplinarity', and it states that the cooperation of a professional team with backgrounds in different sciences is necessary and, most importantly, that experts need to exchange their ideas rather than working independently (Lopez-Menchero Bendicho 2013).

The workflow that I am going to present in this chapter is the result of an interdisciplinary approach applied to the study and the valorisation of the Roman theatres in Crete. This innovative methodology combines archaeology, architecture, acoustics and computer science. The methodology developed takes into account several disciplines and focuses on two human senses: sight and hearing. The main aim of this chapter is to demonstrate the fruitful results that archaeologists can achieve by implementing an interdisciplinary and multisensory approach.

Senses have only recently become part of archaeological investigation, with senses beyond sight being recognised as instruments that can enhance our knowledge of the past cultures (Betts 2017; Day 2013; Hamilakis 2011). Visibility has been examined extensively in archaeology since the 1980s and a good review is presented by Lake and Woodman who explain the two main groups in this field: non-GIS visibility studies and GIS visibility studies (Lake and Woodman 2003). Visibility studies are generally considered useful to investigate the distribution of sites and relationships among them (Wheatley 1995), to understand the defensive techniques of ancient populations (Loots et al. 1999), to study the likely rituals connected to prehistoric monuments (Fisher et al. 1997; Wheatley 1995) and to examine the connection between monuments/sites and astronomical events (Ruggles et al. 1993).

Sight has often been considered by archaeologists the main sense of human beings useful to investigate archaeological sites but, more recently, some scholars (Hamilakis 2013; Wheatley 2014) observed the bias for this approach and the consequent inaccuracy in the results and interpretations.

While sight has largely been privileged in archaeology, 'archaeoacoustics' (Scarre and Lawson 2006) is an emerging sub-field, often having a focus on the role and behaviour of sound within prehistoric sites (Devereux 2001), mainly in order to deduce the rituality connected to those spaces.

One of the first case studies in which a combined approach was applied is the sixth-century Byzantine church of San Vitale in Ravenna (Italy) (Paliou and Knight 2013). This study combined visibility and acoustics analyses, intending to obtain more information about the sensations the worshippers were feeling and the stimuli they were receiving within the church during the liturgy. Paliou and Knight created a combined map (visual data obtained by visibility analysis plus acoustics data derived from the in situ measurements) representing the sensory catchment[1] inside the church, to deduce which were the privileged positions in the building to assist the liturgy. In particular, they wanted to examine the social differences between men and women, according to the area they occupied within the church (floor and *matroneum*). In this case, the combination of visibility and acoustics analyses allowed a meaningful and valuable conclusion to be reached about which social discriminations were determined by the church's architecture.

This chapter applies a similar methodology in order to verify possible architectural reconstructions of the Roman theatres of Crete. The acoustics analysis in this research also helped to formulate hypotheses about the kind of performance that was represented in those spaces.

In particular, the research question is: how can we obtain more information about the architecture of monuments that nowadays are destroyed? Can new technologies be a fruitful instrument to improve the knowledge of what is left of a glorious past? and, since the subject of my research are ancient buildings for entertainment (where people

[1] Paliou and Knight were inspired by Frieman and Gillings definition of 'sensory envelop' to carry out their research. According to the authors, a sensory envelop identifies 'an area where all the senses are engaged' (Frieman and Gillings 2007).

used to go mainly[2] to watch and to listen to a performance) 'can the examination of the sensorial aspect help in the reconstruction of the architecture and the history of those monuments?'.

This chapter aims to investigate the potentialities of an interdisciplinary and multisensory approach in archaeology. In particular, the proposed methodology and workflow will demonstrate its effectiveness for obtaining information about the architecture of ancient theatres and for raising new questions.

The study required several steps to be completed. First, all the documents about the Roman theatres of Crete were collected and examined. Then, several 3D models for each chosen theatre were realised according to reconstructive hypotheses based on the combination of available data, comparisons with well-known Roman theatres and Vitruvian rules. These 3D models were used to inspect the visibility of the stage from the cavea and the quality of sound in the seating area.

2 The Roman Theatres in Crete

There are 12 known Roman theatres in Crete, located around the island. In the prefecture of Chania (west side of the island), there were four: the one in Chania and the one in Kissamos are now respectively destroyed and under the modern village, the one in Aptera is well known and still visible in the archaeological site, and the one in Lissos is in the archaeological area but excavations have started only very recently. In the prefecture of Heraklion (central-east part of the island), there were five: three of them are located in the ancient Roman capital of Crete, in Gortyna, one is in Chersonissos, one is supposed to be in Lyttos but it has not been identified yet. In the prefecture of Lassithi (the eastern part of the island), there were three: two of them are located within the town of Ierapetra, and one is on the little island of Koufonissi. It is still uncertain if there was another theatre in Tsousouros (south Heraklion).

For a long time, the Roman theatres in Crete have been neglected, while a large part of attention was addressed towards the rich Minoan past of the island. This initial attitude of the archaeologists might surprise considering that the relevance of several Roman remains (including theatres) was already witnessed at the end of the sixteenth century. Italian (Beschi 1999), British (Pashley 1837; Pococke 1745; Spratt 1865) and French (Pitton de Tournefort 1717) travellers documented the presence, and sometimes also the aspect, of some of these monuments. At the very end of the nineteenth century-beginning of the twentieth century, some archaeological investigations, conducted by the Italian Mission of Archaeology in Crete, started, above all in Gortyna, always considered the most interesting Roman site of the island because it was the capital of the Roman province of Crete and Cyrenaica since 67 AD (Scuola Archeologica Italiana di Atene 1984). Lately, since the beginning of the nineteenth century, systematic archaeological excavations have begun at the site occupied by

---

2 Ancient theatres could be also used as spaces for meetings, ritual ceremonies and as a seat of congregations.

some of the theatres. They allowed to achieve very good results in the understanding of the history and the structure of some of these ancient buildings, as in the case of the theatre of Aptera (Vana Niniou-Kindeli and Chatzidakis 2016), which excavations are carried out by the 23rd Ephorate of Prehistoric and Classical Antiquities of Greece, and in the case of the theatre of the *Pythion* in Gortyna (Bonetto et al. 2019; Bonetto and Francisci 2014) which excavations are conducted by the University of Padua and the Italian School of Archaeology at Athens. Summarising, the Roman theatres in Crete are not very well known, are not very well preserved and only a few of them have been investigated by accurate archaeological excavations. Despite the evident difficulties in trying to extrapolate information from such kind of scenario, these monuments definitely deserve to be examined to restore their honour and to avoid them to be completely forgotten. It is unnecessary to say that archaeological excavations are the main instrument that would allow specialists to have a better understanding of the structure and the history of these theatres, but there are some particular circumstances where archaeological excavations are not enough. Often, as in the case of the Roman theatres in Crete, the ancient buildings are not fully preserved and it is not always easy to deduce their original aspect from the collapsed remains since they could have been pillaged or destroyed. In these cases, the new technologies can be of great help because we can virtually reconstruct such buildings according to our hypotheses and verify their accuracy or validity through 3D visualisation and virtual analyses. In this specific case study, 3D visibility analysis and virtual acoustics analysis have been considered to be, at the moment, the most meaningful ones to apply in order to enhance the knowledge about the architecture and the function of the theatres. The idea to implement this typology of analyses derived from the main function of the theatre itself: it is made to watch and to listen to a performance. The Greek word *θέατρον* (theatre) comes from the ancient Greek verb *θεάομαι* which means 'to see, to watch' (Pappalardo 2007), while the Romans used to call it *auditorium*, from the Latin verb *audio*, that is 'to listen' (Bieber 1981). These observations lead to assume that the spectators were able to see what was happening on the stage and to follow the movements of the actor/s and that they were able to understand the words of the performer/s or to enjoy the music. Consequently, the structure of the theatres needed (and still needs) to respect these prerequisites, that is to allow the visibility of the stage from the seating area and the good perception of the sound (both music or talk). The observance of these requisites in the reconstructive hypotheses of the Roman theatres in Crete have been verified through 3D visibility analysis and virtual acoustics analysis.

3 Methodology

Before I go into detail about the innovative tools (3D visibility analysis and virtual acoustics analysis) used during this study, I want to underline that the traditional approach has been implemented too. The research started with the collection and the analysis of all available data: archaeological reports, images, aerial pictures, ancient plans, descriptions of travellers, surveys and results of geophysical prospection. The combined study of all these documents (Manzetti et al. 2015) enabled to formulate the first hypothesis about the structure of each theatre. If there was not enough information to reconstruct their height, comparisons with well-preserved theatres (as Aspedos and Orange) and the Vitruvian's rules described in '*De Architectura*' (Morgan 1914) were considered. AutoCad and 3D Studio Max were used to draw the plan of the theatres and to extrude it to create 3D models of the reconstructive hypotheses of the monuments. Since these are only hypotheses, each theatre has been represented in more than one 3D model with some possible variations in its structure. All 3D models of each theatre were analysed through 3D visibility and virtual acoustics in order to verify which hypothesis is the most reliable one and if they are accurate reconstructions.

3.1 3D Visibility Analysis

As it has been already mentioned, the visibility analysis in archaeology has been widespread for more than thirty years. Many things changed since then and more quantitative and accurate methods have been developed. One of the main issues about visibility analysis has always been the bi-dimensional approach since we live in a three-dimensional world (Bishop et al. 2000; Paliou et al. 2011). As Tufte reminds us, studying 'flatlands' (maps, drawings and pictures) is not the solution, we have to reproduce objects as they are if we want to understand them (Tufte 1990). Finally, a method for visibility analysis in a fully 3D environment was conceived a few years ago and one of the very first examples is the study of visibility within the *Insula* V 1 of Pompeii, under the Swedish Pompeii Project (Landeschi et al. 2016).

The 3D visibility analysis can be performed through ArcScene which allows creating lines of sight between the observer and the target in a 3D environment, thus it considers the height of the buildings and any other obstacle in the field of view.

Once the 3D models of the Roman theatres of Crete have been realised, a grid of points (representing the observers) has been placed in the seating area. Each grid is composed of four lines dislocated in the cavea (two lines are placed next to the side retaining walls and the other two are toward the centre) with a point over each row of seats.[3] Each point is located 75 cm above the seat, to simulate the average height of a seated person. A target line (representing the actor/s) was placed approximately at the centre of the stage, 160 cm above the floor to simulate the average height of a standing person. The 3D models, the grid of points and the lines were imported into ArcScene where the lines of sight were constructed. The lines of sight are composed of lines of two colours that are built between all the observer points and the target. The green lines represent the visible trajectories, that means the observer points from which the green lines originate can see the area of the target that the lines hit. The red lines are the not visible trajectories, so the observers cannot see

[3] The number of points varies according to the number of rows of seats of the cavea of each theatre.

the target or part of it. The visualisation of the lines of sight in a 3D environment allows us to understand from which area of the building the green and red lines originated and which part of the target is more or less visible. It is also possible to visualise the obstruction points derived from the construction of the lines of sight. The obstruction points are marking the exact location where the lines of sight hit an object that impedes the visibility. In the case of the theatres, this tool is useful to verify that some architectural structures have not been reproduced in an uncorrected position and/or size (for instance: retaining walls too high, stage too high, *basilicae* too close to the cavea).

Besides, another analysis is possible through ArcScene which is called 'visibility', similar to viewshed analysis. The implementation of this tool produces a visual map of frequencies, which is a 2D file but during the calculations, it takes into account the three-dimensional aspect of the objects. Several colours on the map represent the different levels of visibility: each colour corresponds to a specific number of spectators, thus it is possible to understand how many spectators see a specific area of the theatre. In our case, we are interested to know how many spectators can see the stage or part of it.

3.2 Virtual Acoustics Analysis

Already since the sixth century BC, sound (its generation, its behaviour and its effects) was investigated by ancient Greeks. Pythagoras was interested in the pitch of sounds. He conducted some experiments and he finally conceived the Pythagorean tuning, that means the attribution of a series of numbers to the notes according to their pitch. Aristotle (*De Anima*) as well examined sound, its propagation and its creation by the man. Thus, already in fourth century BC, Greeks knew that an auditory body, a knock and the air were the necessary elements to generate a sound, as it was already mentioned by Plato (*Timeo*). These studies, along with the one by Aristoxenus[4] (*Aristoxenou Armonika Stoicheia*), demonstrate that ancient Greeks had quite extensive knowledge about sound and acoustics. They were applying their precious awareness for the construction of buildings where the sound was a fundamental element, as demonstrated by Plutarch (*Moralia*). He narrates that the architect of the theatre of Pella dissuaded Alexander the Great to build a *proscaenium* made out of bronze because such material would have negatively influenced the acoustics of the space.

During the centuries, the knowledge about acoustics increased: the Romans were able to give a more specific description of the effects of the sound. In our case, it is useful to take as an example the architect Vitruvius who, while he was suggesting a proper place where to build a theatre, described different possible sounds, which one to avoid and which one to pursue. He depicts four distinct spaces that influence the behaviour of the sound and therefore its perception. A *desonans* space is where the first sound obstacles the second; a *circumsonans* space is where it is not possible

[4] He studied the perception of the sound.

to discern the different meanings of the sound; the *resonans* space is where echo is generated; a *consonans* space is where the words are distinct and clear in tone. Vitruvius recommends looking for a *consonans* space to build a theatre that can satisfy the need of the spectators to understand the performances.

This brief excursus of ancient literature about sound is useful to understand the utility of analysing the acoustics of ancient theatres. It shows the importance that acoustics had already in the past and therefore nowadays it can give meaningful signs, helpful to interpret ancient architectures. The precious contribution that the study of acoustics in ancient theatres can bring is so evident that in the last 50 years some scholars already systematically investigated this aspect. François Canac carried a detailed and thorough study about the acoustics of ancient theatres, taking measurements in situ (in France, Italy and Asia Minor) and also simulated measurements in scaled models (Canac 1967). He managed to identify the acoustics role of architectural elements such as niches, corridors, roof, walls, seats and orchestra's floor. Only short and sporadic studies were conducted since then, mainly on the well-preserved theatres. A large project on the 'Identification, Evaluation and Revival of the Acoustical Heritage of Ancient Theatres and Odea', ERATO, came out only in 2003–2006. It allowed the discovery of numerous acoustics characteristics of ancient theatres such as Aspendos (Turkey), Aphrodisia (Turkey), Jerash (Jordan) and Syracuse (Italy) (Erdogan 2006). During the ERATO project, in situ measurements were not the only data collected. The software Odeon Room Acoustics was also used to virtually analyse some of the theatres and to compare the real measurements with the simulated ones. The application and the results of virtual acoustics analysis have been presented during the conference Acoustics of Ancient Theatres at Patras in 2011 as well (Foteinou and Murphy 2011; Iannace et al. 2011a, b; Lokki et al. 2011). These previous studies are very useful to this research since they allow to compare methods and results, and consequently to achieve a more accurate outcome.

The software Odeon Room Acoustics was used to analyse the Roman theatres of Crete as well as to facilitate the comparisons with the previous publications. The simplified versions of the 3D models of the theatres were imported into Odeon Room Acoustics. A grid of receivers was placed in the cavea (75 cm above the seats) corresponding to the spectators, and an omnidirectional source was approximately placed at the centre of the stage (160 cm above the floor) corresponding to the actor. The overall gain of the source was set at 60 dB that is equivalent to the human voice. In this research, the value of the sound corresponding to the human voice only has been considered because the theatres in Roman times were principally used for plays rather than musical performances.[5] Before starting with the analysis, it is necessary to adjust the main settings to obtain reliable results, according to the characteristics of the object, as it is suggested by the software handbook (Christensen and Koutsouris 2015). One of the main aspects to consider is that the Roman theatres are open-air

[5] The geometrical evolution of the theatre, from Greek to Roman times, (and of the theatrical texts as well) testifies indeed the passage from a performance with dancers and a chorus (which used to take place in the orchestra that from a circle becomes a semicircle) to a performance where the main character was the actor (located on the stage which became deeper and less high) (Bieber 1981).

theatres, they did not have any roof, not like in modern theatres, or ancient *odêia*, and to do fundamental calculations, like the reverberation time, it is indispensable to have a volume.[6] Therefore, it is necessary to build a bounding-box that 'seals' each theatre and to give each one of its surfaces a total absorption so that the sound rays would pass through them and the open-air characteristic is preserved. The other important step to take before starting the calculations is to assign the correct material to each surface of the 3D model.[7] We need to know which part of the theatre was made out of stone, wood, bricks, marble, etc. Odeon Room Acoustics offers a rich library of materials along with their absorption coefficients for each frequency. Once the calculations are done, we obtain results from many acoustic parameters that indicate different characteristics of the sound; to have a good quality of acoustics, the values of such parameters should fall into a specific range and the verification of these values enables to judge the acoustics of a room. The parameters that have been considered in this research are five: reverberation time, early decay time, clarity, definition, speech transmission index (for more acoustic parameters used for archaeological investigations, see also the research about the soundscape of the streets in Ostia (Veitch 2017)). The reverberation time and the early decay time are parameters related to the reverberation of sound.[8] More precisely, the reverberation time (RT) is the time a sound takes to decrease by 60 dB after it stops. For speech, the ideal time of reverberation is around 1 s, for music is around 2 s (Spagnolo 2014). If the reverberation time lengthens, it gives origin to the phenomenon of the echo. While the reverberation time is an objective value (it represents the real reverberation), the early decay time represents the subjective perception of the reverberation time, that means the feeling of how much the first reflections annoy the listener. It corresponds to the first 10 dB of decay and ideally should be the same as the reverberation time, but it is usually a little lower and the level of disparity between them is a signal of good or bad diffusion of the sound. Previous research dedicated to open-air and well-preserved theatres (Aspendos, Epidaurus, Jerash) demonstrated that in such spaces the difference between RT and EDT is between 0.2 and 0.4 s (Gade and Angelakis

[6] The reverberation time is equal to volume divided by the sum of the absorption coefficients of all the materials.

[7] Each material has a different absorption coefficient which influences the quality of the sound (see note 6).

[8] It is important to underline that sound is generally characterised by three components: direct sound, early reflections and late reflections. The direct sound is the part that directly reaches the ears of a listener, travelling in a straight line from the source, and it arrives before the other components. The early reflections come from sound hitting obstacles (such as walls, ceiling, floor, etc.) that reflect the received acoustic impulse; these are the first reflections that arrive after the direct sound. They cannot be distinguished by the ears but if they arrive within 20 ms after the direct sound, they improve the subjective intensity of the sound. The late reflections arrive after the early reflections: they contribute having the pleasant perception of the vastness of a room and enjoying a full experience of sound but, when reflections keep arriving for a long time, we have a reverberant sound that invalidates its comprehension. This happens because a long/repeated time of reflections makes a sound longer than it should be and when a second sound (that, for instance, can be the second syllable of a word) is emitted, the first sound is still audible, so that the two sounds are not identifiable and distinguishable, therefore they are not comprehensible.

2006). Clarity and definition are parameters connected to energetic criteria. Clarity (C80) represents the comprehension of a single sound within a complex signal. It consists of the ratio between the energy that arrives within 80 ms (that is the energy of the direct sound plus the energy of the early reflections) to the energy that arrives later. If the energy of the late reflections is higher than the energy of direct sound and early reflections, clarity (that is comprehension) is not very good. We may have appropriate acoustics for speech when the value of C80 is equal or greater than 3 dB, while, for a good listening of the music, we should need values under 3 dB (Spagnolo 2014). Definition (D50) indicates the level of clarity of the speech, the ease for the listener to understand the message of the speaker. The index of D50 is the ratio between the energy that arrives within the first 50 ms (direct sound plus early reflections) and the remaining energy of the signal. Also, in this case, the first energy has to be superior to the late energy to have an acceptable quality of the acoustics for the speech. The desirable value of D50 for speech is higher than 0.50, for music lower than 0.50 (by definition is included within 0 and 1) (Spagnolo 2014). The Speech Transmission Index (STI) is related to spoken intelligibility. It establishes objectively the quality of spoken, calculating the combined effect of background noise and reverberation on the intelligibility of the speech. When there are no interferences in the characteristics of modulation of the signal, there are suitable conditions of intelligibility. Values of STI between 0.60 and 0.75 are good; greater than 0.75 are excellent (Spagnolo 2014).

Summarising, through virtual acoustics analysis, we achieve quantitative results which contribute to adopting an objective and scientific approach that can be easily compared with similar studies and that allows judging the acoustics quality of a space. However, since we are in the field of senses, we have to consider also the subjective perception. Senses are always related to emotions, memories and cultures (Hamilakis 2013). The way we perceive sounds, landscapes, smells and materials is strictly connected to our previous experiences and also to our capabilities and sensibility. This is the reason why it is also important to consider the auralisation, which is the convolution between an anechoic file and the impulse response. Odeon Room Acoustics enable us to do the auralisation, producing audio files that sound how they would have sounded if they were directly recorded in situ. This process enables to listen to the reproduction of ancient performances as if we were physically in the space corresponding to the 3D model where the auralisation has been performed and therefore to live a subjective experience of the sound (Manzetti 2018a). To obtain some auralised files from the 3D models of the Roman theatres of Crete, an anechoic file, representing a monologue from the 'Trojan Women' by Euripides, was recorded at the Laboratory Of Sensors and Acoustics Orso Mario Corbino of the CNR in Rome thanks to Dr Calicchia, Dr Pace and Martina Giovanetti.

4 Case Study and Results

The most ancient theatre of Gortyna (the ancient capital of the Roman province of Crete and Cyrenaica) is placed on the south-east slopes of the acropolis of the ancient town. It is known as a Roman theatre but it has been originally built during the Greek times and was modified by the Romans at a later time. This probably explains the structure of the theatre, which is half-dug in the ground and half-built, as it was typical in Greek times. The theatre is currently under investigation by the Ephorate of Prehistoric and Classical Antiquities of Heraklion; archaeological excavations have started in 2011 (Kanta et al. 2014). The information about the theatre is quite numerous: an ancient drawing (Beschi 1999) and its old reinterpretation (Falkener 1854), descriptions by a British traveller (Spratt 1865), plan and section of the cavea by an early archaeologist of the Italian Mission of Archaeology in Crete (Taramelli 1902), recent studies (Barresi 2004), geophysical prospection (Sarris and Papadopoulos 2010) satellite images and recent archaeological excavations. However, unfortunately, this information is fragmentary and still does not clarify the original structure of the Roman theatre at the acropolis of Gortyna. In this case, 3D visibility analysis, virtual acoustics analysis and auralisation can contribute to shed light on the architecture of the theatre or to formulate new questions and raise problems that would not be evident without such kind of analyses.

Through the combination of all the above-mentioned information, also taking into account the Vitruvian's proportions and analogies with well-preserved Roman theatres, two hypothetical reconstructions of the theatre of the acropolis of Gortyna have been attempted. The difference between the two reconstructions is the presence of *parodoi* (the side entrances to the theatre) in the first one, determining a distance between seating area and scene building[9] (model N.1), and the presence of *basilicae* (rooms that flank the stage) connected to the cavea in the second one, which create an enclosed space,[10] together with a portico in *summa* cavea (model N.2).

To verify the visibility from the cavea to the stage, 120 observer points were placed in the seating area (Figs. 1 and 2) and lines of sight were constructed between this grid of observer points and the target line on the stage (Figs. 3 and 4). As it is expected, in both models, the non-visible trajectories are between the observer points located at the sides of the seating area and the extremities of the target line. The central part of the target line, which corresponds to the central part of the stage, is connected through visible trajectories to all the observer points, in both models.

[9] The presence of *parodoi* was typical in Greek theatres. This hypothesis, here, is justified by the apparent absence of traces of structures between the seating area and the scene building. Barresi testifies the presence of vaulted blocks in that area that were probably necessary to cover the *parodoi* (Barresi 2004), but no *tribunalia* are documented that would have connected the cavea and the scene building. Moreover, as it was mentioned before, the theatre at the acropolis of Gortyna was originally built in Greek time and it might be possible that some of its characteristics have been preserved during the Roman modifications.

[10] This kind of structure is typical of the Roman theatres and it has also been proposed by the archaeologists who excavate the theatre at the conference Ergo Kritis in November 2016 in Rethymno, Greece.

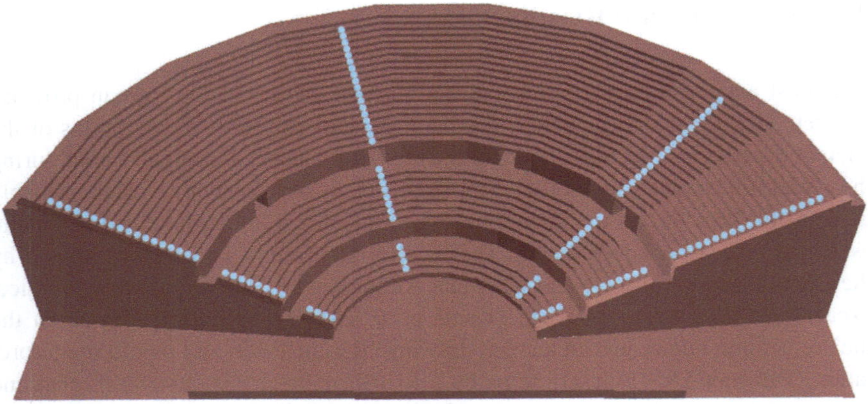

Fig. 1 Model N.1 together with the observer points

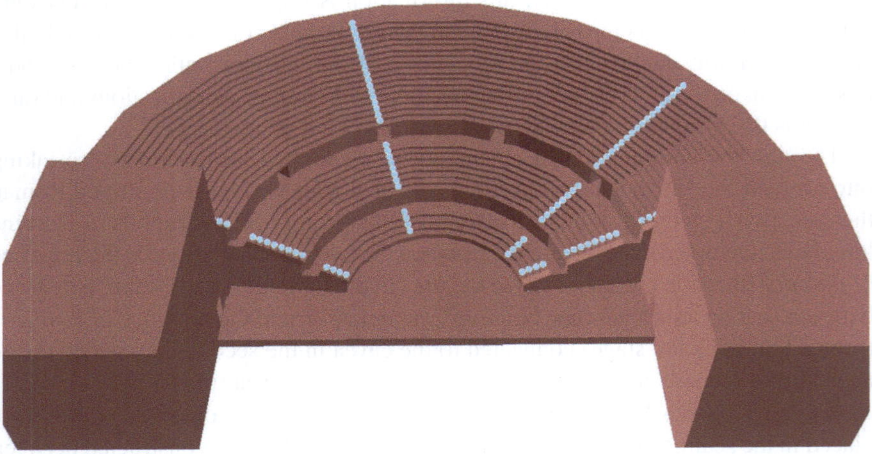

Fig. 2 Model N.2 together with the observer points

More exactly, if we calculate the percentage of visible and non-visible trajectories for both models, we see that the difference between the two hypothetical reconstructions is negligible the model N.1 presents the 17% of non-visible trajectories, model N.2 the 18%. However, differences are more noticeable in the 'maps of frequency of visibility'. From the frequency of visibility map of model N.1, it is clear that the central part of the stage is completely visible to all 120 observer points (Fig. 5). While, the map of frequency of visibility of model N.2 shows that the visible area of the stage, to all observer points, is only the very frontal part of it (Fig. 6). The centre and the back of the stage is still visible to a high number of 'spectators' but no to all of them (between 95 and 115).

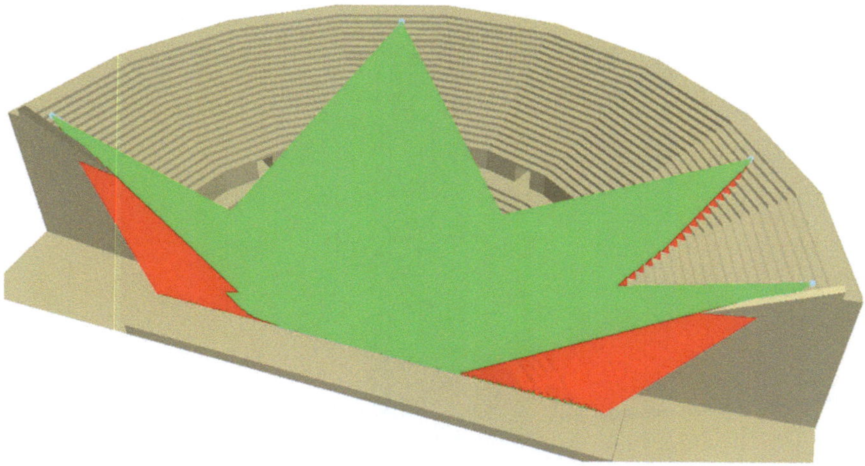

Fig. 3 Lines of sights built from the observer points in the seating area and the target line on the stage (model N.1). The green lines correspond to visible trajectories and the red lines correspond to non-visible trajectories

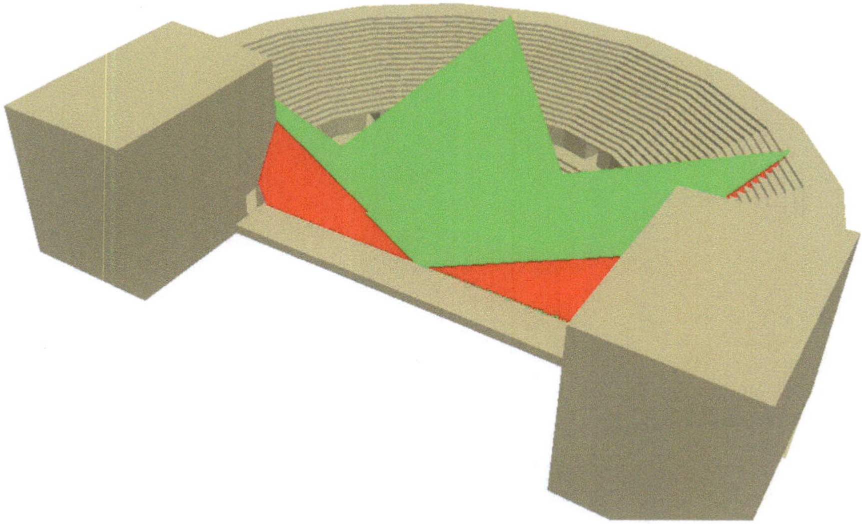

Fig. 4 Lines of sights built from the observer points in the seating area and the target line on the stage (model N.2). The green lines correspond to visible trajectories and the red lines correspond to non-visible trajectories

The same 3D models were examined through the virtual acoustics analysis as well, with 30 receivers placed in the seating area (Fig. 7). For each receiver, the obtained values of RT, EDT, C80, D50 and STI, at the range of frequencies 125–2000 Hz, were considered. Tables 1 and 2 show the average values of all 30 receivers

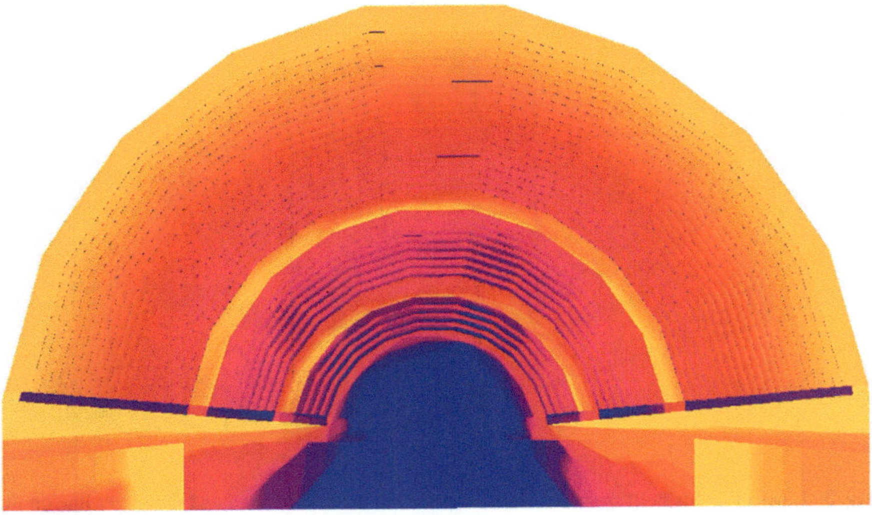

Fig. 5 Map of frequency of visibility of the theatre at the acropolis of Gortyna (model N.1). The blue colour indicates the areas that are visible by all observer points and the yellow colour indicates the areas that are visible to none

Fig. 6 Map of frequency of visibility of the theatre at the acropolis of Gortyna (model N.2). The blue colour indicates the areas that are visible by all observer points and the yellow colour indicates the areas that are visible to none

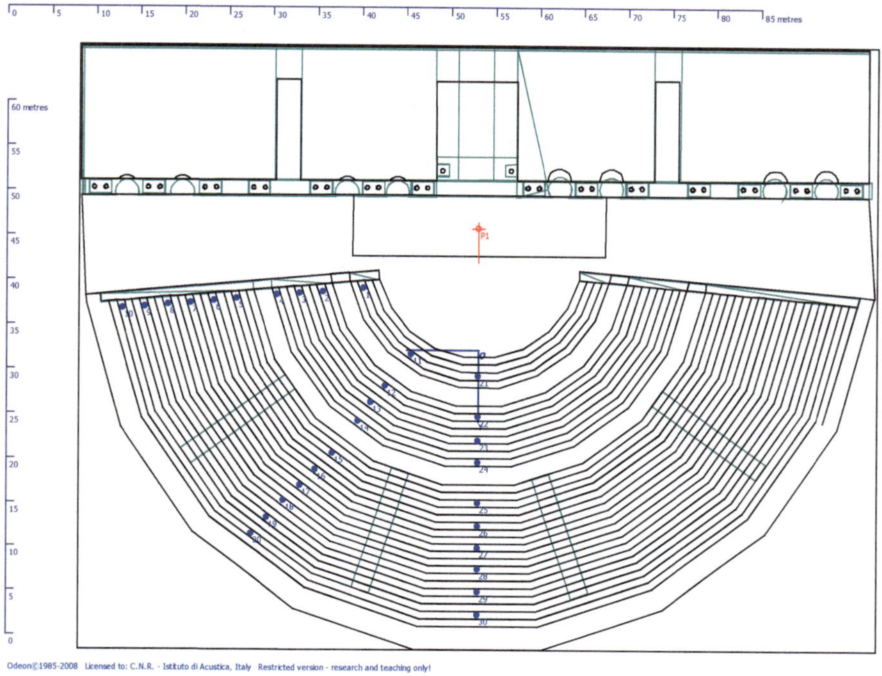

Fig. 7 Representation of model N.1 together with the receivers and the source in Odeon Room Acoustics

for RT, the difference between RT and EDT, C80 and D50, of the two 3D models. Table 1 points out that the reverberation time, in model N.1, is around 1 s and it is then suitable for spoken performances. The difference between reverberation time and the early decay time is between 0.18 and 0.44: it seems consistent with the analyses made in other theatres where the difference was between 0.2 and 0.4 (Gade and Angelakis 2006). The clarity is above 4 dB and the definition is above 0.57; both values indicate a space where speech is easy to comprehend. Moreover, the average value of the speech transmission index of model N.1 is 0.69, suggesting good intelligibility of the spoken language.

Table 1 Average values of all the receivers of RT, difference between RT and EDT, C80 and D50, at each frequency, of model N.1

	RT	RT-EDT	C80	D50
125 Hz	1.40	0.18	4	0.57
250 Hz	1.23	0.35	6.10	0.66
500 Hz	1.10	0.44	7.79	0.73
1000 Hz	1.04	0.37	7.56	0.72
2000 Hz	1	0.37	7.79	0.73

Table 2 Average values of all the receivers of RT, difference between RT and EDT, C80 and D50, at each frequency, of model N.2

	RT	RT-EDT	C80	D50
125 Hz	1.82	−0.1	0.64	0.42
250 Hz	1.65	−0.05	2.27	0.50
500 Hz	1.49	0.07	3.60	0.57
1000 Hz	1.43	0.11	3.60	0.57
2000 Hz	1.41	0.16	3.91	0.58

Table 2 shows that the reverberation time of model N.2 is between 1 and 2 s. The difference between reverberation time and the early decay time is singular, it is very low and does not conform to how it was demonstrated in the previous research above mentioned. The clarity is also anomalous. Its low-frequency values are under 3 dB, which would be suitable for musical performances, but its high-frequency values are above 3 dB (but not too much, between 3.60 and 3.91) as it is suggested for spoken performances. The definition has a similar trend as the clarity: at 125 Hz goes under 0.50 and then it raises till 0.58. The average value of the speech transmission index of model N.2 is 0.60.

The auralisation of several receivers was made for both models. Listening to the auralised files of model N.2, it is possible to perceive a slight echo that is enough to influence the good comprehension of speech. In the auralised file of model N.1, the echo is absent.

5 Discussion and Conclusion

The 3D visibility analysis demonstrated that the structure of model N.1 (the one with *parodoi* between cavea and scene building, and without portico in *summa* cavea) ensures the visibility of the central part of the stage to each spectator. High visibility of the stage is still maintained with the structure of model N.2 (characterised by cavea and scene building forming an enclosed space and by the portico in *summa* cavea), but the stage is not visible by all spectators. Such results may suggest that model N.1 is more reliable than model N.2 but we should also consider that maybe not every seat was supposed to be occupied and that maybe the side areas of the cavea, from which there is limited visibility, were not used. The virtual acoustics analysis seems to confirm the reliability of the reconstruction of model N.1 rather than the one of model N.2. All resulting values of each parameter analysed of model N.1, and the auralisation too, are consistent in demonstrating that such a space would be ideal for acting a spoken performance. While the values obtained from the virtual acoustics analysis of model N.2 do not indicate a clear identification of the possible role of that space, they are inconsistent among them and an echo is perceived from several auralised files in different positions of the seating area.

We may conclude that this research demonstrated that the Roman theatre at the acropolis of Gortyna maintained some Greek characteristics as the presence of the *parodoi* and the absence of the portico in *summa* cavea (Fig. 8). At the same time, we may consider that 3D visibility analysis and virtual acoustics analysis are tools that incite us to think about the architectural structure of the Roman theatres and about its exact function, rather than instruments useful to formulate new conclusive hypotheses. We should wonder if really everyone in a theatre was able to completely see the stage and if the performances were totally clear. We should also contemplate the possibility of mistakes made by the ancient architects. Moreover, we should not forget that, in particular in Roman times, the cavea of the theatres was organised according to the social status of the spectators, so there were probably privileged seats. At the same time, it is not realistic to think that the poorest groups of the society used to go to watch a performance without the possibility to see it and listen to it. 3D visibility analysis, virtual acoustics analysis and auralisation produce suggestions and encourage specialists to investigate more on some aspects. Furthermore, the comparisons of the results obtained analysing both Greek and Roman theatres would help us to understand if the architectural evolution of these monuments was also due to the need to enhance the visibility and the acoustics of these places of entertainment.

The combination of the three instruments is a further step to ensure valuable and meaningful research. However, improvements to this methodology need to be done. First of all, psychoacoustics needs to be considered in such kind of research since the

Fig. 8 Virtual reconstruction of the hypothetical architectural structure of the theatre

perception of sound (as for other senses) is subjected to different factors (age, gender, culture, memories, etc.) (Kolar 2013). To judge the auralised files more extensively and accurately, it would be necessary to create an evaluation test to be filled by a group of people of different ages, cultures and education. The questionnaire can be primarily based on three elements: the expectations on acoustical factors (how much they are considered important), the perception of sound in the different positions in the cavea (rating of annoyance or pleasure), the reaction to the sound (provoked feelings) (Yorukoglu and Kang 2017). Something else that should be considered is the background noise or any other sound that could happen during the performance, even if theatres were not generally placed in the crossroad of very dynamic and populated areas and the retaining wall of the Roman theatres were supposed to acoustically isolate the space from outside noises as stated by Canac. It would be interesting to test such scenario: recreating external soundscape (voices, animals and chariots) and also internal soundscapes (as hubbubs and background music) and including them in the auralisation to verify the quality of the sound and the comprehension of the performance.

This kind of methodology can be applied not only to theatres but also to amphitheatres, stadiums, circuses and all other buildings or monuments where visibility and acoustics play an important role.

Moreover, the results of such kind of study can be useful not only to investigate and interpret the architectural structure of some monuments, but they can be used as an educational instrument as well. The visualisation through 3D models and the listening of auralised files can facilitate the understanding and the memorisation of historical contexts by non-experts. These elements have been combined to develop a Virtual Reality application for head-mounted display to be used onsite or in the museums (Manzetti 2018b). This experience can be improved and can be made more meaningful by stimulating the sense of smell as well (Day 2017).

The research and the methodology presented here have the aim to demonstrate the advantages to adopt an interdisciplinary and multisensory approach. Some results, such as the level of visibility and the acoustics values of monuments or sites that are not fully preserved, can be obtained until now only with this kind of approach. The information collected through this methodology not only enhances our knowledge about ancient buildings but also raises new questions and stimulates new investigations. Hopefully, this methodology will be integrated in the future with approaches that consider the rest of the senses (smell, touch, skin and body sensations) to improve the accuracy of the research and also to expand our vision of ancient societies and not to be limited to the modern conception of the world.

Acknowledgements I would like to thank Dr Landeschi and Dr Betts for giving me the opportunity to contribute with my research to this book.

This research was carried out under the funding of IKY State Scholarship for Foreigners in Greece.

Thanks to Dr Calicchia for her assistance in the acoustics aspect of this research.

Thanks to Dr Sarris for his helpful suggestions.

Thanks to the two referees who enriched the manuscript with their useful comments.

References

Barresi, P., 2004. Gortyna: la sistemazione del teatro all'Acropoli in età Severiana, in: Creta Romana e Protobizantina, Atti Del Convegno (Iraklion 2000). Bottega D'Erasmo, Padova, pp. 557–572.

Beschi, L., 1999. Onorio Belli a Creta: un manoscritto inedito della Scuola Archeologica Italiana di Atene (1587). Scuola Archeologica Italiana di Atene, Atene.

Betts, E., 2017. Senses of the Empire. Multisensory approaches to Roman Culture. Routledge Taylor & Francis Group, London and New York.

Bieber, M., 1981. The History of the Greek and Roman Theatre. Princeton University Press, Princeton.

Bishop, I.D., Wherrett, J.R., Miller, D.R., 2000. Using Image Depth Variables as Predictors of Visual Quality. Environ Plann B Plann Des 27, 865–875. https://doi.org/10.1068/b26101.

Bonetto, J., Francisci, D., 2014. Il teatro del Pythion di Gortina: storia di un teatro romano a Creta, in: Proceedings XVIII International Congress of Classical Archaeology. Presented at the Centro y periferia en el mundo clasico, Museo Nacional de Arte Romano, Merida, pp. 941–944.

Bonetto, J., Francisci, D., Mazzochin, S., 2019. Gortyna IX. Il teatro del Pythion. Scavi e ricerche 2001–2013., Monografie della SAIA. Scuola Archeologica Italiana di Atene, Atene.

Canac, F., 1967. L'acoustique des théatres antiques. Ses enseignements. Centre National de la Recherche Scientifique, Paris.

Christensen, Koutsouris, 2015. Odeon Room Acoustics Software, Version 13, Full User's Manual.

Day, J., 2017. Scents of place and colours of smell. Fragranced entertainmentin ancient Rome, in: Senses of the Empire. Multisensory Approaches to Roman Culture. Routledge Taylor & Francis Group, London and New York.

Day, J., 2013. Making Senses of the Past: Toward a Sensory Archaeology. Southern Illinois University Press.

Devereux, P., 2001. Stone Age Soundtracks: The Acoustic Archaeology of Ancient Sites. Vega, London.

Erdogan, S., 2006. ERATO Project Symposium. Audio visual conservation of the architectural spaces in virtual environment. Proceedings. Yildiz technical University, Istanbul, Turkey.

Falkener, E., 1854. A description of some important theatres and other remains in Crete, from a ms. History of Candia by Onorio Belli in 1586, Supplement to the Museum of Classical Antiquities. Trübner & Co., London.

Fisher, P., Farrelly, C., Maddocks, A., Ruggles, C., 1997. Spatial Analysis of Visible Areas from the Bronze Age Cairns of Mull. Journal of Archaeological Science 24, 581–592.

Foteinou, A., Murphy, D.T., 2011. Perceptual validation in the acoustics modelling and auralization of heritage sites: the acoustic measurement and modelling of St Margaret's Church, York, UK, in: Proceedings of The Acoustics of Ancient Theatres Conference. Presented at the The Acoustics of the Ancient Theatres Conference, Patras.

Frieman, C., Gillings, M., 2007. Seeing is perceiving? World Archaeology 39, 4–16. https://doi.org/10.1080/00438240601133816.

Gade, Angelakis, 2006. Acoustics of ancient Greek and Roman theatres in use today. The Journal of Acoustical Society of America 120, 3148–3156.

Hamilakis, Y., 2013. Archaeology and the Senses. Human Experience, Memory, and Affect. Cambridge University Press.

Hamilakis, Y., 2011. Archaeologies of the Senses [WWW Document]. The Oxford Handbook of the Archaeology of Ritual and Religion. https://doi.org/10.1093/oxfordhb/9780199232444.013.0016.

Iannace, G., Maffei, L., Aletta, F., 2011a. Computer simulation of the effect of the audience on the acoustics of the Roman theatre of Beneventum (Italy), in: Proceedings of The Acoustics of Ancient Theatres Conference. Patras.

Iannace, G., Maffei, L., Trematerra, P., 2011b. The Acoustics Evolution of the large Theatre of Pompeii, in: Proceedings of The Acoustics of Ancient Theatres Conference. Patras.

Kanta, A., Lirintzis, A., Nikolopoulou, K., 2014. Το Μεγάλο Θέατρο της Γόρτυνας-Τα πρώτα αποτελέσματα, in: 1° ΔΙΕΘΝΕς ΔΙΕΠΙΣΤΗΜΟΝΙΚΟ ΣΥΝΕΔΡΙΟ ΓΟΡΤΥΝΑΣ. Presented at the ΄Εν Γορτυνη και 'Αρκαδια εγενετο...,' Εφη Ψιλακη, Μανωλης Δρακακης, Ηρακλειο, pp. 91–99.

Kolar, M., 2013. Archaeological Psychoacoustics at Chavin du Huantar, Peru (Doctoral dissertation). Stanford University, Stanford.

Lake, M.W., Woodman, P.E., 2003. Visibility Studies in Archaeology: A Review and Case Study. Environ Plann B Plann Des 30, 689–707. https://doi.org/10.1068/b29122.

Landeschi, G., Dell'Unto, N., Lundqvist, K., Ferdani, D., Campanaro, D.M., Leander Touati, A.-M., 2016. 3D-GIS as a platform for visual analysis: Investigating a Pompeian house. Journal of Archaeological Science 65, 103–113. https://doi.org/10.1016/j.jas.2015.11.002.

Lokki, T., Southern, A., Siltanen, S., Savioja, L., 2011. Studies of Epidaurus with a hybrid room acoustics modeling method, in: Proceedings of The Acoustics of Ancient Theatres Conference. Patras.

Loots, L., Nackaerts, K., Waelkens, M., 1999. Fuzzy viewshed analysis of the Hellenistic city defence system at Sagalassos, Turkey. Presented at the Archaeology in the age of the internet - CAA97: computer applications and quantitative methods in archaeology. 25th anniversary conference, British archaeological reports, Birmingham, p. ?–?.

Lopez-Menchero Bendicho, V.M., 2013. International Guidelines for Virtual Archaeology: The Seville Principles, in: Good Practice in Archaeological Diagnostics., Natural Science in Archaeology. Springer, Switzerland, pp. 269–283.

Manzetti, M.C., 2018a. Experiencing an Ancient Performances in a Roman theatre, in: Archaeoacoustics III - More on the Archaeology of Sound: Publication of Papers from the Third International Multi-Disciplinary Conference. Presented at the Archaeoacoustics III, The OTS Foundation, Myakka City, Florida, pp. 122–126.

Manzetti, M.C., 2018b. An interdisciplinary approach for the study and the valorization of the Roman theatres of Crete (Doctoral dissertation). School of Architectural Engineering, Technical University of Crete, Chania, Greece.

Manzetti, M.C., Parthenios, P., Sarris, A., 2015. Integrating traditional methods with new technologies, in: 2015 Digital Heritage. Presented at the 2015 Digital Heritage, pp. 173–176. https://doi.org/10.1109/DigitalHeritage.2015.7419480.

Morgan, M.H., 1914. Vitruvius. The ten books on architecture. Harvard University Press, Cambridge.

Paliou, E., Knight, D.J., 2013. Mapping the senses: Perceptual and Social aspects of Late Antique Liturgy in San Vitale, Ravenna, in: Proceedings of CAA 2010, Computer Applications and Quantitative Methods in Archaeology, International Conference, Granada 6-9 April, 2010. Presented at the Computer Applications and Quantitative methods in Archaeology, F. Contreras, M. Farjas and F.J. Melero, Granada, Spain, pp. 229–236.

Paliou, E., Wheatley, D., Earl, G., 2011. Three-dimensional visibility analysis of architectural spaces: iconography and visibility of the wall paintings of Xeste 3 (Late Bronze Age Akrotiri). Journal of Archaeological Science 38, 375–386. https://doi.org/10.1016/j.jas.2010.09.016.

Pappalardo, U., 2007. Teatri Greci e Romani. Arsenale Editore, San Giovanni Lupatoto, Verona.

Pashley, R., 1837. Travels in Crete. John Murray, London.

Pitton de Tournefort, J., 1717. Relation d'un voyage du Levant fait par ordre du Roy. De l'Imprimerie Royale, Paris.

Pococke, R., 1745. Description of the East and some other countries. Bowyer W., London.

Reilly, P., 1991. Towards a Virtual Archaeology, in: Computer Applications and Quantitative Methods in Archaeology 1990, 565. Tempus Reparatum, Oxford, pp. 132–139.

Ruggles, C.L.N., Medyckyj-Scott, D.J., Gruffydd, A., 1993. Multiple viewshed analysis using GIS and its archaeological applications: a case study in northern Mull, in: Andresen, J., T. Madsen and I. Scollar (Eds.), Computing the Past. Presented at the Computer Applications and Quantitative Methods in Archaeology. CAA92, Aarhus University Press, Aarhus, pp. 125–132.

Sarris, A., Papadopoulos, N., 2010. Τεχνική Έκθεση της Γεωφυσικής Έρευνας & Χαρτογράφησης των Αρχαίων Θεάτρων της Ιεράπετρα; & Κουφονησίου (2010). Εργαστήριο Γεωφυσικής-Δορυφορικής Τηλεπισκόπησης & Αρχαιοπεριβάλλοντος. Ινστιτούτο Μεσογειακών Σπουδών, Ρέθυμνο.

Scarre, C., Lawson, G., 2006. Archaeoacoustics, McDonald Institute Monographs. ed. McDonald Instituire for Archaeological Research, Cambridge.

Scuola Archeologica Italiana di Atene, 1984. Creta antica. Cento anni di archeologia italiana, 1884–1984. De Luca, Roma.

Spagnolo, R., 2014. Manuale di acustica applicata. CittàStudi, Torino.

Spratt, T.A.B., 1865. Travels and researches in Crete. John Van Voorst, London.

Taramelli, A., 1902. Cretan Expedition: XXI Gortyna. American Journal of Archaeology 6, 101–165.

Tufte, E., 1990. Envisioning Information. Graphic Press, Michigan University.

Vana Niniou-Kindeli, Chatzidakis, N., 2016. The Roman theatre at Aptera: a preliminary report, in: Roman Crete: New Perspectives. Oxford: Oxbow Books, pp. 127–153.

Veitch, J., 2017. Soundscape of the street. Architectural acoustics in Ostia, in: Senses of the Empire: Multisensory Approaches to Roman Culture. Routledge Taylor & Francis Group, New York, NY, USA, pp. 54–70.

Wheatley, D., 2014. Connecting landscapes with built environments: visibility analysis, scale and the senses, in: Spatial Analysis and Social Spaces. Interdisciplinary Approaches to the Interpretation of Prehistoric and Historic Built Environments. De Gruyter, Boston, pp. 115–134.

Wheatley, D., 1995. Cumulative viewshed analysis: a GIS-based method for investigating inter-visibility, and its archaeological application, in: Archaeology and GIS: A European Perspective. Routlege, London, pp. 171–186.

Yorukoglu, P.N.D., Kang, J., 2017. Development and testing of Indoor Soundscape Questionnaire for evaluating contextual experience in public spaces. Building Acoustics 24, 307–324.

Maria Cristina Manzetti is an archaeologist with a Ph.D. in architecture. She is currently a YUFE postdoc researcher at the Department of History and Archaeology at the University of Cyprus. Her specialty is virtual analyses in archaeological contexts.

"Please, Touch the Exhibits": 3D Archaeology for Experiential Spatialisation

Eleni Bozia

1 Introduction

Recent advances in image capturing and 3D scanning technologies, along with their significant reduction in production costs, have brought to the general public handheld devices equipped with several useful sensors and data collection instruments. As a result, large numbers of artifacts and spaces are 3D digitized. When one moves beyond the "coolness" factor of a 3D model, though, how do they harvest its abundance of information, exploit their digital physicality productively, ultimately reexperiencing the object not through the lens of history but as a "tangible" object? Furthermore, this renewed physicality intrudes in and affects our sense of space, thus making historical artefacts more approachable while also enriching our actual spatiality. Foucault explored this concept of heterogeneous emplacement in his work *Of Other Spaces*. This chapter discusses the mission of digitization projects and particularly the Digital Epigraphy and Archaeology Project (DEA) (www.digitalepigraphy.org) and its collection of 3D digitised material and applications of virtual and augmented reality alongside the Foucauldian notion of heterotopia and heterochrony. I argue that digital archaeology affords us a transcendent understanding of the ancient and the modern world, as it enables us to move beyond ourselves through virtuality while extending ourselves and our perception via augmented reality and advanced physicality. Ultimately, the goal of the chapter is to contextualise epigraphy and archaeology within the concept of spatialisation and open a discussion of the possibilities for "physical contact", reappreciation of the concept of physicality, and the study of digital artefacts.

The chapter first lists briefly a number of digitisation projects of various types that focus on different types of material, eras and areas, all indicative, though, of

E. Bozia (✉)
Department of Classics, University of Florida, Gainesville PO Box 117435, USA
e-mail: bozia@ufl.edu

G. Landeschi and E. Betts (eds.), *Capturing the Senses*,
Quantitative Methods in the Humanities and Social Sciences,
https://doi.org/10.1007/978-3-031-23133-9_7

scholarly attempts towards preservation and dissemination. They all endeavour to answer people's unequivocal need to situate themselves closer to and more meaningfully alongside historical objects, thus necessitating a more consistent and conscious approach to space. The second section explores the significance of space, focusses on the theory of space as a concept and an actuality, and presents Foucault's philosophy to emplace virtual and augmented reality in our experience domain. The following section then discusses the DEA project as a case study. The project's digital repositioning of the 3D artefacts in their original physical context increases accessibility and "tangibility" through interaction design, virtual and augmented reality, and 3D printing, thus reconceptualizing space and reappreciating the user's place within the ancient and modern world. The three *foci* of the project discussed are: 1. natural interaction, 2. spatialised contextualisation and 3. physicality. Advanced interaction design aims at recreating the circumstances of physical interaction with an object, albeit on a digital level, namely, on a computer or a tablet. With regard to contextualisation, an artefact is a mere vessel of a whole gamut of experiences and is intrinsically connected to its findspot. To this end, we work with virtual and augmented reality to reposition the objects back in their surroundings or simply "in front of" the scholar to enhance the possibilities for thorough analysis and better apprehension of their actual role in the history of a place. Finally, concerning physicality, the project reauthenticates the 3D model and reinstitutes its existence, as we consistently resort to 3D printing, offering the possibility for hands-on study of and engagement with the artefacts.

2 Spatialising Archaeology

High-resolution cameras can be found in smartphones along with several user-friendly software applications that process the captured video sequences and produce photorealistic 3D models through photogrammetry without the need for additional expensive equipment. Additionally, low-cost handheld 3D sensors (such as the Structure Sensor by Occipital, Inc.; the RealSense camera by Intel, Inc. and others) can be mounted on portable electronic devices and produce accurate 3D scans of historical objects and other articles of interest.

In this industry-led 3D digitization revolution, hundreds of humanities scholars, such as archaeologists, historians, classicists and conservation specialists as well as enthusiasts, digitise on a regular basis a large number of historical artefacts and publish their 3D digitisation-related findings (Ramírez-Sánchez et al. 2014). The 3D artefacts populate online collections that host thousands of digitally preserved objects of historical significance. In order to understand the magnitude of these industry-led crowd-sourcing initiatives, we could group these projects into two categories: (A) Individual and institution-based initiatives that create and maintain focussed and typically smaller online collections of historical objects. (B) Online repositories of high-resolution and high-polygon-count 3D digitised objects not necessarily focussed on archaeology, such as Sketchfab and Glovius. I briefly mention here some representative projects.

- African Fossils: http://africanfossils.org/search.
- Archaeology Data Service (ADS). ADS provides a viewer for rendering and interacting with 2D and 3D data: http://archaeologydataservice.ac.uk/archives/view/amarna_leap_2011/downloads.cfm?obj=yes&obj_id=38819&CFID=46546&CFTOKEN=FDFFB482-1807-4B58-91F2D23D46220951.
- Cultural Informatics Research Group: http://www.culturalinformatics.org.uk/.
- Digital Libraries for 3D Documents, Institute of Computer Science II, Computer Graphics, Universität Bonn: http://cg.cs.uni-bonn.de/en/activities/digital-libraries-for-3d-documents/.
- Dotty View: http://dotdotty.com/.
- Glovius: https://cloud.glovius.com/.
- London Charter for the Computer-based Visualization of Cultural Heritage: http://www.londoncharter.org/.
- MorphoMuseum: http://morphomuseum.com/.
- Scan the World Initiative that is a collection of printable 3D models: https://www.myminifactory.com/scantheworld/.
- Spatial Models of Great Buildings: http://www.greatbuildings.com/types/models/spatial_models.html.
- The Annual Conference of Museums and the Web in 2016 addressed these very issues. http://mw2016.museumsandtheweb.com/paper/collections-cubed-into-the-third-dimension/.
- The Digital Epigraphy and Archaeology Project: www.digitalepigraphy.org.
- The Dynamic collections project at Lund University, which is based on 3DHop technology, was developed by the ISTI Visual Computing Lab, an open-source solution to upload and create WebGL-like 3D contents: https://portal.research.lu.se/portal/en/projects/dynamic-collections(9a034d5a-e9e0-4688-93d0-ec272beaee1e).html?fbclid=IwAR009Jnt5ORd7_xpHp_Qv70gLl6w2jNvH0e98hHloOrLpWcmCzUc_ck0wrE.
- The Smithsonian has a 3D data collection (https://dpo.si.edu/) featuring Autodesk's x3d viewer.
- The Stanford 3D Scanning Repository: http://graphics.stanford.edu/data/3Dscanrep/.
- The University of Michigan Online Repository of Fossils: http://umorf.ummp.lsa.umich.edu/wp/.
- 3D Heritage Online Presenter with an open-access viewer: http://3dhop.net/.
- There are commercial services (by Google, SketchFab, Autodesk, Verold, etc.) for hosting and sharing digital models that do not restrict their content in any particular topic such as archaeology. Nevertheless, collections of 3D models of archaeological artefacts can be created within such services with free and unlimited uploads/downloads.
- Contrary to the aforementioned free commercial services, the Digital Archive Record (tDAR) is a paid service for the storage and preservation of archaeological

research meant to improve access to these data. tDAR is developed and maintained by Digital Antiquity. Currently, the user can pay to upload files with metadata or browse and download files for free. However, tDAR provides no functionality for viewing or interacting with this kind of data online, limiting the potential reach of these materials.

The mere number of developed projects indicates the magnitude of scholarly efforts to engage with artefacts more closely and, in the case of archaeology, preserve antiquity. Initially, such projects were exciting for the possibility of engaging with technology and determining whether it could accommodate traditional humanities fields and objects that, under any other circumstances, would have been considered diametrically opposite to technological devices. The significance of the collaboration and its results rests in the simple irony of the coexistence of two, by definition, disparate research *foci* and scientific methodologies. How does one not only bridge the chasm between an object that embodies the human record, essentially a part of life that no longer exists, and an object that redefines daily existence but also creates a space that needs both the above to bring about a meaningful experience? This very experience or reexperience, if you will, signifies the elimination of time and place barriers, thus effectuating a heterotopia and heterochrony for historical artefacts alongside their recreators.

3 Digitisation and Virtuality as Heterotopias

In this section, I discuss 3D digitisation and virtual and augmented reality as forms of a body-centred approach that does not mean to replace the real artefact or simply enhance reality. I argue instead that such an embodiment—both on behalf of the user and the object—brings about a sense of the Foucauldian heterotopic and heterochronic reality.

What makes space as both a concept and a reality so important and so multi-modal to have been politicised, legitimised and illegitimised, glorified and condemned to infamy? Space engulfed in and beyond its ubiquity cannot avoid its existence and the bearing it has on human existence. There have been several philosophical problematisations and explorations of the concept of space—internal and external, social, public and private. Bachelard (1994) examines interior space and intimate spaces, such as the house, as a means of prefiguring and understanding the soul. Blanchot, in *The Space of Literature* (1989), presents language as creating and constituting space.[1] Heidegger (1927) and Ingold (2000) present geographical space. And Harvey (1991), following Schivelbusch, credits the role of transportation systems for the shaping of space and time. Lefebvre (1992) discusses space as a social construction of capitalist societies. Low (2014) considers culture spatialisation and space as social production and social construction. McKittrick (2014) discusses space along racial and sexual

[1] Bakhtin also discusses space in literature and introduces the concept of chronotope in *Theory of the Literary Chronotope Reflections, Applications, Perspectives*. Gent: Academia Press. 2010.

lines, and Woolf (2005) criticises and problematises gendered space in A *Room of One's Own*. This chapter focusses on Foucault's theorization, as it accommodates a consideration of the real and unreal that then, in turn, makes us rethink established knowledge and, during this process, creates new knowledge as well. Against this backdrop, I argue that 3D digitised worlds constitute their own space—reviving a world that used to exist differently and now survives both through a recreation but also within contemporary reality as an actual place.

Foucault outlined the concept of heterotopia on three occasions. In the preface of "Les Mots et Les Choses" (The Order of Things), he described literary space. He then discussed the topic in a radio broadcast followed by a lecture to a group of architects in 1967. In both cases, he explored the social constructions of space. The foundational precepts of this analysis did not appear until 1984 when he published "Des Espaces Autres", which was translated into English under the title "Of Other Spaces" or "Different Spaces" in 1986. Foucault redefines—or perhaps better, defines—space as not simply our emplacement in the world but also as conceived beyond sensory perception. He avoids the reductionism of locality by exploring the essence of a space and its representational and interpretational power that moves beyond the sensory homogeneity that limits us as observers. His delineation moves the person into a more participatory role, experiencing the space. According to this theory, heterotopias are spaces outside of all places, even though one may be able to pinpoint their locale. For Foucault, space is malleable and constantly constructible; it is an organic system of relations, differences, similarities, agreement, resistance and change. It is, above all, dialectical. When he defines heterotopia, he describes it as the space of the outside (*du dehors*)[2] and says that it is the space that is "outside of all places"[3] (p. 3–4). In his insightful analysis of heterotopia, Topinka also pinpoints that the concept of space in the Foucauldian universe is more meaningful when we examine it against the backdrop of his ideas about knowledge and knowledge production. Based on the philosopher's analysis of Borges' Funes and the exigency to rearrange our knowledge by inverting the operating table, Topinka argues that: "Knowledge, for Foucault, emerges in a clash of forces. Heterotopias, even as they contest received knowledge, participate in this battle, producing knowledge by problematizing order and space" (2010, 64). Johnson (2006, 78) also argues that heterotopias: "Like utopias, these sites relate to other sites by both representing and at the same time inverting them". Deleuze (1980) also embraces and explores this order of things, the production of knowledge and the need to step outside or move beyond known formations to fully understand. The "outside" or "beyond" do not necessarily denote separation, but it is the concept of comparing and contrasting, thus reconceiving and rethinking.[4] In his discussion of virtual space, Maggini comprehensively concludes that: "Late modern virtual places open new possibilities for territoriality without necessarily succumbing

[2] The concept of the experience of the outside and the role of the subject was also analysed in his essay *La pensée du dehors* (1966).

[3] I am using the translation by Miskowiec (1986).

[4] Colebrook (2003) provides a comparative reading of Deleuze and Foucault on the concept of space.

to the false dilemma of digital utopia or dystopia. Hence, fully immersive digital environments are to be experienced both as an everyday lived experience and as a challenge to it…Digital virtual places are heterotopias in the sense of Char Davies' 'changing spaces' that are at once like and unlike real ones, therefore allowing for transformational processes to take place".

According to Foucault, a mirror is a perfect example; it is a no-place (a utopia), but also a heterotopia, as it actually exists. He says: "Starting from this gaze that is, as it were, directed toward me, from the ground of this virtual space that is on the other side of the glass, I come back towards myself I begin again to direct my eyes toward myself and to reconstitute myself there where I am. The mirror functions as a heterotopia in this respect: it makes this place that I occupy at the moment when I look at myself in the glass at once absolutely real, connected with all the space that surrounds it, and absolutely unreal, since in order to be perceived it has to pass through this virtual point which is over there" (p. 4).

Foucault then defines five heterotopic principles, the third and fourth of which serve as a framework for our virtual (re)creation of objects and space. According to the third principle: "The heterotopia is capable of juxtaposing in a single real place several places, several sites that are in themselves incompatible" (p. 6). By this definition, when we recreate a space virtually, we do not simply recreate the past or leave behind the space we inhabit. There is within the user the sense of multiplicity and a set of coexisting realities. There have been extensive discussions on the authenticity of the reproduced artefact, the authenticity of experience in the cases of virtually recreated spaces and an overall impugning of augmented spaces that part of the scholarly community has defended, arguing the advantages of experiential learning and the opportunities to increase the user's perception of space, place and culture within.[5] All these are undeniable qualities of new technologies but inevitably focus on the concept of the user as an impostor. The primary goal of recent advances is to help people further their understanding of past civilisations. But what about the user as a participant? What about the coexistence of spaces of the past with the space that the user is holding at present? I believe that these technologies contribute to a much more meaningful participatory actuality that combines past and present social production in the forms of the artefacts and the historical places on the one hand and modern devices and places on the other. This mixed reality also produces a mixed social construction. Erwine (2016), in her book *Creating Sensory Spaces,* confirms the importance of sight and observation but also acknowledges what she calls "sensory homogeneity" that is incurred. She insists on the accumulation and collaboration of all the senses as well as the necessity for the individual's participatory role, stating: "As Western culture has become the culture of the eye, the separation this creates between observer and that which is observed has contributed to the culture of 'I'…This action disembodies us" (2016, 16). This disembodiment is precisely what the DEA's NUI and augmented reality options try to overcome, offering the user a wholesome and

[5] For discussions of authenticity, see Benjamin (1999), Di Giuseppantonio Di Franco's edited volume (2018) and particularly Chap. 8 for further bibliography on the topic.

consequential experience instead.[6] The project focusses on advancing the tangibility of artefacts and on reentering them into everyday experiences, thus redefining ancient artefacts within the contemporary experiential culture. Ultimately the user's sense of space is altered through interaction with objects that are not generally part of their environment through an increasingly alert, conscious, contentious, critical or even benign engagement with them.

In her ethnographic work, Setha Low defines social construction as referring to: "Spatial transformations through peoples' social interactions, conversations, memories, feelings, imaginings, and use—or absences—into places, scenes and actions that convey particular meanings" (2014: 35). Mixed realities—the amalgamation of digitisation and augmented virtuality—could fit the above description. Engagements with exhibits in more casual settings can bring about ferments between the past and the present but also procure a set of current experiences that relate to the user's understanding of the self, giving another dimension to the artefact and/or the historical construction. This aspect of involvement then breaks the time continuum and brings us to the fourth principle of Foucault's heterotopia, namely, heterochrony, which is defined as: "Beginning to function at full capacity when men arrive at a sort of absolute break with their traditional time...there are heterotopias of indefinitely accumulating time, for example, museums and libraries. Museums and libraries have become heterotopias in which time never stops building up and topping its own summit...yet the experience is just as much the rediscovery of time, it is as if the entire history of humanity reaching back to its origin were accessible in a sort of immediate knowledge" (p. 7).[7]

In the cases of individual databases and projects that provide advanced digital sensory exploration and apprehension of objects, these digitised realities substantiate exactly that, namely, the condition of the rediscovery of time through and against the backdrop of the rediscovery of space(s). Essentially no geographical place or place in time has a standalone existence. Instead, they all acquire their essence through and in relation to one another, transcending not only boundaries but also substantialising themselves thus. Foucault describes this as "simultaneity", a notion that summarises the interconnecting realities of post-structuralism. Albeit written several decades before the birth of these technologies, the French philosopher notices the changes in technology and people's inherent interpretational socio-cultural constructions of

[6] Similarly, Harding et al. (2002) present a method to explore multi-sensory data in geospatial visualisation. Also, Betts in her edited volume *Senses of the Empire* (2017) daringly attempts to summarise methodological efforts to recapture the sensorial attributes of the Empire based on historical sources and archaeological findings. She does admit, though, that: "Recapturing sensory data is difficult since '[t]he senses seldom leave a direct imprint in the archaeological record and most typically must be implicitly inferred' ...in both qualitative discourses and quantitative analyses the evidence from textual and visual sources can be combined with archaeology to construct multi-sensory interpretations of particular aspects of Roman life" (2017, 7–8). On the exploration of the senses towards reconstructive and more experiential archaeology, see also Pellini et al. (eds.) (2015). See Skeates and Day (2020) for scholarship on sensory archaeology and culture studies.

[7] Radford et al. (2015, 733) explore the library against the backdrop of this Foucauldian concept and argue that: "Drawing together the constructs of heterotopia and serendipity can enrich the understanding of how libraries are experienced as sites of play, creativity, and adventure".

place and time. At the beginning of his treatise, he says: "We are in the epoch of simultaneity: we are in the epoch of juxtaposition, the epoch of the near and far, of the side-by-side, of the dispersed. We are at a moment, I believe, when our experience of the worlds is less that of a long life developing through time than that of network that connects points and intersects with its own skein" (p. 1).

4 Digital Databases: Preserving, Validating and Completing the Archaeological Record

Preservation and dissemination of archaeological material is, of course, a *sine qua non* for the experiential spatialisation I discussed above. However, there are existential issues that hinder this type of meaningful engagement and have also contributed to archaeology's distance from contemporary audiences. On the one hand, the focus usually turns to highvisibility sites and constructions. Such choices validate and consequently may also invalidate certain aspects of the archaeological record, as they "condemn" certain types of objects.[8] On the other hand, the fragility of the material is a prohibitive factor. As a result, as such material is housed in museums, libraries and institutions worldwide, their location significantly thwarts their accessibility. Technology, high-resolution 2D pictures and electronic databases attempt to overcome the aforementioned limitations. However, issues that put projects and databases at a disadvantage are the use of cumbersome or expensive equipment as well as the fact that they are not designed as dynamic databases that can cater to the needs and questions of each user. Moreover, the lack of contact with the physical object as a tridimensional structure still significantly obstructs research.

The Digital Epigraphy and Archaeology group (DEA) argues the significance of dynamic digital libraries of 3D digitised artefacts enhanced with an advanced Natural User Interface (Barmpoutis and Bozia 2016). The project focusses both on ektypa and other historical objects. The significance of ektypa (squeezes, *Abklatsch*, *estampages*) lies in their inherent qualities as media and mediators of culture and literature. However, due to their location on other artefacts (statue bases, columns, etc.), they can be overlooked, an oversight that is, in turn, reductive to the entire artefact. However, their study is more often than not the way *par excellence* to contextualise the artefact. It is also a unique way to bring cultural understanding through language. Therefore, preservation and thorough analysis of ektypa are the unequivocal means to breaking the space-time continuum that obstructs our appreciation of the past by means of its expressive verbal powers. It should also be pointed out that ektypa, albeit copies of inscriptions, are themselves artefacts, and, in cases when the original inscription is lost or severely weathered, they preserve a better record of the inscribed text.

[8] For instance, ektypa have not been considered important carriers of information or worth preserving when compared to the actual artefact. So, there are not many projects focussing on their digital preservation and/or study.

Regarding other kinds of artefacts, archaeologists tend to focus on the digitisation of sites or larger constructions as the means for cultural appropriation of ancient civilisations. The DEA has refocused scholarly attention on reexamining fragments of those civilisations and emplacing them within our everyday surroundings. Thus far, under the auspices of the project and its collaborators, the Rosetta Stone,[9] collections of renaissance statues, British coins of the age of Henry III, lace[10] and embossments on Abraham Lincoln's letters, among other objects, have been digitised and offered for modern analysis and contextualisation. Moreover, advanced visualisations, virtual and augmented reality, and 3D printing have repositioned them, making them accessible for closer study. At the same time, the users familiarise themselves with them and appreciate them as carriers of the aura of the past while situating them within their cultural context.

4.1 Procedural Facilitation

Thus far, several projects, including but not limited to the EAGLE consortium, the Center for Epigraphical and Palaeographical Studies at Ohio State University; the Aleshire Center at the University of California, Berkeley and the US Epigraphy Project at Brown University, among others, feature digital libraries of squeezes. Also, 3D digitisation projects have been undertaken by museums, including the Epigraphic Museum of Athens (Papadaki et al. 2015; Sullivan 2011), Museo Arqueológico Nacional de Madrid (Ramírez-Sánchez et al. 2014), Museo Nazionale Romano di Palazzo Altemps (Barmpoutis et al. 2015), Museo Geologico Giovanni Capellini di Bologna (Abate and Fanti 2014), St. George's Hall in Liverpool (Cooper and Sportun 2007), the Archaeological Museum of Milan (Gonizzi and Guidi 2013) and several other museums and institutes (Landon and Seales 2006; Levoy et al. 2000).

Additionally, several novel methods for scanning, processing and analysing 3D models of inscriptions have been developed, including methods for text extraction from inscriptions (Aswatha et al. 2014; Sullivan 2011), accurate 3D scanning of inscriptions (Papadaki et al. 2015), visualisation of inscriptions (Bozia et al. 2014), 3D visualisation for better contextualisation (Greggio and Salemi 2016) and 3D digitisation of rock surfaces (Vavulin et al. 2019) as well as 3D applications for other archaeological artefacts (Babeu 2011; Esteban and Schmitt 2004; Malzbender et al. 2001; Pollefeys et al. 2001). Comparative studies of 3D scanning methods for cultural heritage can be found in (Pavlidis et al. 2007; Wachowiak and Karas 2009; Böhler and Marbs 2004).

The DEA project has addressed the issue in its foundation by developing and exploring cost-effective methods for digitisation. More specifically, the project employs the shape-from-shading (SFS) 3D digitization of ektypa, using a flatbed scanner, various visualisation modes, and options for measurements and analysis of

9 Amin et al. (2018).

10 Farmer et al. (2015).

lettering techniques and constructional characteristics, respectively, depending on the artefact (Barmpoutis et al. 2010). Such options facilitate dating, attribution, fragment identification, text or even structure reuse. Jameson (2004) eulogises the inclusion of images of manuscripts in digital databases. She states: "The images dramatically increase access to source materials, reduce the power of the scholar as 'gatekeeper', expose the scholar's judgments to wider scrutiny, and make it more likely that readers or users will actually collaborate in the work of perfecting the state of scholarship". The DEA espouses this precept, as the database is not only meant as a repository of artefacts but also aims at disseminating the ektypa and inviting new readings of the inscribed text.

For the digitisation of other artefacts, we have used the Structure Sensor™ by Occipital, which was attached in front of a tablet computer (iPad Air™ by Apple). The resolution of the depth sensor was 640 × 480 pixels at 30 frames per second and was calibrated so that it records depth in the range from 0.4 to 3.0 m, which is adequate for capturing life-size statues. Another depth sensor, Kinect™ by Microsoft, has also been used in our depth fusion experiments, which were performed on a 64-bit computer with an Intel Core i7™ CPU at 2.80 GHz and 8 GB RAM. Both Kinect and Structure sensors had a similar resolution, range of operation and field of view.

In all cases, the equipment utilised is not financially burdensome. The DEA constantly explores methodological approaches and devices that can be accessible to all users. The main goal is not only to explore technological advances but also to achieve a sustainable machine user interaction/dependency that can ultimately bring about more projects and digitised artefacts.

4.2 *The User as a Participant in the Archaeological Record*

Another feature that contributes to active engagement with the artefacts is the option to virtually imitate actual physical interaction between an epigraphist, scholar or student and the paper copy of the inscription. Thus, the user can better visualise the object of study and reexamine weathered parts of the ektypon by manipulating the perspective and the lighting. These methodologies do not enhance physicality and tangibility in the traditional sense, but increase interactivity with the artefact. The user should also be able to engage in a dialogue with the objects and ultimately pursue their study and understanding from their scholarly perspective without being impeded or guided by technological constraints. The artefacts' metadata record is an integral part of their contextualisation and the cultural understanding they can afford. To this end, the DEA database includes all the relevant (contextual) fields of information about the inscription and links to all other online resources containing information about the artefact. The user also has the option to add any field from a drop-down menu list. Additionally, the editable metadata fields provide more options for each database.[11] Being in the position to have a collective record of the ektypon

[11] http://research.dwi.ufl.edu/www.digitalepigraphy.org/edit.php?heightmap=4uk52idgb0a3xlnf.

and the inscription, the researcher has the opportunity to pose new questions or old questions on a new basis. So, instead of a simple hyperlink that guides the user towards other resources and has been described by Bodel as crude contextualisation (Bodel 2012, 280), one can comprehensively study the artefact. Compiling such records also facilitates comparative studies of large numbers of artefacts.

More specifically, the DEA database features an editor where the user can add, delete and work on metadata fields according to the available information, of course, but also their research focus. The editor is also provided in different languages so that the user may not have to choose between the technological facility and language fluency. The *foci* of the metadata are the following:

1. Preservation of the traditional nature of the data—terminological accuracy along with the possibility for keyword search.
2. Accommodation of every type of format of the data—both the digitised and the metadata.
3. Providing an all-encompassing database that will not direct the type of research one can conduct but will instigate new questions instead.
4. Effective communication between computer scientists and humanists to find a common point of reference between creating efficient algorithms and databases while retaining the nature of epigraphic and archaeological studies.
5. Option to add all existing information about the digitised artefact that could highlight other or even broader cultural and political aspects. So, the user can include images, scans of the monument, or the site where the artefact is/was located, museum information and other data that will generate a holistic record of the artefact.

Finally, the DEA facilitates the dissemination of the 3D digitised objects by providing users with an embeddable 3D viewer, which can be easily imported into third-party databases, collections and personal websites (Fig. 1).

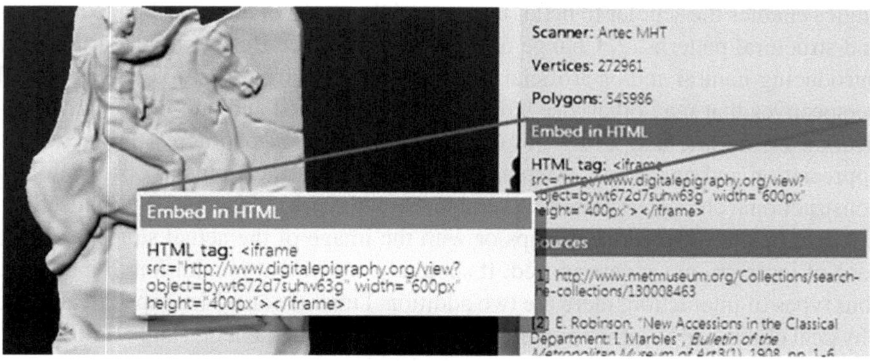

Fig. 1 Screenshot of the DEA metadata environment

4.3 Bridging the Gap Between Users and Usability

The DEA also attempts to remedy issues of usability, as there seems to be a notable disconnect between the research on these technologies and the actual use in the professional epigraphic and archaeological practice, and it has been hard for non-technology-oriented audiences to handle and manipulate tridimensional data, using conventional computer equipment (Barmpoutis and Bozia 2016).[12] Under such circumstances, one cannot fully utilise all the additional information that a 3D model affords, making technology a mere fancy addition without obvious advantages. To this end, the DEA provides an interface that allows the users to naturally "hold" digitised inscriptions and interact actively with them as if they were real physical objects. They also interact with metadata and multi-modal data, such as text and images.

Technological advances alone, though, cannot guarantee enhanced research possibilities, as usability is concomitant with the human factor. So, the DEA is also concerned with enhancing user facility and gearing technology towards imitating natural human interaction. The DEA team has been interacting with adopters of the toolbox, users, scholars who are uploading their collections, and finally, students, inquiring about the movements that accompany actual physical interaction with artefacts. How does one handle an ektypon? What does it take to read it more closely? How close does one need to be depending on its letter size or even its condition? What are the most common statues' postures, and how can we spot a renaissance copy from a Greek or Roman original? The goals of our interaction were threefold: (a) study the various forms of physical interaction that epigraphists and archaeologists have with their object of study as a real physical object; (b) expose scholars to a digital interface that imitates their interaction routine, using digital replicas of physical objects and (c) explore the kinds of questions that researchers ask to design interactions and options that open up their fields of inquiry. The three main types of interaction are 1. Change of point of view: Observation of the artefact from different viewing angles enables the scholar to better understand the shape of the inscribed letterforms and structural patterns. 2. Change of lighting conditions: Relighting the artefact by introducing natural and/or artificial light and shadows from multiple angles reveal perspectives that may otherwise have remained obscured and unnoticed. 3. Magnification of the artefact: Close observation of any region of interest brings a new appreciation and opens new avenues for fragment identification and observation of constructional characteristics. 4. Several levels and types of 3D and 2D visualisations as edge, height or fingerprint maps or with the image of the actual squeeze (in the case of inscriptions) superimposed. It should be noted that in addition to the above four types of interaction, there are two additional interactions. More specifically, the physical object can be either portable, such as a small fragment or a large rigid object. In the first case, the inscription can be moved with respect to the fixed observer or the fixed light source, while in the case of large rigid objects, the observer and the light

[12] http://www.digitalepigraphy.org/museum/collection/draghi-E-leoni/.

source move with respect to the fixed inscription, thus maintaining a more intuitive engagement with the object or area of interest.

According to the above analysis, in the case of digitised inscriptions, a Natural User Interface (NUI) should provide the means for an epigraphist to create and enjoy an experience that closely resembles real physical interaction, thus eliminating assumed time and spatial barriers. Ultimately, such interactions effectuate renewed experiences—new lives for the artefacts and enhanced conception of the objects, the space, and the self. The type of physicality the project promotes transcends the notion of reality, as the user experiences an enhanced tangible interaction with the digital artefact. The DEA is not concerned with the sensory aspects of physicality but with the latter's reconsideration through digital methodologies. It is not a matter of replicating the physical object along with its tactile attributes but of reestablishing the concept of the tangibility of the object and reexploring its potential through a virtual environment. To the same end, the DEA is also working with 3D printing with a view to reconstituting the "tangibility" of the digital object.

5 Augmented Reality for Epigraphy and Archaeology, or How to Bring Holograms of Artefacts to the Classroom

Hamilakis, in his book *Archaeology and the Senses,* describes the concept and, subsequently the practice of sensory archaeology as: "[Not] the rejection of thinking in favour of feeling and lived experience, but rather the reconstitution of thinking as another form of felt experience, as sensorial and affective practice, interwoven with all other embodied practices—thinking through the living and sensing body" (2013, 196).

However, most projects are limited either by the modality of the content or by the delivery mechanism of the educational material. Additionally, they lack the synaesthetic parameter that can grant a degree of reality and understanding that can be afforded through the stimulation of more senses than vision.[13] Flynn criticises the lifelessness of 3D digitised virtual replicas of places and artefacts and proceeds with an extensive discussion of the lack of embodiment that results in a lack of understanding (Flynn 2007, 354–364). Therefore, an advanced solution to this limitation that would also enhance the perception of an object within the user's space is the creation of mixed reality (Milgram and Kishino 1994), a virtual world that would also allow for the embodied participation of the users. Brondi et al. (2016) discuss mixed reality and natural interaction in two cultural heritage applications with the use of an accessible infrastructure.[14]

Such an affordance also affects the educational parameter through experiential learning. The latter is a well-studied research area, and the connection between embodied action and learning outcome has been extensively examined (Alibali and

[13] See above n. 6.

[14] See also Hervy et al. (2015) who present an interface for a scale model of Nantes' harbour activity.

Fig. 2 Interactive visual inspection of a 3D digitised inscription along with the inscription bearer. The user can view the object from different perspectives using natural motions

Nathan 2009; Eisenberg and Pares 2014, 344–8; Goldin-Meadow 1999). Several researchers emphasise the contribution of embodiment to learning (Abrahamson and Lindgren 2014; Eisenberg and Pares 2014, 347–8; Goldin-Meadow 2009). Additionally, there is substantial scholarship in different academic fields to demonstrate that mixed-reality environments enhance educational experiences, leading to better learning outcomes. Lindgren and Johnson-Glenberg (2013) discuss the advantages of mixed reality extensively and present guidelines as to how this is to be achieved within a learning environment.

To this end, the DEA interface allows for interactive manipulation of a 3D digitised inscription bearer to better contextualise both the inscribed text and the artefact. It should also be noted that the user can perform an interactive manipulation of the perspective simultaneously with the interactive relighting to achieve a more realistic interaction that causes relighting and a change of point of view at the same time. The user can also interact with the 3D object using touch gestures and select regions of interest. This action initiates other data tools, such as the image viewer or the edge filter, as shown in this example (Fig. 2).

5.1 3D Holographic Database

Aiming to reconstitute the physicality and naturalness of experience, the DEA interface has effectuated the enhanced sensorial and affective qualities of 3D digitisation and virtuality by using augmented reality head-mounted displays, such as Microsoft's Hololens glasses.

The system enables the users to browse through 3D databases of inscriptions and visualise the inscription within their actual physical space, such as an office or classroom. Once the user positions the hologram of the inscription in a particular location, such as the top of the desk, it remains there, allowing them to move around the inscription and study the artefact as a whole, up close and from different perspectives. Similarly, multiple inscriptions can be positioned next to one another, providing the opportunity for comparative readings, a profound study of lettering techniques, and the potential identification and pairing of fragments. Such an enhanced rendering enables the user to work with their hands, "touching" the digital objects and reinstating in a way their physical presence.

In the current phase of the project, 3D models from the Digital Epigraphy and Archaeology database were imported into the Hololens Augmented Reality headset. The user can browse the 3D database of inscriptions by performing natural hand gestures, such as pointing, picking, moving and dragging. Once the user selects an inscription, they can place its hologram within the physical space, for example, on the top of a desk. The user can study the inscription by naturally walking around the hologram. Fine details of the inscription can be studied by scaling up the hologram using natural hand gestures. In addition, the user can rotate, scale and move the hologram in the real space, as well as open multiple holograms simultaneously. This feature is useful, especially for the comparative study of objects. For example, multiple inscribed fragments can be brought together as holograms on the top of a table and studied next to one another. Furthermore, the benefits of this project are numerous, as it allows the inscriptions to be studied along with their bearer, thus contextualising the inscription and providing a holistic record of the artefact to the scholar. Finally, classrooms, libraries and museums are a few examples of environments that can be augmented using the models from our database, offering a unique learning experience to students, scholars and visitors in general. A live demo of the holographic interface is available to watch at: https://www.youtube.com/watch?v=yh6MyLLFSTo.

The facility to study artefacts through this virtual physicality while having a creating and participatory role resembles Borges' table in the story of Funes, which I mentioned above. In this work, the protagonist suffers an accident that leaves him unable to forget anything. Therefore, he needs to find a non-linear form of memory and knowledge and attempts to create a new language to be in a position to examine, store and work through knowledge. Similarly, Foucault presents heterotopia as a space where one examines many spaces in one. Therefore, in addition to preservation, dissemination and the multiple other advantages of 3D digitisation and augmented reality, one needs to also reappreciate the production of new knowledge. The DEA focusses on advanced visualisations and enhanced physicality to enable the user to study the artefact closely but also reexperience it by reembodying its physical existence within virtuality that, to some extent, involves the user as well.[15] Rousseaux and Thounevin embrace Foucault's theory, on the basis of which they reconstruct virtually an abbey in Compiègne that was partially destroyed in 1790. Their approach, contrary to the DEA, chose to effectuate the philosopher's claim to the rebelliousness of heterotopy. They decided that "Anachronisms were not necessarily problematic and that an air of fiction or even scandal could be maintained" (Rousseaux and Thounevin 2009, 180). The case of the abbey, which is still part of contemporary life to some extent, and therefore is still being experienced by people,

[15] Landeschi (2019, 8), on a similar note, argues: "Considering the human body as a 'universal measurement' (Betts 2017, 23) whose physiological characteristics are almost unchanged from antiquity, it makes sense to use it as a proxy for exploring the perceptual activity of past human agents". See also Richards-Rissetto et al. (2012).

Fig. 3 On the left: a photograph captured by our holographic application, showing the hologram of an inscription rendered on top of a real table. On the right: a photograph of the physical space is shown for comparison without any holograms

may necessitate a certain degree of liberty. On the other hand, the DEA has utilised Foucault's rebelliousness more practically, as the project considers digital tangibility, physicality and the augmented degree of realism as the major immanent factors of reconsideration and rebellious reappreciation of knowledge.[16] So, the DEA focusses on a type of advanced physicality that may lack the sensory aspects of tactility but provides options for study and visualisation that are not available in real life and can facilitate and reconstitute physicality and its affordances (Fig. 3).[17]

5.2 *Reconstituting Physicality Through 3D Printing*

The last component of the DEA's attempts to re-physicalise the past is 3D printing, an attempt towards actual physical presence that still stems from the digital object. Benjamin's words on authenticity may be ringing heavily in our ears, but, as I have argued elsewhere, modern technologies can now claim a different type of originality (Bozia 2018). Additionally, one cannot be reductive when recreating experiences for present and future generations and finding a renewed physicality and locale for objects that would otherwise be considered simply remnants of the past and irrelevant to modern audiences. Sloan (2012), as well as Neely and Langer (2013), among

[16] Chen et al. (2013) experiment with an augmented reality information system to enhance the museum experience in Taiwan. Hoang and Cox (2017) also stress the exigency for an "interweaved reality", as they call it, where virtual reality mixes with physical environment thus: "Allow[ing] the visitors to draw the connection between the two sources of information" (402).

[17] There are haptic technologies that can recreate the sense of a physical object more closely, but such a discussion is beyond the scope of this chapter. For information on the topic and studies on haptic technologies and their advantages, see Israr et al. (2016), Ryu et al. (2006).

others, extol the contributions of 3D printing to the embodiment, engagement and understanding.[18]

The DEA has been working with the Marston Science Library at the University of Florida that uses Fusion F400s, F306s, Lulzbot Taz6, and Ultimaker 3 Extended 3D printers. The printers offer options for different materials, such as ceramics and metal. Such possibilities advance the sense of touch and reality of experience even further. The DEA, cognizant of the above analyses and the patent need for physical interaction, has been using 3D printing as another means of experiential spatialisation. Several artefacts have already been re-physicalised thus and brought to classrooms and research meetings.

As Erwine (2016, 88) points out, "When our hands probe the texture of a surface, we don't register a simple feeling of "touch." Instead, we experience an intricate combination of stimuli relating to pressure, skin stretch, vibration, temperature, etc."; and later, "As this process is extended to our participation in the built environment, we come to understand objects and structures in relation to the measure and form of our own bodies" (2016, 99). This chapter makes a case for a different type of physicality that explores other aspects of the digital object and the advantages of digital technologies. Sensorial apprehension is undeniably seminal for our understanding of the world. With this in mind, the DEA explores the affordances of a digital-physical existence and its unique sensorial presence.

6 Conclusion

In conclusion, technological advances have afforded us unique opportunities for research, teaching, preservation and dissemination. A crucial aspect that has evaded archaeological studies, though, as we have focussed solely on rediscovering and understanding the past, is that, when we view historical artefacts only as objects of study, we are being reductive to their existence and transhistorical significance. The concept of cultural presence was developed in the early 2000s and explored as a *sine qua non* for historical understanding, the notion, as Pujol-Tost (2017, 249) puts it, of: "Being there and making sense there and then together". Within this framework, the DEA aims to re-physicalise artefacts, giving them a contemporary afterlife, promoting their relevance in modern cultural understanding, and ultimately creating our own here and now and bringing the past to it.

Peter Aronsson, the European National Museums Project Coordinator, said: "A museum isn't a house. It is an idea in debate". The DEA has embraced this very premise. Enhanced visualisations, augmented reality and 3D printing enable users to connect with each object, reach their own understandings and apprehend the artefact

[18] For further bibliography on 3D printing, see Bozia (2018).

within their own culture.[19] Such a meaningful, engaged, active and participatory presence can guarantee a cosmopolitan shared future that will enrich the lives and experiences of future generations.

References

Abate, D., and F. Fanti. 2014. La valorizzazione digitale del Museo Geologico Giovanni Capellini di Bologna. *Archeomatica* 5.1:6–9.

Abrahamson, D., and R. Lindgren. 2014. Embodiment and embodied design. In *The Cambridge Handbook of the Learning Sciences*, ed. Robert Keith Sawyer, 358–376. Cambridge, MA: Cambridge University Press.

Alibali, M. W., and Mitchell, J. Nathan. 2009. Teachers' gestures as a means of scaffolding students' understanding: Evidence from an early algebra lesson. In *Video Research in the Learning Sciences*, ed. Ricki Goldman, Roy Pea, Brigit Barron, and Sharon Derry, 349–365. Mahwah, NJ: Erlbaum.

Amin, M., Barmpoutis, A., Berti, M., Bozia, E., Hensel, J., and Naether, F. 2018. Depthmap of the Rosetta Stone. *Humanities Commons*. https://doi.org/10.17613/t1e2-0w02.

Aswatha, S.M, A. N., Talla, J. Mukhopadhyay, and P.A. Bhowmick. 2014. Method for extracting text from stone inscriptions using character spotting. In ACCV 2014 Workshops, 598–611.

Babeu A. 2011. *Rome wasn't digitized in a day: Building a cyberinfrastructure for digital classics.* Council on Library and Information Resources.

Bachelard G. 1994. *The poetics of space.* Translated by Jolas, M. Boston, USA: Beacon Press.

Barmpoutis A, Bozia E, and Wagman R.S. 2010. A novel framework for 3D reconstruction and analysis of ancient inscriptions. *Journal of Machine Vision and Applications* 21.6:989–998.

Barmpoutis A, Bozia E, Fortuna D. 2015. Interactive 3D digitization, retrieval, and analysis of ancient sculptures, using infrared depth sensors for mobile devices. In *Universal Access in Human-Computer Interaction. Access to the Human Environment and Culture,* eds. M. Antona, C. Stephanidis, *Lecture Notes in Computer Science* 9178:3–11. Springer, Cham.

Barmpoutis A, Bozia E. 2016. Augmenting the workspace of epigraphists: An interaction design study. In *Digital and Traditional Epigraphy in Context. Proceedings of the EAGLE 2016 International Conference on Digital and Traditional Epigraphy in Context,* eds. Liuzzo, P.M., Mambrini, F., Orlandi, S., Santucci, R., 171–182. Rome: Sapienza Università Editrice.

Benjamin W. 1999. The work of art in the age of mechanical reproduction. In *Illuminations,* ed. Arendt H. London: Pimlico.

Betts, E. ed. 2017. *Senses of the empire.* Routledge: Abington, OX and New York.

Blanchot M. 1989. *The space of literature.* Translated by Ann Smock. Nebraska, USA: University of Nebraska Press.

Bodel J. 2012. Latin epigraphy and the IT revolution. In *Epigraphy and the Historical Sciences*, eds. J. Davies, J. Wilkes J., 275–296. Oxford, UK: Oxford University Press.

Böhler W, Marbs A. 2004. 3D scanning and photogrammetry for heritage recording: a comparison. In Proceedings of the 12th International Conference on Geoinformatics, 291–298.

Bozia. E. 2018. Ektypa and 3D models of ektypa: The reality(ies) of a digital object. In *Authenticity and Cultural Heritage in the Age of 3D Digital Reproductions,* eds. Di Giuseppantonio Di Franco, P., Galeazzi, F., Vassallo, V., 97–110. MacDonald Institute for Archaeological Research. University of Cambridge.

Bozia, E., Barmpoutis, A., & Wagman, R. 2014. Open-access epigraphy: Electronic dissemination of 3D digitized archaeological material. In Proceedings of the International Conference on

[19] Landeschi (2019) discusses how GIS and its inherent information can unveil even more of the environmental characteristics and also allow for the embedding of 3D objects in simulation projects to enhance the experience of the past.

Information Technologies for Epigraphy and Digital Cultural Heritage in the Ancient World, 421–435.

Brondi R, Carrozzino M, Lorenzini C, Tecchia F. 2016. Using mixed reality and natural interaction in cultural heritage. *Informatica* 40:311–316.

Chen C.Y., Chang, B.R., Huang, P.S. 2013. Multimedia augmented reality information system for museum guidance. *Personal and Ubiquitous Computing* 18:315–322. https://doi.org/10.1007/s00779-013-0647-1.

Colebrook C. 2003. The sense of space: on the specificity of affect in Deleuze and Guattari. *Postmodern Culture* 13.2.

Cooper M., Sportun S. 2007. The Application of laser cleaning in the conservation of twelve limestone relief panels on St. George's Hall. In *Lasers in the Conservation of Artworks, eds.* Nimmrichter J., Kautek W., Schreiner M. Springer proceedings in physics, vol 116. Berlin, Heidelberg: Springer. https://doi.org/10.1007/978-3-540-72310-7_7.

Deleuze, G. 1980. *Mille plateaux* (Paris: Minuit); tr. as *A Thousand Plateaus*, by Brian Massumi. 1987. Minneapolis: University of Minnesota Press.

Di Giuseppantonio Di Franco, P., Galeazzi, F., and Vassallo, V. 2018. eds. Authenticity and cultural heritage in the age of 3D digital reproductions. MacDonald Institute for Archaeological Research. University of Cambridge. https://www.repository.cam.ac.uk/handle/1810/279665. Accessed September 22, 2020.

Eisenberg, M. and Pares, N. 2014. Tangible and full-body interfaces in learning. In *The Cambridge Handbook of the Learning Sciences,* ed. R. K. Sawyer, 339–357. Cambridge, MA: Cambridge University Press.

Erwine B. 2016. *Creating sensory space: The architecture of the invisible.* New York, USA and London, UK: Routledge.

Esteban, C. H., & Schmitt, F. 2004. Silhouette and stereo fusion for 3D object modeling. *Computer Vision and Image Understanding* 96.3:367–392.

Farmer, R., Eastop, D., Bozia, E., Barmpoutis, A. 2015. 'Shape-from-shading' to document and examine lace, seals and metal. *Journal of Institute Conservation* 38.1:41–53. https://doi.org/10.1080/19455224.2014.999004.

Foucault M. 1986. Of other spaces: utopias and heterotopias. Translated by Miskowiec J. http://web.mit.edu/allanmc/www/foucault1.pdf. Accessed January 18, 2019.

Flynn, B. 2007. The Morphology of Space in Virtual Heritage. In *Theorizing Digital Cultural Heritage*, eds. F. Cameron and S. Kenderdine, 349–368. Cambridge, MA: MIT Press.

Goldin-Meadow, S. 1999. The role of gesture in communication and thinking. *Trends in cognitive sciences* 3.11:419–429.

Goldin-Meadow, S. 2009. How gesture promotes learning throughout childhood. *Child Development Perspectives* 3:106–111.

Gonizzi Barsanti, S. and Guidi, G. 2013. 3D digitization of museum content within the 3D icons project. *ISPRS Annals of Photogrammetry, Remote Sensing and Spatial Information Sciences* II-5/W1:151–156.

Greggio, S. and G. Salemi. 2016. A mobile augmented-reality system integrating 3D model and radiance scaling to enhance epigraphic inscriptions. In *Proceedings of the 20th International Conference on Cultural Heritage and New Technologies.* http://www.chnt.at/wp-content/uploads/eBook_CHNT20_Greggio_Salemi_2015.pdf. Accessed September 22, 2020.

Hamilakis Y. 2013. *Archaeology and the senses.* New York, USA: Cambridge University Press.

Harding C, Kakadiaris I, Casey J, and Bowen Loftin R. 2002. A multi-sensory system for the investigation of geoscientific data. *Computers & Graphics* 26.2:259–269.

Harvey D. 1991. *The condition of postmodernity: an enquiry into the origins of cultural change.* Maiden, MA, USA: Wiley-Blackwell.

Heidegger M. 1927. *Sein und Zeit.* Tübingen, Germany: Klostermann.

Hervy, B., Laroche, F., Kerouanton, J.L., Berbard, A. 2015. Museum augmented interface for historical scale models: Towards a new way for cultural heritage promotion. *International Journal of Virtual Reality* 15.1:3–9. https://doi.org/10.20870/IJVR.2015.15.1.2863.

Hoang T, Cox T. 2017. Alternating reality: an interweaving narrative of physical and virtual cultural exhibitions. *Presence* 26.4:402–419.

Ingold T. 2000. *Perceptions of the environment. Essays in livelihood, dwelling and skill.* London, UK: Routledge.

Israr, A., Zhao, S., Mcintosh, K., Schwemler, Z., Fritz, A. 2016. Stereohaptics: A haptic interaction toolkit for tangible virtual experiences. ACM SIGGRAPH 2016 Studio, Anaheim, United States. https://doi.org/10.1145/2929484.2970273ff.

Jameson, M. 2004. Promises and challenges of digital libraries and document image analysis: A humanist's perspective. In Proceedings of the First International Workshop on Document Image Analysis for Libraries (Dial'04). IEEE Computer Society, Washington, DC, USA. https://doi.org/10.1109/DIAL.2004.1263237.

Johnson P. 2006. Unravelling Foucault's 'different space.' *History of the Human Sciences* 19(4):75–90.

Landeschi G. 2019. Rethinking GIS, three-dimensionality and space perception in archaeology. *World Archaeology* 51.1:17–32. https://doi.org/10.1080/00438243.2018.1463171.

Landon, G. V. and Seales, W. B. 2006. Petroglyph digitization: Enabling cultural heritage scholarship. *Machine Vision and Applications* 17:361–371.

Lefebvre, H. 1992. *The production of space.* New Jersey, USA: Wiley-Blackwell.

Levoy, M. et al. 2000. The digital Michelangelo project: 3D scanning of large statues. In Proceedings of the 27th annual conference on Computer graphics and interactive techniques, 131–144.

Lindgren, R. and Johnson-Glenberg, M. 2013. Emboldened by embodiment: Six precepts for research on embodied learning and mixed reality. *Educational Researcher* 42.8:445–452.

Low S. 2014. Spatializing culture. An engaged anthropological approach to space and place. In *The people, place and space reader,* eds. Gieseking J, Mangold W, Katz C, Low S., 34–38. New York, USA and London, UK: Routledge.

Maggini G. 2017. Digital virtual places: Utopias, atopias, heterotopias. In *Place, Space and Hermeneutics,* ed. Janz, B.B., 465–477. New York, USA: Springer.

Malzbender, T., Gelb, D., and Wolters, H. 2001. *Polynomial texture maps.* In Proceedings of the 28th annual conference on Computer graphics and interactive techniques, 519–528.

McKittrick K. 2014. The last place they thought of: black women's geographies. In *The people, place and space reader,* eds. Gieseking J, Mangold W, Katz C, Low S., 309–313. New York, USA and London, UK: Routledge.

Milgram, P and Kishino, A.F. 1994. Taxonomy of mixed reality visual displays. *IEICE Transactions on Information and Systems* E77-D(12):1321–1329.

Neely, L., & Langer, M. 2013. Please feel the museum: The emergence of 3D printing and scanning. In *Museums and the Web 2013,* eds N. Proctor & R. Cherry. Silver Spring, MD: Museums and the Web.

Pavlidis, G., Koutsoudis, A., Arnaoutoglou, F., Tsioukas, V., Chamzas, C. 2007. Methods for 3D digitization of cultural heritage. *Journal of Cultural Heritage* 8.1:93–98.

Papadaki, A. I., Agrafiotis, P., Georgopoulos, A., & Prignitz, S. 2015. Accurate 3D Scanning of damaged ancient Greek inscriptions for revealing weathered letters. *International Archives of Photogrammetry, Remote Sensing and Spatial Information Sciences,* 1:237–243.

Pellini J, Zarankin A, Salerno M., 2015. eds. *Coming to senses.* Topics in sensory archaeology. Newcastle, UK: Cambridge scholars publishing.

Pollefeys, M., Van Gool, L. J., Vergauwen, M., Cornelis, K., Verbiest, F., and Tops, J. 2001. Image-based 3D acquisition of archaeological heritage and applications. In Proceedings of the 2001 conference on Virtual reality, archeology, and cultural heritage, 255–262.

Pujol-Tost, L. 2017. Cultural presence in virtual archaeology: An exploratory analysis of factors. *Presence* 26.3:247–263.

Radford G, Radford M, Lingel J. 2015. The library as heterotopia Michel Foucault and the experience of library space. *Journal of Documentation* 71.4:733–751.

Ramírez-Sánchez, M., Suárez-Rivero, J. P., & Castellano-Hernández, M. Á. 2014. Epigrafía digital: tecnología 3D de bajo coste para la digitalización de inscripciones y su acceso desde ordenadores y dispositivos móviles. *El profesional de la información* 23.5:467–474.

Richards-Rissetto H, Remondino F, Agugiaro G, Von Schwerin J, Robertsson J, Girardi G. 2012. Kinect and 3D GIS in archaeology. In Proceedings of the 18th International Conference on Virtual Systems and Multimedia, 331–337.

Rousseaux F, Thounevin I. 2009. Exploring informed virtual sites through Michel Foucault's heterotopias. *International Journal of Humanities and Arts Computing* 3.1–2:175–191.

Ryu, D., Moon, K., Kang, S., Kim, M., & Song, J. B. 2006. Development of wearable haptic system for tangible studio to experience a virtual heritage alive. In *2006 IEEE/RSJ International Conference on Intelligent Robots and Systems,* 466–471. https://doi.org/10.1109/IROS.2006.282266.

Skeates, R. and J. Day. 2020. Ed. *The Routledge handbook of sensory archaeology*. London and New York: Routledge.

Sloan, R. 2012. Dance the flip-flop. Hi: I'm Robin Sloan, a writer × media inventor in California. March. http://www.robinsloan.com/note/flip-flop/. Accessed August 21, 2016.

Sullivan, S. M. 2011. Analytical methods for the extraction of content from high resolution 3D data sets: Epigraphical applications to the Drakon Stele. Doctoral dissertation, University of Arkansas.

Topinka R.J. 2010. Foucault, Borges, heterotopia: producing knowledge in Other Spaces. *Foucault Studies* 9:54–70.

Vavulin, M., Nevskaya, I., Tybykova, L. 2019. Digital macro-photogrammetry in documentation of old Turkic runiform inscriptions in the Altai mountains. *Mediterranean Archaeology and Archaeometry* 19.2:81–104.

Wachowiak, M. J. and Karas, B. V. 2009. 3D scanning and replication for museum and cultural heritage applications. *Journal of the American Institute for Conservation* 48.2:141–158.

Woolf, V. 2005. *A Room of one's own.* New York & London: Harcourt, Inc.

Eleni Bozia is an Associate Professor of Classics and Digital Humanities at the University of Florida. She also serves as the Associate Director of the Digital Epigraphy and Archaeology project and the Center for Greek Studies. Bozia is also the founder and Head of the Data-Driven Humanities Research Group. She holds two doctoral degrees: a Ph.D. in Classical Studies and a Dr. phil. in Digital Humanities. Her research interests include linguistic and cultural diversity in Imperial Greek and Latin literature and its intersection with modern globalism, digital preservation and the collaboration between the humanities and the sciences.

Sailing Along the Coast of North Etruria: Ancient Perceptions Versus Multidisciplinary Coastal Landscape Studies

Marinella Pasquinucci and Giacomo Landeschi

Abstract Aim of this contribution is to demonstrate how digital methods, in combination with traditional sources, can effectively contribute to reconstruct a narrative of the past based on a sensory account of a few coastal landscapes in Northwestern Etruria as they were perceived and described by ancient authors. A few passages by Strabo (Geogr. 5.2.5, 222C, Augustan period) and Rutilius Namatianus (de reditu suo, early fifth-century CE) are examined, in order to understand how these authors perceived, either through previous sources or by autopsy, the river network and some coastal landscapes in Northwestern Etruria. The study of these passages is compared with the output of recent integrated research in the same districts described by the ancient authors. Areas of particular interest have been selected, for which landscape archaeology provides evidence of their long-term history, based on integrated palaeogeographic, historical and archaeological research including geomorphologic and palaeoenvironmental changes, exploitation of natural resources, urban forms, type and distribution of settlements. As for Strabo and Claudius Rutilius Namatianus, both authors relayed on their personal experience and on previous writers, but certainly chose to describe specific aspects characterising our case-study areas. In the frame of different literary genres, they provide descriptions based on their perceptions and also on their culture.

Keywords Coastal landscape · Ancient harbours · Ancient sources · Remote sensing · Satellite imagery

M. Pasquinucci (✉)
Department of Civilizations and Forms of Knowledge, University of Pisa, Pisa, Italy
e-mail: pasquinuccimarinella@gmail.com

G. Landeschi
Department of Archaeology and Ancient History, Lund University, Lund, Sweden

G. Landeschi and E. Betts (eds.), *Capturing the Senses*,
Quantitative Methods in the Humanities and Social Sciences,
https://doi.org/10.1007/978-3-031-23133-9_8

1 Research Overview

Starting from the 1980s, research conducted by the University of Pisa has enabled the acquisition of a significant amount of geospatial data, producing a source of information to validate and complement what was described by ancient authors' accounts. A series of integrated methods were employed to investigate the study areas, which include the harbour sites of Vada Volaterrana and Portus Pisanus; they consisted of satellite remote sensing, GIS-based analysis, geophysics and geo-archaeology. The digital output derived from these analyses dramatically increased our understanding and interpretation of the landscape as it was described by the ancient authors.

Similarly, interdisciplinary projects run by the University of Siena in the Populonia District provided relevant data to the long-term history of the district, the variety of natural environments, changes in human settlements, farming landscapes, exploitation of resources and differing political strategies (Bianchi and Gelichi 2016; Bianchi and Hodges 2018).

1.1 North Coastal Etruria: Palaeogeography, Landscapes and Settlements

The studied district (Fig. 1) consists of river valleys (Magra, Serchio, Arno, Fine, Cecina, Cornia and minor ones) with their alluvial plains, mountain and hill districts (Apennines, Apuan Alps, Monti Pisani, Colline Livornesi, Colline Metallifere, etc.). In the Etruscan and Roman periods, the local economies were based primarily on agro-pastoral activities, woodland exploitation, mining and quarrying, manufacturing and trading activities (Pasquinucci and Menchelli 2017). The coastline (Fig. 2) consists of different morphological features which shaped the location and activities of ports and landings. The Luni-Livorno segment is characterised by a low shoreline; it was almost stable from the eight to the second-first centuries BCE, then prograded until c. 1860. The Livorno terrace and Livorno-Castiglioncello coastal strip are rocky and stable; the Vada-Cecina shoreline is low and substantially stable (Pasquinucci and Menchelli 2012) except for the ancient Cecina River Delta (Bresci et al. 2006; Benvenuti et al. 2008). In the Populonia/Piombino District, the high rocky Populonia promontory dominates the Baratti Bay and alluvial plains resulting from the progressive geomorphological evolution in the district (Pasquinucci et al. 2004; Giroldini 2012).

In the Etruscan and Roman periods, the coast was dotted with ports and landings located in sites (gulfs/bays, inlets, coastal lagoons) naturally protected from the prevailing winds and waves, nearby the ancient rivers mouths and in other suitable sites where the boats could land/dock, load/unload wares and/or stock up on food and water. Coastal and inland navigation had to conform to the seasonal floods and to the constant and usually intense geomorphologic evolution which characterised some coastal districts and river courses. Sea and river routes were sailed by vessels and

Fig. 1 Study area including river valleys and their alluvial plains, mountain and hill districts (map by Giacomo Bonino)

boats/crafts of various typology, size and draught and were connected by a hierarchy of roads.

From the seventh/sixth to the early second-century BCE, Northwestern Etruria was dominated by three city-states, Pisa (Pisae), Volterra (Velathri, Volaterrae) and Populonia, with their territories dotted with minor settlements (including ports and landings, rural sites, etc.).

The Roman conquest of the early third-century BCE had a strong impact on both major and minor settlements, territories and related economies. Moreover, in the early second-century BCE two "new" cities, Lucca (Luca, Latin colony, 180 BCE) and

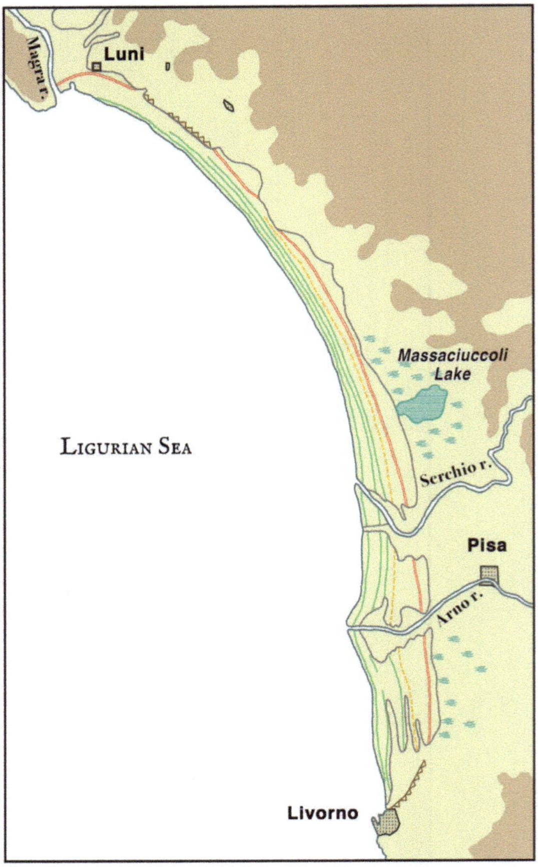

Fig. 2 Coastline characterised by different morphological features in which activities of harbours and landing places were located (map by Giacomo Bonino)

Luni (Luna, a citizen's colony, 177 BCE), were founded North of Pisa in the frame of the Roman wars against the Ligures. The Roman road network, in part following previous itineraries, was constructed on stable soils with attention paid to the local morphology, and provided efficient North–South and East–West connections which linked the sea- and river waterways (Pasquinucci 2014a, b) (Fig. 3).

Later, in the last decades of the first-century BCE, areas of North Etruria were affected by intense veteran colonisation that shaped or re-shaped the rural districts and marked the beginning of new manufacturing activities both in the coastal district (Luni, Pisa) and in inner Etruria, especially in the Serchio and Arno Valleys (Ciampoltrini 1981; Pasquinucci and Menchelli 2003, 2017). As was usual in the Roman colonisation process, such territories were in large part centuriated and assigned to the colonists. The practice entailed deforestation, increased agricultural and manufacturing activities, construction of roads and channels, therefore induced soil erosion. The marked increase in alluvial sedimentation from the second-first-century BCE caused the westwards progradation of the Luni-Livorno coastline

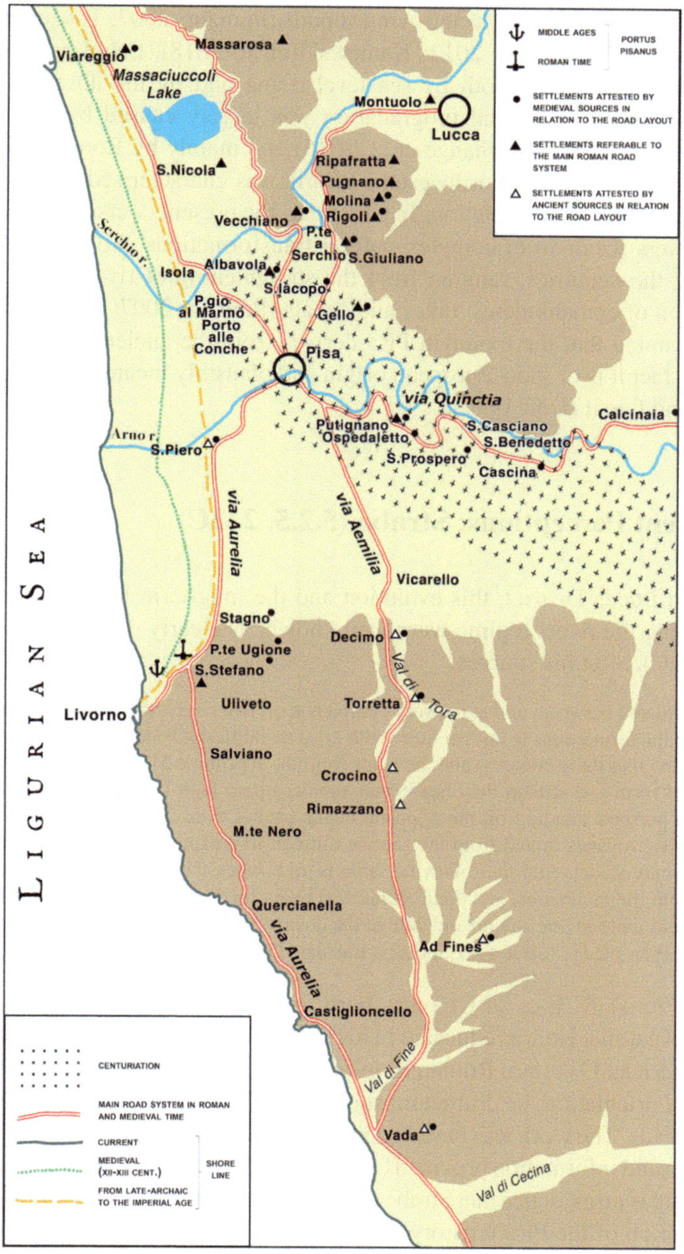

Fig. 3 Roman road network developed in connection to the conquest of Northwestern Etruria (map by Giacomo Bonino)

(Fig. 2), mostly in relation to the Arno mouth (Pranzini 2007; Pasquinucci 2008; Pasquinucci and Menchelli 2012; Kaniewski et al. 2018). Scholars agree that in this period characterised both by sea level rising and by the absence of drastic climatic changes, the coastal progradation was largely caused by anthropogenic factors (Pranzini 2007; Morhange et al. 2015) and mainly by Roman colonisation. As for the river network, Northwestern Etruria was characterised by a particularly complex hydrogeologic evolution. In particular, the present courses of the Arno and Serchio rivers result from complex natural transformations and anthropic actions taken over the centuries, ranging from the straightening of river meanders to the construction of embankments, dikes and canals (Pranzini 2007; Pasquinucci 2008). It is to be noted that the toponym Pisa derives from the ancient perception of the district: in fact it is of Indo-European origin and plausibly means rich in water, both stagnant and fluent (Dini 1996).

2 Ancient Perceptions: Strabo (5.2.5, 222C)

In the Pisa-Lucca District, this evolution and the long-term human actions aimed at optimising the rivers regime were well known, as clearly documented by Strabo (5.2.5, 222C), after his sources:

> Pisa is situated between, and at the very confluence of, two rivers, the Arnus and the Auser, of which the former runs from Arretium, with great quantities of water (not all in one stream, but divided into three streams) and the latter from the Apennine Mountains; and when they unite and form one stream they heave one another up so high by their mutual resistance that two persons standing on the opposite banks cannot even see each other; and hence, necessarily, voyages inland from the sea are difficult to make; the length of the voyage is about twenty stadia. And the following fable is told: when these rivers first began to flow down from the mountains, and their course was being hindered by the natives for fear that they would unite in one stream and deluge the country, the rivers promised not to deluge it and kept their pledge (Strabo 5.2.5, C223: translated by Jones 1960: 350–353).

Strabo (c. 64 BCE-c. 24 CE) was born to an aristocratic family at Amasia, in northeast Anatolia. He was educated in his hometown, resided in Rome and travelled in the Eastern and Western Roman Empire. A Greek man of letters in education and ideological orientation, he drafted most of his Geography by 3/2 BCE and revised it under Tiberius. The work was based on previous authors, ancient "maps", eyewitness description and information provided by local people (Migliario 2017, passim, 84 and n. 41). There is no evidence that Strabo travelled North of Populonia (Migliario 2017); his description of the Pisa territory is based on previous writers. The parádoxon of the Auser mounding into the Arno in the outskirts of Pisa is most probably derived (Lasserre 1967, 201–202) from Artemidorus (second-first-century BCE: Lasserre 1967, 14–18). This topos goes back to Timaeus (Lycophron, *Alexandra* 1240: fourth-century BCE: translated by André Hurst and Antje Kolde 2008, 71, 284) and Pseudo Aristoteles (*de mirabilibus auscultationibus* 92, translated by Hett 1936, 276–277) and is reported by several authors until Late Antiquity (Pasquinucci 2008, 152).

The legend of the rivers and their "promise" not to deluge the country most probably has the same origin (Lasserre 1967, 202), corroborated by hydrogeologic instability of the Arno and Serchio River Lower Plains, which is well documented by recent research in the Arno and Serchio River Coastal Plains (Pasquinucci and Menchelli 2012; Pranzini 2007). The integrated study of ancient written sources, mediaeval and modern documents, toponyms, maps and drawings, archaeological (Pasquinucci 2008, 152; Ciampoltrini 2007) and environmental evidence, air photo-interpretation, remotely sensed image processing of medium (Landsat TM) to high (Ikonos and Quickbird) resolution data, a LIDAR survey and sedimentologic studies (Pranzini 2007) document changes in the river courses, individual major floods and broader patterns of change in flood frequency in Pisa, Lucca and other specific areas of the studied district and beyond (Alinne et al. 2016; Walsh 2014, 96 ff., 104). As for the Arno splitting in three branches (Strabo 5.2.5, C223), three coarse-grained lobes were detected in the Pisa coastal district at Le Rene and Chiesanuova through satellite image processing and interpreted as possibly corresponding to Strabo's description (Della Rocca et al. 1987, 78; Marchisio et al. 2000, 234 and Fig. 23.1; Pranzini 2007, 401). The course of the Roman Via Quinctia is identified in the plain East of Pisa (Fig. 4) based on the location of the itinerary toponyms deriving from the Roman milestones and quoted in Mediaeval deeds (Ceccarelli Lemut et al. 1991, 125f., 127–129; Pasquinucci 2014a, b). The road layout was not straight, as one would expect given the characteristics of the terrain. Evidently it was constructed on the bank of the second-century BCE Arno, on solid river sediments, following the meanders and connecting the river landing places. Remotely sensed image processing provides possible links between a few identified palaeochannels and the ancient viability (Marchisio et al. 2000, 234 and Fig. 23.3). In the northwestern outskirts of Pisa (San Rossore Railway Station) a riverine site (not a fluvial port in a strict sense: Leucci et al. 2014, 272) with several Roman wrecks and their cargoes has been excavated and studied. The sedimentological evidence and pollen analyses document catastrophic flood flows that occurred between the second-century BCE and the fifth-century CE (Benvenuti et al. 2006; Mariotti Lippi et al. 2007). Geophysical surveys (active/induced polarisation electrical methods) of the site, integrated with remote sensing analyses, largely contribute to the study of the site (Leucci et al. 2014). A cool and relatively damp climate phase characterised the Archaic period to the Late Republic, followed by a warm phase up to the third/fourth-century CE (Liebermann and Gordon 2018, 58–62; cf. Lionello 2012, 110–111; for a new approach to the study of precipitation changes, Peyron et al. 2017).

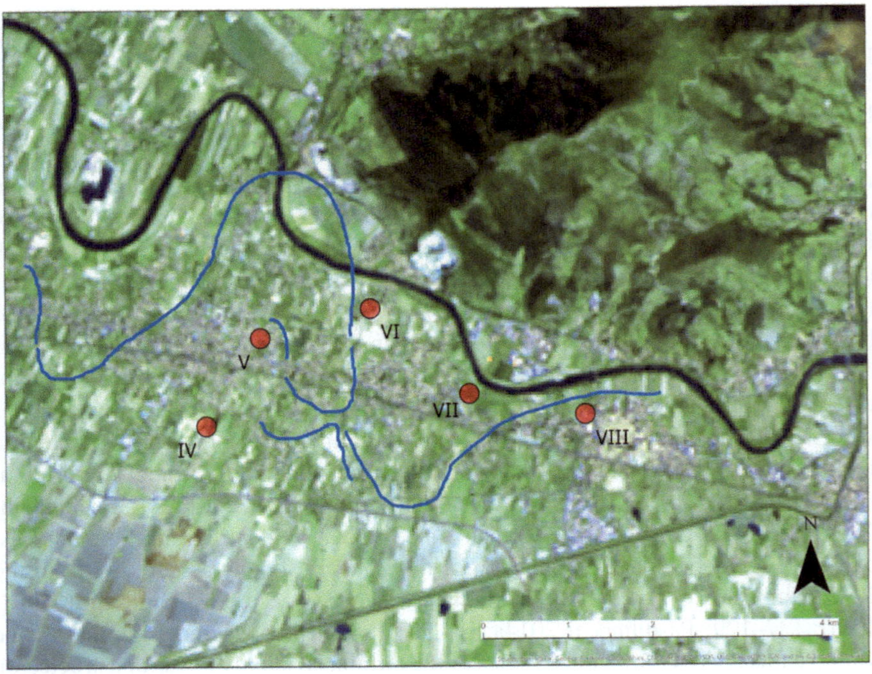

Fig. 4 Landsat TM (acquired on 12 September 1990) colour composite with band combination 7-5-3. Detected palaeorivers are marked with blue lines and spatially related with place names connected to Roman milestones (map by the authors, after Marchisio et al. 2000)

3 Ancient Perceptions: Claudius Rutilius Namatianus

Claudius Rutilius Namatianus was a native of Tolosa (Toulouse) in South Gaul. In his youth, he was well trained in classical rhetoric and literature, most likely in Rome. Like his father Lachanius, he had a highly successful career in the western imperial court (Malamud 2016, 8–9). In 417 CE, in October or early November, Rutilius fled from Rome, where he had held the relevant public offices of magister officiorum and praefectus urbi, and sailed from Portus (in the present Fiumicino area, north of the Tiber mouth) to his homeland in South Gaul coasting Latium, Etruria and Liguria (Fo 1992; Wolff et al. 2007; Pasquinucci 2020).

Shortly after the end of this journey, he described it in the poem in elegiac meter "de reditu suo", the last part of which is lost. He intertwined various aspects of his journey with historical and ideological digressions. The "de reditu" is relevant for all scholars studying Late Antiquity and is particularly rich in topographical data based on Rutilius' autopsy. Rutilius precisely and colourfully described several peculiar aspects of the landscapes he saw, the cities and ports he called at, the sea storms he faced, the people he met, etc.

Hereafter, a few examples of verses expressing what he could observe/perceive:

Good examples of visual perceptions:

1. 179–180 *ad naves gradior, qua fronte bicorni dividuus Tiberis dexteriora secat* "At last I make it to the ships, where two-horned Tiber branches and cuts a channel to the right" (Malamud 2016, 48).

1. 189–192 *respectare iuvat vicinam saepius urbem et montes visu deficiente sequi, quaque duces oculi grata regione fruuntur, dum se, quod cupiunt, cernere posse putant.* "To look back at the nearby city is a joy, to trace the hills that we can barely see, and feast our eyes on those familiar regions, while we think that we can see what we desire" (Malamud 2016, 48).

1. 283–284: *nemorosa viret densis vicinia luci pineasque extremis fluctuat umbra fretis.* "Forests clothe the neighborhood with thickset groves; the water's edge reflects the pine tree's shadow" (Malamud 2016, 51).

1. 431–434: *Incipit obscuros ostendere Corsica montes nubiferumque caput concolor umbra levat; sic dubitanda solet gracili vanescere cornu defessis oculis luna reperta latet.* "Corsica begins to show her dim mountains. Same-colored shadow lifts her cloudy head, just as the puzzling moon with slender horn will fade and even when found will hide from straining eyes" (Malamud 2016, 55).

1. 531: *contiguum stupui portum...mira loci facies: pelago pulsatur aperto...* "the near-by port amazed me…It's a sight to see: the open seas and winds from every quarter pound its exposed shores" (Malamud 2016, 58).

1. 639: *Vidimus exciti pontum flavescere harenis* "We Saw the Stirred up Sea-Sands Turn the Water Gold and Belched-Up Waterspouts Submerge the Fields" (Malamud 2016, 61).

2. 63–68: *candentia moenia...nominis est auctor sole corusca soror. Indigenis superat ridentia lilia saxis et levi radiat picta nitore silex; dives marmoribus tellus, quae luce coloris provocat intactas luxuriosa nives.* "…shining walls: the sun's bright sister gave her name to them…Its native rocks surpass the laughing lilies, the colored stone emits a polished gleam. The earth, so rich in marble and abounding in the color of light, can rival virgin snows" (Malamud 2016, 63).

Audio perceptions:

1. 201–205: *saepius attonitae resonant circensibus aures, nuntiat accensus plena theatra favor, pulsato notae redduntur ab aethere voces, vel quia perveniunt, vel quia fingit amor.* "The Circus often echoes in our startled ears, inflamed applause proclaims the crowded theater: familiar shouts are sent back from the echoing air-do we hear, or only hope we do?" (Malamud 2016, 48).

1. 370 *dum resonat variis vile celeuma modis.* "While the mate shouts out the rower's beat" rower's beat" (Malamud 2016, 53).

1. 456 *dirigit et puppim voce monente regit.* "And guides the stern with many a warning shout" (Malamud 2016, 56).

1. 629–630 *Tum responsuros persulta bucina colle fitque reportando carmine praeda levis;* "The sound of the hunting horn dances through echoing hills and singing lightens the spoil we carry back" (Malamud 2016, 60).

Olfactory perceptions

1. 282 *quas premit aestivae saepe paludis odor.* "A swampy stench sits over it in summer" (Malamud 2016, 51).

Taste/olfactory perceptions

1. 251–254 *non illic gustu latices vitiantur amaro lymphaque fumifico sulphure tincta calet: purus odor mollisque sapor dubitare lavantem cogit…* "The hot springs there are not spoiled with bitter taste, no sulphur-tainted waters boil there: a fresh aroma and sweet taste confuse the bather about which use is better for this water" (Malamud 2016, 50).

Multisensory perceptions

1. 313–316 *Necdum decessis pelago permittitur umbris, natus vicino vertice ventus adest. Tenditur in medias mons Argentarius undas ancipitique iugo caerula curva premit.* "Night' shades have not yet scattered as we set to sea: a breeze, born on a nearby peak, befriends us. Mount Argentarius juts out into the waves, its twofold ridge confines the turquoise bays" (Malamud 2016, 51–52).

Rutilius' description of the Populonia, Vada Volaterrana (present Vada, Livorno) District, of the Portus Pisanus Basin (Livorno) and the way he perceived Luni are of peculiar interest (Pasquinucci 2020).

In these areas, landscape archaeology applying excavations, surveys and non-invasive prospecting techniques (remote sensing, geophysical investigations, geomorphologic and palaeogeographic research, bio- and geosciences) provides evidence of the landscapes, the settlements characteristics and patterns, the infrastructures in a long-term perspective.

3.1 Falesia and Populonia

In the fourth stage of his journey Rutilius coasted the southern Populonia territory in view of the Elba Island and went ashore in the port named Falesia (de red., 1.371–386, cited from "surname" year: page number; cf. Itinerarium Maritimum 501: 'Falesiae portus', edited by Cuntz 1929) (Fig. 1). In the immediate hinterland, he watched people celebrating a spring festivity and reached a villa. Here he wandered in a nearby grove (de red., 1.377, translated by Malamud 2016, 53) and observed a fish farm rich in water and fishes. He perceived and vividly described the joyful celebration dedicated to Osiris, the characteristics of the ponds, the abundance of water and the darting fishes (de red. 1, 373–380, translated by Malamud 2016, 53).

Falesia (Falesiae portus) was located ENE of present Piombino, in the Portovecchio area. The present district is a coastal sedimentation basin formed for the progressive contribution of river debris (Dallai 2016, 94; Dallai 2018). Archaeological surveys and excavations, non-invasive prospecting techniques, historical, cartographic, palaeogeographic and palinolonogical studies document the long-term natural evolution of the territory, the ancient and mediaeval settlements and settlement patterns, the road network, rural and manufacturing economy, the role of fishing, salt production and fish processing (Shepherd 2006; Dallai 2016, 92). In particular, palaeogeographic evidence documents that in Roman and Mediaeval times the district was characterised by permanently flooded areas (some of them deep), alternating with areas just lapped by water and dry ones, linked by major and minor roads: a composite landscape, which provided numerous resources (Dallai 2016, 94–98; Dallai et al. 2018). Although it is impossible to identify the villa and fish farm located not far from Falesiae portus and vividly described by Rutilius (Pasquinucci 2020), landscape archaeology and quantitative researches demonstrate that his verses provide a careful picture of the local environment, settlement and economy characteristics and the way the author perceived them.

3.2 *Vada Volaterrana*

Vada Volaterrana was the main harbour of Volterra, located North of the ancient Cecina river mouth along the coastal road (via Aurelia since the third-century BCE), 25 milia from Populonia and 18 from Portus Pisanus (Itinerarium Maritimum, 501: edited by Cuntz 1929) (Figs. 1, 5 and 6). The Etruscan and Roman settlement lies under present Vada and North of it, where a quarter has been excavated and in part prospected by geo-electrical prospections and multichannel Gpr (Pasquinucci et al. 2001, 2012; Baroni et al. 2014; Benetti et al. 2018). Evidently related to the harbour, it includes horrea, two thermae, a schola, a fountain and other buildings (early decades of the first-century CE-early seventh-century CE). The toponym is derived from the large shoals (Latin vadum/vada) in front of the coastal strip centred on Vada (Aiello et al. 1981), which protected the site and determined the town's seaport function since the most remote antiquity (Fig. 5). The shoals were evidently perceived by the ancients as the peculiar characteristic of the site. In antiquity they provided a higher protection since the sea level was about one metre and a half lower (Lambeck et al. 2004; cf. Pasquinucci 2020). Geomorphologic and archaeological research proves the ancient harbour basin was located in the sheet of water in front of the town, roughly in the area where the mediaeval and modern ports were located (Pasquinucci 2020) (Fig. 6). This area is the most protected and therefore suitable for the harbour; anyway evidence of loading/unloading ships a small distance from the coast has been found both North and South of Vada and landing places were scattered along the coast. The Vada hinterland has been thoroughly surveyed. It was dotted by stationes/mansiones, villas and farmsteads studied and under study in a long-term perspective (Iacopini et al. 2012; Pasquinucci 2014a, b; Repetto et al. 2018). It was characterised by Mediterranean crops, breeding, manufacturing and commercial activities, and many natural resources (sea- and rock-salt, timber, copper, alabaster). A few rural sites were

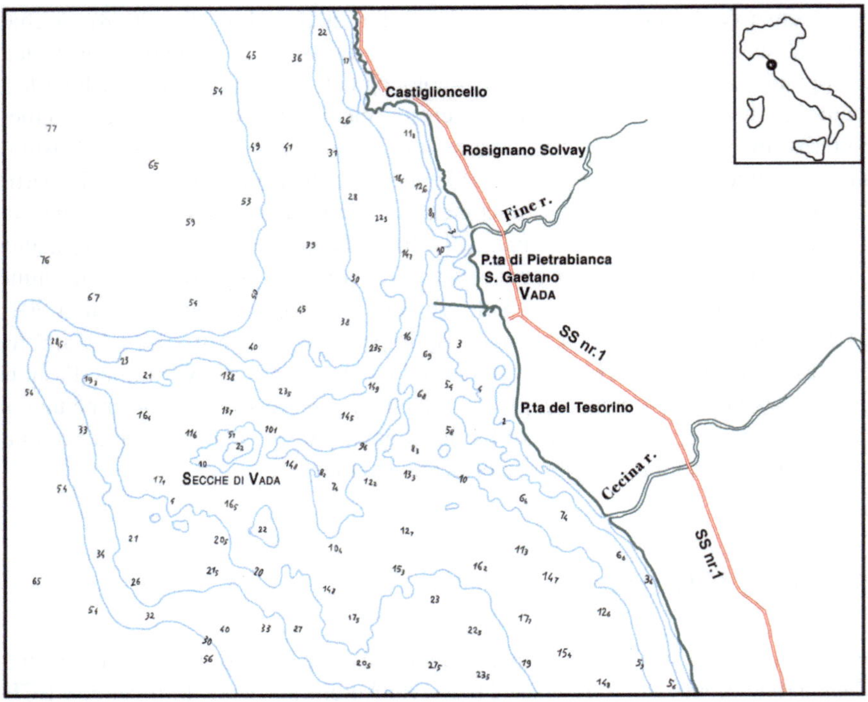

Fig. 5 Large shoals (Latin vadum/vada) in front of the coastal strip centred on Vada (Aiello et al. 1981), which protected the site and determined the town's seaport function since the most remote antiquity (map by Giacomo Bonino)

recently investigated by magnetic prospections employing Fluxgate Gradiometer FM 256 by Geoscan Research as main device; it was used with a dual configuration and a resolution of 0.1 nT (nano-Tesla). In some areas, the Fluxgate data were integrated with a Caesium Gradiometer G-858 by Geometrics, which has been shown more sensitive in detecting weak magnetic anomalies related to archaeological features. Radar survey was carried out with an antenna manufactured by GSSI, with 270 MHz of central frequency. The surveys have been undertaken within a net of georeferenced rectangular grids (20 × 40 m) (Repetto et al. 2018). A GIS has been implemented with data provided by intensive archeological surveys of the area. As for the road network, cost surface analyses (based on slope, altimetry and hydrography) have been applied to the Vada Volaterrana-Pisae pre-Roman and Roman via track. Viewshed analyses prove that a few hillforts built on the Colline Livornesi had a very important strategic role concerning viability thanks to excellent control over large part of the ancient route connecting Vada with Pisa through the Fine and Tora River Valleys which was later run by via Aemilia (Ceccarelli Lemut et al. 1991, 116, 120; Iacopini et al. 2012; Pasquinucci 2014a). Based on these available data, we can deduce that in his description of Vada Volaterrana, Rutilius chose to focus on three aspects, which he evidently perceived as particularly relevant and therefore characterising the area: the

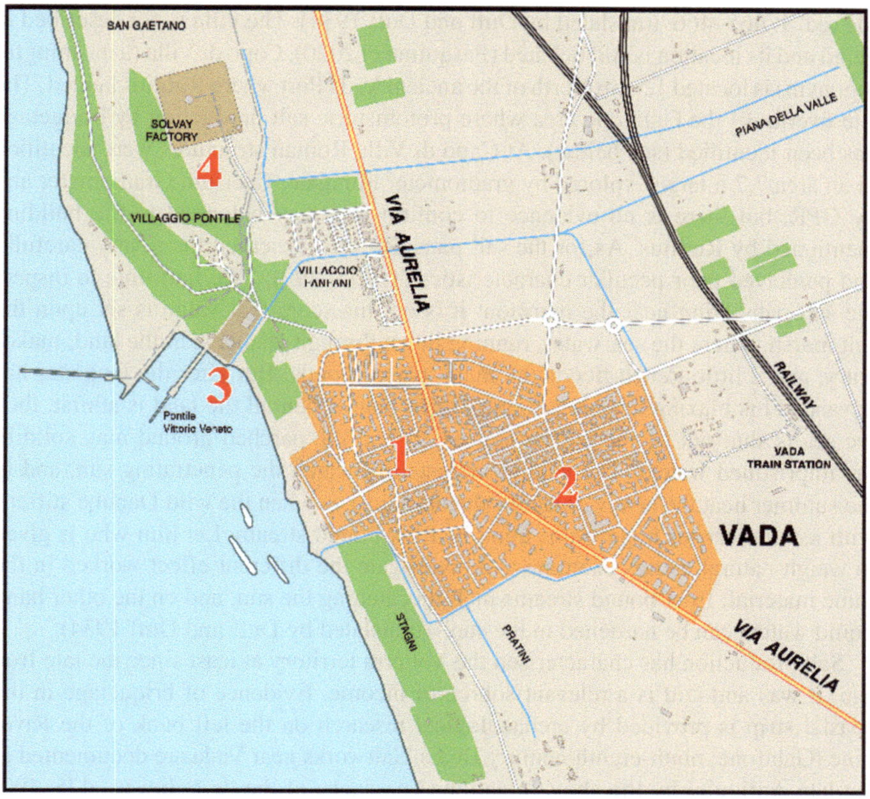

Fig. 6 Probable location of the ancient harbour basin of Vada Volaterrana. This was located in the sheet of water in front of the town (n. 3), roughly in the area where the mediaeval and modern ports were located (map by Giacomo Bonino, after Pasquinucci 2020)

shoals cut through by a narrow canal which provided access to the port, the "nearby" villa belonging to his friend Caecina Albinus and the salt pans visible from Albinus' villa. The first ones are carefully and colourfully described in the poem (1.453–466): "Entering on the region of Volterra, appropriately called "The Shallows", I thread my way through the deep part of the treacherous channel. At the bow the look-out watches the water beneath and gives directions to the helm beyond, guiding the stern with warning shouts. A boundary on each side marks puzzling narrows by a pair of trees, and presents a line of piles hammered in there: to these it is the custom to fix tall laurels easy to see because of their branches and bushy foliage, so that, although the shifting bank of thick mud shows its mass of sea-weed, a clear passage may keep the guiding-signs unstruck" (Duff and Duff 1934). After docking, under heavy rain Rutilius reached a villa near the port belonging to his friend Albinus: "There I was driven to make a halt by a tearing North-western of the sort that is wont to shatter the depths of the woods. Scarce safe beneath a roof did we endure the pitiless rains: the neighbouring country-seat of my own Albinus was placed at my disposal" (de red. 1. 465–466: translated by Duff and Duff 1934). The villa is not described in detail and its location is still debated (Pasquinucci 2020). Capo di Villa (a meaningful toponym) is located 1,5 km North of the ancient Vada Port where Rutilius landed. The site overlooks the Galafone area where protohistoric salt production by briquetage has been identified (see below). At Capo di Villa Roman structures were identified in an area 7,7 h large explored by gradiometer Fluxgate, Caesium Gradiometer and by GPR, but there is no evidence to confirm that they belonged to the building mentioned by Rutilius. As for the salt pans, Rutilius observed them very carefully and perceived their peculiar characteristics (1. 475–490): "We find time to inspect the salt-pans lying near the mansion: it is on this score that value is set upon the salt marsh, where the sea-water, running down through channels in the land, makes entry, and a little trench floods the many-parted ponds. But after the Dog-star has advanced his blazing fires, when grass turns pale, when all the land is athirst, then the sea is shut out by the barrier-sluices, so that the parched ground may solidify the imprisoned waters. The natural incrustations catch the penetrating sun, and in the summer heat the heavy crust of salt cakes, just as when the wild Danube stiffens with ice and carries huge wains upon its frost-bound stream. Let him who is given to weigh natural causes examine and investigate the different effect worked in the same material: frost-bound streams melt on catching the sun, and on the other hand liquid waters can be hardened in the sun" (translated by Duff and Duff 1934).

Salt production has characterised the Volterra territory at least since the late Iron age. It was and still is a relevant source of income. Evidence of briquetage in the coastal strip is provided by archaeological research on the left bank of the River Fine (Galafone: ninth-eighth-century BCE). Saltworks near Vada are documented in the late Antiquity by the above-mentioned passages of the de reditu (1. 475–490) and since the mid-eighth-century CE by archive documents (Ceccarelli Lemut and Maria Luisa 2013, 32–35). In the hinterland (at Saline di Volterra, in the inner Cecina Valley), the brine was exploited since remote times, most probably by the Etruscans and Romans, certainly since the early Middle Ages up to now. To sum up, we can find relevant evidence of the fifth-century landscapes and settlements in the *de reditu*, but only "loose" links between the data derived from quantitative researches in the Vada territory and Rutilius' perceptions. Anyway it is evident that he chose to focus on the aspects he perceived as particularly relevant and therefore characterising the area, and wrote a clear and vivid picture of the local landscapes, as they are outlined by historical, archaeological and quantitative researches.

3.3 Pisa, Portus Pisanus and Livorno

In the seventh/sixth-century BCE, Pisa became an urban entity with the merging of Iron age villages separated by major and minor streams, at the confluence of the river Auser into the Arnus (see par. 02 above; Pasquinucci 2008, 152), on the right bank of the latter, 20 stadia from the sea according to Strabo and his sources (most probably Artemidoros, second-first-century BCE: Migliario 2017, 85), at the intersection of the coastal road with the tracks following the river banks (Figs. 1 and 3). The ancient writers describe the district as rich in agriculture (Pliny, NH 14.39; 18.86–87: translated by Harris Rackham 1961, see below), cattle breeding (Livy 35.3: translated by Sage 1965, 8–9), stone quarries (Strabo 5.2.5: translated by Jones 1960, 352–353), manufacturing activities (ship construction: Strabo 5.2.5: translated by Jones 1960, 352–353) and maritime trade (Rut. Nam. 1.532: translated by Malamud 2016, 58). In particular, the Pisa territory was renowned for the vineyard and grain cultivation (Pliny, NH 14.39: translated by Harris Rackham 2005, 212–13; Pliny, NH 18.86–87: translated by Harris Rackham 1961, 244–245) still widespread today. The archaeological data matches with the literary one and adds evidence of relevant pottery, Graeco-Italic and Dressel 1 amphoras, marble and alabaster artefacts productions (Pasquinucci and Menchelli 2017, 327–330). The city and its territory were served by a well-integrated system of sea and river ports and landings, well connected by the Roman roads system since the mid-third-century BCE (Pasquinucci 2014a, b). The main maritime harbour was situated NNE of present Livorno. The coastal lagoon where it was located was frequented since the archaic period (see below), but the toponym Portus Pisanus is not mentioned before Late Antiquity, when it is documented by Rutilius Namatianus (*de reditu suo* 2.12; cf. 1. 527–540: early fifth-century CE: translated by Malamud 2016, 58) and by the *Itinerarium maritimum* (501, 1–4: early sixth-century CE: Arnaud 2004). According to the latter source Portus Pisanus was located eighteen Roman miles North of Vada Volaterrana (present Vada) and nine Roman miles South of the Arno river mouth of the time: "a Vadis portum Pisarum m(ilia) p(assuum) XVIII, a portu Pisano Pisis, fluvius, m(ilia) p(assuum) VIIII", therefore in the present silted up area ENE of Livorno (Figs. 1 and 2). Recent interdisciplinary research in this district (S. Stefano ai Lupi, La Paduletta, Il Deserto) confirms the ancient Portus Pisanus location and provides evidence of several characteristics of the site in its changing environment, based on palaeogeography, archaeology, geophysical prospections, ancient, mediaeval and post-mediaeval written sources, post-mediaeval drawings and maps (Pasquinucci et al. 2018; Kaniewski et al. 2018).

Following the coastal dynamics, the Mediaeval Portus Pisanus kept the ancient name but developed WSW of the Late Roman one. It was the main port of the Pisan Republic, protected by towers and closed by a chain. South of it, another Mediaeval harbour (porto di Livorno) was located nearby the small settlement ("castello") Livorno. It coexisted with the Mediaeval Portus Pisanus until the latter was gradually silted up and abandoned. The Florentine Government progressively transformed the Livorno settlement in a new town planned by the preeminent architect Buontalenti and the Livorno Port in a very innovative one (Pasquinucci et al. 2018).

4 Portus Pisanus: Archaeological Evidence

In 2004–2009, rescue excavations carried out in the NNE outskirts of Livorno by the Soprintendenza per i Beni Archeologici della Toscana and the University of Pisa have identified some small but very meaningful areas of the ancient Portus Pisanus Basin and of a few structures belonging to the port facilities and settlement (Pasquinucci et al. 2018). A few zones of a well-preserved sandy seabed were brought to light, covered with artefacts (pottery fragments, amphorae, ballast stones, etc.) dated from the late seventh/sixth-century BCE (bucchero, Samian and Etruscan wine amphorae) to the second-century BCE; the finds layout shows that the coastline prograded westwards and the loading and unloading of goods progressively followed this progradation (Pasquinucci et al. 2018). Since the mid-second-century BCE the ancient stretch of shallow water was progressively and rapidly silted up by alternate sand and posidonia layers. A few artefacts date this specific silting up phase between the first half of the first-century BCE and the fifth-century CE. In the late first-century BCE activities connected with navigation could no longer be performed in this area and were therefore shifted westwards. The silting chronology matches the above-mentioned data (par. 02) according to which the North Etruscan coast progradation was a consequence of the late Republican colonisation impact on the hinterland and possibly of a phase characterised by intense rainfalls. The presence of clay deposits testifies to a gradual process of continentalisation which started in the early Middle Ages (Kaniewskii et al. 2018) and came to an end only during the eighteenth–nineteenth centuries. A few Roman buildings were also excavated in the area. They are located immediately below the edge of the natural terrace called Gronda dei Lupi, on a sandy soil that can be interpreted as an ancient shoreline. The oldest structures date back to the third-second-century BCE: some walls line two rooms, whose function is hard to identify. Around the mid-first-century BCE this building was replaced by a new one, characterised by an open courtyard and a porch surrounded by at least 13 rooms, for commercial and warehousing use. The different orientation of the structures is perhaps due to a change in the shape of the shore where the buildings lay (Pasquinucci et al. 2018). The building entered a crisis in the second quarter of the fifth-century CE, shortly after Rutilius Namatianus' journey. As documented by a small coin hoard of the Emperors Anthemius (AD 467–472) and Leo I (AD 452–474) hidden inside the southwest corner of a room used as a Mithraeum, and by other data, this room and the whole commercial building were abandoned around the mid-fifth-century AD. A few fragments of pottery show a weak recovery between the end of the fifth- and the mid-sixth-century CE. Links with the main trade routes coming from Rome and Ostia had not yet completely dissolved in the sixth-century CE, as proved by the presence of African amphorae, South Italian Keay 52 and Eastern Late Roman 2 type amphorae. This phase was followed by the final abandonment of the building and, presumably, of other port facilities.

As for the environmental changes, between the fifth- and the sixth-century CE, the silting process went on (Kaniewski et al. 2018; Pasquinucci et al. 2018). Summing up, based on written sources, archaeological and geoarchaeological evidence Portus Pisanus was a large and probably not so deep coastal lagoon opened directly to the sea from the seventh-sixth-century BC to the sixth-century CE. This stretch of shallow water was navigated by appropriate crafts in order to load and unload wares. The port structures and buildings (wooden piers, warehouse, etc.) were located along a sandy shoreline, as proved by archaeological research. The ancient landing area and port activities were progressively shifted westwards due to the remarkable Luni-Livorno coastal progradation dated from the second-first-century BCE to around 1830 (see above par. 02); Pasquinucci and Menchelli 2012).

4.1 *Portus Pisanus: Claudius Rutilius Namatianus versus Palaeogeographic and Archaeological Evidence of the Site*

In the seventh stage of his journey Rutilius left Vada Volaterrana and sailed North in view of the Gorgona Island. While coasting the Livorno rocky promontory northwards, he watched (on his right) a villa maritima (Triturrita) overlooking the sea (1, 527–531: *sic villa vocatur, quae latet expulsis insula paene fretis*: translated by Malamud 2016, 58), evidently located at the NW edge of the promontory, most probably in the area of the present graveyard Cimitero dei Lupi (Livorno) (Fig. 8). Immediately later he saw the harbour Basin which he defined well sheltered and impressive (1. 533–540; 1. 559). He perceived and described Portus Pisanus as a wide open sea basin, a "maritime" port with windswept beaches and port facilities (de reditu 1. 527–540) and a safe one (1. 559). Of particular interest is the mention of the extensive seagrass meadows through which his boats (cymbae) navigated to reach the landing area (see below). The description is lively and detailed:

> From there we make for Triturrita: that is the name of a residence, a peninsula lying in the wash of baffled waves. For it juts out into the sea on stones which man's hand has put together, and he who built the house had first to make sure building ground. I was astonished at the haven close by, which by report is thronged with Pisa's merchandise and sea-borne wealth. The place has a marvellous appearance. Its shores are buffeted by the open sea and lie exposed to all the winds: here there are not sheltering piers to protect any inner harbour-basin capable of defying the threats of Aeolus. But, fringing its own deep-water domain, the tall sea-weed is like to do no damage to a ship that strikes it without shock; and yet in giving way it entangles the furious waves and lets no huge roller surge in from the deep (de red. 1. 527–540) … So, then I moor my ships in the safe anchorage (1. 559) (Duff and Duff 1934).

4.2 *Satellite Remote Sensing Contribution*

Indeed, a series of integrated methods of archaeological prospection confirms what Rutilius Namatianus observed for this complex landscape. His verses provide important clues about the appearance of the natural environment in which the harbour was located. Whereas it is now apparent the contribution provided by satellite remote sensing to the investigation of archaeological landscape (Campana 2002; Lasaponara and Masini 2012; Parcak 2009; Mozzi et al. 2016; Kaimaris et al. 2017, 2018), the Pisa coastal plain has been one of the pioneering case studies for the application of multispectral imagery-based techniques.

Multispectral images were employed to identify the presence of palaeolagoons characterising the Portus Pisanus Harbour System in antiquity (Marchisio et al. 2000). Based on the capability of sediments to retain water that strongly reduces bare soil reflectance, lithological recognition allowed scientists to detect and define areas with different levels of soil wetness. The importance of using infra-red spectral bands resided in their suitability to capture any small variation in moisture presence. The combination of different bands allowed to better mark those swampy areas that formed the lagoon system in which several landing points developed in antiquity (Fig. 7). Bright colours indicate concentrations of fine sediments which can be related to the presence of swampy areas. Different algorithms including PCA and NDVI allowed to confirm the presence of palaeolagoons and channels in the area between Pisae and its harbour Portus Pisanus (Marchisio et al. 2000).

4.3 GIS-Based Legacy Data Integration

Around 1760 the Florentine medicine doctor and naturalist G. Targioni Tozzetti saw ancient ruins and abundant artefacts in this area which he correctly attributed to the Portus Pisanus Harbour settlement based on his excellent knowledge of the Latin sources. He commissioned the engineer A. Morozzi a map showing the location of the Portus Pisanus settlement ruins and the Roman age hypothetical coastline in comparison with the late ones (Targioni Tozzetti 1768). The same district is visible in several seventeenth and eighteenth-century maps illustrating the basin undergoing a slow but constant silting up process and the Mediaeval and Modern ports of Livorno (Frati 2000). As usual in the de reditu, Rutilius didn't describe the port settlement in detail but observed a "villa" placed on a promontory and partially constructed on stone blocks projecting into the sea (de red. 1. 527–531) as in a proximal position to the harbour Portus Pisanus. By integrating multiple map sources in a GIS environment it was possible to spatially connect different layers providing an accurate picture of the area occupied by the described villa and the harbour structures located in its closest proximity (Fig. 8). What is particularly worth to mention is the impressive correspondence between the small peninsula's contour line drawn by Morozzi (Targioni Tozzetti 1768) and the same contour line clearly visible in a historical orthorectified aerial image of the area acquired during the 1950s. The possibility to visualise in a diachronic perspective multiple cartographic sources allows us to detect important features of the landscape that are no longer visible. The case of Portus Pisanus area is emblematic in this respect, as the area nowadays lies in the very densely urbanised portion of Livorno, where it is almost impossible by looking at present-day satellite imagery to discern those features that characterised the ancient landscape.

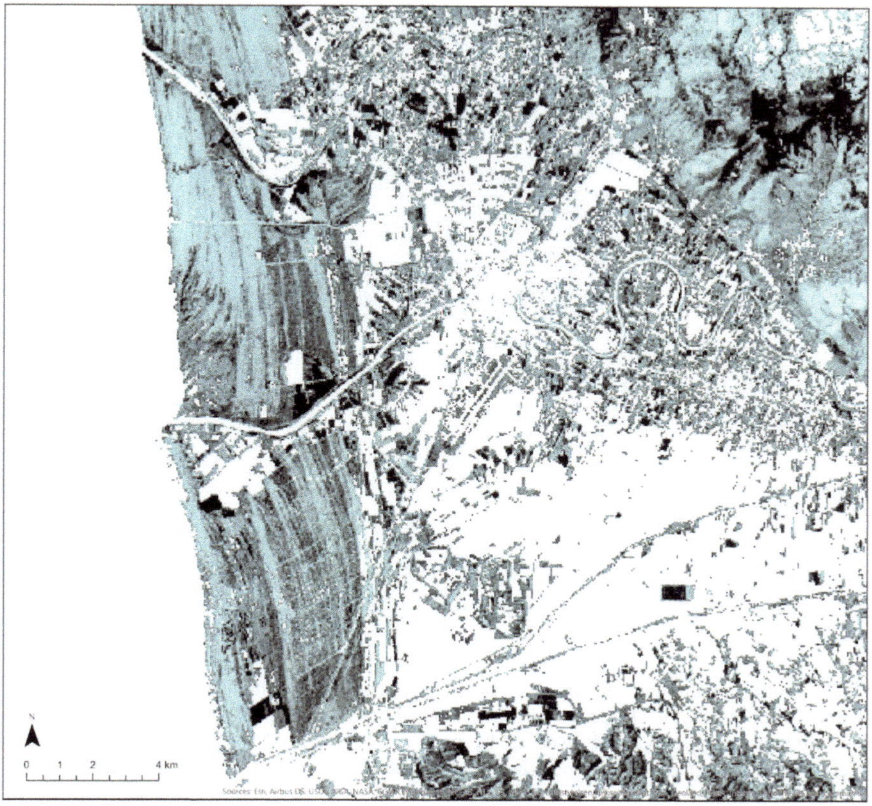

Fig. 7 Landsat TM image resulting from the difference between Principal Component Analysis (PC2) and Vegetation Index. Bright colours indicate fine sediment areas corresponding to ancient swamps (map by the authors, after Marchisio et al. 2000)

4.4 Geophysical Prospecting

Between the third- and the mid-fifth-century CE the Portus Pisanus lived an intense phase of commercial activities. The high number of amphora fragments reveals the relevant trade with the African provinces, the Iberian Peninsula and the Eastern part of the Mediterranean Sea (Genovesi 2010; Ducci et al. 2011; Genovesi 2014).

An important contribution to investigate the extension of this commercial area was provided by Ground Penetrating Radar (GPRS) technology that was intended to provide a complete map for interpreting the original function of the building (Pasquinucci et al. 2012). Geophysics has been widely applied in urban contexts and this is due to the clear advantages it brings on when it comes to the possibility of prospecting areas with no chance of undertaking stratigraphic excavations (Basile et al. 2000; Papadopoulos et al. 2009). Combined use of geophysical prospection and aerial photo-interpretation has also been extensively presented and discussed (Campana

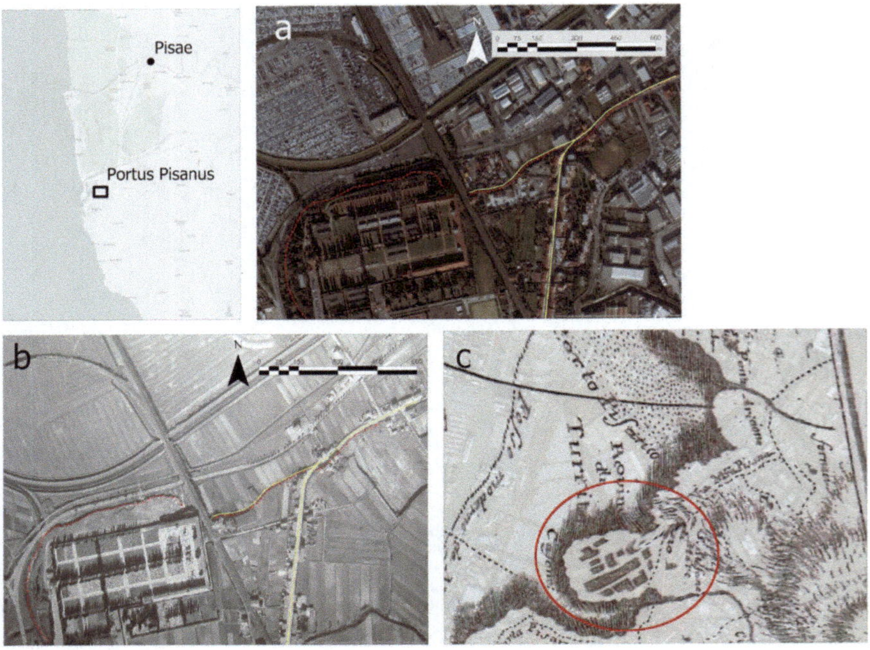

Fig. 8 Portion of the ancient Portus Pisanus area located in northern outskirts of Livorno (**a**). Historical aerial imagery (**b**) clearly shows the Pleistocene terrace profile (red line) named Gronda dei Lupi that was observed and described by Targioni Tozzetti (**c**). The crossroad of two historical roads probably datable to the Roman time is also visible (yellow line, map by the authors)

and Forte 2001; Sarris et al. 2013; Verdonck et al. 2012). Such an integration, in which satellite remote sensing provides an additional contribution, allows archaeologists to explore more effectively issues connected to the landscape palaeoenvironmental evolution (Keay et al. 2014). Concerning the area of Portus Pisanus, GPRS was employed to prospect an area of about 2000 m^2 where linear elements were interpreted as wide walls shaping a sequence of rooms (Pasquinucci et al. 2012). Interestingly, this prospection seems to confirm what has been observed and described by Rutilius Namantianus, who mentions an intense commercial activity while he approached the harbour as recalled by the use of the terms "emporio divitiisque maris" (Fig. 9) "port… full…with Pisa's stores and riches gained at sea" (de red. 1. 531–532: Malamud 2016, 59). By observing the data collected in the archaeological excavation, commercial activities are documented by the artefacts and by this commercial building, which was interpreted as an horreum (Pasquinucci and Menchelli 2010; Ducci et al. 2011, 43–45, Fig. 3). This was articulated in a central courtyard lined by a portico faced by quadrangular rooms. It is dated to the first-century BCE-sixth-century CE and was constructed on a previous building (third–second-century BCE) (Ducci et al. 2011, 43–45).

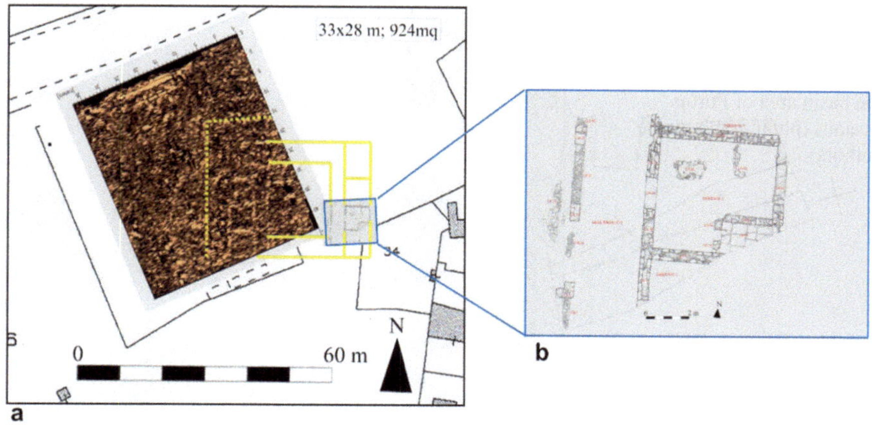

Fig. 9 Area of the geophysical prospection performed by using a Ground Penetrating Radar (GPR). The excavated portion of a commercial building (interpreted as a horreum) consistently matches the linear anomalies identified during the prospection and interpreted as possible walls (map by the authors, after Pasquinucci et al. 2012; Ducci et al. 2011).

4.5 Geoarchaeology Contribution

Concerning further observations made by Rutilius, it is worth to underline the description of the Posidonia seagrass. Geoarchaeological prospection in the Portus Pisanus area and archaeological excavations confirmed its presence at different chronological stages in the stratigraphic sequence. Recent geoarchaeological research (Alinne et al. 2016; Kaniewski et al. 2018) based on coring confirms the major changes in the geomorphological asset of the area. Cores have been extracted both in the area immediately West of the mentioned archaeological excavations and North of it. The presence of a large lagoon in the Etruscan and Roman time period is confirmed by the above-mentioned (par. 4) excavations. Based on the most recent study (Kaniewski et al. 2018), within the end of the second millennium BCE, the area West of the harbour settlement was occupied by sediments likely to be due to the existence of a marine bay protected from the main waves of the open sea. As the archaeological excavations show, at least since the Etruscan age (seventh-sixth-century BCE) the area with sandy seabed proved to be a good landing area for the boats sailing along the North Tyrrhenian Coast. This marine area, characterised by the presence of Posidonia and substantial fluvial deposits, would have tended to silt up in later centuries, to be interested by a major continentalisation process starting during the early Middle Ages (Fig. 10) (Kaniewski et al. 2018).

Fig. 10 Section of a natural sequence showing continentalisation process in the basin area of Portus Pisanus (photograph by the authors)

5 From Ancient Perception to Archaeological Interpretation: A Multidisciplinary Investigation

This chapter has sought to demonstrate the importance of connecting narratives of ancient authors to the archaeological evidence retrieved through combined approaches based on conspicuous amounts of digital data. The accounts of Strabo and Rutilius Namatianus, who provided insightful descriptions of the coastal regions examined in this study, have been compared against the data collected in over 30 years of archaeological investigation conducted by the authors of this contribution. Some case-study areas located along the North Coastal Etruria were chosen as they were described by these authors who used either their own perception or previous authors' descriptions to make a detailed account of important features connected to the natural environment and the social landscape. The Portus Pisanus area, in particular, was intensively investigated in the last 15 years and the collected data seem to confirm the picture drawn by Rutilius Namatianus in his poem, who described with his own eyes a lively and prosperous harbour strategically positioned in a wide coastal lagoon. The complexity of the transformations that affected those spaces through the centuries is enormous and therefore it is crucial to reflect on the urgency of defining innovative

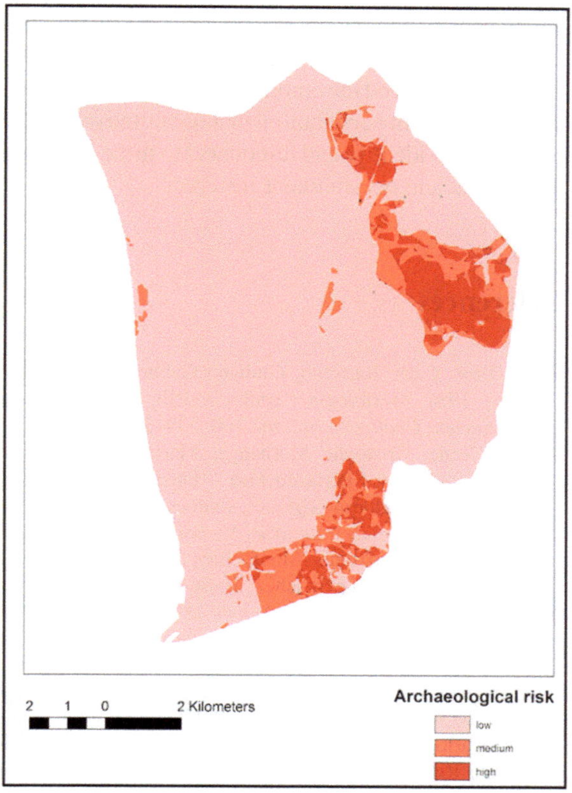

Fig. 11 Predictive model for the alluvial coastal plain between the ancient city of Pisae and the main harbour site of Portus Pisanus. Red-coloured areas express higher archaeological risk/potential and are quite expectedly spatially related to that portion of land along the ancient coastline viewed and described by Rutilius Namatianus (map by the authors, after Landeschi and Carrozzino 2011)

strategies for dealing with uncertainties due to the lack of information in areas that are nowadays heavily urbanised and affected by new development. In this respect, the data collected through multiple and integrated methods and techniques in more than 30 years of research allowed also to define an interpretative predictive model that was used to better understand the archaeological potential in the southernmost portion of the Pisa alluvial coastal plain (Fig. 11) (Landeschi and Carrozzino 2011). Interestingly, areas with higher archaeological potential matched very well with the portion of the landscape described by Rutilius as being part or at least proximal to the harbour system and the villa, and located on the Pleistocenic terrace boundary known as "Gronda dei Lupi" (Ciampalini et al. 2006). To sum up, multidisciplinary methods of investigation have proven to be crucial in confirming the account made by Strabo and Rutilius Namatianus, by enabling archaeologists to get a deeper insight into the ancient landscape not just as a physical space but also as a lived-in, social landscape made by people, encounters and relations. By combining traditional and digitally based methods it is possible at least to attempt to simulate that "sense of place" as it has been described in the "de reditu". The experiential approach to the space/place is mediated through the eyes of an ancient traveller/author who provides us with an invaluable source of information for understanding significant transformations which occurred in the observed landscape. Accounts from ancient authors/travellers are an invaluable source of information about the mindset of people living in a certain context. It is indeed the emotional and affective dimension that it is quite hard to grasp and an important contribution that quantitative and digital methods can provide is the possibility to identify and re-connect to these accounts the conditions and affordances that the ancient environment fostered.

References

Aiello, Eros, Carlo Bartolini, Giuliano Gabbani, Renzo Mazzanti, Enzo Pranzini, and Gigliola Valleri. 1981. Morfologia e geologia delle Secche di Vada (Provincia di Livorno). *Bollettino della Società Geologica Italiana* 100: 339–368.

Alinne, Cecile, Cristophe Morhange, Marinella Pasquinucci, and Camille Roumieux. 2016. Géoarchéologie des Ports de Pise – Stazione Ferroviaria San Rossore et de Portus Pisanus. Dynamiques géomorphologiques, sources antiques et données archéologiques. In *Les ports dans l'espace méditerranéen antique. Narbonne et les systèmes portuaires fluvio-lagunaires.* Actes du Colloque international, Montpellier, 22 May 2014. Revue Archéologique de la Narbonnaise, suppl XIV, ed. Corinne Sanchez, Marie-Pierre Jézégou: 321–338.

Arnaud, Pascal. 2004. Entre Antiquité et Moyen-Âge: l'Itinéraire Maritime d'Antonin In *Rotte e porti del Mediterraneo dopo la caduta dell'impero romano d'Occidente. Continuità e innovazioni tecnologiche e funzionali, Atti IV Seminario Progetto ANSER (Anciennes routes maritimes méditerranéennes, Interreg IIIB MEDOCC), Genova-2004*, eds. Lorenza De Maria and Rita Turchetti, 3–19. Soveria Mannelli: Rubbettino Editore.

Baroni, Carlo, Monica Bini, Simonetta Menchelli, Marta Pappalardo, Marinella Pasquinucci, Adriano Ribolini, Maria Rosaria Salvatore and Paolo Sangriso. 2014. Landscape changes in north coastal Tuscany : the Vada Volaterrana Project. In Atti del Quinto Simposio Il monitoraggio costiero Mediterraneo: problematiche e tecniche di misura, Livorno 17-18-19 giugno 2014. CNR-IBIMET ed. Fabrizio Benincasa, 261–268.

Basile, Vito, Maria Teresa Carrozzo, Sergio Negri, Luigia Nuzzo, Tatiana A. M. Quarta, and Aurélien Villani. 2000. A ground penetrating radar survey for archaeological investigations in an urban area (Lecce, Italy). *Journal Applied Geophysics* 44: 15–32.

Benetti, Ilaria, Fulvia Donati, Simonetta Menchelli, Marinella Pasquinucci, and Paolo Sangriso. 2018. Indagine sulla diffusione del terzo stile in Etruria, Il caso di Vada Volaterrana. In Antiqua 55. Pictores per Provincias II - Status quaestionis, Actes du 13e Colloque de l'Association Internationale pour la Peinture Murale Antique (AIPMA) organisé par Yves Dubois, Michel E. Fuchs, Alexandra Spüler. Lausanne, Anthropole, 12–16 septembre 2016: 555–566.

Benvenuti, Marco, Marta Mariotti Lippi, Pasquino Pallecchi, and Mario Sagri. 2006. Late-Holocene catastrophic floods in the terminal Arno River (Pisa, Central Italy) from the story of a Roman riverine harbour. *The Holocene* 16 (6): 863–876.

Benvenuti, Marco, Marco Bonini, Giovanna Moratti, Marianna Ricci, and Chiara Tanini. 2008. Tectonic and climatic controls on historical landscape modifications: The avulsion of the lower Cecina River (Tuscany, central Italy). *Geomorphology* 100: 269–284.

Bianchi, Giovanna, and Sauro Gelichi. eds. 2016. *Un monastero sul mare. A Monastery by the Sea. Ricerche archeologiche a San Quirico di Populonia (Piombino, LI) Archaeological Research at San Quirico di Populonia (Piombino, LI).* Sesto Fiorentino (FI): Edizioni All'Insegna del Giglio.

Bianchi, Giovanna, and Richard Hodges, eds. 2018. *Origins of a new economic union (7th.-12th. Centuries). Preliminary results of the nEU-Med project: October 2015-March 2017.* Biblioteca di Archeologia Medievale 25. Firenze: All'Insegna del Giglio.

Bresci, Deborah, Sara Carli, Pranzini Enzo, and Lorenzo Rossi. 2006. Studio geomorfologico delle dune costiere di marina di Cecina (Toscana) con rilievi Lidar da aereo. *Studi costieri*: 17–29.

Campana, Stefano. 2002. Ikonos-2 Multispectral satellite imagery to the study of archaeological landscapes: An integrated multi-sensor approach in combination with "traditional" methods. In *The Digital Heritage of Archaeology, CAA 2002. Computer Applications and Quantitative Methods in Archaeology*, eds. Doer Martin and Apostolos Sarris, 219–225. Proceedings of the 30 Conference, Heraklion, Crete, 2–6 April 2002. Archive of monuments and publication: Hellenic Ministry of Culture.

Campana, Stefano, and Maurizio Forte, eds. 2001. *Remote sensing in archaeology*. XI Ciclo di lezioni sulla ricerca applicata in archeologia. Certosa di Pontignano (Siena), 6–11 dicembre 1999. Firenze: All' Insegna del Giglio.

Ceccarelli Lemut, Maria Luisa. 2013. Il paesaggio costiero della Maremma Pisana medievale. In *Paesaggi e proiezione marittima. I sistemi adriatico e tirrenico nel lungo periodo. Marche e Toscana a confronto*, eds. Gabriella Garzella, Roberto Giulianelli, Giuseppe Petralia, Olimpia Vaccari, 25–45. Pisa, Centro di studi storici mediterranei. Pisa: Pacini Editore.

Ceccarelli Lemut, Maria Luisa, and Marinella Pasquinucci. 1991. Fonti antiche e medievali per la viabilità del territorio pisano. *Bollettino Storico Pisano* 60: 111–138.

Ciampalini, Alessandro, Lorenzo Ciulli, Giovanni Sarti, and Giovanni Zanchetta. 2006. Nuovi dati geologici del sottosuolo del "Terrazzo di Livorno". *Atti della Società Toscana di Scienze Naturali, Memorie* 111: 75–82.

Ciampoltrini, Giulio. 1981. Note sulla colonizzazione augustea nell'Etruria settentrionale. *Studi Classici e Orientali* 31: 41–55.

Ciampoltrini, Giulio. 2007. *Ad limitem. Paesaggi d'età romana nello scavo degli Orti del San Francesco in Lucca*. Lucca: Tipografia Menegazzo.

Ciampoltrini, Giulio, Carlotta Cianferoni, and Antonella Romualdi. 1982–83. La raccolta archeologica e numismatica Enrico Chiellini. Il Museo Civico Archeologico di Livorno ed i materiali dal Portus Pisanus. *Rassegna di Archeologia* 3:183–241.

Cuntz, Otto (ed.). 1929. *Itineraria Romana, Volumen prius, itineraria Antonini Augusti et Burdigalense*. Leipzig: Teubner

Dallai, Luisa. 2016 Paesaggio e risorse: il monastero di San Quirico di Populonia, la pianura ed il promontorio di Piombino/ Landscape and resources: the monastery of San Quirico di Populonia, the plain, and the promontory of Piombino. In *Un monastero sul mare. Ricerche a San Quirico di Populonia (Piombino, LI) / A Monastery by the Sea. Archaeological Research at San Quirico di Populonia (Piombino, LI)*, eds. Giovanna Bianchi and Sauro Gelichi, 89–108. Firenze: All'Insegna del Giglio.

Dallai, Luisa, Andrea Bardi, Arianna Briano, Mauro Paolo Buonincontri, Mirko Buono, Gaetano Di Pasquale, Stefania Fineschi, Giulio Poggi, Elisabetta Ponta, Marta Rossi, Luisa Russo and Vanessa Volpi. 2018. Investigations at Carlappiano: new archaeological findings in anthropic and natural landscapes. In: *Origins of a new economic union (7th.-12th. Centuries). Preliminary results of the nEU-Med project: October 2015-March 2017*, eds. Giovanna Bianchi and Richard Bianchi et Hodges, 29–55. Biblioteca di Archeologia Medievale 25. Firenze: All'Insegna del Giglio.

De Maria, Lorenza, and Rita Turchetti, eds. 2004. *Evolución paleoambiental de los puertos y fondeaderos antiguos en el Mediterráneo occidental,* Atti I Seminario Progetto ANSER (Anciennes routes maritimes méditerranéennes, Interreg IIIB MEDOCC), El patrimonio arqueológico submarino y los puertos antiguos, Alicante-2003. Soveria Mannelli: Rubbettino Editore.

Della Rocca, Bruno, Renzo Mazzanti and Enzo Pranzini. 1987. Studio geomorfologico della Pianura di Pisa. *Geografia fisica dinamica quaternario* 10: 56–84.

Dini, Pietro Umberto. 1996. Sul toponimo Pisa in una prospettiva indoeuropea. *Annali dell'Istituto Orientale di Napoli* 16: 283–306.

Ducci, Silvia, Marinella Pasquinucci, Stefano Genovesi. 2011. Portus Pisanus nella tarda età imperiale (IIIVI secolo): nuovi dati archeologici e fonti scritte a confronto. In *I sistemi portuali della*

Toscana mediterranea. Infrastrutture, scambi, economie, dall'antichità ad oggi, eds. Maria Luisa Ceccarelli Lemut, Gabriella Garzella, Olimpia Vaccari, 11–56. Pisa: Pacini Editore.

Duff, John Wight, and Arnold M. Duff. 1934. *Namatianus, Rutilius*, Loeb Classical Library: Volume II: Minor Latin Poets: de Reditu suo. London: Heinemann.

Fo, Alessandro. 1992. *Rutilio Namaziano. Il ritorno*. Torino: Giulio Einaudi Editore.

Frati, Piero. 2000. *Livorno nelle antiche stampe: piante e vedute della città dalla fine del secolo XVI alla fine del secolo XIX*. Livorno: Cassa di Risparmi di Livorno.

Genovesi, Stefano. 2010. Materiali tardoantichi dal Portus Pisanus (S. Stefano) ai Lupi, Livorno. In *Late Roman Coarse Wares, Cooking Wares and Amphorae in the Mediterranean, Archaeology and Archaeometry. Comparison between western and eastern Mediterranean*, eds. Simonetta Menchelli, Sara Santoro, Marinella Pasquinucci, and Gabriella Guiducci, 337–344. LRCW 3, Atti del Congresso Internazionale, Parma-Pisa marzo 2008, Oxford: BAR Int. Series 2185, I–II.

Genovesi, Stefano. 2014. Contenitori da trasporto dall'area del Portus Pisanus e rotte commerciali tirreniche tra IV e VI sec. d. C.: nuove evidenze dalla campagna 2009. In: *Late Roman Coarse Wares, Cooking Wares and Amphorae in the Mediterranean, Archaeology and Archaeometry. The Mediterranean: a market without frontiers* 1, eds. Natalia Poulou-Papadimitriou, Eleni Nodarou e Vassilis Kilikoglou, 993–1003. Proceedings 4th Conference on Late Roman Coarse Wares, Cooking Wares and Amphorae, Thessaloniki, 7–10 April 2011, BAR Int. Ser 2016. Oxford: BAR Publishing.

Giroldini, Pierluigi. 2012. Between Land and Sea: A GIS Based Settlement Analysis of the Ancient Coastal Lagoon of Piombino (Tuscany, Italy). In *Landscape Archaeology*, eds. Wiebke Bebermeier, Robert Hebenstreit, Elke Kaiser – Jan, 383–389. Proceedings of the International Conference Berlin, 6–8 June 2012. Berlin: Excellence Cluster Topoi.

Hett, W.S. 1936. Aristotle. *Minor Works: On Colours. On Things Heard. Physiognomics. On Plants. On Marvellous Things Heard. Mechanical Problems. On Indivisible Lines. The Situations and Names of Winds. On Melissus, Xenophanes, Gorgias*. The Loeb Classical Library, 1936, repr.1963. London-Cambridge MA: W. Heinemann Ldt - Harvard University Press.

Iacopini, Eleonora, Antonella Del Rio, Linda Cherubini, Simonetta Menchelli, and Marinella Pasquinucci. 2012. Il Sistema Informativo Territoriale dell'*ager Volaterranus*: metodologia e metadati. In *Laboratorio Universitario Volterrano 2010–2011, Quaderno* 15, ed. Costantino Caciagli, 55–64. Pisa: Tipografia di Agnano

Kaimaris, Dimitris, Petros Patias, and Olga Georgoula. 2017. Google Earth Revisited: Case Studies at the Plain of Larissa (Thessaly, Greece). *International Journal of Computational Methods in Heritage Science* 1(1): 77–88.

Kaimaris, Dimitris, George Karadedos, Charalampos Georgiadis, and Petros Patias. 2018. Locating and Mapping the Traces of the Covered Ancient Theater of Amphipolis (Eastern Macedonia, Greece). *Heritage* 1: 306–319.

Kaniewski, David, Nick Marriner, Christophe Morhange, Matteo Vacchi, Giovanni Sarti, Veronica Rossi, Monica Bini, Marinella Pasquinucci, Cecile Alinne, Thierry Otto, Frédéric Luce, and Elise Van Campo. 2018. Holocene evolution of Portus Pisanus, the lost harbour of Pisa. *Scientific Reports* 8: 11625 (2018). https://doi.org/10.1038/s41598-018-29890-w.

Keay, S.J., S.H. Parcak, and K.D. Strutt. 2014. High resolution space and ground-based remote sensing and implications for landscape archaeology: The case from Portus, Italy. *Journal of Archaeological Science* 52: 277–292.

Lambeck, Kurt, Fabrizio Antonioli, Antony Purcell, and Sergio Silenzi. 2004. Sea-level change along the Italian coast for the past 10,000 yr. *Quaternary Science Reviews* 23: 1567–1598.

Landeschi, Giacomo and Marcello Carrozzino (accepted/in press). Detecting and Communicating archaeology in the Pisa coastal plain: new tools to reach this aim. In *Porti antichi e retroterra produttivi*. Atti del Convegno Internazionale (Livorno 2009), eds. Antoinette Hesnard and Marinella Pasquinucci.

Landeschi, Giacomo and Marcello Carrozzino. 2011. Communicating archaeological risk with web-based virtual reality: a case study. *Internet Archaeology* 31.

Lasaponara, Rosa, and Nicola Masini, eds. 2012. *Satellite remote sensing: A new tool for archaeology* 16. Springer Science & Business Media.

Lasserre, Francois. 1967. *Strabon. Geographie Tome III (Livres V-VI).* Paris: Les Belles Lettres.

Leucci, Giovanni, Lara De Giorgi, and Giuseppe Scardozzi. 2014. Geophysical prospecting and remote sensing for the study of the San Rossore area in Pisa (Tuscany, Italy). *Journal of Archaeological Science* 52: 256–276.

Liebermann, Benjamin, and Elisabeth Gordon. 2018. *Climate Change in Human History: Prehistory to the Present.* New York: Bloomsbury Academic.

Lionello, Piero. 2012. *The Climate of the Mediterranean Region: from the past to the Future* Amsterdam Boston Tokio: Elsevier.

Livy. The History of Rome, 10, Books 35–37. Translated by Evan T. Sage (reprinted 1939, 1950, 1958, 1965). The Loeb Classical Library. London-Cambridge, MA: William Heinemann Ltd. - Harvard University Press.

Lycophron. *Alexandra:* translated by André Hurst and Antje Kolde 2008. Paris: Les Belles Lettres.

Malamud, Martha. 2016. *Rutilius Namatianus' Going home: de reditu suo.* Abingdon-New York, Routledge.

Marchisio, Mario, Marinella Pasquinucci, Enzo Pranzini, and Guido Vigna Guidi. 2000. The Pisa territory Project. In *Non-destructive Techniques Applied to Landscape Archaeology*, eds. Marinella Pasquinucci and Fréderic Trément: 233–244. The Archaeology of Mediterranean Landscapes 4, (series eds. Graeme Barker and David Mattingly). Oxford: Oxbow Books.

Mariotti Lippi, Marta, Cristina Bellini, Chiara Trinci, Marco Benvenuti, Pasquino Pallecchi, and Mario Sagri. 2007. Pollen analysis of the ship site of Pisa San Rossore, Tuscany, Italy: the implications for catastrophic hydrological events and climatic change during the late Holocene. *Vegetation History and Archaeobotany* 16, 6: 453–465.

Migliario, Elvira. 2017. Strabo, Italy and the Italian peoples. In *The Routledge Companion to Strabo*, ed. Daniela Dueck. Abingdon: Routledge.

Morhange, Christophe, Nick Marriner, Maria Luisa Blot, Guénaëlle Bony, Nicolas Carayon, Pilar Carmona, Clément Flaux, Matthieu Giaime, Jean-Philippe Goiran, Mourad Kouka, Anna Lena, Ameur Oueslati, Marinella Pasquinucci and Alexeï Porotov. 2015. Dynamiques géomorphologiques et typologie géoarcheologique des ports antiques en contextes lagunaires. *Quaternaire* 26, 2: 117–139.

Mozzi, Paolo, Alessandro Fontana, Francesco Ferrarese, Andrea Ninfo, Stefano Campana, and Roberto Francese. 2016. The Roman City of Altinum, Venice Lagoon, from remote sensing and geophysical prospection. *Archaeological Prospection.* 23, 1: 27–44.

Neumann, James E. 1985. Climate change as a topic in the classical Greek and Roman literature. Climatic Change 7:441–454. https://doi.org/10.1007/BF00139058.

Papadopoulos, N., A. Sarris, M.J. Yi and J.H. Kim. 2009. Urban archaeological investigations using surface 3D ground penetrating radar and electrical resistivity tomography methods. *Exploration Geophysics* 40, 1: 56–68.

Parcak, Sarah H. 2009. *Satellite remote sensing for archaeology.* London: Routledge.

Pasquinucci, Marinella. 2007. I porti di Pisa e Volterra. Breve nota a Strabone 5.2.5, 222C. *Athenaeum* 95: 677–684.

Pasquinucci, Marinella. 2008. Water Management practices and risk management in North Etruria (Archaic period to Late Antiquity): a few remarks. In *Vers une gestion intégrée de l'eau dans l'histoire environnementale: savoirs traditionnels et pratiques modernes*, ed. Ella Hermon, 147–156. Actes du Colloque International, Université Laval, october 2006. Atlante Tematico di Topografia Antica, XVI Supplemento. Roma: L'Erma di Bretschneider.

Pasquinucci, Marinella. 2014a. An efficient communication network: Roman land, sea and river routes in North Western Etruria. In *Honesta missione. Festschrift für Barbara Pferdehirt.* Römisch-Germanischen Zentralmuseum Mainz Monographien 100: 33–48. Mainz: RGZM Verlag.

Pasquinucci, Marinella. 2014b. Vada Volaterrana e il suo territorio: siti costieri e popolamento rurale fra romanizzazione e tardoantico. In *Amore per l'antico. Dal Tirreno all'Adriatico, dalla*

Preistoria al Medioevo e oltre. Studi di antichità in ricordo di Giuliano de Marinis, eds. Gabriele Baldelli and Fulvia Lo Schiavo, 1: 281–292. Roma: Scienze e Lettere.

Pasquinucci, Marinella. 2020. Fra osservazione puntuale e percezione: la fascia costiera nord-etrusca nel de reditu. In *Rutilius Namatianus, aristocrate païen en voyage et poète.* Actes Colloque Int. Paris- Nanterre 2018, ed. Étienne Wolff, 99–123. Scripta Antiqua 131. Bordeaux: Éditions Ausonius.

Pasquinucci, Marinella, and Simonetta Menchelli. 2003. Porti, approdi e dinamiche commerciali nell'ager Pisanus e nella valle dell'Arno (III sec. a.C.-VI sec. d.C.). In *Puertos Fluviales Antiguos: Ciudad, Desarrollo e Infraestructuras, Actas IV Jornadas de Arqueología Subacuática, Valencia-2001,* eds. Guillermo Pascual Berlanga, José Pérez Ballester, 237-249. Valencia: Universitat de València, Facultat de Geografia i Història.

Pasquinucci, Marinella, and Simonetta Menchelli. 2010. Il sistema portuale di Pisa: dinamiche costiere, import-export, interazioni economiche e culturali (VII sec. a.C.-I sec. d.C.). *Bollettino di Archeologia online, Numero Speciale* www.beniculturali.it/bao. https://bollettinodiarcheologiaonline.beniculturali.it/.

Pasquinucci, Marinella, and Simonetta Menchelli. 2012. Landscape transformations in North Coastal Etruria. In eds. Sjoerd. J. Kluiving and Erica B. Guttmann-Bond: *Landscape Archaeology between Art and Science. From a multi- to an interdisciplinary approach.* Proceedings First International Landscape Archaeology Conference, Amsterdam 2010: 179–196. Amsterdam: Amsterdam University Press.

Pasquinucci, Marinella, and Simonetta Menchelli. 2017. Rural, urban and suburban communities and their economic interconnectivity in Coastal North Etruria (2nd cent.BC-2nd cent.AD). In *The economic integration of Roman Italy. Rural communities in a globalizing world,* eds. Gijs Tol and Tymon de Haas: 322–341. Mnemosyne Supplements, History and Archaeology of Classical Antiquity 404. Leiden-Boston: Brill.

Pasquinucci, Marinella, Simonetta Menchelli, Renzo Mazzanti, Mario Marchisio, and Laurent D'Onofrio. 2001. Coastal Archaeology in North Etruria. Geomorphologic, Archaeological, Archive, Magnetometric and Geoelectrical researches. *Revue d'Archéometrie* 25: 187–201.

Pasquinucci, Marinella, Enzo Pranzini, and Sergio Silenzi. 2004. Variazioni del livello marino ed evoluzione della costa toscana in epoca storica: opportunità di porti e di approdi. In *Evolución paleoambiental de los puertos y fondeaderos antiguos en el Mediterráneo occidental,* eds. Lorenza De Maria and Rita Turchetti, 87–102. Atti del I Seminario Progetto ANSER (Anciennes routes maritimes méditerranéennes, Interreg IIIB MEDOCC El patrimonio arqueológico submarino y los puertos antiguos, Alicante-2003. Soveria Mannelli: Rubbettino.

Pasquinucci, Marinella, Silvia Ducci, Simonetta Menchelli, Adriano Ribolini, Alessandro Bianchi, Monica Bini, and Simone Sartini. 2012. Ground penetrating radar survey of urban sites in North Coastal Etruria: Pisae, Portus Pisanus, Vada Volaterrana. In *Urban Landscape Survey in Italy and the Mediterranean,* eds. Frank Vermeulen, Gert-Jan Burgers, Simon Keay, and Cristina Corsi, 149–159. Oxford: Oxbow Books.

Pasquinucci, Marinella, Silvia Ducci, and Stefano Genovesi. 2018. Portus Pisanus and Livorno: environmental, archaeological and historical interdisciplinary research. In *Monitoring of Mediterranean Coastal Areas. Problems and measurement techniques,* ed. Fabrizio Benincasa, 13–30. Proceedings Seventh International Symposium, Livorno (Italy) June 19–21. Firenze: FU Press.

Peyron, Odile, Nathalie Combourieu-Nebout, David Brayshaw, Simon Goring, Valérie Andrieu-Ponel, Stéphanie Desprat, Will Fletcher, Belinda Gambin, Chryssanthi Ioakim, Sébastien Joannin, Ulrich Kotthoff, Katerina Kouli, Vincent Montade, Jörg Pross, Laura Sadori, and Michel Magny. 2017. Precipitation changes in the Mediterranean basin during the Holocene from terrestrial and marine pollen records: a model–data comparison. *Climate of the Past* 13: 249–265. https://doi.org/10.5194/cp-13-249-2017.

Pliny. Natural History, Volume IV: Books 12–16. Translated by Harris Rackham. 1945, repr. 2005. Loeb Classical Library 370. Cambridge, MA - London: Harvard University Press, W. Heinemann Ltd.

Pliny. Natural History, Volume V: Books 17–19. Translated by Harris Rackham. Loeb Classical Library 371 (1950.repr 1961). London-Cambridge, MA: W. Heinemann Ltd-Harvard University Press.

Pranzini, Enzo. 2007. Airborne LIDAR survey applied to the analysis of historical evolution at the Arno River delta (Italy). *Journal of Coastal Research* 50: 400–409.

Repetto, Ivan, Klaus Freitag, Marinella Pasquinucci, Stefan Groh, Antonella Del Rio, Linda Cherubini, Simonetta Menchelli, and Helga Sedlmayer. 2018. Indagini geofisiche nell'Etruria settentrionale costiera. I siti di Capo di Villa, Vallescaia e Poggio Fiori. *Journal Ancient Topography* 28: 43–66.

Sarris, Apostolos, Nikos Papadopoulos, Athos Agapiou, Maria Cristina Salvi, Diofantos G. Hadjimitsis, William Arthur Parkinson, Richard. W. Yerkes, Attila Gyucha, and Paul R. Duffy. 2013. Integration of geophysical surveys, ground hyperspectral measurements, aerial and satellite imagery for archaeological prospection of prehistoric sites: the case study of Vésztő-Mágor Tell, Hungary. *Journal of Archaeological Science* 40 (3): 1454–1470.

Shepherd, Elisabeth Jane. 2006. La tonnara di Baratti". In eds. Maria Aprosio and Cynthia Mascione, *Materiali per Populonia,* 5, 271–280. Pisa: Edizioni ETS.

Strabo. The Geography, Volume II: Books 3–5. Translated by Horace Leonard Jones. Loeb Classical Library 50 (1923 repr 1949, 1960). London - Cambridge MA: W. Heinemann Ltd- Harvard University Press.

Targioni Tozzetti, Giovanni. 1768. *Relazioni d'alcuni viaggi fatti in diverse parti della Toscana per osservare le produzioni naturali, e gli antichi monumenti di essa,* II. Firenze: Cambiagi.

Verdonck, L., D. Taelman, & F. Vermeulen. (2012). 3-D GPR investigation of a residential area in the Roman town Ammaia (Portugal). In *Recent Work in Archaeological Geophysics, Abstracts,* 34–36. London, UK: Near-surface Geophysics Group.

Walsh, Kevin. 2014. The Archaeology of Mediterranean Landscapes: Human-environment Interaction from the Neolithic to the Roman period. Cambridge: Cambridge University Press.

Wolff, Étienne, Serge Lancel, and Joëlle Solers. 2007. *Rutilius Namatianus. Sur son retour.* Paris: Les Belles Lettres.

Marinella Pasquinucci is a former full professor of ancient topography, professor of maritime archaeology, professor for doctoral courses in classical archaeology and in ancient history (the University of Pisa), professor of ancient topography for specialised courses in archaeology (the University of Pisa and the University of Florence). Her main research interests are landscape archaeology, Roman town planning, western Mediterranean trade, and archaeometry of Roman pottery.

Multisensory Experiences in Archaeological Landscapes—Sound, Vision, and Movement in GIS and Virtual Reality

Heather Richards-Rissetto, Kristy E. Primeau, David E. Witt, and Graham Goodwin

Abstract Archaeologists are employing a variety of digital tools to develop new methodological frameworks that combine computational and experiential approaches which is leading to new multisensory research. In this article, we explore vision, sound, and movement at the ancient Maya city of Copan from a multisensory and multiscalar perspective bridging concepts and approaches from different archaeological paradigms. Our methods and interpretations employ theory-inspired variables from proxemics and semiotics to develop a methodological framework that combines computation with sensory perception. Using GIS, 3D, and acoustic tools we create multisensory experiences in VR with spatial sound using an immersive headset (Oculus Rift) and touch controllers (for movement). The case study simulates the late eighth and early ninth-century landscape of the ancient Maya city of Copan to investigate the role of landscape in facilitate movement, send messages, influence social interaction, and structure cultural events. We perform two simulations to begin to study the impact of vegetation on viewsheds and soundsheds of a stela at ancient Copan. Our objectives are twofold: (1) design and test steps towards developing a GIS computational approach to analyse the impact of vegetation within urban agrarian landscapes on viewsheds and soundsheds and (2) explore cultural significance of Stela 12, and more generally the role of synesthetic experience in ancient Maya society using a multisensory approach that incorporates GIS and VR.

H. Richards-Rissetto (✉)
School of Global Integrative Studies, Nebraska College of Arts and Sciences, Old Father Hall (OLDH) 840, Lincoln, NE, USA
e-mail: richards-rissetto@unl.edu

K. E. Primeau
New York State Office of Renewable Energy Siting, Albany, NY, USA
e-mail: keprimeau@alumni.albany.edu

D. E. Witt
Department of Anthropology, University at Buffalo, Buffalo, NY, USA
e-mail: dwitt@buffalo.edu

G. Goodwin
University of California, Merced, CA, USA
e-mail: ggoodwin@ucmerced.edu

G. Landeschi and E. Betts (eds.), *Capturing the Senses*,
Quantitative Methods in the Humanities and Social Sciences,
https://doi.org/10.1007/978-3-031-23133-9_9

Keywords Ancient Maya · Multisensory · GIS · Virtual reality (VR) · Archaeoacoustics

1 Introduction

Archaeologists began using computers in the 1950s and 1960s, contributing to the subsequent rise of New Archaeology (Cowgill 1967; Gardin 1971). However, only since the turn of the twenty-first century with the emergence of many off-the-shelf software packages have digital technologies played a larger role in shaping archaeological practice and scholarship. When archaeologists began employing Geographic Information Systems (GIS) in the 1980s, GIS had a non-GUI interface requiring users to code in GRASS (Geographic Resources Analysis Support System) with a Unix shell (https://grass.osgeo.org/home/history/). In 1981, ESRI (Environmental Science Research Institute released ARC/INFO, the first commercial GIS, but it also had a non-GUI interface requiring users to code with the ARC Macro Language (AML). In 1992, ESRI released ArcVIEW providing a user interface for GIS that did not require coding. However, wide-spread adoption of GIS did not occur until the early 2000s with the introduction of ArcGIS Desktop in 1999 (ESRI) along with a push to provide low-cost and free educational licenses for the software and greater access via the internet. Post-processual archaeology and the addition of extensions such as Spatial Analyst and 3D Analyst moved digital archaeology beyond data management and mapping to human-centred approaches by affording greater analytical functionality for non-expert users (i.e. coding was no longer an essential skill) (Llobera 2000, 2001, 2003; Lock 2000; Wheatley and Gillings 2000; Wheatley 1993, 1995). By the early 2000s developers began work on a variety of open-source GIS solutions, including Quantum GIS/QGIS and JUMP/OpenJUMP, both released in 2002, and gvSIG and SAGA, both released in 2004. By 2009, many archaeologists had become familiar with the open source QGIS providing greater access to GIS.

In the 1990s a few archaeologists began to use Virtual Reality (VR) (e.g. Barceló et al. 2000; Dingwall et al. 1999; Forte and Siliotti 1997a, b; Reilly 1991). While the purpose of VR is to create *interactive* 3D reconstructions, in the 1990s and early 2000s archaeologists primarily employed VR to create 3D reconstructions that were viewed as static 2D illustrations or non-interactive animations (Bentkowska-Kafel et al. 2012). In 2005, Unity—a 3D gaming engine—was released making the development of 3D interactive content more accessible. Currently unity works on over 25 platforms and along with rapid software and hardware development of immersive virtual reality (e.g. Oculus Rift, Samsung Gear VR and HTC Vive headsets), archaeologists have increasingly used VR to *intentionally* create interactive 3D environments that facilitate embodied experiences of archaeological sites and landscapes (Forte and Bonini 2010; Forte and Gallese 2015; Richards-Rissetto et al. 2012, 2014; Rubio-Tamayo et al. 2017). Recently, software and hardware have been released inviting archaeologists to experiment with approaches to enhance embodiment in VR.

In this vein, cyberarchaeology integrates computer science, engineering, and archaeology (Levy et al. 2012) to simulate potential past environments in 3D affording multisensory interaction with data in VR. Cyberarchaeology is therefore leading to new methods and knowledge that are beginning to influence archaeological practice (Forte 2010, 2016b; Forte and Pietroni 2009; Forte and Siliotti 1997a, 1997b; Jones and Levy 2018; Smith and Levy 2014). While archaeologists have carried out many visibility analyses using GIS (e.g. Doyle et al. 2012; Howey and Burg 2017; Kosiba and Bauer 2013; Lake and Woodman 2003; Lambers and Sauerbier 2006; Richards-Rissetto 2010, 2017a, b; Wernke et al. 2017; Wheatley 1995), they are only recently performing acoustic analyses (e.g. Goodwin and Richards-Rissetto 2020; Lake 2013; Primeau 2022; Primeau and Witt 2018; Witt and Primeau 2019; Zalaquett 2010; Zalaquett Rock 2015). Other scientists have explored acoustics using technologies outside of GIS and VR (e.g. Azevedo et al. 2013; Díaz-Andreu et al. 2017; Iannace et al. 2014; Kolar 2017; Liwosz 2018; Loose 2008; Reznikoff 2008; Watson and Keating 1999). Despite these advancements, there are very few computational and experiential *multisensory* studies of the past; however, archaeologists are increasingly integrating complex heterogeneous datasets into various digital technologies moving us forward in human-centred analyses that are expanding understanding of the past (Jones and Levy 2018).

2 Research Overview

Bringing together cyberarchaeology, geospatial modelling and an immersive embodied experience, we engage in a multisensory study of vision, sound, and movement in archaeological landscapes using GIS and VR. We initially represent the ancient landscape as 2.5D GIS data created using analogue maps and airborne LiDAR (von Schwerin et al. 2016). Next, we integrate these GIS data along with 3D models acquired via terrestrial laser scanning and photogrammetry as well as 3D Computer Aided Design (CAD) models to simulate built and natural components in VR. Using both GIS and VR, we investigate the ancient Maya landscape from a multisensory and multiscalar perspective using computational and embodied approaches to construct spatial narratives of potential past experiences. Computational methods in GIS generate viewsheds and soundsheds and acoustic tools allow us to process sound data from the field to integrate into VR to create multisensory experiences with spatial sound using an immersive headset and touch controllers. Our methods and interpretations employ theory-inspired variables from proxemics (Hall 1966; Moore 2005; Gillings and Wheatley 2020) and semiotics (Buchler 1978; Richards-Rissetto 2010, 2017a, b) to develop a methodological framework in which different scales of representation can be defined to specifically target a variety of sensory perceptions.

The case study simulates the late eighth and early ninth-century landscape of the ancient Maya city of Copán to investigate from a multisensory perspective the role of landscape in facilitating movement, sending messages, influencing social interaction, and structuring cultural events (Richards-Rissetto 2010, 2012, 2017a, b; Richards-Rissetto and Landau 2014). While most sensory analyses focus on either individual buildings or non-urban landscapes, we employ GIS and VR to bring together both *built and natural* elements of the landscape to explore the combined cultural and ecological impacts on multisensory experience. Combining urban structures with vegetation is particularly important for the Ancient Maya given that they viewed settlements as "populated earth", or *kahkab* (Marcus 2000), likely representing Maya cities as urban agrarian places with urban gardens and orchards intermixed with residences (Ashmore 2004; Chase et al. 2016; Isendahl 2012; Isendahl and Smith 2013; Fletcher 2009; Graham 2008).

To investigate the multipurpose roles of vision, sound and movement for the ancient Maya, we generate viewsheds and soundsheds from Stela 12 situated in the southeastern part of Copán. We explore the cultural significance of Stela 12 its physical surroundings by performing two simulations in GIS and VR. Simulation #1 models viewsheds and soundsheds from Stela 12 using an Urban Digital Elevation Model (Urban DEM) generated from LiDAR and pedestrian mapping data (von Schwerin et al. 2016) that includes bare earth (terrain) and archaeological structures without vegetation. Simulation #2 builds on this by incorporating vegetation modelled from paleoenvironmental, botanical, and ethnobotanical data (House 2007; McNeil et al. 2010; Richards-Rissetto et al. 2016). The objectives are threefold: (1) augment the Soundshed Analysis Toolbox computational approach to account for additional ecological variables (beyond temperature, humidity, etc.) to include groundcover such as urban gardens or orchards, maize fields, forests, etc., (2) analyse the impact of vegetation within urban agrarian landscapes on viewsheds and soundsheds, and (3) explore the cultural significance of Stela 12 using a multisensory approach, and more generally the role of synesthetic experience in ancient Maya society (Houston et al. 2006).

3 Theoretical Foundations

Shifting paradigms and new technologies lead to innovative approaches to archaeology. In the 1950s, settlement pattern studies emerged as archaeologists expanded research beyond site-level analysis to regions (Sears 1956; Willey 1953, 1956; Williams 1956). This shift impacted archaeological practice by expanding research questions and methodologies. Archaeologists began to carry out pedestrian surveys, mapping large areas to investigate regional interaction and patterns of land use (Chisholm 1979), and spatial analysis burgeoned. Spatial concepts (often stemming from geography) such as central places, thresholds and ranges became integral, along with quantitative methods (Clarke 1972, 1977; Christaller 1933; Foley 1977; Vita-Finzi and Higgs 1970). In the 1980s, archaeologists adopted Geographic Information Systems (GIS) for data management and as we entered into the 1990s, archaeological uses for GIS expanded to include cost surfaces, resource allocation, predictive modelling, and other computational approaches (Kvamme 1988; Lock et al. 2014; Lock and Stancic 1995; Wheatley and Gillings 2013).

In the 1990s, in part as a backlash to processual archaeology, post-processual or interpretative archaeology emerged, asking questions about human agency, indigenous perspectives, gender and perception (Brady and Ashmore 1999; Conkey and Gero 1997, 2002; Wylie 1992). Phenomenology began to explore human perception in the past (Tilley 1994) serving as a major driver/impetus to creating narratives of human experiences in ancient landscapes (Llobera 2012). For example, archaeologists began to use GIS to investigate the role of vision and movement in the past to understand human agency, social interactions, etc. (Kantner 1997; Wheatley 1995; Wheatley and Gillings 2000). In the early twenty-first century, archaeologists have been developing GIS computational methods to employ viewsheds and cost surfaces to investigate past human experience in new ways (Llobera 2001, 2003, 2007; Llobera et al. 2011; Richards-Rissetto 2010, 2017a, b; Richards-Rissetto et al. 2012; Richards-Rissetto and Landau 2014; Verhagen et al. 2013; Wheatley and Gillings 2000; Whitley and Hicks 2003).

While GIS applications were gaining momentum, Paul Reilly (1991) introduced the concept of virtual archaeology. In 1997, Forte and Siliotti published the first publication exploring the potential of virtual archaeology, and while VR applications have been increasingly utilised in the past two decades (Barceló et al. 2000; Bruno et al. 2010; Champion 2015, 2017; Dakouri-Hild and Frischer 2009; Richards-Rissetto et al. 2012), it is only in the last decade with the growth of Cyberarchaeology that we are witnessing multisensory interaction and analysis in 3D environments affording increased embodiment (Pujol and Champion 2012). Cyberarchaeology crosses archaeology, computer science and engineering (Levy et al. 2012) to simulate "potential past" in a 3D "cyber-environment" (Forte and Siliotti 1997b) affording innovative approaches and leading to new questions and knowledge as well as changing archaeological practice (Forte 2003, 2010, 2016b; Forte and Pietroni 2009; Jones and Levy 2018; Smith and Levy 2014). In regard to landscape archaeology, VR in archaeology has focused primarily on built environments for projects such as Rome Reborn (Dylla et al. 2010), Digital Revival of Cham's Architecture (Guidi et al. 2012), Depicting Çatalhöyükness (Pujol 2017), Ultraset 3D (http://patrimoni.gencat.cat/en/ullastret3D) and Funerals on the Rostra (Saldaña and Johanson 2013), or paleoenvironmental reconstructions with little to no built architecture (Spada et al. 2017). Recently, archaeologists have been bringing together the built and natural components of the landscape in VR environments for more holistic analysis. They are also integrating a variety of digital tools to develop new methodological frameworks that combine computational and experiential approaches leading to new multisensory research (Chalmers and Zányi 2010; Gillings and Goodrick 1996; Richards-Rissetto 2017a).

4 Digital Affordances and Material Culture: GIS and VR

Digital technologies provide certain opportunities to perform, create, and otherwise represent the potential sensory environment of the past in faster and newer ways. In other words, they have affordances, or offer *possibilities* for specific action(s) by users that may extend beyond their original intended use(s) (Conole and Dyke 2004; Gibson 1979; Norman 1988). In regard to digital, affordances relate to human-computer interaction and computer-mediated communication; for example, affordances of web 1.0 centred on consumers, while the web 2.0 expanded affordance to provide opportunities for participation and collaboration, or producers of information (i.e. user-generated content).

In 1977, James J. Gibson coined the concept of affordance originating from his research on visual perception. Gibson (1979) argues for a direct theory of perception, which means the environment that an animal is situated in encodes meaning that is directly perceived by that animal. In other words, the environment is meaning-laden and sensory engagement extracts that meaning. Affordance is not a static concept, and there is an ongoing debate within psychology about its exact meaning (Heft 1989; Jones 2003; Michaels 2003). Gibson's own descriptions of affordances were somewhat vague.

As for archaeology, Gillings (2012) argues that spatial technologies such as GIS should focus on experiential affordances rather than attempting to model human perception or sensory modalities. Gillings notes that using affordance, as a framework for GIS-based analyses does not mean anyone is attempting to actually map and analyse affordances. Instead he contends it is more important to generate framing heuristic in order to study relations. As a case study Gillings takes a GIS-based approach to study the placement of early Neolithic monuments. In order to understand the importance of ocean views in the location of these monuments, he explored the question: "Where on the island does the relationship between an active viewer and topographical configuration afford these qualities?" (Gillings 2012, 608). His analysis was primarily based on GIS derived viewsheds.

However, these were not generated to understand sensory perception, instead they were generated in order to investigate the relation between people and landscape (affordance). In other words, Gillings is not visualising an affordance but using GIS to begin the investigation of one. He concludes that GIS has a key part in experiential landscape research but the time for dialogue between GIS and experiential landscape theory is past. Instead of a middle ground, he believes archaeologists should develop new frameworks that take current trends into account to initiate new debates, while also embracing emerging spatial technologies.

In the late 1990s archaeologists began to promote the idea that VR afforded opportunities for embodiment in past places (Forte 2000; Forte and Siliotti 1997a, b). VR encompasses a wide range of technologies (past, present, and future), reconstructions (schematic, photorealistic, human actors, etc.) and affordance differs amongst them (Forte 2016b). Since the turn of the twenty-first century, debate has ensued about the technological affordances for embodiment (Champion 2011; Forte and

Bonini 2010; Forte and Gallese 2015; Forte 2016a). Technically, embodiment refers to the representation or expression of something in tangible or visible form; however, archaeologists, and others, contend that more than simply being visible is necessary to create embodiment. Instead, for a person to feel embodied requires a multisensory experience allowing for real-time feedback and interaction (Forte 2016b). Additionally, questions as to the degree of actual embodiment in VR environments persist, in great part related to multisensorial capabilities and interactive experiences derived from real-time feedback (Champion 2011; Pujol and Champion 2012; Forte 2016b).

Cyberarchaeology offers a potential for enriching embodiment using VR (Forte 2016b); and GIS and VR allow for specific affordances, two of which we discuss here. One affordance is the ability to utilise technology for the development of various interpretations (Opitz et al. 2022); the other is the ability for technology to draw upon various sources of evidence and to invite researchers to incorporate evidence that they may not have otherwise considered (Forte 2016b, 117). Both these affordances are present in this study as the authors incorporate various evidences for Maya political and ritual performance: not only does the technology allow for the exploration of the importance of performance within a particular case study, it also requires an explicit consideration of the ephemeral aspects of performance. These aspects, such as sights, sounds and movement, are inherently difficult for archaeologists to study, but evidence for them is present within the archaeological record (Katz 2017, 2018; Sanchez 2007). The incorporation of these phenomena within GIS and VR allows researchers to more fully understand and interpret the experience of previous performances, constructing a phenomenological account based more firmly upon evidence (Gillings 2011; Witt and Primeau 2019).

5 Case Study: Ancient Maya

5.1 Perspectives of Sight, Sound, and Movement

The Classic Maya regarded sound, sight and other senses as tangible yet imperceptible phenomena that were important to ancient Maya interaction and experience. Archaeological and ethnographic evidence support this interpretation (Garza et al. 2008; Katz 2018; Sanchez 2007; Vogt 1976). Vision was proactive to the ancient Maya; it affected and changed the world around it. Observers validated and authorised what they saw, the gaze of Classic Maya rulers was crucial for moral validation and projection of power (Houston et al. 2006). This concept is evident in sculptures, which were viewed as extensions of the person represented and capable of affecting the space around them. For this reason, when monumental architecture was destroyed, the eyes and other areas of the face of sculptures were often intentionally mutilated (Clancy 1999; Freidel 1986; Just 2005). This understanding of Maya perceptions suggests that elevation and vision are important aspects of city planning, and that there is an association between visibility and authority amongst the ancient Maya

(Hammond and Tourtellot 1999; Doyle et al. 2012; Landau 2015; Richards-Rissetto 2010).

In Mesoamerica, sight and sound were conceptually linked (King and Sánchez Santiago 2011) and sound was equally important as a vision to the ancient Maya. A diverse array of instruments is depicted in ancient Maya artwork and uncovered in archaeological excavations (Katz 2017, 2018; Kerr et al. 1998; Sanchez 2007). They range from percussion instruments like drums and rattles to wind instruments such as flutes. The sound of instruments was used to enhance visual spectacles, mimic wildlife, direct dancers, and awaken supernatural entities (Houston et al. 2006; Katz 2018; Looper 2009; Ramos and Medina 2014; Zalaquett Rock 2015; Zalaquett et al. 2014).

Like sight and sound, movement was also important to the ancient Maya, especially in the context of ritual processions (Keller 2009; Palka 2014; Reese-Taylor 2002; Sanchez 2007). Ritual processions are focused on movement from one locale to another over the course of a ceremony. Movement in a ritual procession is interrupted by stops to engage in ritual acts at certain stations. These processions were a specialised rite performed for a specific reason such as the symbolic establishment of land ownership or promotion of social cohesion. Ancient Maya cities provided a locale for public performances such as ritual processions that mimic the cosmos and the actions of the supernatural (Ashmore and Sabloff 2002; Coggins 1980; Sanchez 2007; Takeshi 2006; Tate 2019).

5.2 *Ancient Maya City of Copán*

Today Copán is a UNESCO World Heritage Site in Honduras and the city's landscape is dramatically different from the past. During the fluorescence of the Maya Kingdom of Copán (427–820 CE), a series of sixteen dynastic kings ruled over the city and its surroundings (Fash 2001). For over four hundred years, the city's population and infrastructure grew. At its peak about 22,000–25,000 people lived in the city (Webster 2005) manufacturing and trading goods, growing crops, maintaining households, attending ceremonial events as well as carrying out political and administrative duties. By the late eighth century, the main civic-ceremonial precinct (Principal/Main Group) had undergone many construction phases resulting in a sequence of large temples, palaces, and freestanding monuments (Fash 2001). Not only did the Main Group and urban core experience growth and change, but surrounding suburbs (sub-communities) developed and grew (Fig. 1).

Scholars have argued that the ancient Maya viewed their cities as *kahkab,* a concept combining *kah* (earth) and *kab* (community). This concept implies that both built and natural features were integral to Maya landscapes, including cities (Marcus 2000). Supporting this idea is the hypothesis that they practiced urban agrarianism (Isendahl 2012; Isendahl and Smith 2013). Households typically had garden orchards with cultivated plants and suburbs outside the urban core also likely grew patches of maize, along with beans and squash (Fedick 1996; Ford and Nigh 2009; Graham

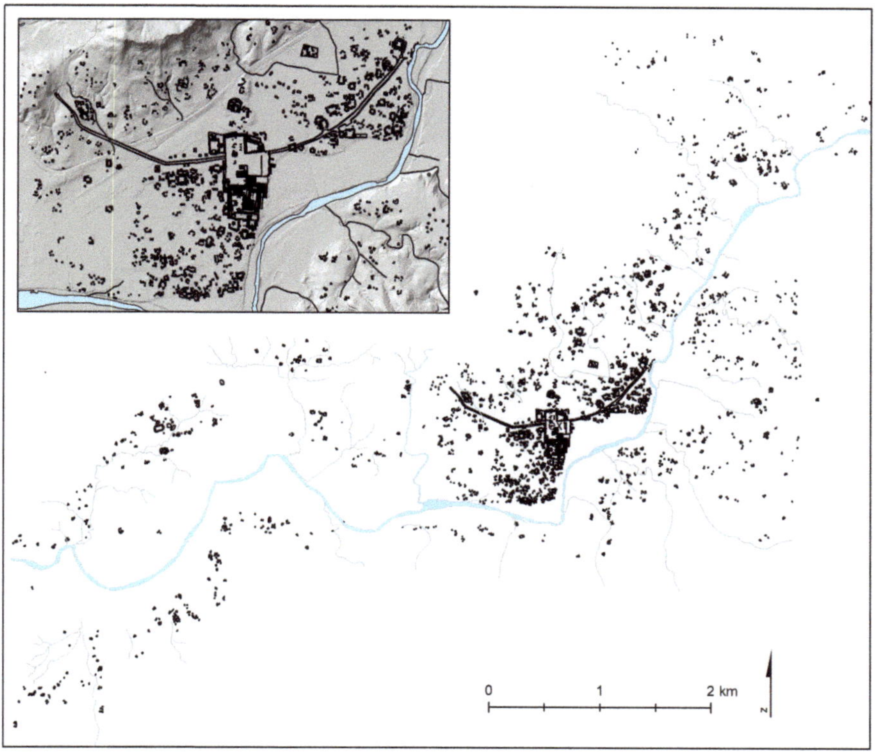

Fig. 1 Map of archaeological structures and sub-communities, Copán, Honduras

2008; Killion 1992). While Copán had two *sacbe* (causeways) leading to the Main Group, they only extended about 0.75 km to the east and west. Thus, most movement outside the Main Group was along informal (travel-worn) paths, and while plaza floors were cleared of vegetation, and some plastered, spaces beyond the plazas would have had varying degrees of vegetation. Thus vegetation along with topography is essential to consider in analyses of sight, sound, and movement through ancient Maya landscapes.

In our simulations we compare the potential impact of vegetation on acoustics during a ritual performance held at a stela outside Copán's urban core. The case study is Stela 12, erected by Ruler 12 to celebrate the 9.11.0.0.0 period (Maya Long Count notation) ending on Oct. 9, 652 CE (Morley 1920) outside the city's urban core in an area with low-density settlement, and yet archaeologists believe it played an important role in the city's past (Fig. 2). Several hypotheses exist about Stela 12's significance: (1) it was a sun marker, along with Stela 10 that identified the onset of planting season (Morley 1920), (2) it formed part of a line-of-sight communication system for relaying smoke signals (Fash 2001), (3) it served as a territorial marker for the Copán polity (Fash 1983, 2001), (4) it was a locus for ritual

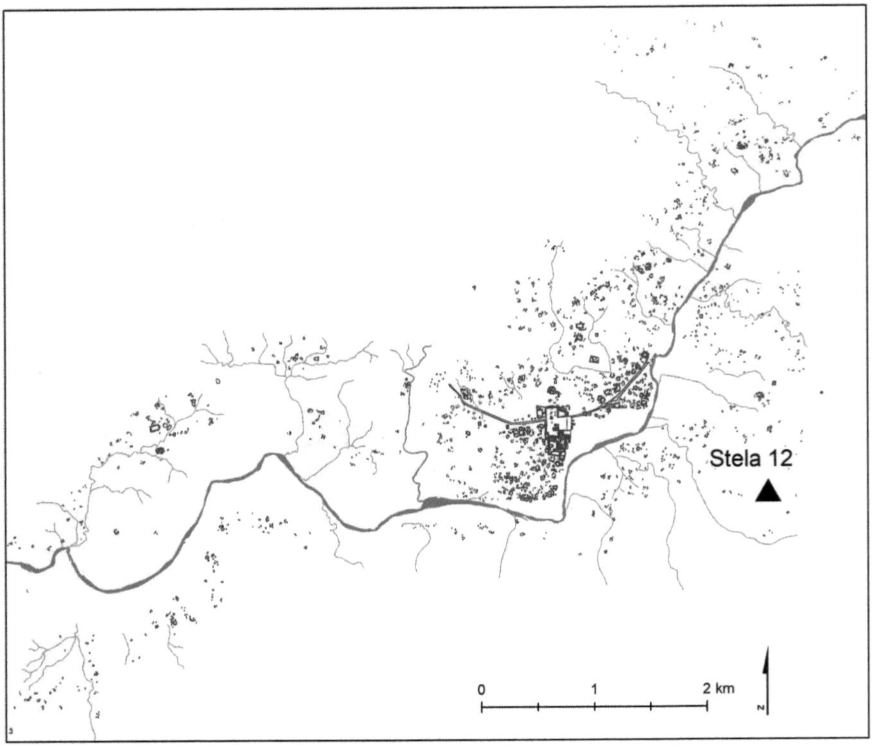

Fig. 2 Location of Stela 12, Copán (right)

and community events, and (5) it served as a destination for ritual processions (Carter 2010; Richards-Rissetto 2010).

Our intent (at this time) is not to interrogate each of these hypotheses, but rather begin to gather new (multisensory) data to deepen understanding of ancient Maya processions. Iconographic, archaeological, ethnohistoric, and ethnographic evidence indicates that the ancient Maya practiced three main types of processions: Circum-ambulation, Core-Periphery, and Base to Summit (Keller 2009; Palka 2014; Reese-Taylor 2002; Vogt 1969). Each type of employed elements of performance involving stimulating the senses to achieve specific sociopolitical and ideological outcomes. Our research seeks to contribute to scholarship on ancient Maya processions and more broadly, to offer empirical and experiential approaches for archaeologists to explore the role of sound and vision in performance within past urban agrarian (and other) landscapes.

6 Materials (Data Sources)

6.1 Data Acquisition and Integration

Using GIS and VR, we integrate various datasets including survey, excavation, ethnographic data, architectural drawings and LiDAR (Fash and Long 1983; Hohmann 1995; Hohmann and Vogrin 1982; Richards-Rissetto 2010, 2013; von Schwerin et al. 2016; Wisdom 1940) with paleoenvironmental, botanical and ethnobotanical data (McNeil 2009, 2010, 2012; McNeil et al. 2010; Richards-Rissetto et al. 2016) to simulate the ancient landscape. Ambient sounds captured in the field along with reproduced sound sources such as a conch shell, whistles and flutes (Goodwin 2018; Katz 2017) provide acoustical data.

We create simulations of Copán in the mid to late eighth century during the reign of *Yax Pasah*, Copán's 16th and final dynastic ruler. The data collection and reconstruction process began with the built environment and terrain and recently turned to adding vegetation to refine simulations of ancient Maya urban agrarian landscapes (Richards-Rissetto et al. 2016).

Architecture and Terrain: Previous publications discuss the datasets and process employed to create GIS and 3D data we use to simulate ancient Copán (Goodwin 2018; Goodwin and Richards-Rissetto 2020; Richards-Rissetto 2010, 2013; Richards-Rissetto and Landau 2014; Richards-Rissetto et al. 2016; von Schwerin et al. 2016). Our archaeological settlement data came from excavations, photogrammetric mapping, pedestrian surveys and airborne LiDAR (Fash and Long 1983; Hohmann and Vogrin 1982; von Schwerin et al. 2016). Initially paper maps (scale 1:2000) were georeferenced and manually digitised to create vector GIS data (shapefiles) of archaeological structures and contour lines (Richards-Rissetto 2010). In 2013 the MayaArch3D Project commissioned airborne LiDAR for 25 km^2 surrounding Copán's main civic-ceremonial complex (Fig. 3) (von Schwerin et al. 2016). 3D points were post-processed to identify archaeological features and compare to existing analogue-derived GIS data as well as generate a 0.5 m Digital Elevation Model (bare earth with archaeological mounds) and a 0.5 m Digital Terrain Model (with archaeological mounds removed). The DTM was integrated with rasterized structures assigned height using a trigonometric formula (Richards-Rissetto 2013) to create an Urban DEM to simulate the city (scape) of Copán in the mid to late eighth century with terrain but without vegetation that we use for computational analysis in GIS.

Vegetation: Vegetation is classified according to five physiographic zones, low terrace, intermountain pocket, high terrace, foothills and floodplain, designated for Copán in the 1980s (Baudez et al. 1983), as well as two additional zones, water and urban. Vegetation data originate from multiple sources. Palynological (pollen and spore) data from pond sediment cores provide plant species classifications with associated AMS dates (McNeil et al. 2010). Using these raw data, we aggregated the data into specific time periods (e.g. Preclassic, Early Classic, and Late Classic) to isolate plant types for landscape simulation. In future research we will use percentages of

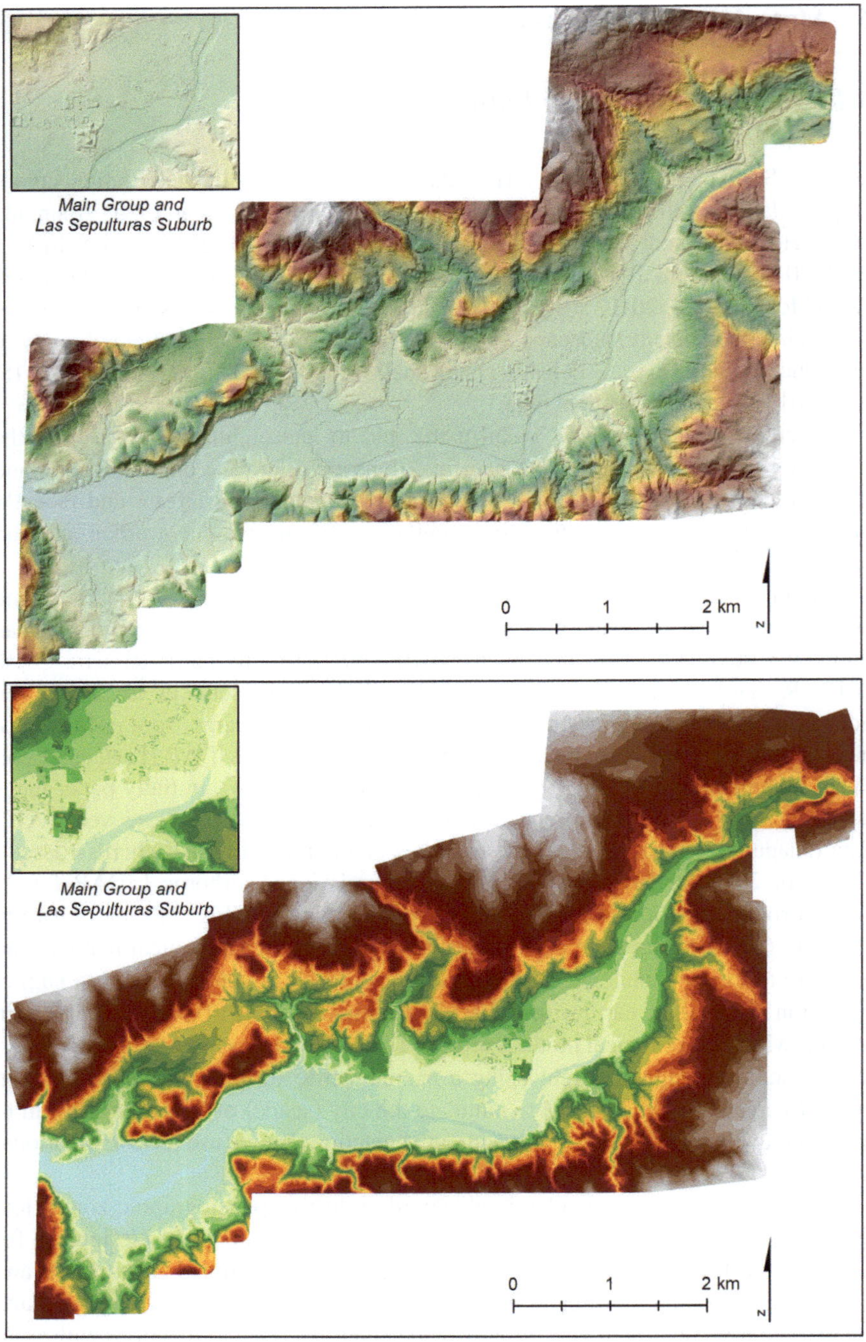

Fig. 3 Digital elevation model (top); urban digital elevation model (bottom)

pollen and spores classified as arboreal, herb or aquatic to begin to determine vegetation composition for the mid to late eighth century (McNeil et al. 2010). Additionally, we will employ ethnographic, ethnobotanical, and archaeological studies on land use to provide context for interpreting and integrating plant, terrain, and settlement data for the simulation. A key resource is The Maya Ethnobotanical Report—a quantitative ecological study for Copán Archaeological Park with data on species density, frequency, and dominance—and information on indigenous plant uses (House 2007).

The GIS data as well as airborne LiDAR and photogrammetric data are the building blocks for the current VR environment. All GIS data and 3D models are georeferenced (i.e. they have real-world spatial reference). We generated the terrain from airborne LiDAR, (with a decimated/optimised resolution) (von Schwerin et al. 2016) and the archaeological structures, monuments, and architectural sculpture from four sources: shapefiles, photogrammetry, SketchUP and 3D Studio Max (Goodwin and Richards-Rissetto 2020; Lyons 2016; Remondino et al. 2009; Richards-Rissetto 2010, 2013; Richards-Rissetto and Plessing 2015; von Schwerin 2011). Figure 4 illustrates the photogrammetric data integrated into their spatial surroundings comprising extruded GIS models as 3D models generated using the software SketchUP and 3D Studio Max (www.youtube.com/watch?v=XEXZJHNpn4c; www.youtube.com/watch?v=B9U3y0CbVh0). The vegetation data comprise initial simulations using a range of temperate and tropical plants rendered in the gaming engine Unity using GIS footprints (Day and Richards-Rissetto 2016). Future 3D and VR modelling will provide more accurate plant types, communities and spatial distribution for VR simulations (see the MayaCityBuilder Project for a sample of vegetation data http://mayacitybuilder.org/?page_id=1219).

Using this VR environment, we integrated captured ambient sounds of spaces at Copan with 3D and VR models for a more immersive experience. The recorded ambient sounds were captured through on-site recordings utilising a handheld Zoom H4n stereo recorder with adjustable microphones that are adaptable to numerous fieldwork situations. Once recorded, sounds were utilised to create ambience in the VR environment with the DearVR plugin. The plugin enables a greater sense of position and reality through spatial sound. For instance, with the DearVR plugin the audibility of bird calls in the VR environment are relative to the user position. DearVR has several features that contribute to spatial sound. The first is occlusion, which is the manipulation of sound waves upon being fully blocked by a surface or feature. The second is obstruction, which like occlusion may result in a partial blocking of sound waves, however, some sound may be reflected around the obstruction altering sound source loudness and reverberation. Obstruction is generally applicable only to objects near the listener. Third is distance correction, which can increase or decrease the perceived distance of a sound source relative to the user. Together, the GIS and VR data allow us to create multiple simulations using different technologies to explore multisensory experience in the past.

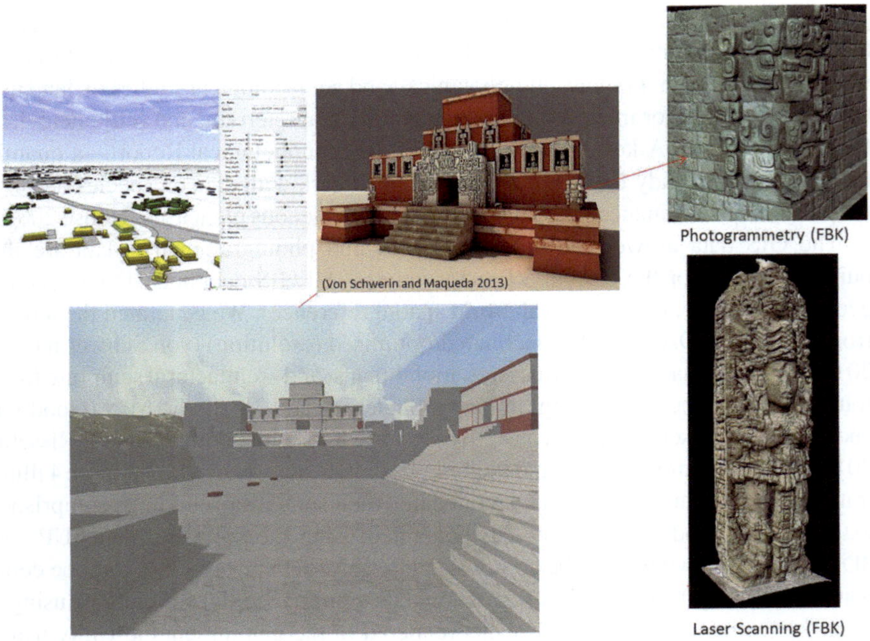

Fig. 4 VR environment integrating multiple data types-GIS, 3D StudioMax, Photogrammetry, and LiDAR

7 Methods

7.1 Soundshed Analysis Toolbox

In 2016, the Soundshed Analysis Tool, beta version 0.9.2, was developed as part of an Archaeoacoustics Toolbox written in the Python programming language for ArcGIS 10.3 (Primeau 2022; Primeau and Witt 2018; Witt and Primeau 2019). The Soundshed Analysis Tool models how sound spreads throughout a landscape and is based upon "SPreAD," developed to calculate the effects of noise in US National Forests (Harrison et al. 1980), and "SPreAD-GIS," an open source script that first converted SPreAD into a GIS tool (Reed et al. 2009, 2010). The tool operates by creating a raster layer of the resultant A-weighted Decibel (dBA) Sound Pressure Level (SPL) observed by a listener when a sound is made outdoors (i.e. in a "free-field"). Several factors that contribute to losses or "attenuation" of SPL are calculated by acoustical formulae which include: atmospheric absorption loss as described in ANSI 1.26 (1995), topographic loss as described in ISO 9613-2 (1996), and barrier attenuation as described by Maekawa's optical diffraction theory (Maekawa 1968; Primeau 2022; Primeau and Witt 2018; Witt and Primeau 2019).

The Soundshed Analysis tool was initially applied to study archaeoacoustics in Chaco Canyon, New Mexico, using a variety of acoustical and environmental inputs

Table 1 Soundshed analysis tool v0.9.2 input variables, from Witt and Primeau (2019)

Environmental inputs	Cultural inputs
Percentage of relative humidity	Location of Sound Source
Air temperature (°F)	Height of sound source (ft)
Ambient sound pressure level (dBA)	Sound pressure level of source (dBA)
LiDAR-based DEM	Measurement distance of source (ft)
	Frequency of source (Hz)

(see Table 1) and employing 1.5 m LiDAR data to provide base modelling elevations (Primeau and Witt 2018; Witt and Primeau 2019). These studies captured the way that sound spreads through the landscape, recreating potential experiences; however, as noted they did not accurately reflect potential impacts of old, no longer extant structures on audibility. When the Soundshed Analysis Tool was first used to explore two case studies at Copán's principal group, this limitation was overcome through the addition of Urban Digital Elevation Models which, as noted previously, recreate the original structure dimensions, most notably their heights (Goodwin et al. 2018a, b). Soundsheds created using the Urban DEM could therefore be compared chronologically to reveal how the construction or demolition of a structure could alter the sonic environment.

However, anthropogenic modification is not limited to the built environment. Whereas Chaco Canyon presents a fairly homogeneous semi-arid desert landscape of scrub and grasses, Copán presents a landscape of ecotones with both vegetative and urban modifications. These differences revealed further opportunity to enhance and modify options within the Soundshed Analysis Toolbox. The Soundshed Analysis—Variable Cover tool was therefore developed to incorporate vegetation attenuation and includes the optional assignment of multiple ambient SPLs based on cover type: for example, one ambient SPL in a dense semi-tropical forest, and another in garden orchards. While the utilisation of reconstructed vegetation models is a source of debate (e.g. Cummings and Whittle 2003; Lyon et al. 1977; Peng et al. 2014), land cover and vegetation may have impacted the experience of past soundscapes. Recent reconstructions (e.g. Goodwin and Richards-Rissetto 2020; Guth 2009; Llobera 2007) support the inclusion of vegetation in analyses to produce a full range of potential reconstructions, particularly in study areas where past ecosystems and flora have persisted, essentially unchanged.).

The Soundshed Analysis—Variable Cover tool currently models attenuation based on four general categories of vegetation. These cover type categories correspond to formulae used by the US Forest Service (Harrison et al. 1980; Reed et al. 2009, 2010) and were further informed by the work of Aylor (1972). Category A consists of open or cleared areas (approximately 80% cleared or greater). These areas may include open water, barren soils, open urban spaces, or low grasses, crops and shrubs (<0.5 m tall). Category A areas may include trees or other tall vegetation but these are sparse and do not result in major breaks in line of sight between the sound source and observer; structures or other features are visible on the landscape beyond. Category B areas correspond to denser (approximately 50–80% cleared) vegetation between 1.3 and 2.0 m tall (e.g. thick maize). This vegetation is not much taller than a person, however, the average person would have a difficulty seeing through it as visibility is restricted by dense stems. Category C and D areas both consist of dense forested areas (<50% cleared) that a person cannot see through. Type C areas consist of dense coniferous vegetation or "old growth" forests where attenuation is primarily due to tree trunks causing breaks in the line of sight. Type D areas consist of full growth trees with a high density of branches, leaves, and undergrowth. These areas provide the greatest amount of attenuation.

7.2 Project Specific Environmental Inputs

For this analysis the seven physiographic zones within the Copán study area were divided into vegetation attenuation categories as follows: Category A included water, urban areas, low terrace, intermountain pocket and high terrace; and Category B included foothills and floodplains. No category C or D areas were modelled based on the data resolution.

To analyse the impact of vegetation on sight and sound, both the Soundshed Analysis Tool and the Variable Cover tool were provided the same environmental input values, including the use of a single ambient Sound Pressure Level of 31 dB. The models assume the conch shell trumpet is being played on a warm, humid day (26 °C, 90% humidity) during the wet season (May–November) in the early morning. Therefore, the only difference between the models is that the Variable Cover tool includes formulae to calculate vegetation attenuation based on the categories assigned to the physiographic zones (Fig. 5).

8 Results and Analysis

8.1 GIS Results and Interpretation

Stela 12 and its modelled soundsheds are located entirely within the foothills' physiographic zone. The presence of vegetation in the area surrounding Stela 12 results in a degree of sound attenuation that would have ranged between the two mapped possibilities created by the soundshed tools; therefore, the experience of the listener should be interpreted as a reality somewhere between these extremes. The soundshed created with the Soundshed Analysis tool which encompasses a larger and more multi-directional area (Fig. 6) illustrates how far the conch could be heard without

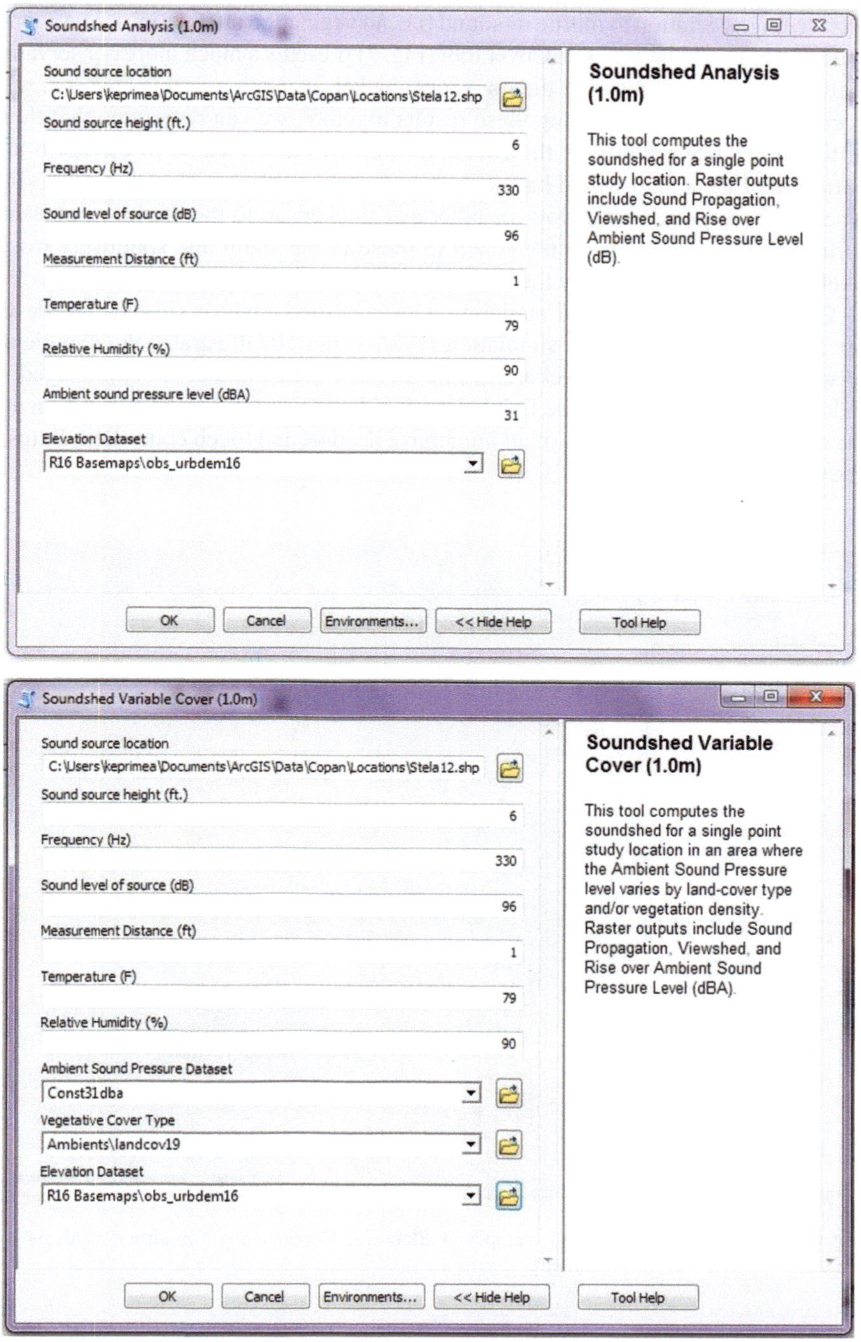

Fig. 5 Inputs for Stela 12: (top) Soundshed analysis tool; (bottom) Soundshed variable cover tool

intervening vegetation to muffle its sound (i.e. no vegetation attenuation). The soundshed created with the Variable Cover tool (Fig. 7) presents a much more conservative auditory experience showing the impact of thicker vegetation in this area (i.e. with vegetation attenuation). Taking these results together, we can determine that those in the immediate vicinity of the conch, as well as those located to the north and northeast of the sound would have heard the instrument being played regardless of whether the vegetation was low, or taller and thicker, up to the thickness of dense shrubbery. The audibility of the conch to those in the south and southwest would likely have been impacted by the intervening vegetation.

Combining the soundshed modeling with viewshed analysis (Fig. 8), we developed a VR simulation. This simulation (Figs. 9 and 10) illustrates the experience of walking through the project area while a conch shell trumpet is being played. A video is available online at the link below that demonstrates the VR simulation and the spatial sound capabilities of an immersive headset and touch controllers (https://youtu.be/qHUnxNn4C3g).

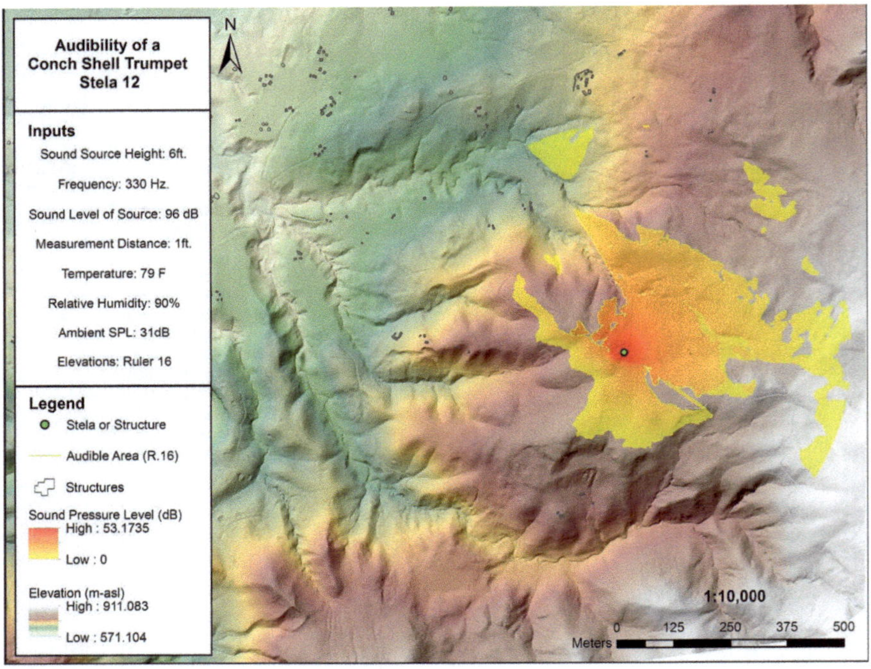

Fig. 6 Soundshed of conch shell trumpet at Stela 12, Copán using soundshed analysis tool [vegetation attenuation not included]

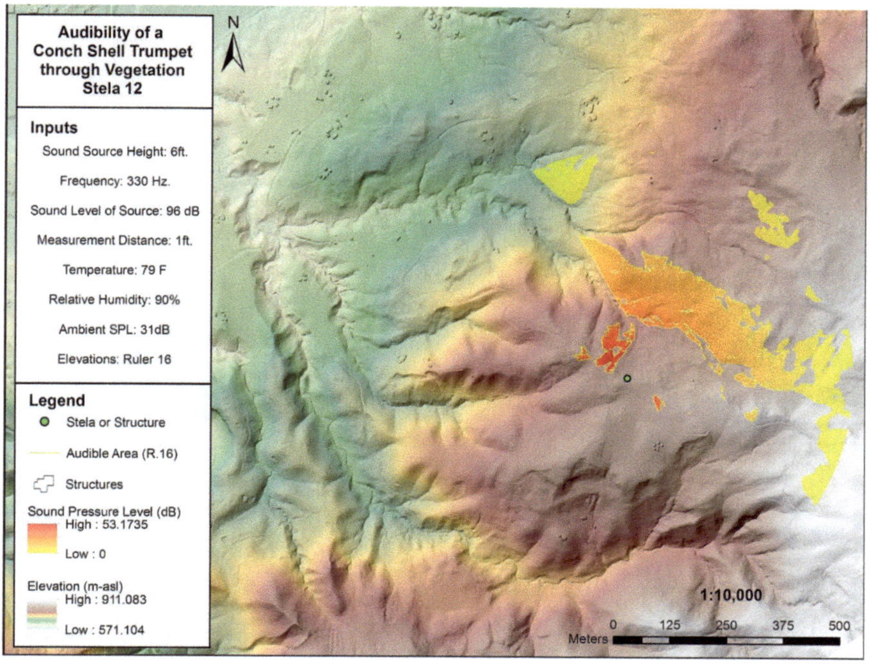

Fig. 7 Soundshed of conch shell trumpet at Stela 12, Copán using the soundshed analysis—variable cover tool [vegetation attenuation included]

9 Conclusions and Future Direction

This study represents a preliminary exploration of the impacts of vegetation on the spread of sound. The Copan Archaeological Project (PAC 1) delineated five physiographic zones (Baudez et al. 1983) that provide an established baseline for vegetation reconstruction at Copan, further refinement of the landscape reconstruction will be necessary to achieve the most accurate modelling results. Category C and D vegetation, as described above, will be added to a high resolution (up to 1 m) land cover reconstruction raster, capturing the vegetative variability within the physiographic zones. Viewsheds will also be updated to reflect the irregular patches of vegetation.

As illustrated by the above discussion, vegetation played an important part in both everyday life and special events in the past. Often considered only on a surface level, if at all, vegetation impacted visibility, sound and movement across the landscape. When considered in the context of processions and other political or ritual events, vegetation limited the reach, and thus the audience, of those events. It remains to be seen if those events were modified to take this effect into account, but as the events themselves were meant to be experienced by an audience—indeed, gain their meaning from the fact that an audience is present—it seems likely that this would have been a key consideration (Inomata and Coben 2006).

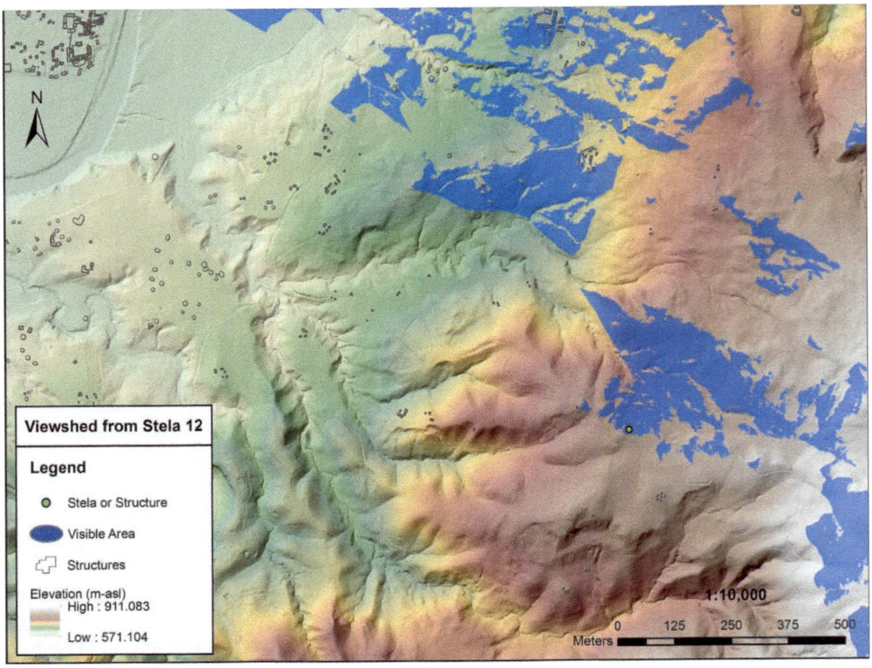

Fig. 8 Viewshed from Stela 12, Copán, Honduras

Fig. 9 Screenshot from the VR simulation as the user approaches Stela 12 with the city's urban core in the background

Fig. 10 Screenshot from the VR simulation after the user has moved past Stela 12 and towards the civic core and residentials groups visible in the background

Technologies such as GIS and VR allow researchers to explore visibility, audibility and movement, and how they may have affected the performance of events. Rather than recreating the paths of events themselves, the technologies provide affordances and open up the ability to question the past, allowing archaeologists and other researchers to engage sensorially with the past, albeit grounded on the evidence of material culture. This provides for a human-centred form of analysis, rather than one dictated by the specificities of local geography and resource availability.

However, going beyond this specific affordance, digital technologies lead researchers to other questions: if GIS and VR are being used to develop accurate models of the past, in order to allow for a sensorial engagement with that past, then what information needs to be included in these models? Beyond the presence or absence of structures and surrounding terrain, or visibility, or even audibility of events, what other aspects of the past need to be considered? Is there evidence within the archaeological record to provide clues to answering this question? Digital technologies guide us to both of these questions and the research needed to answer them.

References

American National Standards Institute. 1995. *ANSI S1.26-1995 Method for Calculation of the Absorption of Sound by the Atmosphere*. New York City: Acoustical Society of America.

Ashmore, Wendy. 2004. "Classic Maya Landscapes and Settlement." In *Mesoamerican Archaeology: Theory and Practice*, edited by Julia A. Hendon and Rosemary A. Joyce, 169–191. Malden, MA; Oxford: Blackwell Publishing.

Ashmore, Wendy, and Jeremy A. Sabloff. 2002. "Spatial Orders in Maya Civic Plans." *Latin American Antiquity* 13 (2): 201–215. https://doi.org/10.2307/971914.

Aylor, Donald. 1972. "Noise Reduction by Vegetation and Ground." *The Journal of the Acoustical Society of America* 51 (1B): 197–205. https://doi.org/10.1121/1.1912830. https://asa.scitation.org/doi/abs/https://doi.org/10.1121/1.1912830.

Azevedo, Matthew, Benjamin Markham, and John N. Wall. 2013. "Acoustical Archaeology - Recreating the Soundscape of John Donne's 1622 Gunpowder Plot Sermon at Paul's Cross." *Proceedings of Meetings on Acoustics* 19 (1): 015133. https://doi.org/10.1121/1.4799054.

Barceló, Juan A., Maurizio Forte, and Donald Hugo Sanders, eds. 2000. *Virtual Reality in Archaeology, BAR International Series*. Oxford: Archaeopress.

Baudez, Claude F., William L. Fash, and Kurt Z. Long, eds. 1983. *Introduccion a la arqueologia de Copán, Honduras*. Tegucigalpa: Proyecto arqueológico Copán, Secretaría de estado en el despacho de cultura y turismo.

Bentkowska-Kafel, Anna, Hugh Denard, and Drew Baker, eds. 2012. *Paradata and Transparency in Virtual Heritage, Digital Research in the Arts and Humanities*. Farnham, Surrey, England: Ashgate.

Brady, James E., and Wendy Ashmore. 1999. "Mountains, Caves, Water: Ideational Landscapes of the Ancient Maya." In *Archaeologies of Landscape: Contemporary Perspectives*, edited by Wendy Ashmore and Arthur Bernard Knapp, 124–145. Malden, MA: Blackwell.

Bruno, F., S. Bruno, M. L. Luchi, M. Muzzupappa, G. De Sensi, and S. Mancuso. 2010. "From 3D Reconstruction to Virtual Reality: A Complete Methodology for Digital Archaeological Exhibition." *Journal of Cultural Heritage* 11 (1): 42–49.

Buchler, J. 1978. *Philosophical Writings of Peirce*. New York City: Dover Publications.

Carter, Nicholas. 2010. "Paleographic Trends and Linguistic Processes in Classic Ch'olti'an: A Spatiotemporal Distributional Analysis." MA thesis, Anthropology, Brown University.

Chalmers, Alan, and Eva Zányi. 2010. "Multi-Sensory Virtual Environments for Investigating the Past." *Virtual Archaeology Review* 1 (1): 13–16. https://doi.org/10.4995/var.2010.4750.

Champion, Erik. 2011. *Playing with the Past.Human–Computer Interaction Series*. London: Springer.

Champion, Erik. 2015. *Critical Gaming: Interactive History and Virtual Heritage*. Farnham, Surrey, England: Ashgate.

Champion, Erik. 2017. "Bringing Your A-Game to Digital Archaeology: Issues with Serious Games and Virtual Heritage and What We Can Do About It." *The SAA Archaeological Record* 17 (2): 24–27. https://www.onlinedigeditions.com/publication/?i=392992&article_id=2740714&view=articleBrowser&ver=html5.

Chase, Arlen F., Kathryn Reese-Taylor, Juan C. Fernandez-Diaz, and Diane Z. Chase. 2016. "Progression and Issues in the Mesoamerican Geospatial Revolution: An Introduction." *Advances in Archaeological Practice* 4 (3): 219–231https://doi.org/10.7183/2326-3768.4.3.219.

Chisholm, Michael. 1979. *Rural Settlement and Land Use: An Essay in Location*. London: Hutchinson.

Christaller, Walter. 1933. *Die zentralen Orte in Süddeutschland*. Jena: Fischer.

Clancy, Flora S. 1999. *Sculpture in the Ancient Maya Plaza: The Early Classic Period*. Albuquerque: University of New Mexico Press.

Clarke, David L., ed. 1972. *Models in Archaeology*. London: Methuen.

Clarke, David L., ed. 1977. *Spatial Archaeology*. London; New York: Academic Press.

Coggins, Clemency. 1980. "The Shape of Time: Some Political Implications of a Four-Part Figure." *American Antiquity* 45 (4): 727–739. https://doi.org/10.2307/280144.

Conkey, Margaret W., and Joan M. Gero. 1997. "Programme to Practice: Gender and Feminism in Archaeology." *Annual Review of Anthropology* 26: 411–437. https://doi.org/10.1146/annurev.anthro.26.1.411.

Conkey, Margaret W., and Joan M. Gero. eds. 2002. *Engendering Archaeology: Women and Prehistory*. Oxford: Blackwell.

Conole, Gráinne, and Martin Dyke. 2004. "Understanding and Using Technological Affordances: A Response to Boyle and Cook." *Research in Learning Technology* 12 (3). https://doi.org/10.3402/rlt.v12i3.11261.

Cowgill, G. L. 1967. "Computer Applications in Archaeology." International Workshop on Managing Requirements Knowledge, November 14–16, 1967.

Cummings, Vicki, and Alasdair Whittle. 2003. "Tombs with a View: Landscape, Monuments and Trees." *Antiquity* 77 (296): 255–266. https://doi.org/10.1017/S0003598X00092255.

Dakouri-Hild, Anastasia, and Bernard Frischer, eds. 2009. *Beyond Illustration 2D and 3D Digital Technologies as Tools for Discovery in Archaeology*. Oxford: Archaeopress.

Day, Zachary, and Heather Richards-Rissetto. 2016. "Creating Interactive Landscapes with Multi-Method Modeling." 81st Annual Meeting Society for American Archaeology, Orlando, FL, April 8, 2016.

Díaz-Andreu, Margarita, Gabriel García Atiénzar, Carlos García Benito, and Tommaso Mattioli. 2017. "Do You Hear What I See? Analyzing Visibility and Audibility in the Rock Art Landscape of the Alicante Mountains of Spain." *Journal of Anthropological Research* 73 (2): 181–213. https://doi.org/10.1086/692103.

Dingwall, Lucie, Sally Exon, Vince Gaffney, Sue Laflin, and Martijn van Leusen, eds. 1999. *Archaeology in the Age of the Internet: CAA 97: Computer Applications and Quantitative Methods in Archaeology: Proceedings of the 25th Anniversary Conference, University of Birmingham, April 1997, British Archaeological Reports*. Oxford: Archaeopress.

Doyle, James A., Thomas G. Garrison, and Stephen D. Houston. 2012. "Watchful Realms: Integrating GIS Analysis and Political History in the Southern Maya Lowlands." *Antiquity* 86 (333): 792–807. https://doi.org/10.1017/S0003598X0004792X.

Dylla, K., B. Frischer, P. Mueller, A. Ulmer, and S. Haegler. 2010. "Rome Reborn 2.0: A Case Study of Virtual City Reconstruction Using Procedural Modeling Techniques." In *Making History Interactive. 37th Proceedings of the CAA Conference March 22–26, 2009, Williamsburg, Virginia*, edited by B. Frischer, J. Webb Crawford and D. Koller, In BAR International Series, 62–66. Oxford: Archaeopress.

Fash, William L. 1983. "Maya State Formation: A Case Study and its Implications (Volumes I-III)." Ph.D. dissertation, Anthropology, Harvard University.

Fash, William L. 2001. *Scribes, Warriors and Kings: The City of Copán and the Ancient Maya*. London; New York: Thames and Hudson.

Fash, William L., and Kurt Z. Long. 1983. "Mapa Arqueologico del Valle de Copán." In *Introduccion a la arqueologia de Copán, Honduras*, edited by Claude F. Baudez, William L. Fash and Kurt Z. Long. Tegucigalpa: Proyecto arqueológico Copán, Secretaría de estado en el despacho de cultura y turismo.

Fedick, Scott L., ed. 1996. *The Managed Mosaic: Ancient Maya Agriculture and Resource Use*. Salt Lake City: University of Utah Press.

Fletcher, Roland. 2009. "Low-density, Agrarian-based Urbanism: A Comparative View." *Insights* 2: 2–19. https://doi.org/10.1017/CBO9781139022712.013.

Foley, Robert. 1977. "Space and Energy: A Method for Analysing Habitat Value and Utilization in Relation to Archaeological Sites." In *Spatial Archaeology*, edited by David L. Clarke, 163–188. London; New York: Academic Press.

Ford, Anabel, and Ronald Nigh. 2009. "Origins of the Maya Forest Garden: Maya Resource Management." *Journal of Ethnobiology* 29 (2): 213–236. https://doi.org/10.2993/0278-0771-29.2.213.

Forte, Maurizio. 2000. "About Virtual Archaeology: Disorders, Cognitive Interactions and Virtuality." In *Virtual Reality in Archaeology*, edited by Juan A. Barceló, Maurizio Forte and Donald H. Sanders, In BAR International Series, 247–259. Oxford: Archaeopress.

Forte, Maurizio. 2003. "Mindscape: Ecological Thinking, Cyber-Anthropology and Virtual Archaeological Landscapes." In *The Reconstruction of Archaeological Landscapes through Digital Technologies: Proceedings of the 1st Italy-United States Workshop, Boston, Massachusetts, USA, November 1–3, 2001*, edited by Maurizio Forte and P. Ryan Williams, In BAR International Series, 95–108. Oxford: Archaeopress.

Forte, Maurizio. ed. 2010. *Cyber-Archaeology, BAR International Series*. Oxford, England: Archaeopress.

Forte, Maurizio. 2016a. "Cyber Archaeology: 3D Sensing and Digital Embodiment." In *Digital Methods and Remote Sensing in Archaeology: Archaeology in the Age of Sensing*, edited by Maurizio Forte and Stefano Campana, 271–289. Cham: Springer.

Forte, Maurizio. 2016b. "Virtual Reality, Cyberarchaeology, Teleimmersive Archaeology." In *3D Recording and Modelling in Archaeology and Cultural Heritage: Theory and Best Practices*, edited by Fabio Remondino and Stefano Campana, In BAR International Series, 113–127. Oxford: Archaeopress.

Forte, Maurizio, and E. Bonini. 2010. "Embodiment and Enaction: A Theoretical Overview for Cybercommunities." In *Heritage in the Digital Era*, edited by Marinos Ioannides and A. Addison, 45–56. Brentwood, Essex: Multi-Science Publishing.

Forte, Maurizio, and Vittorio Gallese. 2015. "Embodiment and 3D Archaeology: a Neolithic House at Çatalhöyük." In *Breaking Barriers: Proceedings of the 47th Annual Chacmool Archaeological Conference*, edited by Robyn Crook, Kim Edwards and Colleen Hughes, 35–55. Calgary, Alberta: Chacmool Archaeological Association.

Forte, Maurizio, and Eva Pietroni. 2009. "3D Collaborative Environments in Archaeology: Experiencing the Reconstruction of the Past." *International Journal of Architectural Computing* 7 (1): 57–76. http://papers.cumincad.org/data/works/att/ijac20097104.content.pdf.

Forte, Maurizio, and Alberto Siliotti, eds. 1997a. *Virtual Archaeology: Great Discoveries Brought to Life through Virtual Reality*. London: Thames and Hudson.

Forte, Maurizio, and Alberto Siliotti, eds. 1997b. *Virtual archaeology: Re-Creating Ancient Worlds*. New York: H.N. Abrams.

Freidel, David. 1986. "The Monumental Architecture." In *Archaeology at Cerros, Belize, Central America*, edited by R.A. Robertson and D.A. Freidel, 1–22. Dallas, TX: Southern Methodist University Press.

Gardin, Jean Claude. 1971. "Archaeology and Computers: New Perspectives." *International Social Science Journal* 23 (2): 189–203.

Garza, Clara, Andrés Medina, Pablo Padilla, Alejandro Ramos, and Francisca Zalaquett. 2008. "Arqueoacústica maya. La necesidad del estudio sistemático de efectos acústicos en sitios arqueológicos." *Estudios de cultura maya* 32: 63–87.

Gibson, James J. 1977. "The Theory of Affordances." In *Perceiving, Acting and Knowing: Toward an Ecological Psychology*, edited by Robert E. Shaw and John D. Bransford, 67–82. Hillsdale, N.J: Erlbaum.

Gibson, James J. 1979. *The Ecological Approach to Visual Perception*. Boston: Houghton Mifflin.

Gillings, Mark. 2011. "Chorography, Phenomenology and the Antiquarian Tradition." *Cambridge Archaeological Journal* 21 (1): 53–64. https://doi.org/10.1017/S0959774311000035.

Gillings, Mark. 2012. "Landscape Phenomenology, GIS and the Role of Affordance." *Journal of Archaeological Method and Theory* 19 (4): 601–611.

Gillings, Mark, and Glyn Thomas Goodrick. 1996. "Sensuous and Reflexive GIS: Exploring Visualisation and VRML." *Internet Archaeology* (1). https://doi.org/10.11141/ia.1.2.

Gillings, Mark, and David Wheatley. 2020. "GIS-Based Visibility Analysis." In *Archaeological Spatial Analysis: A Methodological Guide*, edited by Mark Gillings, Piraye Hacigüzeller and Gary Lock, 313–332. London: Routledge.

Goodwin, Graham. 2018. "Modeling Sound in Ancient Maya Cities: Moving Towards a Synesthetic Experience using GIS & 3D Simulation." MA thesis, Anthropology, University of Nebraska-Lincoln.

Goodwin, Graham, and Heather Richards-Rissetto. 2020. "Modelling acoustics in ancient Maya cities: Moving towards synesthetic experience using GIS & 3D Simulation." Digital Archaeologies, Material Worlds (Past and Present). Proceedings of the 45rd Annual Conference on Computer Applications and Quantitative Methods in Archaeology edited by J. Glover, J. Moss, and D. Rissolo, pp. 73-86. Tubingen University Press.

Goodwin, Graham, Heather Richards-Rissetto, Kristy E. Primeau, and David E. Witt. 2018a. "Bringing Sound into the Picture: Experiencing Ancient Maya Landscapes with GIS and 3D Modeling." Computer Applications and Quantitative Methods in Archaeology (CAA) International Conference, Tübingen, Germany, March 19–23, 2018.

Goodwin, Graham, Heather Richards-Rissetto, Kristy E. Primeau, and David E. Witt. 2018b. "Soundscapes and Visionscapes: Investigating Ancient Maya Cities with GIS and 3D Modeling." 83rd Annual Meeting of the Society for American Archaeology, Washington, DC, April 11–15, 2018.

Graham, Elizabeth. 2008. "Stone Cities, Green Cities." *Archaeological Papers of the American Anthropological Association* 9 (1): 185–194. https://doi.org/10.1525/ap3a.1999.9.1.185.

Guidi, G., M. Russo, D. Angheleddu, and P. Zolese. 2012. "A Virtual Connection between Past and Present: The Digital Revival of Cham's Architecture (Vietnam)." In *18th International Conference on Virtual Systems and Multimedia: Proceedings of the VSMM 2012 Virtual Systems in the Information Society*, edited by Gabriele Guidi and Alonzo C. Addison, 361–368. Piscataway, NJ: Institute of Electrical And Electronics Engineers, Inc.

Guth, Peter L. 2009. "Incorporating Vegetation in Viewshed and Line-of-Sight Algorithms." ASPRS/MAPPS 2009 Specialty Conference, San Antonio, Texas, November 16–19, 2009.

Hall, Edward T. 1966. *Hidden Dimension*. New York: Anchor Books.

Hammond, Norman, and Gail Tourtellot. 1999. "Shifting Axes: Spatial Expressions of Power at La Milpa." 64th Annual Meeting of the Society for American Archaeology, Chicago, IL, March 27, 1999.

Harrison, R. T., R. N. Clark, and G. H. Stankey. 1980. *Predicting Impact of Noise on Recreationists. ED&T Project No. 2688: Noise Pollution Prediction Method* San Dimas, CA: USDA Forest Service, Equipment Development Center.

Heft, Harry. 1989. "Affordances and the Body: An Intentional Analysis of Gibson's Ecological Approach to Visual Perception." *Journal for the Theory of Social Behaviour* 19 (1): 1–30. https://doi.org/10.1111/j.1468-5914.1989.tb00133.x.

Hohmann, Hasso. 1995. *Die Architektur der Sepulturas-Region von Copán in Honduras der Siedlungsraum nordöstlich des Hauptzentrums: Vermessung, Plandarstellung, Rekonstruktion, Untersuchung der baulichen Elemente und der räumlichen Zusammenhänge*. Graz: Academic Publishers.

Hohmann, Hasso, and Annegrete Vogrin. 1982. *Die Architektur von Copan/Honduras: Vermessung, Plandarstellung, Untersuchung der baulichen Elemente und des räumlichen Konzepts 2 2*. Graz: Academic Publishers.

House, Paul R. 2007. "Etnobotánica Maya, Parque Arqueológico Ruinas de Copán." August 31, 2007.

Houston, Stephen D., David Stuart, and Karl A. Taube. 2006. *The Memory of Bones: Body, Being, and Experience among the Classic Maya*. Austin, TX: Univ. of Texas Press.

Howey, Meghan, and Marieka Brouwer Burg, eds. 2017. *Archaeological GIS Today: Persistent Challenges, Pushing Old Boundaries, and Exploring New Horizons., Special issue, Journal of Archaeological Science 84: 1–136.*

Iannace, Gino, Amelia Trematerra, and Ahmad Qandil. 2014. "The Acoustics of the Catacombs." *Archives of Acoustics* 39 (4): 583–590. https://doi.org/10.2478/aoa-2014-0062.

Inomata, Takeshi, and Lawrence S. Coben. 2006. "Overture: An Invitation to the Archaeological Theater." In *Archaeology of Performance: Theaters of Power, Community, and Politics*, edited by Takeshi Inomata and Lawrence S. Coben, 11–44. Lanham, MD: Altamira Press.

Isendahl, Christian. 2012. "Agro-Urban Landscapes: The Example of Maya Lowland Cities." *Antiquity* 86 (334): 1112–1125. https://doi.org/10.1017/S0003598X00048286.

Isendahl, Christian, and Michael E. Smith. 2013. "Sustainable Agrarian Urbanism: The Low-Density Cities of the Mayas and Aztecs." *Cities* 31: 132–143. https://doi.org/10.1016/j.cities.2012.07.012.

Jones, Ian W. N., and Thomas E. Levy. 2018. "Cyber-archaeology and Grand Narratives: Where Do We Currently Stand?" In *Cyber-Archaeology and Grand Narratives: Digital Technology and Deep-Time Perspectives on Culture Change in the Middle East*, edited by Thomas E. Levy and Ian W. N. Jones, 1–17. Cham: Springer.

Jones, Keith S. 2003. "What Is an Affordance?" *Ecological Psychology* 15 (2): 107–114. https://doi.org/10.1207/s15326969eco1502_1.

Just, Bryan R. 2005. "Modifications of Ancient Maya Sculpture." *Res: Anthropology and Aesthetics* (48): 69–82. https://doi.org/10.1086/RESv48n1ms20167678.

Kantner, John W. 1997. "Ancient Roads, Modern Mapping: Evaluating Chaco Anasazi Roadways Using GIS Technology." *Expedition* 39 (3): 49–61. https://www.penn.museum/documents/publications/expedition/PDFs/39-3/Ancient.pdf.

Katz, Jared C. 2017. "Digitized Maya Music: The Creation of a 3D Database of Maya Musical Artifacts." *Digital Applications in Archaeology and Cultural Heritage* 6: 29–37. https://doi.org/10.1016/j.daach.2017.08.004.

Katz, Jared C. 2018b. "Gentle Flutes and Blaring Horns: An Analysis of Ancient Maya Music and Musical Instruments in Daily and Ceremonial Activities." Ph.D. dissertation, Anthropology, University of California Riverside.

Keller, Angela H. 2009. "A Road by Any Other Name: Trails, Paths, and Roads in Maya Language and Thought." In *Landscapes of Movement: Trails, Paths, and Roads in Anthropological Perspective*, edited by James E. Snead, Clark L. Erickson and J. Andrew Darling, 133–157. Philadelphia, PA: University of Pennsylvania Press.

Kerr, Justin, Barbara Kerr, and Nikolai Grube. 1998. The Maya Vase Book: A Corpus of Rollout Photographs of Maya Vases. New York, NY: Kerr Associates.

Killion, Thomas W. 1992. "Residential Ethnoarchaeology and Ancient Site Structure: Contemporary Farming and Prehistoric Settlement Agriculture at Matacapan, Veracruz, Mexico." In *Gardens of Prehistory: The Archaeology of Settlement Agriculture in Greater Mesoamerica*, edited by Thomas W. Killion, 119–149. Tuscaloosa, Ala.: University of Alabama Press.

King, Stacie M., and Gonzalo Sánchez Santiago. 2011. "Soundscapes of the Everyday in Ancient Oaxaca, Mexico." *Archaeologies* 7 (2): 387–422. https://doi.org/10.1007/s11759-011-9171-y.

Kolar, Miriam A. 2017. "Sensing Sonically at Andean Formative Chavín de Huántar, Perú." *Time and Mind* 10 (1): 39–59. https://doi.org/10.1080/1751696X.2016.1272257.

Kosiba, Steve, and Andrew M. Bauer. 2013. "Mapping the Political Landscape: Toward a GIS Analysis of Environmental and Social Difference." *Journal of Archaeological Method and Theory* 20 (1): 61–101. https://doi.org/10.1007/s10816-011-9126-z.

Kvamme, Kenneth L. 1988. "Development and Testing of Quantitative Models." In *Quantifying the Present and Predicting the Past: Theory, Method, and Application of Archaeological Predictive Modeling*, edited by W. James Judge and Lynne Sebastian, 325–428. Denver, Colo.; Washington, D.C.: Bureau of Land Management.

Lake, Mark W. 2013. "Trends in Archaeological Simulation." *Journal of Archaeological Method and Theory* 21 (2): 258–287. https://doi.org/10.1007/s10816-013-9188-1.

Lake, Mark W., and Patricia E. Woodman. 2003. "Visibility Studies in Archaeology: A Review and Case Study." *Environment and Planning B: Planning and Design* 30 (5): 689–707. https://doi.org/10.1068/b29122.

Lambers, Karsten, and Martin Sauerbier. 2006. "GIS-based visibility studies of the Nasca geoglyphs at Palpa, Peru." In *Recording, Modeling and Visualization of Cultural Heritage*, edited by

Emmanuel Baltsavias, Armin Gruen, Luv Van Gool and Maria Pateraki, 249–262. London: Taylor & Francis.

Landau, Kristin. 2015. "Spatial Logic and Maya City Planning: The Case for Cosmology." *Cambridge Archaeological Journal* 25 (1): 275–292. https://doi.org/10.1017/S09597743140 0105X.

Levy, Thomas, Neil Smith, Mohammad Najjar, Thomas Defanti, Albert Yu, Min Lin, and Falko Kuester. 2012. *Cyber-Archaeology in the Holy Land: The Future of the Past*. San Diego, CA: California Institute for Telecommunications and Information Technology (Calit2), UC San Diego. https://www.biblicalarchaeology.org/free-ebooks/cyber-archaeology-in-the-holy-land-the-future-of-the-past/.

Liwosz, Chester R. 2018c. "Benchmarks: Ontological Considerations at Two Mojave Desert Petroglyph Labyrinths." Ph.D. Dissertation, Department of Anthropology, University of California Santa Cruz.

Llobera, Marcos. 2000. "Understanding Movement: A Pilot Model towards the Sociology of Movement." In *Beyond the Map: Archaeology and Spatial Technologies*, edited by Gary R. Lock, In NATO ASI Series A: Life Sciences, 65–84. Amsterdam: IOS Press.

Llobera, Marcos. 2001. "Building Past Landscape Perception With GIS: Understanding Topographic Prominence." *Journal of Archaeological Science* 28 (9): 1005–1014. https://doi.org/10.1006/jasc.2001.0720.

Llobera, Marcos. 2003. "Extending GIS-based Visual Analysis: The Concept of Visualscapes." *International Journal of Geographical Information Science* 17 (1): 25–48. https://doi.org/10.1080/713811741.

Llobera, Marcos. 2007. "Modeling Visibility through Vegetation." *International Journal of Geographical Information Science* 21 (7): 799–810. https://doi.org/10.1080/136588106011 69865.

Llobera, Marcos. 2012. "Life on a Pixel: Challenges in the Development of Digital Methods Within an "Interpretive" Landscape Archaeology Framework." *Journal of Archaeological Method and Theory* 19: 495–509. https://doi.org/10.1007/s10816-012-9139-2.

Llobera, Marcos, Pastor Fábrega-Álvarez, and César Parcero-Oubiña. 2011. "Order in Movement: A GIS Approach to Accessibility." *Journal of Archaeological Science* 38 (4): 843–851. https://doi.org/10.1016/j.jas.2010.11.006.

Lock, Gary, ed. 2000. *Beyond the Map: Archaeology and Spatial Technologies, NATO Science Series A: Life Sciences*. Amsterdam: IOS Press.

Lock, Gary, Mariza Kormann, and John Pouncett. 2014. "Visibility and Movement: Towards a GIS-based Integrated Approach." In *Computational Approaches to the Study of Movement in Archaeology: Theory, Practice and Interpretation of Factors and Effects of Long Term Landscape Formation and Transformation*, edited by Silvia Polla and Philip Verhagen, 23–42. Berlin: de Gruyter GmbH.

Lock, Gary, and Zoran Stancic, eds. 1995. *Archaeology And Geographic Information Systems: A European Perspective*. London: Taylor & Francis.

Looper, Matthew George. 2009. *To Be Like Gods: Dance in Ancient Maya Civilization*. Austin: University of Texas Press.

Loose, Richard W. 2008. "Tse'Biinaholts'a Yalti (Curved Rock That Speaks)." *Time and Mind* 1 (1): 31–49. https://doi.org/10.2752/175169608783489080.

Lyon, Richard H., Christopher N. Blair, and Richard G. DeJong. 1977. "Evaluating Effects of Vegetation on the Acoustic Environment by Physical Scale-Modeling." In *Proceedings of the Conference on Metropolitan Physical Environment, General Technical Report NE-25*, edited by Gordon M. Hesler and Lee P. Herrington, 218–225. Upper Darby, PA: U.S. Department of Agriculture, Forest Service, Northeastern Forest Experiment Station.

Lyons, Michael. 2016. "A 3D Reconstruction of Structure 10L-18 in Copan, Honduras: Data Structuring for Transparency." MA thesis, University of Bonn, Germany.

Maekawa, Zyun Iti. 1968. "Noise Reduction by Screens." *Applied Acoustics* 1 (3): 157–173. https://doi.org/10.1016/0003-682X(68)90020-0.

Marcus, Joyce. 2000. "Toward an Archaeology of Communities." In *The Archaeology of Communities: A New World Perspective*, edited by Marcello A. Canuto and Jason Yaeger, 231–242. London; New York: Routledge.

McNeil, Cameron L. 2009. "The Environmental Record of Human Populations and Migrations in the Copan Valley, Honduras." In *Cho'rti' Maya Area: Past and Present*, edited by B. Metz, C. McNeil and K. Hull, 47–59. Gainesville: University Press of Florida.

McNeil, Cameron L. 2012. "Deforestation, Agroforestry, and Sustainable Land Management Practices among the Classic Period Maya." *Quaternary International* 249: 19–30. https://doi.org/10.1016/j.quaint.2011.06.055.

McNeil, Cameron L., David A. Burney, and Lida Pigott Burney. 2010. "Evidence Disputing Deforestation as the Cause for the Collapse of the Ancient Maya Polity of Copan, Honduras." *PNAS: Proceedings of the National Academy of Sciences* 107 (3): 1017–1022. https://doi.org/10.1073/pnas.0904760107.

Michaels, Claire F. 2003. "Affordances: Four Points of Debate." *Ecological Psychology* 15 (2): 135–148. https://doi.org/10.1207/S15326969ECO1502_3.

Moore, Jerry D. 2005. *Cultural Landscapes in the Ancient Andes: Archaeologies of Place.* Gainesville: University Press of Florida.

Morley, Sylvanus Griswold. 1920. *The Inscriptions at Copan.* Washington: Carnegie Institution of Washington.

Norman, Donald A. 1988. *The Psychology of Everyday Things.* New York: Basic Books.

Organización Internacional de Normalización. 1996. *ISO 9613-2:1996, Acoustics: Attenuation of Sound During Propagation Outdoors. General Method of Calculation.* Geneva: International Organization for Standardization.

Opitz R., H. Richards-Rissetto, K. Dalziel, J. Dussault, and G. Tunink. 2022. Affording archaeological data reinterpretation: exploring 3d data reuse & repurposing through procedural modeling. In *Critical Archaeology in the Digital Age*, edited by Kevin Garstki, pp. 123–139. Costen Institute Press.

Palka, Joel W. 2014. *Maya Pilgrimage to Ritual Landscapes: Insights from Archaeology, History, and Ethnography.* Albuquerque: University of New Mexico Press.

Peng, Jeffrey, Rob Bullen, and Simon Kean. 2014. "The Effects of Vegetation on Road Traffic Noise." Inter.noise 2014 Conference, Melbourne, Australia, November 16–19, 2014.

Primeau, Kristy E. 2022. "A GIS Approach to Landscape Scale Archaeoacoustics." Ph.D. dissertation, Anthropology, SUNY Albany. https://www.proquest.com/openview/1a935d9ea5e463d4be15d55303103b17/1?pq-origsite=gscholar&cbl=18750&diss=y

Primeau, Kristy E., and David E. Witt. 2018. "Soundscapes in the Past: Investigating Sound at the Landscape Level." *Journal of Archaeological Science: Reports* 19: 875–885. https://doi.org/10.1016/j.jasrep.2017.05.044.

Pujol, Laia. 2017. "Depicting Çatalhöyükness." Accessed August 27, 2020. http://www.catalhoyuk.com/content/depicting-catalhoyukness.

Pujol, Laia, and Erik Champion. 2012. "Evaluating Presence in Cultural Heritage Projects." *International Journal of Heritage Studies* 18 (1): 83–102. https://doi.org/10.1080/13527258.2011.577796.

Ramos, Alejandro, and Andres Medina. 2014. "Parámetros de utilidad en la caracterización acústica de espacios mesoamericanos." In *Entramados sonoros de tradición mesoamericana : identidades, imágenes y contextos*, edited by Francisca Zalaquett Rock, Martha Ilia Nájera C and Laura Sotelo, 149–175. Mexico City: Instituto de Investigaciones Filológicas.

Reed, S. E., J. L. Boggs, and J. P. Mann. 2010. *SPreAD-GIS: An ArcGIS Toolbox for Modeling the Propagation of Engine Noise in a Wildland Setting. Version 2.0.* San Francisco: The Wilderness Society.

Reed, S. E., J. P. Mann, and J. L. Boggs. 2009. *SPreAD-GIS: An ArcGIS Toolbox for Modeling the Propagation of Engine Noise in a Wildland Setting. Version 1.2.* San Francisco: The Wilderness Society.

Reese-Taylor, Kathryn. 2002. "Ritual Circuits as Key Elements in Maya Civic Center Designs." In *Heart of Creation: The Mesoamerican World and the Legacy of Linda Schele*, edited by Andrea Joyce Stone, 144–165. Tuscaloosa: University of Alabama Press.

Reilly, P. 1991. "Towards a Virtual Archaeology." In *Computer Applications and Quantitative Methods in Archaeology 1990*, edited by S. Rahtz and K. Lockyear, In BAR International Series, 132–139. Oxford: Tempus Reparatum.

Remondino, Fabio, Armin Gruen, Jennifer von Schwerin, H. Eisenbeiss, Alessandro Rizzi, Stefano Girardi, Martin Sauerbier, and Heather Richards-Rissetto. 2009. "Multi-Sensor 3D Documentation of the Maya Site of Copán." 22nd CIPA Symposium, Kyoto, Japan, October 11–15, 2009.

Reznikoff, Iegor. 2008. "Sound Resonance in Prehistoric Times: A Study of Paleolithic Painted Caves and Rocks." *The Journal of the Acoustical Society of America* 123 (5): 3603. https://doi.org/10.1121/1.2934773.

Richards-Rissetto, Heather. 2010. "Exploring Social Interaction at the Ancient Maya City of Copán, Honduras: A Multi-Scalar Geographic Information Systems (GIS) Analysis of Access and Visibilty." Ph.D. Dissertation, Anthropology, The University of New Mexico. https://search.proquest.com/docview/734287221.

Richards-Rissetto, Heather. 2012. "Social Interaction at the Maya Site of Copán, Honduras: A Least Cost Approach to Configurational Analysis." In *Least Cost Analysis of Social Landscapes: Archaeological Case Studies*, edited by Devin A. White and Sarah L. Surface-Evans, 109–127. Salt Lake City: University of Utah Press.

Richards-Rissetto, Heather. 2013. "From Mounds to Maps to Models: Visualizing Ancient Architecture across Landscapes." 2013 Digital Heritage International Congress, 28 Oct.–1 Nov. 2013.

Richards-Rissetto, Heather. 2017a. "An Iterative 3D GIS Analysis of the Role of Visibility in Ancient Maya Landscapes: A Case Study from Copan, Honduras." *Digital Scholarship in the Humanities* 32 (2): 195–212. https://doi.org/10.1093/llc/fqx014.

Richards-Rissetto, Heather. 2017b. "What Can GIS + 3D Mean for Landscape Archaeology?" *Journal of Archaeological Science* 84: 10–21. https://doi.org/10.1016/j.jas.2017b.05.005.

Richards-Rissetto, Heather, and Kristin Landau. 2014. "Movement as a Means of Social (Re)production: Using GIS to Measure Social Integration across Urban Landscapes." *Journal of Archaeological Science* 41: 365–375. https://doi.org/10.1016/j.jas.2013.08.006.

Richards-Rissetto, Heather, and Rachel Plessing. 2015. "Procedural Modeling for Ancient Maya Cityscapes: Initial Methodological Challenges and Solutions." 2015 Digital Heritage, 28 Sept.–2 Oct. 2015.

Richards-Rissetto, Heather, F. Remondino, G. Agugiaro, J. von Schwerin, J. Robertsson, and G. Girardi. 2012. "Kinect and 3D GIS in Archaeology." 2012 18th International Conference on Virtual Systems and Multimedia, 2–5 Sept. 2012.

Richards-Rissetto, Heather, Jim Robertsson, Jennifer von Schwerin, Giorgio Agugiaro, Fabio Remondino, and Gabrio Girardi. 2014. "Geospatial Virtual Heritage: A Gesture-Based 3D GIS to Engage the Public with Ancient Maya Archaeology." In *Archaeology in the Digital Era: Proceedings of the 40th Annual Conference of Computer Applications and Quantitative Methods in Archaeology (CAA)*, edited by G. Earl, T. Sly, A. Chrysanthi, P. Murrieta-Flores, C. Papadopoulos, I. Romanowska and D. Wheatley, 118–130. Amsterdam: Amsterdam University Press.

Richards-Rissetto, Heather, Shona Sanford-Long, and Jack Kirby-Miller. 2016. "3D Tool Evaluation and Workflow for an Ecological Approach to Visualizing Ancient Socio-environmental Landscapes." In *Digital Methods and Remote Sensing in Archaeology: Archaeology in the Age of Sensing*, edited by Maurizio Forte and Stefano Campana, 171–198. Cham: Springer International Publishing.

Rubio-Tamayo, Jose, Manuel Gertrudix Barrio, and Francisco García García. 2017. "Immersive Environments and Virtual Reality: Systematic Review and Advances in Communication, Interaction and Simulation." *Multimodal Technologies and Interaction* 1 (4): 21. https://doi.org/10.3390/mti1040021.

Saldaña, M., and C. Johanson. 2013. "Procedural Modeling for Rapid-Prototyping of Multiple Building Phases." *International Archives of the Photogrammetry, Remote Sensing and Spatial Information Sciences* XL-5/W1: 205–210. https://doi.org/10.5194/isprsarchives-XL-5-W1-205-2013.

Sanchez, Julia L. J. 2007. "Procession and Performance: Recreating Ritual Soundscapes among the Ancient Maya." *World of Music* 49 (2): 35–44. https://doi.org/10.2307/41699763.

Sears, William H. 1956. "Settlement Patterns in the Eastern United States." In *Prehistoric Settlement Patterns in the New World*, edited by Gordon R. Willey, 45–51. New York: Wenner-Gren Foundation for Anthropological Research.

Smith, Neil G. , and Thomas E. Levy. 2014. "ArchField in Jordan: Real-Time GIS Data Recording for Archaeological Excavations." *Near Eastern Archaeology* 77 (3): 166–170. https://doi.org/10.5615/neareastarch.77.3.0166.

Spada, Italo, Cesaria Ferdinando, Chionna Francesco, Cucinelli Anna Marina, and Scarano Teodoro. 2017. "The Virtual Reconstruction of Torre Guaceto Landscape (Brindisi, Italy)." *Conservation Science in Cultural Heritage* 16 (1): 277–313. https://doi.org/10.6092/issn.1973-9494/7173.

Takeshi, Inomata. 2006. "Plazas, Performers, and Spectators: Political Theaters of the Classic Maya." *Current Anthropology* 47 (5): 805–842. https://doi.org/10.1086/506279.

Tate, Carolyn Elaine. 2019. *Yaxchilan: The Design of a Maya Ceremonial City*. Austin, TX: University of Texas Press.

Tilley, Christopher. 1994. *A Phenomenology of Landscape*. London: Routledge.

Verhagen, Philip, Tom Brughmans, Laure Nuninger, and Frédérique Bertoncello. 2013. "The Long and Winding Road: Combining Least Cost Paths and Network Analysis Techniques for Settlement Location Analysis and Predictive Modelling." 40th Annual Conference of Computer Applications and Quantitative Methods in Archaeology (CAA), Southampton, March 26–29, 2012.

Vita-Finzi, Claudio, and Eric Sidney Higgs. 1970. "Prehistoric Economy in the Mount Carmel Area of Palestine: Site Catchment Analysis." *Proceedings of the Prehistoric Society* 36 (1): 1–37. https://doi.org/10.1017/S0079497X00013074.

Vogt, Evon Z. 1969. *Zinacantan: A Maya Community in the Highlands of Chiapas*. Cambridge, MA: The Belknap Press of Harvard University Press.

Vogt, Evon Z. 1976. *Tortillas for the Gods: A Symbolic Analysis of Zinacanteco Rituals*. Cambridge, MA: Harvard University Press.

von Schwerin, Jennifer. 2011. "The Sacred Mountain in Social Context. Symbolism and History in Maya Architecture: Temple 22 at Copan, Honduras." *Ancient Mesoamerica* 22 (2): 271–300. https://doi.org/10.1017/S0956536111000319.

von Schwerin, Jennifer, Heather Richards-Rissetto, Fabio Remondino, Maria Grazia Spera, Michael Auer, Nicolas Billen, Lukas Loos, Laura Stelson, and Markus Reindel. 2016. "Airborne LiDAR Acquisition, Post-processing and Accuracy-checking for a 3D WebGIS of Copan, Honduras." *Journal of Archaeological Science: Reports* 5: 85–104. https://doi.org/10.1016/j.jasrep.2015.11.005.

Watson, Aaron, and David Keating. 1999. "Architecture and Sound: An Acoustic Analysis of Megalithic Monuments in Prehistoric Britain." *Antiquity* 73 (280): 325–336. https://doi.org/10.1017/S0003598X00088281.

Webster, David. 2005. "Political Ecology, Political Economy, and the Culture History of Resource Management at Copán." In *Copán: The History of an Ancient Maya Kingdom*, edited by E. Wyllys Andrews and William Leonard Fash, 33–72. Santa Fe, NM: School of American Research.

Wernke, Steven A., Lauren E. Kohut, and Abel Traslaviña. 2017. "A GIS of Affordances: Movement and Visibility at a Planned Colonial Town in Highland Peru." *Journal of Archaeological Science* 84: 22–39. https://doi.org/10.1016/j.jas.2017.06.004.

Wheatley, David. 1993. "Going over Old Ground: GIS, Archaeological Theory and the Act of Perception." In *Computing the Past. Computer Applications and Quantitative Methods in Archaeology. CAA92.*, edited by J. Andresen, T. Madsen and I. Scollar, 133–138. Aarhus: Aarhus University Press.

Wheatley, David. 1995. "Cumulative Viewshed Analysis: A GIS-based Method for Investigating Intervisibility, and its Archaeological Application." In *Archaeology And Geographic Information Systems: A European Perspective*, edited by Gary R. Lock and Zoran Stancic, 171–185. London: Taylor & Francis.
Wheatley, David, and Mark Gillings. 2000. "Vision, Perception and GIS: Developing Enriched Approaches to the Study of Archaeological Visibility." In *Beyond the Map: Archaeology and Spatial Technologies*, edited by Gary R. Lock, In NATO Science Series A: Life Sciences, 1–27. Amsterdam: IOS Press.
Wheatley, David, and Mark Gillings. 2013. *Spatial Technology and Archaeology: The Archaeological Applications of GIS*. New York City: Taylor & Francis.
Whitley, Thomas G., and Lacey M. Hicks. 2003. "A Geographic Information Systems Approach to Understanding Potential Prehistoric and Historic Travel Corridors." *Southeastern Archaeology* 22 (1): 77–91. https://www.jstor.org/stable/40713266.
Willey, Gordon R. 1953. *Prehistoric Settlement Patterns in the Viru Valley, Peru.* Washington, DC: Smithsonian.
Willey, Gordon R. ed. 1956. *Prehistoric Settlement Patterns in the New World*. New York: Wenner-Gren Foundation for Anthropological Research.
Williams, Stephen. 1956. "Settlement Patterns in the Lower Mississippi Valley." In *Prehistoric Settlement Patterns in the New World*, edited by Gordon R. Willey, 52–62. New York: Wenner-Gren Foundation for Anthropological Research.
Wisdom, Charles. 1940. *The Chorti Indians of Guatemala.* Chicago: University of Chicago Press.
Witt, David E., and Kristy E. Primeau. 2019. "Performance Space, Political Theater, and Audibility in Downtown Chaco." *Acoustics* 1 (1): 78–91. https://doi.org/10.3390/acoustics1010007.
Wylie, Alison. 1992. "Reasoning About Ourselves: Feminist Methodology in the Social Sciences." In *Women and Reason*, edited by Elizabeth D. Harvey and Kathleen Okruhlik, 225–244. Ann Arbor: University of Michigan Press.
Zalaquett, Francisca. 2010. "The Northern Group Plaza in Palenque: An Archaeoacoustic Study." *The Journal of the Acoustical Society of America* 128 (4): 2330–2330. https://doi.org/10.1121/1.3508237.
Zalaquett, Francisca, Martha Ilia Nájera, and Laura Sotelo, eds. 2014. *Entramados sonoros de tradición mesoamericana : identidades, imágenes y contextos.* Mexico City: Instituto de Investigaciones Filológicas.
Zalaquett Rock, Francisca. 2015. *Estrategia, comunicación y poder. Una perspectiva social del Grupo Norte de Palenque.* Mexico City: Instituto de Investigaciones Filológicas.

Heather Richards-Rissetto is an Associate Professor of Anthropology in the School of Global Integrative Studies (SGIS) and a Faculty Fellow at the Center for Digital Research in the Humanities (CDRH) at the University of Nebraska-Lincoln. She is an archaeologist who employs geospatial and 3D technologies to research ancient Maya landscapes.

Kristy Primeau is the Agency Preservation Officer at the New York State Office of Renewable Energy Siting. They are an archaeologist specialising in archaeoacoustics, the archaeology of the Northeastern United States, and geospatial modeling and analysis.

David Witt is a Research Assistant Professor with the Department of Anthropology at the University at Buffalo, and a Tribal Liaison with Washington State's Department of Archaeology and Historic Preservation. He is an archaeologist who studies hegemony and politics in the American Southwest, as well as the history of anthropology and its relationship with Native peoples.

Graham Goodwin is a Ph.D. student in the Interdisciplinary Humanities group at the University of California-Merced. His research interests focus on the experience of sound in the past and present by utilising digital tools such as GIS and VR to better understand how space and place affect people.

Home-Making in 17th Century Amsterdam: A 3D Reconstruction to Investigate Visual Cues in the Entrance Hall of Pieter de Graeff (1638–1707)

Chiara Piccoli

Abstract This paper investigates the role of 3D modelling in enhancing our understanding of the spatial arrangement and representational character of a room in a 17th century Dutch home. The case study presented here is the entrance hall ("voorhuis" in Dutch) of the house of Pieter de Graeff and Jacoba Bicker located at Herengracht 573 in Amsterdam. This research draws upon a heterogenous dataset which includes the surviving architecture, the probate inventory of De Graeff's properties that was drawn up after his death, and the almanacs in which he recorded some of the construction works in the house. This paper shows how the "materialization" of the inventoried objects in a 3D model suggests otherwise unnoticeable intentions and visual cues underlying their disposition within the room. In addition, this approach offers a non-intrusive and non-destructive way of visualizing past building phases and a room's forgotten function which prompts a more dialogical engagement with architectural heritage in comparison to permanent physical reconstructions.

Keywords 3D reconstructions · Seventeenth-century interiors · Amsterdam

1 Introduction

In the last decades, considerations and reflections from architects, sociologists, and philosophers have expanded our perception of the deeply layered meaning of the house across different times and cultures. A house is not just a construction that responds to the practical necessities of providing shelter and protection, but also a symbolic space designed to reflect, express and reinforce socio-cultural norms and values (Rapoport 1969; Bourdieu 1977, 1979; De Mare 1993, 2003; Heldon 2004). The house has therefore been seen as a proxy to understand the workings of a society at large (Kent 1990). As such, the analysis of the degrees of its architectural complexity has been used to decode the underlying rules of social behaviour which overwrite the purely functional and strictly hierarchical principles of construction (Hanson

C. Piccoli (✉)
Faculty of Humanities, University of Amsterdam, 1012 CX Amsterdam, The Netherlands
e-mail: c.b.m.piccoli@uva.nl

G. Landeschi and E. Betts (eds.), *Capturing the Senses*,
Quantitative Methods in the Humanities and Social Sciences,
https://doi.org/10.1007/978-3-031-23133-9_10

and Hillier 1982; Hillier and Hanson 1984; Hanson 2003). Numerous studies have investigated the symbolic function of the house as a carrier of meanings and messages, such as the display of the owner's wealth and status (see e.g. Hanson and Hillier 1982; Jameson 1990a, 1990b; Fock 1999, 2001; Hales 2003; Purves 2010). According to Goffman's interpretation of social interaction as a dramatic performance, the house is one of the settings in which human action is played out (Goffman 1956). In his view, its layout, furniture and other items in the rooms constitute the "stage props" which shape the scenic aspect of this performance (Goffman 1956, 13–4). Thus, the house can be read as a combination of "front stage" and "backstage" areas which create the prerequisites for what Goffman defines as "impression management": in front stage areas the performers disseminate information to guide and influence the impression they want the viewer to hold about them, while in backstage areas, which are hidden from the intended audience, the performers "behave out of character" and have time to prepare the performance (Goffman 1956, 70).

Loughman and Montias applied Goffman's dramaturgical model to 17th century Dutch interiors and showed a non-casual disposition of works of art in the houses of that period. From their analysis of a selection of six probate inventories[1] from upper middle class houses in Amsterdam and Dordrecht, they recognized an increasing distinction as the century progresses[2] between spaces to receive guests (the "front stage"), where the most expensive items were placed, and rooms with a more private character (the "backstage"), where paintings with moralizing subjects were preferred due to their pedagogical value for the younger generations (Loughman and Montias 2000, 71–104).[3] This change is also observable in the placement of furniture. For example, beds (a typical feature of backstage areas, as noted by Goffman 1956, 73–4) are present in some of the reception rooms until the last quarter of the century. After that they were often replaced by a couch with mattress and pillows following the French fashion (Fock 1999, 41–2).

As "one of the principal venues for front stage activities" (Loughman and Montias 2000, 72), the entrance hall had a marked representational character (Sluijter 2001; Fock 2007a). For this reason, this research focuses on this room to investigate the role of 3D modelling in exploring the choices made by the owner of the house regarding the disposition of furniture and objects. Specifically, this case study is the entrance hall (called "voorhuis" or "voorhuys" in Dutch) of the Amsterdam canal house on the Herengracht 573 at the time when it belonged to Pieter de Graeff (1638–1707), who

[1] Probate inventories recorded personal possessions upon the time of the owner's death. Inventories could also be drawn up by a notary or his clerk(s) in other circumstances, such as when a marriage was stipulated or in case of bankruptcy. As highlighted in Schuurman (1980), they represent an important source to gain insight into personal possessions, wealth patterns and consumer culture although they are affected by biases and limitations (e.g. only middle and upper classes had their goods inventoried, while the lowest social classes are underrepresented, see Faber 1980).

[2] It must be noted that other studies have identified the distinction between front and back stage areas already in 16th century houses (Van Tussenbroek 2016a).

[3] For a brief overview of the layout of Dutch houses in this period, see Loughman and Montias (2000, 22–30). Broader discussions and specific examples can be found in Meischke and Zantkuijl (1969).

Fig. 1 Pendant portraits of Pieter de Graeff and Jacoba Bicker painted by Caspar Netscher (1663), now at the Rijksmuseum (SK-A-3977 and SK-A-3978). Their original location was on a wall of the "Groote Kamer" (Grand Salon), on the upper floor of their house at Herengracht 573

lived there with his wife Jacoba Bicker (1640–1695) (Fig. 1) and their five children Agneta (1663–1725), Joannes (1664–1666), Cornelia (1669–1688), Cornelis (1671–1719) and Jan (1673–1714). The aim of this work is to investigate to what extent the positioning of the objects in this room was purposely chosen and, if this is the case, which messages they meant to convey to the visitors entering the house.

One of the main sources for this research is the probate inventory that was drawn up after De Graeff's death in 1707. As Beaudry pointed out, archaeologists and historians analysing this type of documents almost instinctively "materialize" them when they "read out of the text the physicality of objects—words become things—and immediately begin to furnish in their minds a home (…)" (Beaudry 2015, 7). However, this process remains usually confined in the researcher's mind and lacks the possibility to visualize and test the formulated hypotheses in a real-world measurement environment. This paper aims to demonstrate how by "materializing" the household furnishings and objects with the help of a 3D model it is possible not only to make this mental picture explicit, but also to gain new insight in the use of space and disposition of objects in the room. In this way, the 3D environment is used as an interpretative and exploratory tool which helps in exploring agency in domestic interiors, simulating alternative hypotheses and actively contributing to generating new knowledge (Piccoli 2018, 67–83).

2 At Home at Herengracht 573

The De Graeff's household was part of the Amsterdam elite, as both husband and wife stemmed from powerful and wealthy families who dominated the political scene at that time. Pieter de Graeff was the son of Cornelis de Graeff (Amsterdam Burgomaster several times) and Catharina Hooft (also descendant from an important family). Jacoba Bicker was the daughter of Jan Bicker (a wealthy merchant and political figure) and Agneta de Graeff of Polsbroek (Pieter's aunt). One of Jacoba's sisters, Wendela, married the statesman Johan de Witt, who was a close friend of Pieter de Graeff. De Graeff became a member of the Amsterdam city council ("Vroedschap") in 1662, one of the chief administrators ("bewindhebber") of the Amsterdam chamber of the Dutch East India Company in 1664, and alderman ("schepen") in 1668.[4] As a supporter of Johan de Witt, he was then dismissed by the stadtholder William III of Orange during the eventful year 1672 together with others of his family members with Republican sympathies. Over the years, he inherited numerous possessions from his parents and relatives including the estates of Zuid-Polsbroek (south-east of Utrecht) and Purmerland and Ilpendam (north of Amsterdam), as well as expensive paintings such as a portrait of his uncle Andries made by Rembrandt. Much of his profits came from his possessions of stocks in his lands (Zaandvliet 2006, 94) and from renting out his numerous properties.[5]

The first stone of their house at Herengracht 573 was laid out on the 17th April 1665 and the family moved in one year later.[6] This house was chosen as the case study for this research due to the availability of a heterogeneous dataset which allows us to combine information from different sources. Beside a detailed probate inventory that was drawn after De Graeff's death in 1707 which lists most of the household objects room by room,[7] we can extract additional information about the house interior from the almanacs ("Dagelijkse notities") preserved at the Amsterdam City Archives that he kept for about forty years (Fig. 2).[8] In these accounts, De Graeff recorded the works in the house, including the names of artists and craftsmen from whom he

---

[4] See *Alphabetisch Register van de Naamen der Magistraatspersoonen van Amsterdam 1578–1768*, III boek, VII deel, p. 207.

[5] Amsterdam City Archives, from now on: SAA ("Stadsarchief Amsterdam"), Inventaris van het Archief van de Familie De Graeff (nr. 76), inv. nrs. 186–226, *passim*. De Graeff ranked at nr. 44 in Zandvliet's book on the 250 richest men in the Dutch Golden Age, with a capital of at least 600.000 guilders (Zaandvliet 2006, 93–7).

[6] On 29 April 1666, as recorded in De Graeff's almanacs (SAA, Inventaris van het Archief van de Familie De Graeff (nr. 76), inv. nr. 188 (1666)).

[7] SAA, Inventaris van het Archief van de Notarissen ter Standplaats Amsterdam (nr. 5075), inv. nr. 5001, fols. 425-493, notary Michiel Servaas (nr. 199), 8 March 1709 (the notary signed this inventory as "Michiel Servaas", while his surname is spelled "Servaes" in the list of Amsterdam notaries in the archive nr. 5075). Silver and golden objects are not listed per room but are grouped under a heading of their own and accompanied by their weight (fols. 464–474); the same goes for materials such as tin, copper, iron (fol. 463).

[8] SAA, Inventaris van het Archief van de Familie De Graeff (nr. 76), inv. nrs. 186–226: From 1664 to 1707 (1700 is currently missing).

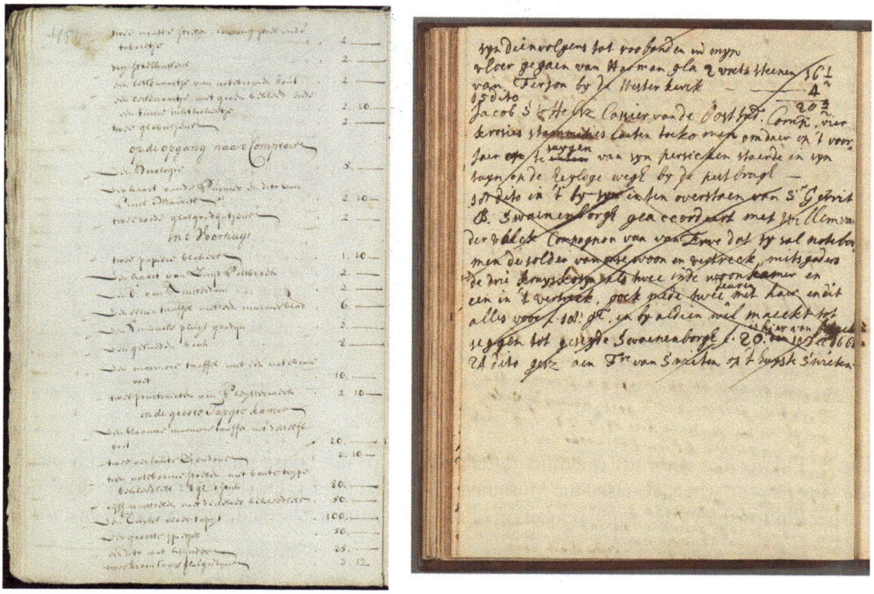

Fig. 2 left: Page from Pieter de Graeff's probate inventory where the items in his *voorhuis* are listed; right: a page from De Graeff's almanacs (November 1666) with one of his notes recording the number of floor tiles that were used in the floor of his *voorhuis*

commissioned them.[9] In addition to this archival documentation, we can also rely on plans and drawings kept at the Monuments and Archaeology office of the City of Amsterdam and on the spatial information provided by the building itself, which still survives and hosted the Museum of Bags and Purses until 2020. Over the course of the generations, the building underwent numerous changes both in the interior and on the façade, of which the earliest and most substantial were made by Pieter de Graeff's grandchild, Gerrit, in the first half of the 18th century.

An 18th century drawing by Caspar Philips and some historical photos show that the entrance was originally located in the central bay on the *bel-etage* and was reached by a flight of steps with a landing. These steps were dismantled in 1868 when a window was created in place of the main entrance. This modification therefore turned the *voorhuis* into a sort of anteroom giving access to two larger side rooms (Fig. 3). The fact that this space's original function is completely unrecognizable

[9] Willemijn Fock provided the first overview of some passages from De Graeff's almanacs, highlighting the importance of this unique source for investigating the owner's personal choices in the house construction and decoration during the early modern period (Fock 2007b). Furthermore, the almanacs contain invaluable information to shed light on the commission of paintings: For example, on 22 July 1673, De Graeff's records the payment to Gerard ter Borch of a copy of his brother Jacob's portrait (SAA, Inventaris van het Archief van de Familie De Graeff (nr. 76), inv. nr. 193 (1673)). One of the two identical portraits on oval-topped wooden panels is now at the Rijksmuseum in Amsterdam (SK-A-3963), the other one at the Saint Louis Art Museum (see Korevaar and Tauber 2014).

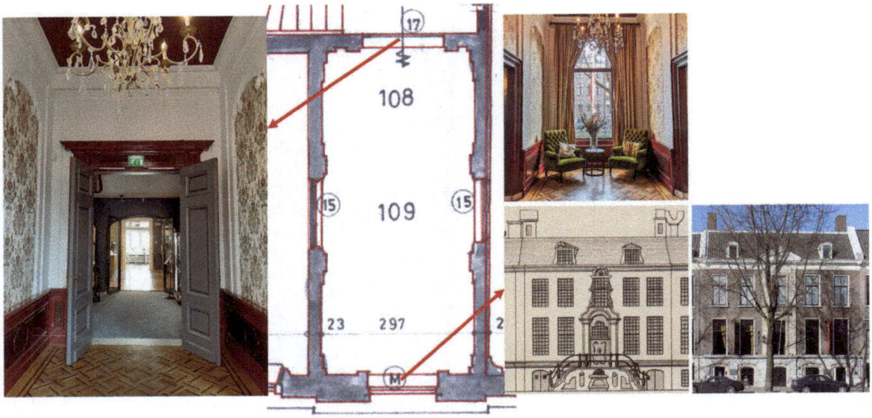

Fig. 3 Plan of the *voorhuis* (modified after the plan of the house made in 1974) with pictures showing its state when it housed the Museum of Bags and Purses. On the right side, the drawing by Caspar Philips shows the original location of the main entrance, turned into a window in 1868

nowadays made it an interesting case study to evaluate the role of 3D modelling in investigating its past appearance. In the next section I will present the sources that are available to reach this goal and then I will discuss the insight provided by the creation of the 3D reconstruction in more detail.

3 The Entrance Hall: Sources for a Reconstruction Hypothesis

3.1 Almanacs, Inventory, and Physical Remains

Pieter de Graeff's almanacs, his probate inventory and the physical remains of the building allow us to integrate the fragmentary information that each of these sources provide to obtain a more complete image of the entrance hall at the time in which the De Graeff family lived in the house. From the almanacs, we know that the construction works on the *voorhuis* started in October 1666 when the floor was laid out. De Graeff recorded in his notes that he used 20.5 "Swedish red stones" of 2 *voeten*[10] (56.6 cm) as bands in the floor and that he bought 6 white marble thresholds, 5 of which measured 3 *voeten* by 10 *duim* (84.9 by 25.7 cm) and a larger one of 4.5 *voeten* by 14 *duim* (ca. 127.3 by 36 cm) for the portal.[11] The Swedish red tiles that

[10] One "voet" (feet) corresponds to 28.3 cm and one "duim" (thumb) to 2.57 cm.

[11] SAA, Inventaris van het Archief van de Familie De Graeff (nr. 76), inv. nr. 188 (1666), 11 October and 13 November. It is not clear whether all these thresholds were meant only for the *voorhuis* or also for the other rooms on this floor. If the former case were true, this would mean that the *voorhuis* had originally two doors on each side, which were then walled up to make space for the grisailles.

De Graeff mentions are to be identified as made of the red Öland stone which was imported from the island of Öland just off the southeast coast of Sweden.[12] From another passage of the almanacs, we know that the remaining tiles were made of white Italian (Carrara) marble.[13] Together with the red Öland tiles, the white marble offered an aesthetically pleasing combination which had been already used in the recently constructed Amsterdam Town Hall. In fact, this imposing building served as the reference point for architectural experimentation in the elite houses constructed in the same period or shortly after.[14]

For several years there are no further mentions of works in the *voorhuis* until 1682 when De Graeff records that he commissioned Paulus de Fouchier to paint its coffered ceiling together with the ceiling of the adjacent room ("Zydelkamer") and staircase.[15] The two latter ceilings are still preserved in their original locations and depict the personification of Amsterdam surrounded by the four continents,[16] and cupids respectively. Unfortunately the almanac's entry does not contain information about the subjects depicted on the ceiling of the *voorhuis*, which nowadays still maintains the coffered construction but has been painted over in white and dark red. Other entries from the almanacs indicate that it had some gilded decorations. In fact, the painter Jacob Smit, who applied gold to the ceiling of the *zydelkamer* a few months earlier,[17] was called again to work in the *voorhuis* in November 1683.[18] Finally, the *voorhuis* is mentioned in 1691 when De Graeff notes that he commissioned the sketches for four oval-topped and six upper grisailles from the painter and draughtsman Romeyn de Hooghe.[19] The four larger ones had allegorical subjects related to edifying properties, namely the Education ("Educatie"), the Dedication ("Applicatie"), the Probity ("Probiteijt") and the Piety ("Pieteijt"), while the themes

[12] Examples of this stone used in floors of 17th century houses are given in Koldeweij (2008) and Groeneveld (2010–2011).

[13] SAA Inventaris van het Archief van de Familie De Graeff (nr. 76), inv. nr. 188 (1666), 6 July. For the international building materials trade in Amsterdam in that period, see Van Tussenbroek (2016b).

[14] See below, section "Visual references for 17th century Dutch interiors". The first stone of the new City Hall was laid in 1648 and the construction lasted for several years. For the history of the city hall's construction works, see Vlaardingerbroek (2011) (esp. pp. 123–9 for the materials) and Vlaardingerbroek (2019).

[15] SAA, Inventaris van het Archief van de Familie De Graeff (nr. 76), inv. nr. 202 (1682), 10 and 12 August and 7 November; inv. nr. 204 (1684), 17 June.

[16] See https://rkd.nl/explore/images/70979 (last accessed August 2021).

[17] SAA, Inventaris van het Archief van de Familie De Graeff (nr. 76), inv. nr. 203 (1683), 15 February. Cf. Fock (2007b, 9).

[18] SAA, Inventaris van het Archief van de Familie De Graeff (nr. 76), inv. nr. 203 (1683), 4, 11 and 24 November. Smit will also work on the gilding of the stairs one year later (SAA, Inventaris van het Archief van de Familie De Graeff (nr. 76), inv. nr. 204 (1684), 25 September and 25 October).

[19] SAA, Inventaris van het Archief van de Familie De Graeff (nr. 76), inv. nr. 211 (1691), 21 August, 19 and 24 November. See also De Graeff's travel journals where he mentions visiting de Hooghe in Haarlem on 30 July, 12 and 17 November and 21 December 1691 to talk about the making of these canvases (SAA, Inventaris van het Archief van de Familie De Graeff (nr. 76), inv. nr. 184A, *passim*).

of the upper ones are not mentioned. This type of wall decorations, for which Gerard de Lairesse is particularly known, was in fashion in palaces, city halls and upper-class private houses in the second half of the 17th century (van Eikema Hommes and Bakker 2008, 223). In this case, neither the original grisailles nor the preparatory sketches have survived, similarly to most of de Hooghe's painting production. The few still preserved include the grisailles that he painted for the city hall of Enkhuizen and for the portal of the new city hall in Alkmaar, which give us an idea of his drawing style.[20]

While the almanacs record the diachronic development of the works on the *voorhuis*, the probate inventory captures the content of this room after De Graeff's death in 1707 (Fig. 2, left). The first items in the list are two paper candleholders ("Twee papiere blakers"), the appearance of which is still uncertain due to the lack of evidence of similar objects. In a passage of his almanacs, De Graeff mentions four gilded candle holders that his wife made with paper as a gift for an acquaintance.[21] This note gives us the closest reference to the items in the inventory, but still leaves some open questions as to how to model them correctly. The following items are two maps, which were common in the *voorhuis* (Loughman and Montias 2000, 59) and were usually chosen according to the specific interests or occupations of the owner.[22] De Graeff had one map of Zuid-Polsbroek ("Een kaart van Zuijd Polsbroek"), the family's estate, and one of the City of Amsterdam ("Een d[it]o van Amsterdam"). The list continues with an oak table with a marble top ("Een eeken taaffel met een marmerblad"), a lint curtain "from Smyrna" ("Een Smirnase pluys gordijn"), a carved wooden bench ("Een gesneden bank") and a marble table with a walnut foot ("Een marmore taaffel met een notebome voet"), and finally closes with two plaster portraits ("Twee pourtraicten van Pleysterwerk"). It must be noted that silver and golden objects are all grouped together towards the end of the inventory instead of being listed room by room. We therefore cannot exclude that some additional objects, for example silver lighting devices, were originally placed in the *voorhuis*. Moreover, the testament that De Graeff and his wife deposited in 1695 mentions paintings ("schilderijen") (unspecified in subject and amount) in the *voorhuis* bequeathed to their eldest son Cornelis.[23] Although it cannot be confirmed with certainty at this moment, the fact that in their previous testament (dated 1688) there is no mention of paintings in the *voorhuis* may indicate that they refer to the above-mentioned grisailles and not to the presence of additional paintings that were not recorded in the inventory.[24] As far as the pieces of furniture mentioned in the inventory, there is no

---

[20] See van Eikema Hommes and Bakker (2008), 222–43, esp. 225 and 227. On Romeyn de Hooghe, see van Nierop (2008).

[21] SAA, Inventaris van het Archief van de Familie De Graeff (nr. 76), inv. nr. 210 (1690), 24 January.

[22] For example, two maps of the West India possessions were hung in the entrance hall of the "Bartolotti house" at Herengracht 170–172, a clear connection with the owner's role as West India company director and Levant trader (Schama 1997 [1987], 313).

[23] SAA, Inventaris van het Archief van de Familie De Graeff (nr. 76), inv. nr. 609 Portefeuille 2, nr. 7, fol. 15 v. (notary Gerrit Steeman, 31 January 1695).

[24] SAA, Inventaris van het Archief van de Familie De Graeff (nr. 76), inv. nr. 609 Portefeuille 2, nr. 6', unpaginated (notary Michiel Servaas, 28 May 1688).

surviving example that can be identified as specifically belonging to this household. For this reason, the visual references for the creation of 3D models of the tables and the bench have been drawn from the types that were in fashion in the second half of the 17th century.[25] Figure 4 displays a part of the workflow to obtain the 3D models of the tables. The description of the curtain can possibly refer to Ottoman velvet, a textile that was much sought after at that time (Lessi 2000). Interestingly, the almanacs contain a reference to the ordering of a large cloth from Izmir: in December 1685, Jacoba Bicker sent a note to the wife of Captain Anthony Colomby asking her to bring them a large Turkish cloth of ca. 6 × 4 m.[26] Due to its dimensions, this cloth might have served as the curtain that we find back in the inventory, perhaps covering both the window and the entrance door.

For two items of the list, specifically the map of Zuid-Polsbroek and the two plaster portraits, the integration of the information derived from the almanacs allows us to provide some more specific visual comparisons. A large manuscript map of Zuid-Polsbroek, which was made in 1668 by the surveyor and draughtsman Johannes Leupenius by request of Pieter de Graeff, is kept at the Amsterdam City Archives (Fig. 5).[27] Two entries in the almanacs more than a decade later record the agreements between De Graeff and Leupenius to make copies of the map of Zuid-Polsbroek.[28] According to the information we can gather from the almanacs, it was indeed around the same time when new interventions were made on the *voorhuis*, namely the painting of the ceiling (see above). It is possible that a renewal of this room took place in this period, and that the item in the inventory therefore refers to one of these copies of the original map made in 1668 which was hung on the wall. Although it is not certain that this map corresponds to the one that is recorded in the inventory as hanging in De Graeff's *voorhuis*, it certainly provides us with the closest comparison to the item listed there.

In the case of the two portraits, the identity of their subjects has not been recorded in the inventory. A hypothesis for their identification is here suggested based on information collected from other documents. The only mention of plaster portraits in the almanacs relates to the commission to an otherwise unknown Master Anthony of plaster casts from two bas-reliefs depicting De Graeff's parents made by the famous sculptor Artus Quellinus (Fig. 6).[29] Although there is no mention of the purpose of this commission nor of the destination of these portraits, the inventory of Catharina Hooft, Pieter's mother, gives us precise indications as to where they were hung. In

---

[25] Van Aalst and Hofstede (2011), Baarsen (2007), Pijzel-Dommisse (2000).

[26] SAA, Inventaris van het Archief van de Familie De Graeff (nr. 76), inv. nr. 205 (1685), 6 December ("(…) van Smirna voor ons noch wil mede brenge een groot Turx kleet langh 9 ellen en breedt 6 ellen (…)"). One Amsterdam *el* corresponds to 68,8 cm.

[27] SAA, Inventaris van het Archief van de Familie De Graeff (nr. 76), inv. nr. 454.

[28] SAA, Inventaris van het Archief van de Familie De Graeff (nr. 76), inv. nr. 201 (1681), 31 October and inv. nr. 202 (1682), 15 June. The commission of this and of De Graeff's other maps is discussed in Otten (1995).

[29] SAA, Inventaris van het Archief van de Familie De Graeff (nr. 76), inv. nr. 190 (1670), 4 August and inv. nr. 191 (1671), 8 April; the original marble bas-reliefs made by Quellinus are kept at the Rijksmuseum (BK-KOG-1458-A and BK-KOG-1458-B).

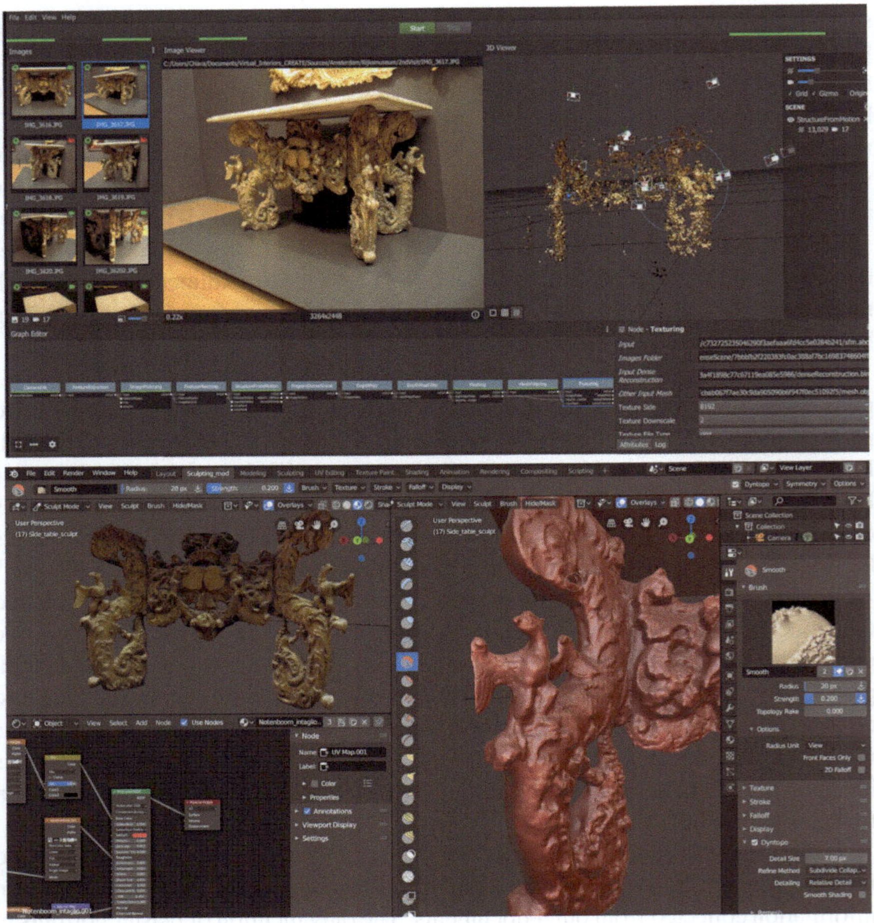

Fig. 4 Part of the workflow for the creation of the 3D models of one of the tables: image-based modelling with the open source software Meshroom (top); retouches and re-texturing in Blender (bottom)

fact, Quellinus' bas-reliefs depicting her husband and herself were listed in the salon ("zaal") of their house at the Herengracht 216,[30] while two plaster portraits of the couple were listed as being in their front room ("voorkamer").[31] The latter are likely those that De Graeff mentions in his almanacs.[32] In this reconstruction I propose

[30] SAA, Inventaris van het Archief van de Familie De Graeff (nr. 76), inv. nr. 605, Serie A 1-34, nr. 34, fol. 45 (notary Dirk van der Groe, 18 August 1692). The two bas-reliefs had gilt frames and were valued at 25 guilders. See also Scholten and Hoyle 2006, 115.

[31] SAA, Inventaris van het Archief van de Familie De Graeff (nr. 76), inv. nr. 605, Serie A 1-34, nr. 34, fol. 105 (see also Scholten and Hoyle 2006, 115). These plaster portraits were valued at 4 guilders.

[32] Scholten and Hoyle 2006, 115.

Fig. 5 The original manuscript map of Zuid-Polsbroek (1,35 m × 75,5 cm on the longest edges) made by Johannes Leupenius for De Graeff in 1668, currently kept at the Amsterdam City Archives (SAA, Inventaris van het Archief van de Familie De Graeff (nr. 76), inv. nr. 454)

to identify the two plaster portraits mentioned in the inventory as being in fact the copies of those made by Quellinus. This suggestion is based on the hypothesis that De Graeff could have brought the two plaster portraits from his parents' house after his mother died in September 1691 and hung them in this prominent location in his own. This hypothesis is supported by the fact that his inventory contains other paintings which were previously listed in his mother's inventory.[33]

3.2 *Visual References for 17th Century Dutch Interiors*

Despite the numerous and, at times, very precise pieces of information that the sources provide, some unknown elements remain. For example, we know the exact dimensions of the doors' thresholds but nothing regarding the appearance of their

[33] See e.g. Bredius 1912.

Fig. 6 The two portraits of Pieter de Graeff's parents made by Artus Quellinus and currently kept at the Rijksmuseum in Amsterdam (BK-KOG-1458-A and BK-KOG-1458-B)

frames, which were changed in the 18th century.[34] Moreover, as already noted, additional challenges arise from the fact that the short-written descriptions of the household properties are often difficult to translate into the corresponding object. Therefore, it is necessary to rely on comparisons to fill in these gaps. The 17th century Dutch house has become familiar to us because of our exposure to domestic scenes in contemporary genre paintings. However, a close comparison between paintings depicting interiors, the household possessions listed in probate inventories, and the domestic architecture of the period shows that such images should not be considered completely faithful renditions of contemporary interiors. As Fock demonstrated, luxury items that are often found in paintings, such as elaborate brass chandeliers, are in fact seldom found in inventories, while other objects that are recurrent in inventories (for example simple floor matting) are in turn systematically overlooked in paintings (Fock 1998). Moreover, the omnipresent black and white floor tiles were less common in reality than what paintings induce us to believe. In addition, some architectural features, such as the "enfilade" of rooms in Emanuel de Witte's "interior with a woman at the virginal", were not typical of the Dutch house of the period but represent a later introduction influenced by the French fashion (Fock 1998). In fact, painters aimed not for realistic representations, but for scenographic effects in their

[34] The almanacs do not contain any information about the doors in the *voorhuis*, but they inform us that some other doors in the house were painted: in November 1666, De Graeff agreed with Willem Jacobsz van der Valck that he would paint two doors with a technique that was used to reproduce the effect of walnut tree wood ("noteboomen") (SAA, Inventaris van het Archief van de Familie De Graeff (nr. 76), inv. nr. 188 (1666), 18 November); at the end of 1685 he asked Paulus Fouchier to paint a Mercurius on the door of his house office (SAA, Inventaris van het Archief van de Familie De Graeff (nr. 76), inv. nr. 205 (1985), 11 December), and six 'room doors' ("Camerdeuren") and two small doors (one of which in the attic) with unspecified subjects in January 1686 (SAA, Inventaris van het Archief van de Familie De Graeff (nr. 76), inv. nr. 206 (1986), 10 January).

compositions and spatial settings and for the expression of their artistic skills when painting challenging subjects, such as light reflections and expensive fabrics (see Wijsenbeek-Olthuis 1996; Fock 1982, 1998; Muurling 2002). This type of source has been therefore considered with caution during the 3D reconstruction process.

In searching for more reliable sources for the appearance of upper-class interiors, we can turn to contemporary doll houses. These very detailed three-dimensional miniature houses were pastimes for upper class wives who assembled their collection of furniture and other household objects with great effort and expenditure over the years. As numerous studies have shown, these doll houses provide us with a reliable representation of contemporary upper-class interiors, albeit with a marked female domestic topography.[35] They present, in fact, a selective view focusing on the female presence and her ideal role in the domestic sphere in which the head of the house is almost completely absent. One example of this is the existence of a dedicated lying-in room for new mothers ("kraamkamer") which was usually set up ad hoc for the occasion in one of the reception rooms and was not a permanent feature in houses of that period. One of the most famous doll houses is the one of Petronella Oortman (dated between ca. 1686 and 1710), now at the Amsterdam Rijksmuseum,[36] for which the painting by Jacob Apple provides contemporary evidence of its state around 1710.[37] Interestingly, the walls of its *voorhuis* are decorated with grisailles (see Fig. 7): an oval-topped one on each side of the longer walls and one smaller one on top of each door. This wall decoration is the closest visual comparison to the appearance of the *voorhuis* of Herengracht 573, as De Graeff describes it in his almanacs. For this reason, pictures of these grisailles have been used as texture images for the grisailles in the 3D reconstruction discussed here. Also, the wooden benches placed on each side of the doll house's entrance hall provided the visual reference for the bench in the De Graeff's *voorhuis*.

Lastly, surviving examples of 17th century architecture provide evidence of the style and the materials in use at the time. The architectural style in fashion during the period when the house at the Herengracht was constructed is Dutch classicism, with architects Jacob van Campen, Pieter Post and Philips Vingboons as main exponents. Van Campen was one of the architects who introduced this style to the Netherlands, his inspiration coming from the ideal Vitruvian rules of proportions and orders in architecture interpreted by Renaissance architects such as Andrea Palladio and Vincenzo Scamozzi. Scamozzi's treatise *Idea dell'Architettura universale* (Venice 1615) had an especially great impact on the development of Dutch classicism and was used as an actual construction manual.[38] Among the surviving evidence of this

[35] Pijzel-Dommisse (2000), Westermann (2001), Koldeweij (2008), Moseley-Christian 2010. Pijzel-Dommisse (2000) provides the most detailed account of the surviving doll houses, with individual descriptions of miniature objects and furniture.

[36] Rijksmuseum, BK-NM-1010.

[37] Jacob Appel, Poppenhuis van Petronella Oortman, ca. 1710 (Rijksmuseum, SK-A-4245).

[38] 4For a more detailed account on the development of the Dutch classicism, see Hopkins and Witte (1996, Ottenheym (2007, 2010). Scamozzi's work was already available in the Netherlands shortly after 1620 (Ottenheym 2007, 188). A number of local editions, starting with the translation of Book VI on the Five Orders of architecture published by Cornelis Danckerts in 1640, made this work

Fig. 7 Petronella Oortman's doll house (ca. 1686–1710), currently at the Rijksmuseum (BK-NM-1010), with the *voorhuis* occupying the central space. This room is decorated by grisailles on the walls and has a wooden bench on each side (see detail in the picture to the right) and it offers a contemporary visual reference for De Graeff's *voorhuis*

style, the most prominent is the already mentioned Town Hall in Dam Square which was designed by Van Campen in mid-17th century using Scamozzi's Roman and Corinthian orders on the façade (Ottenheym 2007). As for domestic architecture, numerous double-width canal houses in Amsterdam were designed around the same period of De Graeff's house according to Scamozzi's principles. They include: the residence of Carel Gerards at Herengracht 386 (built in 1664–5) and the residence of Guillaume Belin la Garde at Herengracht 412 (1664), both designed by Philips Vingboons, as well as the Trippenhuis at Kloveniersburgwal 29, built by Philips' younger brother Justus in 1660–2 under the commission of the two brothers Louis and Hendrick Trip.

Interestingly, there are elements that directly tie Scamozzi's works with the De Graeff's family: the Dutch translation of Scamozzi's Book III on villas and palaces that was published by Dancker Danckerts in 1658 was dedicated to Pieter de Graeff's father, who, Burgomaster of Amsterdam at the time, was one of the initiators of the construction of the new City Hall (Ottenheym 2007, 191). Moreover, as we

more accessible and contributed to its fortune in this country. In fact, it must be noted that this work became available in the Netherlands before Palladio's treatise, whose publication took place in 1646 (Hopkins and Witte 1996, 277). For the catalogue of the various editions of Scamozzi's work published in the Netherlands, see Hopkins and Witte (1996, 295–302).

can gather from his book auction catalogue,[39] Pieter himself owned a copy of the abbreviated version of Scamozzi's Book VI, compiled by the master-mason Joost Vermaarsch (Fig. 8).[40] This edition in a compact quarto format was intended as a proper construction manual and was published in Leiden in 1664, incidentally the same year in which Pieter and his father bought the parcel on the Herengracht where the house was soon to be built. Notably, Vitruvius' *De Architectura* also appears among the books in De Graeff's catalogue.[41] Although the name of the architect who designed the house at Herengracht 573 is not known,[42] it is likely that it was built and decorated according to this style and relying on a workforce and artisans who were already involved in the construction of other buildings. For example, Artus Quellinus, the sculptor from whom De Graeff commissioned the plaster casts, also made the sculptures for the City Hall. In fact, it was Pieter's father, who, together with the architect Jacob van Campen, was responsible for the choice of Quellinus for this important new project (Scholten 2010, 15). The appearance of the reconstructed interior is therefore in line with this architectural style and some of the elements are directly taken from surviving architecture of the period. For example, the door frames here are constructed of wood and painted over to look like marble. This was a common technique used most notably in the Amsterdam City Hall. This choice is also supported by the fact that De Graeff himself showed an interest in this faux marble effect: in August 1666, in the midst of his house's construction works, he noted down the name of Alexander de Ruel (known also as Ruwel) as the painter who used this technique at somebody else's house.[43]

4 "Materializing" Household Objects in a 3D Digital Model

The following paragraphs describe the steps taken for the creation of a 3D visualization of the *voorhuis* and the insights that this process has generated. The preparatory

[39] *Catalogus Librorum Viri Amplissimi Petri De Graaff (dum viveret) Toparchae In Zuydt-Polsbroeck, Purmerland, Ilpendam, &c. &c. Urbis Amstelodamensis Scabini &c. Quorum auctio habebitur in Aedibus Viduae T. Boom, & haeredum H. Boom. Op de Cingel by de Jan-Roonpoorts Tooren. Die Martis 9. Julii MDCCIX. Amstelodami, In Officina Bomiana Ubi Catalogi distribuuntur.* This catalogue is kept at the National Library of Russia in St. Petersburg (Shelf number NL: 16.133.9.36). Its analysis by the author is currently underway and will appear in C. Piccoli, Pieter de Graeff (1638-1707) and his treffelyke bibliotheek: Exploring and reconstructing an early modern private library, Leiden: Brill (accepted for publication).

[40] *Eerste deel der Bouw-Kunst* (…), Leiden, 1664 (*Catalogus Librorum* (…) *Petri De Graaff* (…): p. 35, nr. 294).

[41] Lyon, 1586 (*Catalogus Librorum* (…) *Petri De Graaff* (…): p. 35, nr. 285).

[42] From the almanacs we know the names of De Graeff's master mason (Thomas Munster) and of his master carpenter (Cornelis Adriaensz Verduyn), see e.g. SAA, Inventaris van het Archief van de Familie De Graeff (nr. 76), inv. nr. 187 (1665), 17 April; inv. nr. 188 (1666), 20 or 24 March; inv. nr. 191 (1671), 17 January.

[43] SAA, Inventaris van het Archief van de Familie De Graeff (nr. 76), inv. nr. 188 (1666), August (a specific day is missing; the entry is written between the entries dated 25 and 30 August).

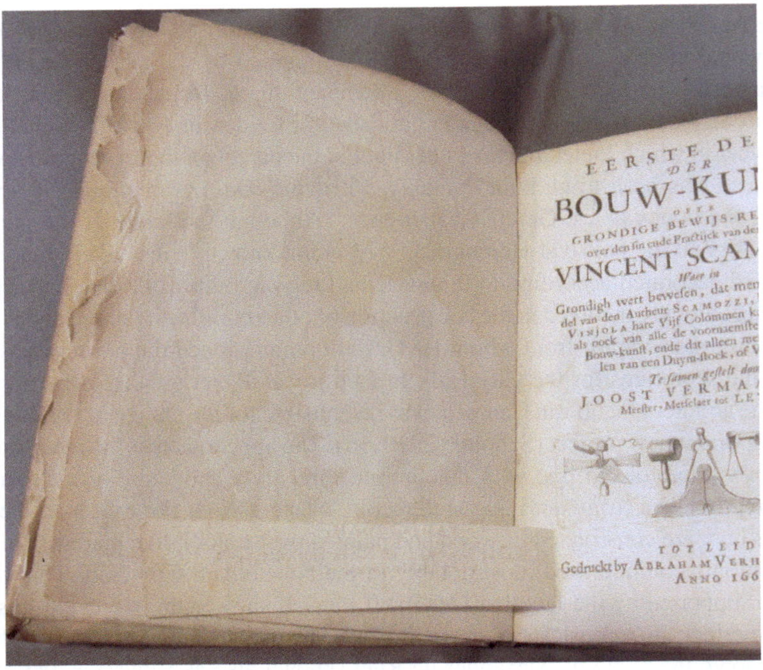

Fig. 8 The title page of the *Eerste deel der Bouw-Kunst*, the construction manual published in 1664 in Leiden that is listed in De Graeff' book auction catalogue. This copy is kept at the Special Collections of the Leiden University Library (call number 1208 F 55)

stage for the 3D reconstruction of the *voorhuis* includes the broader analysis of the whole house, to retrace the original circulation routes within, and to identify from which door the notary and his clerk(s) would have entered. Building plans made in 1974 (see Fig. 3) were a useful starting point for better understanding its structure since they record some of the changes that the house underwent, especially doorways that have been walled up at a certain point in time. Several on-site inspections were carried out to double-check the plans and to start to correlate the rooms listed in the inventory with the corresponding rooms in the current spatial arrangement.[44] The plans made in 1974 were then digitized in AutoCAD, which made it easier to compare the changes made on different floors, and imported into the 3D modelling Open Source software Blender to re-assemble them into the building's 3D frame (Fig. 9). Beside the doorways, part of the main staircase and the dismantled service stairs also needed to be reconstructed in their original location and dimensions. The 3D model allows the exploration of alternative possible reconstructions of both stairs to see how they would interact spatially and visually with the rest of the house.

This approach led to the reconstruction of the route that the notary and his clerks took when entering the *voorhuis*, namely from the door on the most narrow wall of

[44] The surveys of the building were carried out by the author together with Gabri van Tussenbroek and Bart Reuvekamp.

this room.[45] This location offers the first anchor point to start placing the objects listed in the inventory. The other anchor point is the curtain, which is halfway down the list and undoubtedly covered the window on top of the main entrance door (and, as previously mentioned, possibly the door as well).[46] Several alternatives have been explored to find the most plausible disposition in order to fit the maps, the furniture pieces and the plaster portraits in the spaces left by the doorways, the window opening and the grisailles which occupied the walls. The results of this process are displayed in Fig. 10. By maintaining the order of the objects as mentioned in the inventory (thus assuming that it reflects their location within the room), we find out that the two tables that are listed a couple of objects apart (respectively the fourth and the seventh items in the inventory list, see Fig. 2) would have been positioned facing each other along the two longer sides of the room. This disposition gives a sense of symmetry to the *ensemble*, as was indeed in fashion at the time (Fock 2007a, 65). An empty space to the left of the main entrance would have provided enough room for the door shutter to open towards that direction, while on the other side the wooden bench would have accommodated visitors waiting to be received. Given their uncertain identification, the placing of the two candle holders remains ambiguous.

In addition, the scale model made it possible to experiment with various arrangements of the floor tiles to test which one would allow the laying out of 20.5 red tiles, the number that De Graeff recorded in his almanacs as being used in his *voorhuis*' floor. The most likely pattern matching this number mirrors the structure of the coffered ceiling, as it is was in fashion in that period, and allows the most efficient laying down of tiles with minimum need of cutting both red stone and white marble tiles.[47]

By placing the objects listed in the inventory back in their original location, this 3D model provides a qualitative method of assessing which objects visitors would have seen when entering the house. As seen in Fig. 10, after crossing the main entrance door they would have had in front of them the map of the family's estate in Zuid-Polsbroek, the map of the beloved city of Amsterdam and the two portraits. Therefore, the visitor entering the house would have been immediately made aware of the household's status and lineage, even more so if we take the identification of the plaster portraits with De Graeff's parents as plausible. Moreover, the two tables opposite each other would have given a sense of symmetry to the room. This work has demonstrated that the "translation" of the textual information into a visual

[45] A question remains open in relation to the exact position of this door, since a later larger portal has substituted the original doorway. The reconstructed location of the door is therefore inferred by taking into account the symmetry of the room and the volume of the service stairs which were originally behind the right part of the wall.

[46] The presence of a window over the main entrance corresponds to the common design of the time and is confirmed by an entry in the almanacs where De Graeff recorded that he received 90 screws for the windows of the attics, the *voorhuis* and the *zydelkamer* (SAA, Inventaris van het Archief van de Familie De Graeff (nr. 76), inv. nr. 188 (1666), 13 November).

[47] Two alternative reconstruction hypotheses of the floor tile pattern are discussed in more detail in Huurdeman and Piccoli (2021), and can be explored in the prototype Virtual Interiors webviewer at https://www.virtualinteriorsproject.nl/output/ (last accessed August 2021)

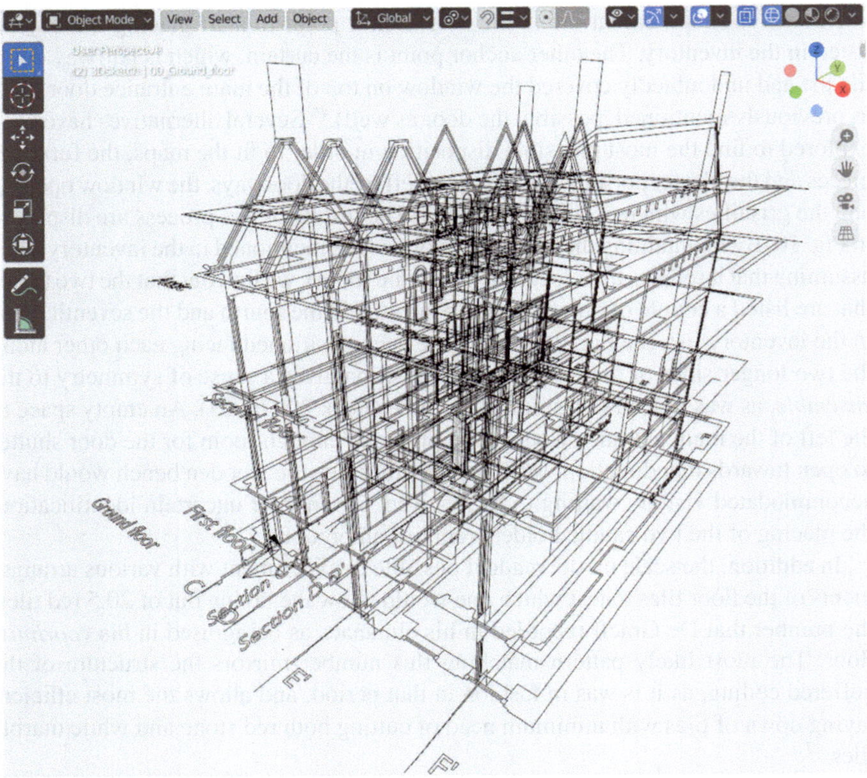

Fig. 9 The plans digitized in AutoCAD are imported into Blender and re-assembled to create the building's 3D frame

representation enables the detection of spatial correlations, prominence and strategic placements of objects, which were not evident from the textual sources alone.

5 Discussion

This paper explored the contribution of a 3D reconstruction to gain insight into the representational character of the entrance hall of De Graeff's grand canal house. The making of this 3D model allowed re-introducing the spatial dimension into the list of objects recorded in De Graeff's probate inventory. This process of "virtually materializing" the room and its furnishing has made it possible to suggest an otherwise unnoticeable visual hierarchy and symmetry within it. At the same time, by transferring the mental image of what this room would have looked like into a digital scale model, the creation process and the results are made explicit and verifiable. In this way, the 3D reconstruction has become both an *interpretative* and an *expressive* means of visualization[48] which enables knowledge creation and sharing.[49] There is no doubt that this type of approach to visualizing past housing phases and lost room functions in historical buildings will be increasingly used in place of on-site physical reconstructions, which usually result in a more intrusive, permanent and often problematic intervention on a heritage site.[50]

The research that was here discussed, driven by the creation of the 3D reconstruction, has shown the importance of collecting and integrating evidence from various sources. In fact, a great deal of information on the appearance of this room (most notably the presence of grisailles on the walls) would have been missed by looking at the inventory alone. The cross-referencing of this multidisciplinary dataset has created new links and relations among previously unconnected pieces of information. The creation process has therefore turned the 3D model into a virtual hub where these data are integrated and spatially visualized. However, the complex relation between the certain, the inferred and the hypothetical is inevitably simplified in the resulting visualization and hidden to the viewer if the latter is exposed only to the end result of this process. As such, challenges arise related to providing an effective knowledge management which guarantees an adequate and long-term access to the underlying data sources and a transparent assessment of the varying degrees of certainty in their identification.

Over the years, photo-realistic 3D visualizations of archaeological and historical sites have been increasingly seen as powerful non-transparent visualization modes which need to be accompanied by sufficient information to enable their evaluation. In fact, 3D reconstructions have been compared to the philological restoration of a fragmentary text (Frischer et al. 2002) and to the creation of an academic paper (Denard 2012) with a common underlying concept: instead of being presented only with the conclusions, the viewer should be able to access the sources and follow the entire reasoning and decision-making process behind the reconstruction. The London Charter for the computer-based visualization of cultural heritage[51] and the Seville Principles,[52] more specifically targeted at virtual archaeology, aimed to raise awareness on the need of quality standards in this field and proposed a set of principles that this kind of visualizations need to comply to. The degree to which the principles have been adopted in the past and current projects still vary greatly, and the development of more applied workflows is needed in order to demonstrate and evaluate possible

[48] See Gordin et al. (1996).

[49] Further on this, see Huurdeman and Piccoli (2021)

[50] See e.g. the physical reconstruction of Rembrandt's house, completed in 1999, which has triggered a debate about the ethics of this type of interventions and the authenticity of the results (e.g. Laan and Vroom 1997; Koelemeijer 1998; van den Boogert 1999). For other case studies and a reflection on this subject, see Nakaris and Avgerinou-Kolonia (2016). In our case, the plan of making the results of this work available on location has been halted by the permanent closure of the museum in 2020.

[51] http://www.londoncharter.org/ (last accessed August 2021).

[52] http://sevilleprinciples.com/ (last accessed August 2021).

ways to tackle the above-mentioned issues in practice.[53] A thorough documentation of the underlying data and reconstruction process is also key to enhance the chances of their long-term availability in the presently still uncertain future of 3D assets' storage and preservation.

This research aims to approach the 3D modelling of the interiors in a documented and consistent way. To this end, the decision-making process and the sources for the reconstruction hypotheses are recorded in a system of related spread sheets and written reports which also keep track of possible alternative reconstructions and record the uncertainty value of the reconstruction hypotheses that are chosen to be represented. For example, two columns in the spreadsheet store a "confidence index": namely a numerical value from 1 (closer to original) to 4 (uncertain) that expresses the degree of certainty for the identification of each object and their location. In this way, it is possible to differentiate between objects for which the location is certain, but their appearance is not (e.g. the curtain) and vice versa. Moreover, a column lists the object taken as comparison for each 3D model in the scene and another contains the explanation of the reasoning behind the choice.

These underlying pieces of information are being integrated into a prototype web-viewer designed as part of the NWO-funded project "Virtual Interiors as Interfaces for Big Historical Data Research Spatially enhanced publications of the creative industries of the Dutch Golden Age", which the research presented here is part of.[54] As the web-viewer directly queries the information in the spreadsheet, this system makes it easy to update the visual references that have been used for representing the items in the room in case new evidence is available. The numerical values describing the uncertainty translate into a color-coded scheme (for the moment from green to red) which visualizes the various degrees of certainty and overlay them onto the reconstruction. As such, the web-viewer acts as a trustworthy interface and research environment for exploring these historical virtual reconstructions, their uncertainty values, alternative hypotheses, underlying data sources and related Linked Data in an interactive and customizable way. In doing so, it enables a more dialogical form of engagement with the proposed 3D reconstruction (Fig. 11).[55]

---

[53] For various project-based ways of visualizing uncertainty see, e.g. the Villa of Livia project for one of the earliest examples in the archaeological domain (Forte 2007), and Noordegraaf et al. (2016) in the history of cinema going. See also Huurdeman and Piccoli (2021) for a more detailed discussion of this topic.

[54] See https://virtualinteriorsproject.nl/ (last accessed August 2021) and Huurdeman (2020).

[55] These aspects related to the case study of the De Graeff's *voorhuis* are further discussed in Huurdeman and Piccoli (2021) and Huurdeman 2021. The proposed 3D reconstruction of De Graeff's entrance hall can be explored at https://www.virtualinteriorsproject.nl/output/ (last accessed August 2021). A screencast showcasing the functionalities that are currently implemented in the prototype web-viewer is available at https://doi.org/10.21942/uva.14424218 (last accessed August 2021). See also Huurdeman et al. 2021 for the Linked Data integration.

Fig. 10 The proposed reconstruction hypothesis of De Graeff's *voorhuis* based on the currently available data and interpretations

Fig. 11 A screenshot of the prototype web-viewer designed as part of the Virtual Interiors project (available at https://www.virtualinteriorsproject.nl/output/). The viewer allows the real-time exploration of the 3D reconstruction, of the decision-making process and of the complex web of underlying data sources (see Huurdeman and Piccoli 2021).

Acknowledgements This work was part of "Virtual Interiors as Interfaces for Big Historical Data Research: Spatially Enhanced Publications of the Creative industries of the Dutch Golden Age" project financed by the NWO Smart Culture—Big Data/Digital Humanities program (2018–2022). The author would like to thank Gabri van Tussenbroek for his advice during this research, Bart Reuvekamp for his help in exploring the De Graeff family archive and for his transcriptions, Judith Brouwer for checking the transcriptions, and Hugo Huurdeman for his feedback on the data spreadsheets' structure. Also, thanks to Gabri van Tussenbroek, Charles van den Heuvel and Julia Noordegraaf for their comments on an earlier version of this text.

References

Aalst, Loek van and Annigje Hofstede. 2011. *Noord-Nederlandse meubelen van renaissance tot vroege barok 1550–1670*. Utrecht: Hes & de Graaf.

Baarsen, Reinier. 2007. *Wonen in de Gouden Eeuw 17de-eeuwse Nederlandse meubelen*. Rijksmuseum Amsterdam: Nieuw Amsterdam Uitgevers.

Beaudry, Mary C. 2015. Households beyond the house. On the Archaeology of Materiality of historical households. In *Beyond the Walls: New Perspectives on the Archaeology of Historical Households*, ed. K. R. Fogle, J. A. Nyman, and M. C. Beaudry, 1–22. Gainesville: University Press of Florida.

Boogert, Bob van den. 1999. Bouwkundige reconstructie van het Rembrandthuis voltooid. *Binnenstad* 179. https://www.amsterdamsebinnenstad.nl/binnenstad/179/rembrandt.html. Accessed August 2021.

Bourdieu, Pierre. 1977. *Outline of a Theory of Practice*. Cambridge: Cambridge University Press.

Bourdieu, Pierre. 1979. *La distinction: Critique sociale du jugement*. Paris: Les Editions de Minuit.

Bredius, Abraham. 1912. Iets over de copie van Gerrit Lundens naar Rembrandt's "Nachtwacht". *Oud Holland* 30 (4), 197–200.

Denard, Hugh. 2012. A New Introduction to the London Charter. In *Paradata and Transparency in Virtual Heritage*, ed. A. Bentkowska-Kafel, H. Denard and D. Baker, 57–71. Farnham: Ashgate.

Eikema Hommes, Margriet van and Piet Bakker. 2008. Hoogachtbaarheid en ontzaglijke grootheid: De burgermeesterskamer van het stadthuis van Enkhuizen. In *Romeyn de Hooghe: de verbeelding van de late Gouden Eeuw*, ed. H. van Nierop, 222–43. Zwolle: Waanders.

Faber, Johannes. 1980. Inhabitants of Amsterdam and their possessions, 1701–1710. In *Probate Inventories. A New Source for the Historical Study of Wealth, Material Culture and Agricultural Development. Papers Presented at the Leeuwenborch Conference (Wageningen, 5–7 May 1980)*, ed. A. van der Woude and A. Schuurman, 149–76. Utrecht: Brill | Hes & DeGraaf.

Fock, C. Willemijn. 1982. Review of Thornton 1978. *Oud Holland* 96: 198–200.

Fock, C. Willemijn. 1998. Werkelijkheid of schijn. Het beeld van het Hollandse intérieur in de zeventiende-eeuwse genreschilderkunst. *Oud Holland* 112: 187–246.

Fock, C. Willemijn. 1999. Het decor van huiselijk vermaak ten tijde van de republiek. In *Vermaak van de elite in de vroegmoderne tijd*, ed. J. de Jongste, J. Roding and B. Thijs, 40–72. Hilversum: Verloren.

Fock, C. Willemijn. 2001. *Het Nederlandse interieur in beeld, 1600–1900*. Zwolle: Waanders.

Fock, C. Willemijn. 2007a. Het interieur in de Republiek 1670–1750: (g)een plaats voor schilderkunst? In *De kroon op het werk. Hollandse schilderkunst 1670–1750*, ed. E. Mai, S. Paarlberg, G. J. M. Weber, 65–84. Dordrecht: Dordrechts Museum.

Fock, C. Willemijn. 2007b. *Het stempel van de bewoner*. Leiden: Leiden University.

Forte, Maurizio. 2007. *La villa di Livia: un percorso di ricerca di archeologia virtuale*. Roma: L'Erma di Bretschneider.

Frischer, Bernard, Franco Niccolucci, Nick Ryan and Juan Antonio Barceló. 2002. From CVR to CVRO: The Past, Present and Future of Cultural Virtual Reality. In *Proceedings of VAST 2000*, ed. F. Niccolucci, 7–18. Oxford: Archaeopress.

Goffman, Erving. 1956. *The Presentation of Self in Everyday Life*. Edinburgh: University of Edinburgh Social Sciences Research Centre.

Gordin, Douglas N., Daniel C. Edison and Louis M. Gomez. 1996. 'Scientific Visualization as an Interpretive and Expressive Medium'. In *Proceedings of the Second International Conference on the Learning Sciences*, July 1996, Evanston, IL, Charlottesville, ed. C. Edelson and E. A. Domeshek, 409–14. VA: AACE.

Groeneveld, Inger. 2010–2011. In goede orde veranderlijk geordineerd. Schriftelijke bronnen over (marmer)stenen vloeren in het Nederlandse interieur van de 17de en 18de eeuw. *Tijdschrift voor Interieurgeschiedenis en Design* 37: 21–51. https://doi.org/10.2143/GBI.37.0.3017262.

Hales, Shelley. 2003. *The Roman House and Social Identity*. Cambridge: Cambridge University Press.

Hanson, Julienne. 2003. *Decoding homes and houses*. Cambridge: Cambridge University Press.

Hanson, Julienne and Bill Hillier. 1982. Domestic space organization. Two contemporary space-codes compared. *Architecture and Behaviour* 2: 5–25.

Havard, Henry. 1887. *Dictionnaire de l'ameublement et de la décoration depuis le XIIIe siècle jusqu'à nos jours*, vol. 1, Paris: Ancienne maison Quantin, Librairies-imprimeries réunies.

Hendon, Julia A. 2004. Living and Working at Home: The Social Archaeology of Household Production and Social Relations. In *A Companion to Social Archaeology*, ed. R. W. Preucel and L. Meskell, 272–86. Oxford: Blackwell.

Hillier, Bill and Julienne Hanson 1984. *The Social Logic of Space*. Cambridge: Cambridge University Press.

Hopkins, Andrew and Arnold Witte. 1996. From deluxe architectural book to builder's manual: the Dutch editions of Scamozzi's *L'Idea della Architettura Universale*. *Quaerendo* 26 (4): 274–302.

Huurdeman, Hugo. 2020. Visualizing a radio of the past using technology of the future. https://www.beeldengeluid.nl/en/knowledge/blog/visualizing-radio-past-using-technology-future. Accessed August 2021.

Huurdeman, Hugo, and Chiara Piccoli. 2021. 3D reconstructions as research hubs: Geospatial interfaces for real-time data exploration of 17th cent Amsterdam domestic interiors. *Open Archaeology* 7: 314–336.

Huurdeman, Hugo. 2021. 'Analyze & Experience: Towards a Research Environment for 3D Reconstructions' https://www.virtualinteriorsproject.nl/2021/08/04/towards-a-3d-research-environment. Accessed August 2021.

Huurdeman, Hugo, Chiara Piccoli and Leon van Wissen. 2021. Linked Data in a 3D Context: Experiential Interfaces for Exploring the Interconnections of 17th-Century Historical Data. Paper presented at the DH Benelux conference (Leiden, 2–4 June 2021) available at https://doi.org/10.5281/zenodo.4889856. Accessed August 2021.

Jameson, Michael. 1990a. Private Space in the Greek City. In *The Greek City from Homer to Alexander*, ed. O. Murray and S. Price. 171–98. Oxford: Clarendon Press / New York: Oxford University Press.

Jameson, Michael. 1990b. Domestic space in the Greek city-state. In *Domestic Architecture and the Use of Space*, ed. S. Kent, 92–113. Cambridge: Cambridge University Press.

Kent, Susan. 1990. *New Directions in Archaeology: Domestic Architecture and the Use of Space: An Interdisciplinary Cross-Cultural Study*. Cambridge: Cambridge University Press.

Koelemeijer, Judith. 1998. Een kijkhuis vol valse meubels Het Rembrandthuis wordt net echt zeventiende-eeuws. *De Volkskrant* 20 februari 1998. https://www.volkskrant.nl/cultuur-media/een-kijkhuis-vol-valse-meubels-het-rembrandthuis-wordt-net-echt-zeventiende-eeuws~be74a666/. Accessed August 2021.

Koldeweij, Eloy. 2008. 'Wat er op de vloer omme-gaet': poppenhuisvloeren en de realiteit. In *Over de vloer. Met voeten getreden erfgoed*, ed. E. Koldeweij, 132–53. Zwolle: Waanders.

Korevaar, Gerbrand and Gwen Tauber. 2014. Gerard ter Borch repeats: on autograph portrait copies in the work of ter Borch (1617–1681). *Bulletin of the Rijksmuseum* 4: 348–81.

Laan, Barbara and Wim Vroom. 1997. Sloop interieur De Bazel van Rembrandthuis te Amsterdam? *Cuypersbulletin* 3: 14–6.

Lessi, Federica. 2000. Velluti Ottomani dei secoli XVI e XVII del Museo Nazionale del Bargello di Firenze, *Emblemata* 6: 113–37.

Loughman, John and John Michael Montias. 2000. *Public and Private Spaces: Works of Art in Seventeenth-Century Dutch Houses* (Studies in Netherlandish Art and Cultural History). Zwolle: Waanders.

Mare, Heidi de. 1993. The Domestic Boundary as Ritual Area in Seventeenth-Century. In *Urban Rituals in Italy and the Netherlands: Historical Contrasts in the Use of Public Space and the Urban Environment*, ed. H. de Mare and A. Vos, 108–31. Assen: Van Gorcum.

Mare, Heidi de. 2003. *Het huis en de regels van het denken. Een cultuurhistorisch onderzoek naar het werk van Simon Stevin, Jacob Cats en Pieter de Hooch*, (4 vols), Vrije Universiteit Amsterdam, PhD thesis (28 January 2003).

Meischke, Rudolph and Henk J. Zantkuijl. 1969. *Het Nederlandse Woonhuis van 1300–1800* (Vijftig jaar Vereniging 'Hendrick de Keyser'). Haarlem: Tjeenk Willink.

Moseley-Christian, Michelle. 2010. Seventeenth century 'pronk poppenhuisen': Domestic space and the ritual function of Dutch dollhouses for women. *Home cultures* 7 (3): 341–64.

Muurling, Sanne. 2002. Huiselijkheid tussen ideaal en materiële werkelijkheid. Een materiële microgeschiedenis van veertien Amsterdamse huishoudens. *Holland* 44 (3): 119–30.

Nakasis, Athanasios and Sofia Avgerinou-Kolonia (ed.). 2016. *Reconstructions: European perspective, Booklet of the ICOMOS Europe Group Meeting, 6–7 June 2016, Athens, Greece*. Athens: Propobos Publications.

Nierop, Henk van (ed.) 2008. *Romeyn de Hooghe: de verbeelding van de late Gouden Eeuw*. Zwolle: Waanders.

Noordegraaf, Julia, Opgenhaffen, Loes and Norbert Bakker. 2016. Cinema Parisien 3D: 3D visualisation as a tool for the History of Cinemagoing. *Alphaville* 11 (3): 45–61.

Otten, Jeanine. 1995. Kaarttekenaars en kaartafzetters in de dagboeken van Pieter de Graeff (1638–1707). *Caert Thresoor* 14 (3): 53–8.

Ottenheym, Konrad. 2007. A Bird's-Eye View of the Dissemination of Scamozzi's Treatise in Northern Europe. *Annali di architettura* 18–19: 187–98.

Ottenheym, Konrad. 2010. *Schoonheid op maat. Vincenzo Scamozzi en de architectuur van de Gouden Eeuw*. Amsterdam: Architectura & Natura Pers.

Piccoli, Chiara. 2018. *Visualizing cityscapes of Classical antiquity: From early modern reconstruction drawings to digital 3D models*. Oxford: Archaeopress.

Pijzel-Dommisse, Jet. 2000. *Hollandse Pronkpoppenhuis interieur en huishouden in de 17de en 18de eeuw*. Zwolle: Waanders.

Purves, Alex C. 2010. *Space and Time in Ancient Greek Narrative*. Cambridge/New York: Cambridge University Press.

Rapoport, Amos. 1969. *House Form and Culture*. Prentice-Hall: Englewood Cliffs, New Jersey.

Scholten, Frits. 2010. *Artus Quellinus. Beeldhouwer van Amsterdam*. Amsterdam: Rijksmuseum.

Scholten Frits and Michael Hoyle. 2006. Quellinus's Burgomasters: A Portrait Gallery of Amsterdam Republicanism. *Simiolus: Netherlands Quarterly for the History of Art* 32 (2/3): 87–125.

Schuurman, Anton. 1980. Probate inventories: research issues, problems and results. In *Probate Inventories. A New Source for the Historical Study of Wealth, Material Culture and Agricultural Development. Papers Presented at the Leeuwenborch Conference (Wageningen, 5–7 May 1980)*, ed. A. van der Woude and A. Schuurman, 19–31. Utrecht: Brill / Hes & DeGraaf.

Schama, Simon. 1997 [1987]. *The Embarrassment of Riches: an interpretation of Dutch culture in the Golden Age*. New York: Vintage Books.

Sluijter, Eric Jan. 2001. "All striving to adorne their houses with costly peeces" Two Case Studies of Paintings in Wealthy Interiors. In *Art and Home: Dutch Interiors in the Age of Rembrandt*, ed. M. Westermann, 103–27. Zwolle: Waanders.

Tussenbroek, Gabri van. 2016a. Functie en indeling van het Amsterdamse woonhuis aan de hand van een aantal zestiende-eeuwse boedelinventarissen. *KNOB* 3: 113–31.

Tussenbroek, Gabri van. 2016b. Assembling the World. The International Building Materials Trade in Amsterdam (1613–1795). In *The Amsterdam Canals: World Heritage*, ed. P. Vlaardingerbroek, 108–47. Amsterdam: Bas Lubberhuizen.

Vlaardingerbroek, Pieter. 2011. *Het paleis van de Republiek. Geschiedenis van het stadhuis van Amsterdam*. Zwolle: Wbooks.

Vlaardingerbroek, Pieter. 2019. An appropriated history: The case of the Amsterdam Town Hall (1648–1667). In *The Quest for an Appropriate Past in Literature, Art and Architecture*, ed. K. A. E. Enenkel and K. A. Ottenheym, 455–81. Leiden: Brill.

Westermann, Mariët. 2001. "Costly and Curious, full off pleasure and home contentment" Making Home in the Dutch Republic. In *Art and Home: Dutch Interiors in the Age of Rembrandt*, ed. M. Westermann, 15–81. Zwolle: Waanders.

Wijsenbeek-Olthuis, Thera Francine. 1996. Het Hollandse interieur in beeld en geschrift. *Theoretische Geschiedenis* 23 (2): 145–163.

Zaandvliet, Kees. 2006, *De 250 rijksten van de Gouden Eeuw*, Amsterdam: Rijksmuseum / Nieuw Amsterdam.

Chiara Piccoli is Research Fellow and Data Scientist at the Faculty of Humanities, University of Amsterdam. Her research interests focus on urban and domestic contexts and on the application of 3D modelling and GIS mapping for data visualization, analysis and communication.

The Embodied City: A Method for Multisensory Mapping

Anna Misharina and Eleanor Betts

Abstract This chapter presents a methodology for recording sensory data in an urban landscape and looks forward to how this might be adapted to enable multisensory mapping of ancient spaces more broadly. The premise is that it is impossible to make a single map of a city without overlapping temporal, monumental, social, and sensory spaces, a premise situated in Henri Lefebvre's philosophy of social space. The focus of the authors' methodology is lived space. Lived space is constructed from the relations between people and their habitation of the physical environment. Recognition of, and attachment to, places is constructed through personal experience and memories. Sight, sound, smell, taste, kinaesthesia, and touch all contribute to the creation of the experience and affectiveness of place. Sensation is complex, and the sensory experience of place is more so. In any discipline, taking a multisensory approach means embracing this complexity, while recognising the myriad variables and finding methods and approaches by which to record them. In order to draw attention to the embodied city, the authors invited a group of workshop participants to work with a map of the Canterbury city centre (Kent, UK) as a critical tool with which to analyse concrete space. Participants were encouraged to map the impressions engendered by their physical environment in the specific moment in which they encountered it. The objective of this exercise was to capture the qualitative experience of sensory space by recording individual perceptions of sensory stimuli. The results were then digitised and are presented in the final section of this chapter.

Supplementary Information The online version contains supplementary material available at https://doi.org/10.1007/978-3-031-23133-9_11.

A. Misharina (✉)
Studio CRIT, P.O. Box 395, CA 94563 Orinda, USA
e-mail: anna@critstudio.com

E. Betts
School of Arts and Humanities, Faculty of Arts and Social Sciences, The Open University, Milton Keynes, UK
e-mail: eleanor.betts@open.ac.uk

G. Landeschi and E. Betts (eds.), *Capturing the Senses*,
Quantitative Methods in the Humanities and Social Sciences,
https://doi.org/10.1007/978-3-031-23133-9_11

Keywords Urban space · Production of space · Lefebvre · Urban mapping · Multisensory mapping methodology

1 Embodied City Mapping

It is a gloomy morning in the late Spring of 2015 when a group of fourteen people, one by one, embark on a journey to explore and map elusive lived space. Exiting the warmth and monotonous humming of the Lodge, they are met with the fierce wind, which makes it difficult not only to record anything but barely to hold onto the thin paper proformas. Proformas flap violently in their hands, threatening to escape at any moment. The contrast between the stillness and controlled detachedness of the building's interior and the anticipated but still somehow unexpected physical force of the wind makes most of them put a colour sticker on a map regardless or probably because of the struggle. The ochre limestone of the Canterbury Cathedral that towers over the participants radiates warmth, contrasting grey sky and piercing wind. A metallic clanking sound of a scaffolding parasitising on the stately Cathedral spreads through the area. Directed by individual intuition, participants disperse through the territory of the Canterbury Cathedral Park and beyond. We follow behind, observing them, recording video, and taking measurements of the natural light's intensity.

Most of the participants turn right and, after a short walk, a birdsong melody and tree fragrance tell them that they enter the precinct's park area. Soon, their bodies relax, relieved by the warmth behind the rough stone walls of a chamber garden that shelters them from the wind. The whiff of honeysuckle tickles their nose. Their bodies carry them further, and the vehicle fumes and sounds hit them as they pass through a gate to a busy road. The smell of fumes mingles for a while after they enter a lively shopping district. The streets are narrow; the echo of their footsteps reminds them of this narrowness when they can hear it through the human chatter, coffee machine whirring, and shop signs squeaking. They brush against the stone pillars, though most buildings are brick, and the cold glass meets them on the ground floors. Their body feels wobbly as their feet suddenly hit uneven cobblestones. The sounds of human voices intensify as participants approach the main Cathedral gateway and return to the precinct. All along their way, participants map their experience of the city (see Fig. 1).

The mapping exercise is a part of a methodology for recording and analysing sensory data in an urban landscape. While conducted in the contemporary setting, the chapter looks forward to how this methodology might be adapted to enable multi-sensory mapping of both modern and ancient urban spaces more broadly. The lived space that participants are mapping is a part of a conceived-perceived-lived triad that constitutes social space as described and explored by Henri Lefebvre, primarily in *The Production of Space* (1991). Lefebvre stressed that space has always been a complex social construct based on values and the social production of meanings. It affects both spatial practices and perceptions: "...space is social: it involves assigning more or less appropriated places to social relations...social space has thus always been a social

Fig. 1 Participant sheltering the map from the wind

product" (Lefebvre 2009, 186–7). He further argued that the social space comprises conceived space, perceived space, and lived space. Conceived space expresses the dominant social order and hence its conceptualisation, signs, and symbols representing that order. It is "the space of scientists, planners, urbanists, technocratic subdividers and social engineers" (Lefebvre 1991, 38). Perceived space, or spatial practice, is a space of everyday life. It "secretes that society's space; it propounds and presupposes it, in a dialectical interaction; it produces it slowly and surely as it masters and appropriates it" (Lefebvre 1991, 38). Lived space is "space as directly *lived* through its associated images and symbols...the dominated—and hence passively experienced—space which the imagination seeks to change and appropriate. It overlays physical space, making symbolic use of its objects" (Lefebvre 1991, 39).

Here it is essential to understand how Lefebvre relates the terms "space" and "place". Interpreting Lefebvre's work, which does not explicitly elaborate on that relation, Merrifield (1993) defines place as practised space. For Lefebvre, he writes, space is a social dynamic, a continuous movement. The place is to space what form is to process: a grounding of a flow. However, the place is not the direct fixation of that flow but its momentary embodiment that is neither constant nor determined. It changes under the flux of social dynamics—it is shaped by the space but shapes it simultaneously. "...space is already flow and place—it is simultaneously a process and a thing" (Merrifield 1993, 521). The place is where the complex triad of space is tangible and can be delineated.[1] A city is an eloquent example of a place epitomising

[1] Lefebvre further drew a relation between each space of the triad to different urban and architectural objects. They "contribute in different ways to the production of space according to their qualities and attributes, according to the society or mode of production in question, and according to the historical period" (1991: 46). Conceived space finds its expression "by way of architecture, conceived of not as the building of a particular structure... but rather as a project embedded in a spatial context and a texture which call for 'representations' that will not vanish into the symbolic or imaginary realms"

social space—it is in the constant process of formation rather than something formed (Ingold 2020).

Exploration, contextualisation, and understanding of places, especially cities, have historically relied heavily on mapping, along with a textual description and theorising (Mayer 2021, 23). Considering that the spatial triad is tangible in a city, we chose the map as our primary tool to reveal lived space. Besides being instrumental in representing and analysing places, mapping is a way of contemplating the very nature of place and time (Kainz 2020). Conceived space can be revealed by mapping power relations and reading city plans, subdivision maps, and other bureaucratic representations of space generally used to manage cities. Mapping flows of everyday life in the urban fabric unveil perceived space. Lived space is harder to capture because it consists of lived experiences, memories, dreams, and aspirations. It is the space of pure subjectivity, embodied and imaginative involvement of people with their surroundings. Lefebvre also pointed out that the bodily experience of space as lived is "strangely different" from when space is conceived or perceived (1991, 40). Based on Lefebvre's theorising of social space, Kinkaid (2020) further argues that lived space is more than merely a part of the triad. It is the phenomenal ground of space, the practico-sensory totality in which people perceive and act in the world. Kinkaid demonstrates that differential embodiment carries the potential for political change through spatial practice. We suggest that exposing and acknowledging differential perceptions of space does as well bear liberating potential. The diverse lived experiences contradict and oppose the hegemony of the dominant social order. To map lived space is daring to take on the present no matter how complex and subjectively perceived it is. Interested in the relationships between fluid social life and the apparent stillness of urban places, we asked participants to listen to their experiences and dare.

Participants held identical A4 format base maps. They were plain and primarily white, except for pale hatches that identified unpaved areas and thin grey shadow strips at the buildings' edges to delineate their height (see Fig. 2). These subtle maps gave participants enough information to locate themselves within the city and provided space for their discoveries and paths. The maps intentionally covered a relatively small area, barely one block beyond the Cathedral walls. This partiality did not invalidate the map as a critical tool. It made the map concise and direct within limited parameters. The duration of the exercise also conditioned the map's coverage area.

Participants wandered around. They listened to their bodies and let sensory stimuli lead them: they followed a smell that caught their attention or moved away from a disturbing sound:

> "I let smells and sounds guide me to areas of interest. Strong smells and sounds drew me to or kept me in one particular area," said participant #11 later, when the group returned to the Lodge for the plenary.

(1991: 42). Lived space is linked to the clandestine side of social life—"bedroom, dwelling, house, or: square, church, graveyard" (1991: 42). Perceived space incarnates in people's daily routes, networks, and patterns of interaction and movement that link places where work, play, and leisure occur in infrastructure.

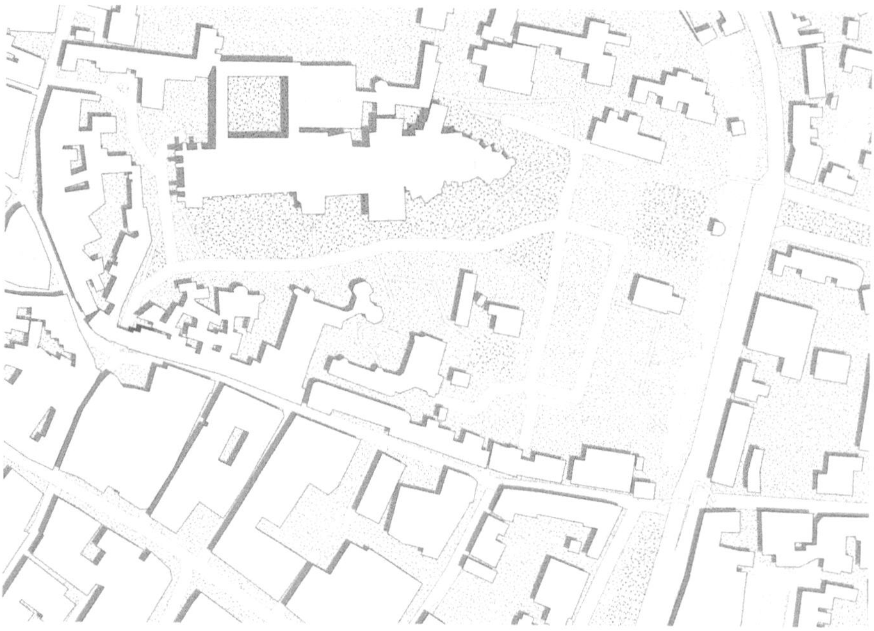

Fig. 2 Base map showing the Cathedral Precinct and adjacent areas

Lefebvre suggested that people can understand the lived experience of space only by examining it through their bodies, without privileging any one of the senses (Lefebvre 2014, 33–4). Bernard Tschumi also emphasises the physical connection between place and body, precisely a sensory encounter before a person consciously analyses their surroundings. At that moment, the "body tries to rediscover its lost unity, its energies and impulses, its rhythms and its flux" (Tschumi 1996, 39). The body communicates with the place through multiple senses. Sight, sound, smell, taste, kinaesthesia, touch, and many more contribute to creating the experience of place. Sensory stimuli can be singular, repeated, or constant, invasive or ambient, situated or directional. While having measurable physiological effects, they are not necessarily consciously observed.[2] When they are indeed consciously observed—in other words, when a human subject perceives them—sensory stimuli become embodied as sensations. Then come perceptions, or how the human subject interprets sensations (Levine and Shefner 1981), often basing these interpretations on the previous experiences. Thus, the way an individual perceives sensory stimuli, a single stimulus or a sensescape of multiple stimuli, is mediated. Sensations are inherently interdependent and can influence and even transform individual characteristics (Stein and Meredith 1993)—a multitude of sensory stimuli thus translates into elaborate coexistence of sensations.

[2] Individual ability to attune various sensory stimuli depends on psychological and physiological characteristics, for example, some people with autism spectrum disorder cannot subconsciously suppress monotonous pervasive sounds that other people can ignore (Sinclair et al. 2017).

"Some streets I will avoid because I do not like the way they feel, not quantifiable, but it may be a combination of visual, sound and smell," participant #7 commented on the indecipherable interrelation of multiple sensations of a place.

Both sensation and perception are also culturally, geographically, and temporally specific and dependent on the individual ability to attune to various sensory stimuli (OpenStax 2020). Perception additionally depends on how human subjects cognitively interpret and attribute stimuli sources (Spence 2020). For example, participant #6 could not initially identify a smell and was "suspicious of it" until associating it with wood and accepting it as pleasant. Perception of sensory stimuli is therefore complex, and the sensory experience of a place is more so. Taking a multisensory approach means embracing the complexity while recognising the myriad variables and finding methods and approaches to recording them.

These sensations gradually appeared on the participants' maps in the shape of out-of-scale colour stickers (see Fig. 3). The stickers marked sensory impressions that an environment gave to an indoctrinated perceiver, such as the following:

- The sound of wheels screeching,
- The smell of wisteria,
- The wind whipping,
- The warmth of the sun on the skin,
- The uneven pavement beneath their feet.

Due to their incommensurability with the map, the stickers could not pinpoint the exact location. They neither outlined a region where the fluid and ambiguous sensory stimulus with often nebulous geographic and temporal borders was present. They did not mark the source of the sensory stimulus but where the participant was standing/sitting/laying when acknowledging the sensation. The disproportionate size of the stickers also lifted the weight of scientific precision and allowed participants to

Fig. 3 Participant's hands holding stickers, map, and proforma

attend more to their feelings than their physical location. However, many participants looked around having a limited non-visual vocabulary in deciphering and describing the stimuli:

> "...there was a very strong 'flower' smell," wrote participant #8, "although I couldn't… figure what the smell was or where it was coming from. It made me look around to try and locate its source but also confused me as I couldn't identify the smell or location of it."

There were five colours of the stickers; each represented a particular sensation: red for touch, blue—kinaesthesia, yellow—sound, and green—smell. The white sticker was a variance sticker symbolising any sensation that did not fall into the other categories in the participant's opinion. We determined categories based on Lefebvre's "sensory field" (2014, 114–15). "Sensory field" included nine types of sensation: (a) visual, (b) auditory, (c) olfactory, (d) gustatory, "(e) mechanical (touch and pressure, penetration), (f) thermal, (g) kinaesthetic (position, resistance, and security, opposing or auxiliary), (h) static (weight, translation, rotation), and finally, (i) the affects (tickling or caressing, pinching, accompanied by sensory pleasure and pain)" (Lefebvre 2014, 15). To simplify the exercise, we retained only auditory (b) as a separate category; we combined the last five categories into two—haptic ((e), (f), and (i)), and kinaesthetic ((g) and (h)). Touch denoted anything felt via the skin; kinaesthesia was instead a muscular sensation (though both may be simultaneously in play). Gustatory (d)—"poorly discernible from olfactory given the ambiguity of the physical" (Lefebvre 2014, 114)—was also eliminated as a separate category in the exercise and merged into olfactory (c). From Lefebvre's "sensory field", the visual was left out intentionally during the exercise. The place in all its complexity cannot be understood until ocularcentrism is undermined[3] (Levin 1993) as generally prioritised sight provides only a partial understanding of a place (Lefebvre 1991, 146). Thus, the five colours and categories: haptic, kinaesthetic,[4] auditory, olfactory, and an undetermined open-ended category. Participants could potentially use the last category for visual sensations, but we did not mention or encourage it in any way during the initial briefing.[5]

In the aftermath, we saw that participants still used the white sticker mainly for the visual sensations. Although, those visual entries were prompted either by the momentary changes of the environment ("the sun suddenly came out and it transformed everything") or the symbolic meaning of places both collective and very personal:

---

[3] We acknowledge that visucentrism is critical for the deaf community but hope to emphasise the importance of "not only visual but embodied and tactile, made so through the embodiment of self and others in the visual-spatial modality" (O'Brien 2021). By concentrating on multiple senses in the exercise, we stressed the need to democratise the hierarchy of sensory experiences, whichever sensory experiences are available to a person considering their physical and mental traits.

[4] The exercise showed that participants had difficulty distinguishing touch and kinaesthesia; there was much blurring between them in the recordings. We advise explaining these two categories extensively and with some physical examples.

[5] For this particular exercise in Canterbury, we excluded the visual sensory stimuli, acknowledging that a different approach should be used with another group of participants, accommodating the individual sensual and perceptual characteristics.

"I used it to mark historical significance—a landmark," participant #4 mentioned.

"There was graffiti, a very historical graffiti on the wall of the Cathedral, and it made me want to touch it", noted participant #2.

"I used the white sticker for memory", and participant #13 continued to tell a personal story.

Kevin Lynch first expounded how the realm of perception conditions an individual subject's actual practices in the city. He pointed out that people acted in their cities according to personal mental images of the urban environment—"the product both of the immediate sensation and the memory of past experience, and it is used to interpret information and to guide action" (Lynch 1977, 4). The image of the city is both a personal and collective way of seeing cities as made not from a collection of objects (buildings, infrastructure) but as a net of places. Lynch distinguished five main categories that constitute this image: paths, edges, districts, nodes, and landmarks. Paths are the channels within which an observer moves through the city (e.g., streets, walkways, and transit lines). Edges are boundaries between two distinguished spaces (e.g., shores, walls, and railroad cuts). Districts are large but distinct urban areas that can be entered and exited (e.g., neighbourhoods, parks, and gated communities). Nodes are strategic public loci often located on paths' intersections (e.g., subway station, plaza, and market). Landmarks are standing-out tangible elements used as a reference point (e.g., monumental buildings, public art, and striking landscape architecture). These five categories intersect and combine in different patterns in any urban environment. The five categories connect the lived experience with the city as a place.[6]

Lynch mentioned that nearly every sense is involved in the production of the image of the city. However, it is not clear how the non-visual qualities of the environment correlate with the categories mentioned above. In his work, Lynch paid most attention to the urban attributes perceived by the eye. Generally, other senses are sidelined in the perception of the urban environment and its production processes (Bille and Sørensen 2018). While sight has always dominated the fields of architecture and urban planning,[7] an even more substantial shift towards a sight-centred paradigm happened in modernity[8]: "modernist design at large has housed the intellect and the eye, but it has left the body and the other senses, as well as our memories, imagination

[6] There also seems to be a relation between Lynch's categories and Lefebvre's architectural and urban most pronounced manifestations of spatial triad. Conceived space is most visible in monuments, perceived space is paths and edges, lived space—within districts and nodes.

[7] Drawings historically are the main tool in conceiving architecture and city; they are more common than models (which often came on the later stages of architectural production) that have a strong tactile quality to them (Empler 2018).

[8] It derived both from the ideology brought forward by influential architects such as Le Corbusier (Le Corbusier 1991, 83) and out of necessity—accompanying large development projects. Enormous scale of architectural and urban projects brought along an incomprehensible amount of information that had to be taken into consideration. Complex multisensory environments had to be simplified to become legible. Simplification for the sake of graspability and increasing speed of design processes lead to the production of spaces that basically disregard perceptions of the environment through any sense beyond sight. Noble at that time intention to provide large parts of the population with new habitation within a short period of time led to homogenous cleared of sensory stimuli spaces.

Fig. 4 Participants in front of the Cathedral

and dreams, homeless" (Pallasmaa 1996, 19). Therefore, for the exercise, we chose the urban setting that has been developed gradually, mainly in the pre-modernist era (see Fig. 4).

While a useful critical tool to analyse a concrete place, a map, both in production and interpretation, also heavily relies on sight.[9] Acknowledging this limitation, we asked the participants to record their experiences in any convenient way. The proforma attached to the back of the map added a linguistic layer[10] to the cartographic representation (see Appendix 1). Proforma consisted of instructions for the exercise and four empty fields repeated several times to accommodate multiple entries: identifier (of the location, where a participant noticed a sensation), time (when it occurred), weather/temperature/wind direction, and description (of the sensation, elaboration on why the participant placed the sticker on the map). The proforma also gave participants some pointers on how to engage with their surroundings. The questions touched on sensory 'stimuli' qualities, sensations' characteristics, emotional responses, and personal sensitivity. They prompted participants to deeply analyse feelings and be as specific as possible in their descriptions. We made the questions as open as possible so as not to direct participants too strongly, in an attempt to avoid biassing the results. None of the questions concerned the urban environment as a material place. They focused on personal bodily experiences and invisible, subtle features of the city as a lived space.

[9] While storytelling, often via non-visual media, plays a large role in documenting and explaining the cities, representation of the human-made environment historically heavily relies on maps (Roth 2021). Models of cities or tactile maps that appeal to touch and GPS-based city soundscapes are quite rare in comparison with the drawn maps.

[10] Language undermined the dominance of the visual, often relying on the hearing.

The proforma enriched the colour stickers' substance and added a temporal factor to the marked locations on the map. The map and the proforma link individual experience with the city form: paths, edges, districts, nodes, and landmarks. However, while graphic and textual recordings provide substantial data for interpretation, we advise using a more multisensory approach to record the experiences. It will make the exercise available to a broader group of people and resolve another map limitation that rests in its two-dimensionality.[11] The complication here lies in not merely recording the sensory stimuli directly (e.g., the sound of the wind) but the participants' perceptions. Additional tools and approaches could include haptic models that elucidate non-architectural features of the urban environment, associative along with descriptive audio recordings, and gathered and juxtaposed objects from the analysed environment to translate an olfactory experience. Besides producing unique individual impressions of urban places, such multisensory recording techniques might also open up this exercise to participants unable to record their experiences with visual means. This further can improve the general understanding of urban spaces as perceived by various people, whose being-in-the-world does not heavily rely on sight.

During the introduction to the exercise, we suggested participants explore three different areas covered on the map. Each of them had a distinct physical and sensory character: a park around the Cathedral enclosed within stone walls (Area 1, see Fig. 5), a monotonous sidewalk along a busy road (Area 2, see Fig. 6), and a dense and lively shopping district (Area 3, see Fig. 7). Later, many participants spoke about the audial sensations that distinguished the areas ("the different kinds of sounds—vegetation, people, and vehicles") besides the strong visual cues. The maps showed that the smells were also quite different in the areas and followed a similar pattern: vegetation, food, and car fumes. These three areas were also clearly related to Lynch's categories[12]: Area 1 was a district with a landmark, Area 2 was a path along a clear linear edge, and Area 3 was a district with nodes and paths.

Each participant used a colour pen to record their path, connecting one sticker to the following on the base maps (see Fig. 8). The starting and ending point was the Cathedral Lodge; it conditioned the initial movement[13] and skewed the routes, which inevitably took a shape of an enclosed loop.[14] All of the participants that left Area 1, the precinct, passed through the Cathedral gate—architecturally articulate entry

[11] The third, vertical, dimension is important in recording of sensory data both because of the prevalent vertical dimension of a human body and of the sensory stimulus perception which may come both from beneath participants and from above them. The time aspect will need more investigation as well.

[12] These three areas also can be related to the direct translation of the triad: conceived—Cathedral, lived—shopping district, and perceived—road.

[13] 7 participants went to the left, 4 to the right, and 2 down.

[14] Most of the participants passed through Nodes A, B, H, M, N, P, Q, and R (the nodes are explained further in the chapter).

Fig. 5 Participant walking in the park

Fig. 6 Participants recording their experiences by the road

point,[15] either at the beginning of the exercise or at the end. When the explorative part of the exercise was over, the participants headed back to the Lodge, where everything started around an hour earlier. Back then, we briefed them on lived space, explained the exercise, and equipped them with maps, proformas, stickers, and pens. Upon return, participants saw a large map awaiting them on the wall. It was an enlarged version of the base maps that participants filled with their impressions of the city.

[15] It was also "a controlled border" in a sense as people had to pay to enter the Cathedral area; participants could move freely across this boundary as part of the workshop having "elevated status" above the general public.

Fig. 7 Participant marking the map at the shopping district

Gathering together around the A0 map, participants replicated their maps. They drew their paths and placed stickers accordingly.[16] Colour pens were instrumental there because they highlighted singular paths in the convoluted net of lines and stickers. While an individual map came from a single perspective, a map produced by several people, a collective map, grasped a more comprehensive range of information. This richness of views, while still subjective, better translated the complexity of the city. Overlapping individual maps created a dialogue between those maps and the experiences they represented. Having the dialogue between numerous viewpoints gave the personal knowledge value and worth (Haraway 1988). While illustrating the multifacetedness and entanglement of the urban environment, the collective map was more about what participants and the city were in the process of becoming than what they were ceasing to be (Braidotti 2002).

The final part of the exercise was a discussion centred on the collective map (see Fig. 9). A new geography of the city appeared on the collective map. We discussed the expected large number of yellow (sound) stickers[17] and unexpected proliferation of the blue (kinaesthesia) stickers and the meaning behind the white (variance) stickers (see Video 1). What sensory stimuli prompted participants to put down stickers in general? How did participants choose their paths? What were the differences they noticed between the three areas? With these and some other questions answered, participant #6 concluded the discussion with the discovered difficulty of attending to one's senses beyond sight:

[16] We advise to draw the paths and place stickers on a tracing paper atop the enlarged base map. In this case, the base map can be removed to reveal alternative urban geography made up purely from sensory fields.

[17] Sound long ago has been accepted as the second most dominating sense in the perception of the city (Blesser and Salter 2007).

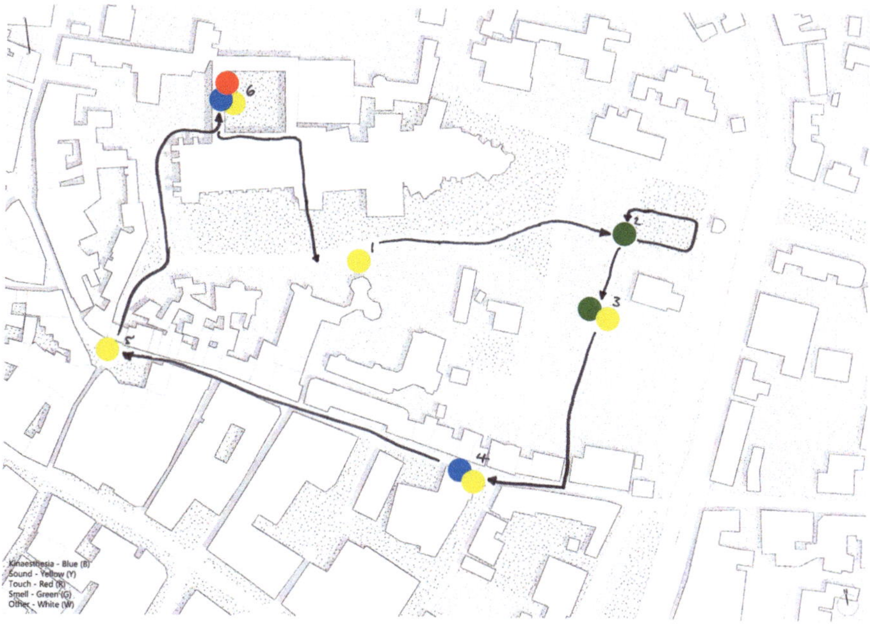

Fig. 8 Participant's individual map with stickers and path at the end of the mapping exercise

> ...I think quite possibly this needs the practice to focus in on the senses.

Not all of the participants were outspoken during the discussion. We followed up with a couple of questions a few months after the exercise (see Appendix 2). The discussion and the retrospective questionnaire gave us more insight into the sensory and mental processes behind the participants' maps.

2 Embodied City Map Analysis

Years later, we review the exercise. Synthesising and analysing the data have somewhat a historical quality to it—we try to reconstruct what had happened a long time ago, ourselves having a weak recollection of the events but with individual and collective maps made by the participants, proformas, and a short video recording.

We begin by systematising the data we have collected by putting it into different forms of spreadsheets, redrawing the collective map in hopes of learning something from the very act of retracing participants' journeys, and building a 3D model.[18] For the clarity of reference and an attempt to relate different recorded sensations to one another and the urban fabric, we divide the map into nodes. First, we attempt

[18] Working on it collaboratively from different geographic locations, we end up making a virtual 3D model but advise producing a physical model as well.

Fig. 9 Map with sensory nodes. Image credit Anna Misharina and Eleanor Betts

to do it following Lynch's categories, but this endeavour renders futile: the sensory experiences are so diverse and often fluid that it is impossible to distribute them neatly among five categories. The categories also appear too large in scale to indicate the sensory subtleties of places picked up by a human body.

We then distinguish nodes based on the patterns of the sensations marked on the map. First, we still try to tie them to some change of the material condition either in vertical or horizontal planes (architecture, landscape), but it does not work for most of the places because the marked sensations do not appear to have a clear relation to the buildings, trees, fences, infrastructure, and other palpable urban elements. In the end, we outline nodes not paying particular attention to the material borders and give them a nebulous form. The amorphous form further emphasises the difficulty to identify an area of influence of various sensory stimuli. Entries from at least two participants in nearby locations define the node. Additionally, several similar or interrelated entries create a node, disregarding a more considerable distance in-between them (for example, a couple of participants commented on the smell of wisteria, and those entries make one node G). The original map transforms from displaying a collection of primarily rectilinear objects to highlighting a net of paths interwoven with irregular beads of nodes (see Fig. 10).

The analysed areas considered on the map—Area 1 (Cathedral park), Area 2 (road), and Area 3 (shopping district)—include the following nodes: Area 1 incorporates nodes A, B, C, D, E, F, G, H, I, L, Area 2—J, K, and Area 3—M, N, P, Q, R, S, T, U, V, W, X. Area 1 is the largest in its coverage but has almost the same

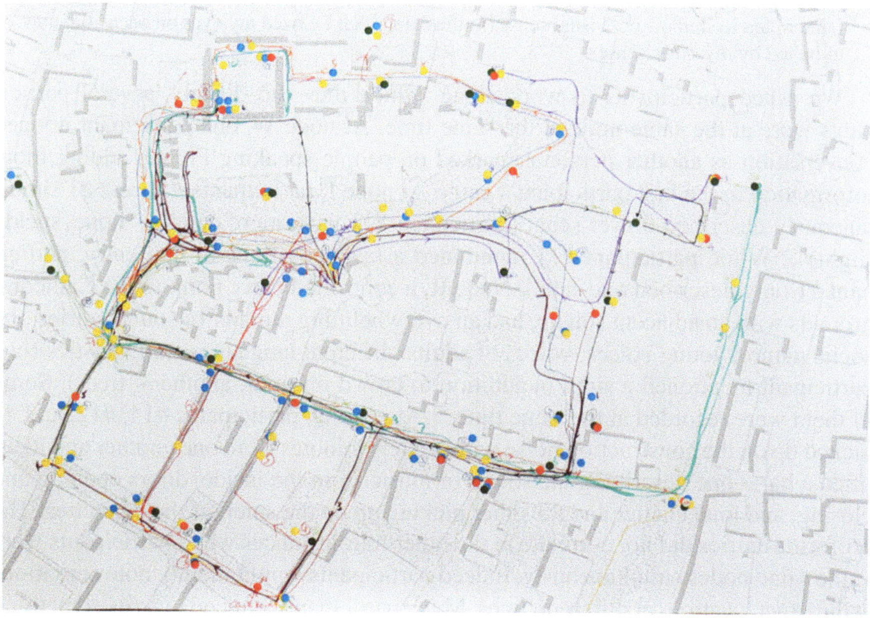

Fig. 10 Collective map with participants' intermingling paths

number of nodes and entries as Area 3 which is the densest. Area 2 is the poorest in the inputs of sensations. It lacks density; its monotony and deprivation of natural elements and people also drove most of the participants away (only 4 participants decided to explore this area; a couple approached it but moved away, not noting any sensations). There is a tentative correlation between the density and the number of sensory stimuli. However, the nature of the exercise might be at fault here to some extent. Participant #6 elaborated on this:

> I think you are aware that you are recording. [I] felt sort of halfway through that street [node B] that there should have been something that should have captured the experience of that street... [in] the Cathedral precinct [nodes H, I, L]... the dots are so much spread out because there is, I suppose, less of the sense of where you naturally stop to make your recording.

Another participant, #12, had a systematic approach to the exercise[19] deciding on the places for the recording before leaving the Lodge in fear of not having enough time to cover the area of interest. Other participants, however, stated that they indeed concentrated on the exercise and tried to attune to the sensory stimuli. They were not consciously attempting to capture the experience of a particular place or cover a specific area but to follow the sensory stimuli of their interest.[20] For example, participant #11 admitted:

---

[19] Systematic approach was not encouraged in the introduction to the exercise.

[20] This type of movement through the city has some similarity with *flaneur/flaneuse* (see works by Guy Debord, Linda McDowell, and others on psychogeography) being in the city but has more sensual directionality to it.

I attempted to shut off my visual sense (to the extent that I closed my eyes on occasion) and to be led by my other senses.

We asked participants to work alone, which they did. Rarely, several participants were at the same node at the same time. At node W, one participant noticed conversation as another person remarked on people speaking French adding more information to the first participant's entry. At node I, participants #11 and #1 simultaneously described flower scent (participant #11 gave more details: "honeysuckle (light)"). While participant #11 mentioned a few sensations in that entry, participant #1 only described one smell. Node R, a controlled entry point to the Cathedral grounds with an adjacent square, had an overwhelming number of sound entries of a social nature: young voices, voices of adults, different languages, and whistles (one participant mentioned a siren in addition to crowd murmur, another—trees). Some of them were recorded at the same time.[21] At node Q, participants #14, #12, and #5 picked up on the construction noise within a few minutes from one another and identified a bar—one describing the sound of music from the inside, doors opening and closing, and loud chatter and the other picking up on the smell of the cigarettes. The proforma entries did not correlate in the other four instances when participants were at the same nodes simultaneously. Indeed participants would mainly note sensations at the exact locations at different times. Many participants stopped to write something down near the Lodge (node A) at the very beginning of the exercise. The contrast between the interior space and the outdoors caused many entries (participant #9: "the change from inside to outside makes me aware of my body and weather"); other entries derived from the sounds of the metal (nearby construction) and a siren from an emergency service vehicle. The only recording at node A later in the exercise was again a kinaesthetic sensation of being "buffeted by the wind" and voices (noted by participant #11).

Participants also had different relations to the analysed site. While some of them were familiar with it, for others, it was a completely new place. Per The Image of the City, an individual knows how to behave in a new environment based on the previous experiences in similar places. The lived space then for some participants was full of symbols and sensations that developed over time, and for others, the lived space had an immediate character, inciting them to project new meanings and the memories of experiential analogies onto the place.

Lynch's categories still appear on the collective map to a certain extent. As mentioned earlier, a few participants observed changes in smells and sounds at the Areas' edges (nodes J, M, and Q). However, more participants traversed the edges without noting anything. The sounds of people's chatter, whistle, and squeaking at node R blurred the delineation between Lynch's edge and node—the sound extended beyond the material edge of the Cathedral walls in all directions. The social noises from the node (the market) and the edge (people waiting to enter the Cathedral grounds at the controlled entry) mixed and spread some distance away. The sound

---

[21] The sounds of chatter ("hustle and bustle of public queuing") continuously appeared at node R—11 out of 14 participants identified it at different times so it is not surprising that several of them noted it simultaneously.

at the edge was so overwhelming that participants did not mention any difference between the Areas. When considered with multiple senses, the edges as physical borders such as walls lose their explicitness in separating one area from another—sounds and scents travel across the walls (for instance, the melody of organ from the Cathedral, the smell of pastries from a bakery; participant #8 heard and saw a group of kids at node J, Area 2, at the same time as participant #11 separated by a stone wall heard their voices at node I, Area 1). The notable material edge is the change of pavement. The urban edges perceived through multisensory lens are closer to "*in-between*" (Grosz 2001, 91–104)—a bodily response to the transformation of a place rather than a mere change in urban structure. The edge is not where one ends and the other begins—they blend and create possibilities of something yet different to form and be perceived.

The paths from The Image of the City on the collective map are fragmented—they do not represent continuous routes. The sensory stimuli appear interrupted; the sound and the smell often appear as an amorphous locus, not as a solid line. Sensory paths are irregular nets of nodes of different sizes. Similar segmentation appears in the district. While there are some repeating sensations within a district, smaller areas with individual sensory characters disintegrate the large urban entity. The node per Lynch is the only category consistent with the definition, yet its sensory footprint expands beyond its physical borders.[22] The landmark[23] blends with the environment having tactile qualities, smells, and sounds similar to those of the other buildings and even the pavement.[24] Fully embodied exploration of the environment then breaks down The Image of the City categories into smaller nodes that are not explicitly related to the urban setting. They emerge as a combination of material form, natural features (including weather), and social happenings.[25]

During the analysis of the collective map, we create several spreadsheets. They add another level of clarity to the maps. The first spreadsheet, count per person (see Appendix 3), shows that sound was the most noticed sensory stimulus. Kinaesthesia followed behind. Smell and touch were almost even in their numbers, and the variance category was the least used. Some participants entirely dismiss touch, smell, or variance in their recordings. The number of sensory entries in the proforma ranges per person from 6 to 16. Often, when participants decided to mark a stimulus that triggered their inner response, they ended up putting more than one marker on the spot. Thus, each proforma entry consisted of one or all five senses, and individual

[22] The stone archway at the edge amplified the sound spreading it in two directions.

[23] The landmark loses its symbolic significance, usually read through sight. Monuments as manifestations of dominant power per Lefebvre then stop imposing the societal order. They are omitted to the level of any other structure in the city, to the human scale. They potentially become the places for the proliferation of lived space. Experienced through the body, monuments step into the space of opposition, "linked to the clandestine or underground side of social life" (Lefebvre 1991, 33).

[24] This, however, also depends on the perceiver: some might be able to distinguish more nuances.

[25] The conceived-perceived-lived triad collapses into one space. They are all felt in place through senses. The conceived and the perceived space descend into the lived space; their distinctions disappear in the sensual realm. Losing their imposing value in the domain outside of symbolism, they become vulnerable to intervention seized on the sensory level.

maps had 10–29 stickers. This wide range of sticker numbers points more to how much descriptive information participants provided for each entry than the number of sensations the participants felt. The number of entries also does not reflect the size of the area covered by the participant.[26]

Single entries (e.g., if a person has only one touch marked on their map among multiple entries for other senses)[27] are indicators of out of the ordinary stimuli. Participant #1 in the only tactile entry mentioned touching the graffiti, which participant #2 did around 20 min earlier in the same location—node C in the cloister. For participant #13, the touch appeared when they were "caught in a sudden crowd", touching arms and coats.[28] Tactile entries could be generally be divided into two kinds. The first was a passive experience of being touched by an object[29] ("hit by flying foam"), human (brushed by "hands and coats"), or weather ("extreme wind whipping face"). The second kind was an experience of intentionally reaching for something (participant #14 "had to touch the gargoyle… to see if it was stone or wood") dealing with the material side of the urban fabric[30] (be that architecture, vegetation, or urban furnishing). It was not an unexpected encounter but a conscious choice that often came with a revelation that actual tactile qualities rarely coincided with visually perceived and assumed tactile qualities. Participant #9 described a street lamp:

> It feels warmer than it looks, I expected cold metal. Instead it is dry and warm… It is very uneven even if it looks shiny and smooth.

This discrepancy echoes Panagia's hypothesis that sensory experience interrupts perceptual givens, creating occasions to question the order of things expanding further into opportunities to suspend authority and reconfigure the arrangement of political order (Panagia 2009). The discrepancies between visually perceived and actual tactile qualities stress the deceitfulness of the assumed accuracy of the visual information. Challenging perceptions through multisensory investigation bring to light hidden processes, lives, and happenings. Visibly solid and formed things in the city are felt as they are—in constant "holomovement" (Bohm 1980, 156–167).

Participant #3 had an only an entry for smell at node G—a mix of sweet wisteria with a distant flavour of fast food. Participant #11 described fragrant wisteria there

---

[26] All participants were able-bodied (no walking sticks or wheelchairs/no obvious mobility problems).

[27] We have to mention here that one of the difficulties of analysing the proformas is a difference in participants' handwriting—we are able to read most of the words in their entries but still have to dismiss some of them.

[28] One more single entry is in participant #10's proforma; they acknowledged the materiality of the clipboard at the beginning of the exercise and did not explore any other tactile surfaces. The tactile exploration begun and ended with what was literally at hand not extending it to the city.

[29] The pavement, soil, grass, or any other surface under the feet is in a rather odd category rarely touched by the open skin but in nearly constant mediated contact with human bodies.

[30] However, one could argue that feelings of warmth from the sun or the cold of the wind are partially conditioned by how the city places are configured whether they obstruct the sun or create "tunnels" for the wind to gain its force, etc.

a bit earlier. Participant #2 picked up a floral smell there but was unsure what it was ("lavender?"). Not being able to identify the fragrance (possibly, not having experiential memory of encountering this floral species), they still found it worth recording—outstanding sensory qualities of the environment caught the perceiver's attention even being only distantly familiar. Similar entries foreground the collective experience and memory (Halbwachs 1992) of the external world as opposed to individual perceptions.

Participant #5 found a herbal whiff at node F that nobody else mentioned, while not distinguishing other odours (including natural) along the way noted by other participants. Participants #7 and #8 were at the same spot at the same time (16:35); participant #8 mentioned the siren, but participant #8 did not, while observing it at other locations and at other times. This highlights the agency of the participants in the act of recording—deliberate selection of sensations at different moments that comes with choices, uncertainties, omissions, and intentions—and the ambiguous subjective nature of mapping, which is often obscured in the final product. The maps represent the external world perceived through a sensorium formed by individual physiology, psychology, and personal, cultural, social, and historical background.

The single kinaesthetic entry that participant #8 had was on the brink of emotion, writing that they "felt 'in the way'... [and] could sense groups approaching or moving out to go around" them. It was both a bodily sensation and an emotional perception.

After working with the count per person spreadsheet, we develop a count per node spreadsheet (see Appendix 4). Besides node A, the initial encounter with the city, node B, had the second largest number of entries, with the majority (16 out of 24) senses recorded on the way back to the Lodge. The question arises whether the participants were impelled to record something, realising that they were approaching the end of the exercise. However, those entries were not remarkably different from the earlier ones. Participant #2 even marked sensations at this node twice—in the middle of the exercise and at the very end—not noting any difference between the entries ("sound of trees, kinaesthetic wind"). Participants #9 (at the beginning of the exercise) and #13 (at the end) noticed a tree with a visibly "wonderful texture" that induced their desire to touch it. One of them followed that desire and felt it by hand; the other did not, avoiding walking over the flower bed. The same object attracted the attention of different people, but only one allowed themselves to build a tactile felt relation (Spuybroek 2016, 112) with it. Most of the city features that provoked intentional tactile connection were made of stone even though the majority of the buildings in the investigated areas were made of brick. Other materials of frequent occurrence were glass and wood and a bit of metal. The perceived and actual historicity of the material was the reason for most of the tactile entries[31]: "radiates history and time, permanence!" Old structures' stone stood out among the more even and flat surfaces of brick, glass, and metal, promising a thrilling sensation.[32]

---

[31] Other tactile entries derive from the moments of rest when participants sat down and noticed the material they landed on, often stone.

[32] Most of the participants noted that it was cold, possibly expecting something else or merely noticing the first most identifiable sensory attribute.

The stone also came out a lot in the proformas as pavement. Participants often marked "cobbles underfoot" when stepping from a smoother surface to a more uneven. They felt "unbalanced", needing to "walk tougher." These material transitions produce subtle edges within the city more readily observed by the body than attended to by the eye.[33] They affect the way people move and experience the environment. Various surfaces point out the socio-economic and cultural qualities of the area (smooth asphalt and muddy road with potholes can tell about the social space as much as architecture or other artefacts) and its place within the context of the city, primarily through comparison with other areas, again underscoring the importance of such transitions.

The other large number of entities was at node M—a transition between Areas 1 and 3, near Area 2. Participant #2 mentioned the loss of natural smell when leaving the park, while participant #4 noted car fumes in the same area. Several participants commented on the cobbles under their feet (change of pavement but not at the very transition point). They also mentioned kids' chatter and vehicle noises; a couple remarked on a police siren. 9 out of 10 participants who passed through node M recorded something, regardless of transitioning from one area to another or just walking by. The conjunction of all three areas provided the node with rich sensory data creating a distinct "sense loci" (Betts 2017, 28).

Some of the participants did not note the time in their entries, so we create one more spreadsheet, count per minute (see Appendix 5), that allows us to calculate approximate times for those participants, marking the time per the distance they covered and the number of entries (see Fig. 11). The exercise took place in the late afternoon: the first entry was at 16:11 and the last was at 16:58. The spreadsheet shows sensations that were recorded at the same time in different locations, for example, the sound of an emergency vehicle. It first appeared at around 16:18-16:20 and was heard from nodes Q, A, and G (Areas 1 and 3—there was no participant in Area 2 at that moment, but presumably, it would be heard there as well). The second time it appeared at 16:35 at the nodes M, K, and T (participants are in all three areas but no mentions of the siren in Area 1; possibly the audial source is far away on the intersection of the road and the furthest Area 3 street where node T is located). The third time it came up around 16:45 for several minutes; the sound seemed to be moving from node M towards X (heard at nodes B, H, L, and M (earliest recording) and N, R, and X (latest recording)).

From working with structured information in spreadsheets, we transition to working with a 3D model and video. The sensations represented as physical forms placed on a map reveal the relations between the urban fabric and individual and collective experiences. The simplified urban model of the three areas shows the overall volumes of the buildings without any detailing.[34] If the architecture is

[33] The change of surfaces is successfully employed as a navigational tool for the visually impaired community and to distinguish pedestrian, vehicular, and other areas within the city but still has the potential for more experiential exploration.

[34] The Cathedral is an exception: its more detailed 3D model is in the open-access online. For this analytical and representational exercise, a less detailed model would have worked just as well.

Fig. 11 Embodied city timelapse map with concurrent sensory entries and paths. Image credit Anna Misharina and Eleanor Betts

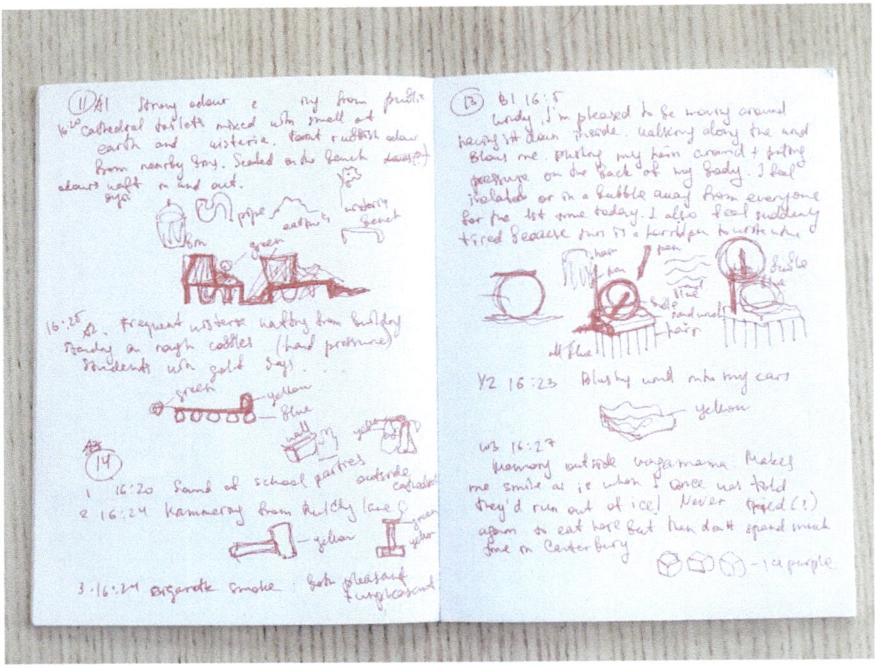

Fig. 12 The process of creating architectonic compositions from participants' sensory entries. Image credit Anna Misharina

commonly perceived as fixed and permanent and thus gains prominence in representing cities, can giving seemingly solid and material form to sensory experiences articulate their inherence to the urban environment? Each proforma entry transforms into an architectonic composition[35] made of ready-made models[36] available online representing described sensations (see Fig. 12). Models do not explicitly portray the "sensory artefacts" (Betts 2017, 26) identified by participants, but a kind of a universal form collectively created and shared online. To further distinguish sensations, qualities of different materials widely present in cities are assigned to the models: red clay of brick or roof tiles to touch, yellow wood to sound, weathered concrete covered in green moss to smell, blue metal to kinaesthesia, and grey marble to a variance sensory category. Each recording then enters the city model in its own right—in the shape of a complex architectural object. While representing simultaneous sensations, it is not inferior to buildings in its monumentality (Fig. 13). The less tangible and stable the described sensation, or its source, the harder it is to translate it into a composition. For example, the concrete model of a tree illustrates the smell of trees, and the metal footprints indicate the kinaesthetic "standing"; the wooden waves signify

[35] Due to the time limitation, we were not able to model all the entries; however, the entries included in the model provide a good sense of the analysed environment.

[36] This analytical and representational approach is inspired by New Cadavre Exquis by NEMESTUDIO though used for a very different type of a project (Turan 2020, 119–131).

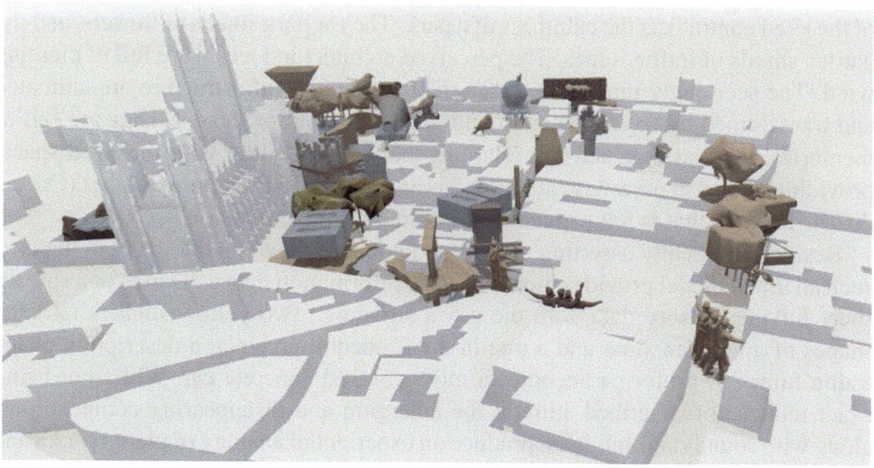

Fig. 13 Embodied city 3D model with volumes representing existing buildings and sensory architectonic compositions. Image credit Anna Misharina and Angelina Voytash

the sound of the wind. While made of often repeating elements (sounds of crowds, bodily sensation of wind, touch of the sun on the skin, smell of wisteria, and view of a monument), each composition is unique. Some elements, experienced through various senses, appear in different materials and colours. For instance, a pram is wooden at node U, being heard there, and of clay material at node R, being accidentally touched; the wind was experienced through sound, kinaesthesia, or touch in different places.

In the video (see Video 2), compositions appear in groups divided by time, accompanied by written descriptions and corresponding sounds.[37] The video shows the abstract representation of the sensations and personal impressions of the urban environment, subjective encounters with the city rather than its material side, and the lived space perceived through the senses, through bodies (Simonsen 2005). The compositions made of irregular forms and multiple materials and colours lack neatness and cohesion. The messiness and intricacy further emphasise the complexity of urban experiences. This new city model brings to light things that are not readily observed: "...focusing on the senses in the configuration of public life reveals an alternative geography of place by offering an insight into narratives, feelings, practices, and experiences often hidden from common view" (Degen 2008, 196). The composure of the old city is agitated by the sounds of kids' voices, and the stink of public toilets and garbage bins disturb the nobility of the Cathedral. The homogeneity of a British town architecture is disaccorded with the diversity of foreign languages.[38] The sound

[37] Ideally, the model would be physical so it could be explored by hand as well. The time aspect, however, would be harder to represent. This needs more investigation and trial.

[38] Several participants commented on specific languages they heard spoken such as French or German (signalled participants' familiarity with that culture) and unspecified foreign languages. These entries marked people out as distinctive.

of the siren contradicts the calmness of a park. The car park smells of flowers, and the garden smells of traffic fumes. The perceived architectural lees[39] are full of piercing wind. The seemingly immobile urban architecture and infrastructure are animated and transformed by the living and nonliving things and processes. They are full of memories, impressions, and felt relations that link the place with the lived space, providing access to otherwise autonomous and violent in their purity places (Coccia 2020). The city that is felt expands and contradicts the city that is seen.

Besides artistically asserting sensory experiences on a tangible level in the city, such an urban model provides more cohesive information than a 2D map or a spreadsheet linking sensory data with the city's structure. Two yellow stickers take the shapes of a wooden siren and a tree in the Cathedral precinct; a description of the traffic fumes in proforma becomes a moss-covered concrete car. While not being exact replicas of described stimuli, the emerging and disappearing compositions, along with sounds and subtitles, produce an experiential analogy of places (Foka and Arvidsson 2016).

Few of the sensory stimuli that come through in all the analysed material are different effects of the weather. prevalent weather conditions were gloomy and cloudy, cold strong wind. Sun breaking through attracted attention and directed it either to the participants' tactile sensations ("warmth of the sun on my cheek") or to architecture ("suddenly aware of the sun shining on the Cathedral as a visual spectacle"). Area 1, the precinct with larger open areas, had most of those moments; participants did not notice the sun effects on the narrow streets: the taller buildings' shade might have conditioned that along with the smaller distances between the perceiver and potentially highlighted objects. The wind muted some of the sensory stimuli:

> "Oddly expect to smell something but nothing prevalent pass due to wind," wrote participant #7 at node B.

Participants remarked on the architecture sheltering them from the wind and the wind dying down. These moments of silence and freedom from bodily resistance to moving air allowed them to concentrate more on their surroundings than on their bodies. The weather and overall climate conditions significantly impact behaviour (looking for shelter) and the perception[40] and experience of a place (including emotional, as a result of comfort or discomfort). These major omnipresent elements of the environment and their influence highlight the importance of non-architectural things in urban life (Jon 2020). The birds,[41] vehicles, hair dryers, trees,[42] stone,

[39] At node Z, two participants looked for shelter from wind, and while participant #11 found "stillness" and "warmth", participant #5 walked away in dismay, not being able to find those qualities (participants #13 and 7 passed through that node but didn't mention anything). A similar condition of perceived shelter from the wind is experienced at nodes C and D, where only one from several participants found protection from wind.

[40] The measurable characteristics of the environment do not always directly translate into "thermo-spatial experience" (Lenzholzer et al. 2018).

[41] Repeatedly mentioned in Area 1.

[42] Appeared in the participants' proformas both as smells and sounds in all three areas.

pastries, wind, Cathedral organ, echo, street signs, sun, hammers, and pollen—all things perceived by the entire sensorium and things that lay beyond human perception—contribute to the construction of places collectively, along with buildings and people: "only because things are joined that the material world can manifest any kind of coherence, and only because of its coherence can this world be inhabited" (Ingold 2020, 17).

3 Possible Application to Past Cities

This chapter has presented a methodology (the theoretical framework, mapping exercise, analysis, and representation technique) that unveils lived spaces by highlighting the multitude of divergent individual experiences.[43] It exposes the myriad corresponding things and processes that create a city through "joint attention and response" (Ingold 2021, XIII). The methodology can be employed in design practices to ameliorate places for human and non-human things and processes. It can stress the plurality and variety of the individual sensory impressions of built (and natural) environments, breaking a hegemonic "objective" image of a city or a place, validating the "abnormal readings" (Boys 2018, 57). It can expose and bring attention to the things and processes that contribute to the production of lived spaces beyond people and architecture. Embodied experience can help answer why this or that place is excluded from social life. It can uncover not readily observed factors that define places negatively or positively and underlying physical, social, and chemical conditions (for example, a smell of mould indicating rotting hidden behind the impassive surface of walls). It smears the physical borders to highlight marginalised events, practices, and circumstances. It brings to light what possibly is not supposed to be seen. Attention to multiple sensory stimuli as a result of the exercise also heightens participants' perception of self as an interwoven part of that world, not an autonomous entity. Emphasising a human body decentralises the human within the social space; it brings to light the evolving intricate contradictory felt relations.

The methodology stresses the value of the full-body experience of the environment in understanding current and past cities. It breaks the noumenal image thereof. The methodology demonstrates the importance of multiple sensory stimuli in the lived space, not merely the visually perceived components. In application to ancient sites, this means reconstructing as many sensory stimuli as possible and experiencing them with the entire sensorium.

First, sensory data from archaeological records, classical literature, and epigraphy should be mapped onto a city or archaeological site (Betts 2011, 121). Then the methodology should be applied several times. Considering it is difficult to pinpoint the source of the stimuli described in the ancient accounts, after analysing the results

[43] The experiment showed that even a group with a similar background (part of academia, able-bodied, aged 25–55, european or of european descent, similar socio-economic status) had different interpretations of their environment and paid attention to different stimuli.

(What sensory stimuli were noticed? What patterns appeared on the collective maps? What were the individual responses? What was the area of influence of different stimuli? To what extent do the proformas correlate with the historical source?), the location and the intensity of the source stimuli should be adjusted every time.[44] Such iterations will bring the environment closer and closer to the one experienced in the past while still underscoring the differential individual perceptions. The participants will be entering these reconstructed lived spaces as tourists, encountering most of the stimuli for the first time and gradually building relations with them. Further, people with various backgrounds and physical abilities should be invited to experience and record the reconstructed space to provide a more comprehensive image of differing perceptions of that space.

Reconstructing the embodied experience of the past lived space and recording, it can become an essential tool in understanding the past, teaching, and making knowledge accessible to a broader public. As suggested in this chapter, ways of recording and representing the impressions of the environment can aid in distributing differing accounts of the site beyond its borders. While there are no universal sensations and perceptions, and it is impossible to replicate both the sensory stimuli and individual responses from the past, multisensory reconstruction of the ancient lived spaces can translate the intensity and fluidity of human and non-human processes by immersing participants in experiential analogy attuned with the help of this methodology.

4 Conclusions

This chapter discussed the methodology for capturing and investigating lived space of modern and past cities. Starting with the premise that the lived space can be understood through a human body, the methodology provided instruments for recording the sensations and perceptions of the urban environment. The chapter further showed how the collected data can be analysed and represented. It also elaborated on Kevin Lynch's urban categories from The Image of the City through a multisensory lens and discovered that they need to be scrutinised further and possibly redefined. The chapter also provided suggestions on how the described methodology could be improved to become more accessible to different groups of people and to highlight a wider variety of individual experiences of the urban environment. This consequently can lead to a more comprehensive understanding of Lefebvrian social space and place, especially cities, as ever-evolving and corresponding to a multitude of human and non-human things and processes.

[44] Omissions will have to be made regarding the differing from the past perceptions of the modern people conditioned by the current being-in-the-world.

References

Betts, Eleanor. 2011. "Towards a Multisensory Experience of Movement in the City of Rome*." In *Rome, Ostia, Pompeii: Movement and Space.*, edited by Ray Laurence and David J. Newsome, 119–133. N.p.: Oxford Scholarship Online. https://doi.org/10.1093/acprof:osobl/9780199583126.003.0005.

Betts, Eleanor. 2017. "The Multivalency of Sensory Artefacts in the City of Rome." In *Senses of the Empire: Multisensory Approaches to Roman Culture*, edited by Eleanor Betts, 23–38. Abingdon: Routledge.

Bille, Mikkel, and Tim F. Sørensen. 2018. "Atmospheric architecture: Elements, processes and practices." In *Senses and sensation: Critical and primary sources*, edited by David Howes, 137–154. Vol. 4. London: Bloomsbury.

Blesser, Barry, and Linda-Ruth Salter. 2007. *Spaces Speak, Are You Listening?* Cambridge: The MIT Press.

Bohm, David. 1980. *Wholeness and the Implicate Order*. London: Routledge.

Boys, Jos. 2018. "Cripping Spaces? On Dis/abling Phenomenology In Architecture." *Log* 42:55–66.

Braidotti, Rosi. 2002. *Metamorphoses : towards a materialist theory of becoming*. Malden: Polity Press in Association with Blackwell Publishers.

Coccia, Emanuele. 2020. "Reversing the New Global Monasticism." *Log*, no. 49 (Summer), 9–17.

Degen, Mónica M. 2008. *Sensing Cities: Regenerating Public Life in Barcelona and Manchester*. London: Routledge.

Empler, Tommaso. 2018. "Representation in architecture as idea, physical model, 3D modeling, BIM." In *Handbook of Research on Form and Morphogenesis in Modern Architectural Contexts*, edited by Domenico D'Uva, 93–107. Hershey: IGI Global.

Foka, Anna, and Viktor Arvidsson. 2016. "Experiential Analogies: A Sonic Digital Ekphrasis as a Digital Humanities Project." *Digital Humanities Quarterly* 10 (2): 24.

Grosz, Elizabeth. 2001. *Architecture from the Outside: Essays on Virtual and Real Space*. Cambridge: The MIT Press.

Halbwachs, Maurice. 1992. *On Collective Memory*. Edited by Lewis A. COser. Chicago: University of Chicago Press.

Haraway, Donna. 1988. "Situated Knowledges: The Science Question In Feminism And The Privilege Of Partial Perspective." *Feminist Studies* 14 (3): 575–599.

Ingold, Tim. 2020. "In the gathering shadows of material things." In *Exploring Materiality and Connectivity in Anthropology and Beyond*, edited by Marlen Elders, Martin Saxer, and Philipp Schorch, 17–35. London: UCL Press.

Ingold, Tim. 2021. "Foreword." In *Architectural Anthropology: Exploring Lived Space*, edited by Marie Stender, Claus Bech-Danielson, and Aina Landsverk Hagen, XIII-XVII. New York: Taylor & Francis.

Jon, Ihnji. 2020. "Deciphering posthumanism: Why and how it matters to urban planning in the Anthropocene." *Planning Theory* 19 (4). https://doi.org/10.1177/1473095220912770.

Kainz, Wolfgang. 2020. "Cartography and the others – aspects of a complicated relationship." tandfonline.com. https://doi.org/10.1080/10095020.2020.1718000.

Kinkaid, Eden. 2020. "Re-encountering Lefebvre: Toward a critical phenomenology of social space." *Environment and Planning D: Society and Space* 38, no. 1 (June). https://doi.org/10.1177/0263775819854765.

Le Corbusier. 1991. *Precisions*. Cambridge: The MIT Press.

Lefebvre, Henri. 1991. *The Production of Space*. Oxford: Blackwell.

Lefebvre, Henri. 2009. *State, Space, World*. London: University of Minnesota Press.

Lefebvre, Henri. 2014. *Toward an Architecture of Enjoyment*. Edited by Łukasz Stanek. Minneapolis: University of Minnesota Press.

Lenzholzer, Sanda, Wiebke Klemm, and Carolina Vasilikou. 2018. "Qualitative methods to explore thermo-spatial perception in outdoor urban spaces." *Urban Climate* 23 (March): 231–249. https://doi.org/10.1016/j.uclim.2016.10.003.

Levin, David M., ed. 1993. *Modernity and the Hegemony of Vision.* Berkeley: University of California Press.
Levine, Michael W., and Jeremy M. Shefner. 1981. *Fundamentals of Sensation and Perception.* New York: Random House.
Lynch, Kevin. 1977. *The Image of the City.* Cambridge: The MIT Press.
Mayer, Felix. 2021. "Landmarks in a History of Spatial Mapping." In *Mapping Urban Spaces: Designing the European City*, 15–25. New York: Routledge.
Merrifield, Andrew. 1993. "Place and space: a Lefebvrian reconciliation." *Transactions of the Institute of British Geographers* 18 (4): 516–531.
O'Brien, Dai. 2021. "Theorising the deaf body: using Lefebvre and Bourdieu to understand deaf spatial experience." *Cultural Geographies*, (March). https://doi.org/10.1177%2F14744740211003632.
OpenStax. 2020. *Psychology 2e.* Ann Arbor: XanEdu Publishing. https://openstax.org/details/books/psychology-2e.
Pallasmaa, Juhani. 1996. *The eyes of the skin: Architecture and the senses.* London: Academy Editions.
Panagia, Davide. 2009. *The Political Life of Sensation.* Durham: Duke University Press.
Roth, Robert E. 2021. "Cartographic Design as Visual Storytelling: Synthesis and Review of Map-Based Narratives, Genres, and Tropes." *The Cartographic Journal* 58 (1). https://doi.org/10.1080/00087041.2019.1633103.
Simonsen, Kirsten. 2005. "Bodies, Sensations, Space and Time: The Contribution from Henri Lefebvre." *Geografiska Annaler. Series B, Human Geography* 87 (1): 1–14. http://www.jstor.org/stable/3554441.
Sinclair, D., B. Oranje, K. A. Razak, S. J. Siegel, and S. Schmid. 2017. "Sensory processing in autism spectrum disorders and Fragile X syndrome—From the clinic to animal models." *Neurosci Biobehav Rev* 76(Pt B) (May): 235–253. https://doi.org/10.1016/j.neubiorev.2016.05.029.
Spence, Charles. 2020. "Senses of place: architectural design for the multisensory mind." *Cognitive Research: Principles and Implications* 5 (46). https://doi.org/10.1186/s41235-020-00243-4.
Spuybroek, Lars. 2016. *The Sympathy of Things: Ruskin and the Ecology of Design.* 2nd ed. London: Bloomsbury Academic.
Stein, Barry E., and M. A. Meredith. 1993. *The Merging of the Senses.* Cambridge: The MIT Press.
Tschumi, Bernard. 1996. *Architecture and Disjunction.* Cambridge: The MIT Press.
Turan, Neyran. 2020. *Architecture as Measure.* New York: Actar Publishers.

Anna Misharina (M.A. Umea School of Architecture) is an independent scholar with a background in architecture and digital humanities. She is a co-founder of architectural Studio CRIT based in the San Francisco Bay Area.

MIX
Papier aus verantwortungsvollen Quellen
Paper from responsible sources
FSC® C105338

If you have any concerns about our products,
you can contact us on
ProductSafety@springernature.com

In case Publisher is established outside the EU,
the EU authorized representative is:
Springer Nature Customer Service Center GmbH
Europaplatz 3, 69115 Heidelberg, Germany

Printed by Libri Plureos GmbH
in Hamburg, Germany